B   Eubanks, Bob.
EUB   It's in the
              book, Bob!

IT'S IN THE BOOK, BOB!

IT'S IN THE BOOK, BOB!

BOB EUBANKS

with
Matthew Scott Hansen

BENBELLA BOOKS
Dallas, Texas

BenBella Books
6440 N. Central Expressway
Suite 617
Dallas, TX 75206
Send feedback to feedback@benbellabooks.com
www.benbellabooks.com

Printed in the United States of America

10 9 8 7 6 5 4 3 2 1

Library of Congress Cataloging-in-Publication Data

Eubanks, Bob.
 "It's in the book, Bob" / by Bob Eubanks with Matthew Scott Hansen.
     p. cm.
 Includes bibliographical references and index.
   ISBN 1-932100-28-8
 1. Eubanks, Bob. 2. Television personalities—United States—Biography. I. Hansen,
Matthew Scott, 1953- II. Title.
 PN1992.4.E93A3 2004
 791.4502'8'092--dc22

                                                              2004008575

Interior design and composition by John Reinhardt Book Design
Cover design by Andy Carpenter and Melody Cadungog
Cover Photography by Ron Derhacopian Photography
The Newlywed Game promo shot courtesy of Capital Cities/ABC Publicity
Photo from *Ozzie & Harriet* courtesy of ABC Publicity
Photo of Bob Eubanks at KRLA courtesy of Publicity Photo Service
Photo of Bob Eubanks and Merle Haggard courtesy of Michael Ochs Archives
All other back cover photos courtesy of the Bob Eubanks Archive

Distributed by Independent Publishers Group
To order call (800) 888-4741
www.ipgbook.com

To my children: Trace, Theresa, Corey and Noah.
Only God knows how much I love each of you.
—

To Irma: She was always there
through the good times and bad times.
The world was a better place when Irma was alive.
—

To my grandchildren:
Tyler Ann, Casey, Cole, Kelly and Christopher.
One of the reasons I wrote this book
is to show you what Grandpa Bum did
before you were born.
—

To my darling Debbie, my wife, my friend, my love:
I know what it's like to wake up in the morning
with a smile and to appreciate the value
of God in my life.
Oh, how I love you.

ACKNOWLEDGMENTS

The Beatles • Mick Jagger • Cary Grant Merle Haggard • Dolly Parton • David Letterman • The Rolling Stones • The Be... ...za Gibbons • Jerry Lee Lewis • Gene Autry Roy Rogers • Monty Hall • Roy Orbison Buddy Hackett • Barbara Mandrell

When your career spans over forty years, so many people contribute.

I would first like to thank Matthew Scott Hansen, who poured his life into the writing of this book. Thanks Matt, for your patience.

To Stephanie Bianca: I appreciate all your hard work in editing this book.

Thanks to Mickey Brown, my partner for so many years. He deserves as much credit as I do for pioneering the early concert promotion business including the Cinnamon Cinders, the Beatles, Rolling Stones, Merle Haggard and Dolly Parton.

To Teri Brown, whose loyalty and talent were a major part of my success. Her tremendous memory helped to fill in the holes of this book.

To Kim Richardson, who worked with me for so many years. She helped keep my life in order during some of the bad times.

To my agent Fred Wostbrock who believes in me even when I don't. His talent and loyalty have helped keep my career alive. His collection of pictures has been invaluable to this book.

To Joanie Perciballi, my assistant and friend: She suffered through most of the writing of this book. Her smile always keeps my office hours a joy.

To Charlene Trichon: Our many years on the road together were both fun and profitable. She is one of my true friends.

To my business manager, Gary Schneider: God, Gary, what can I say but "thanks." I can't imagine my life without you and Sherry Alef and your remarkable talents. I know I am a pain in the ass, but thanks for being so patient.

To my good and loyal partner, Larry Donizetti and his wife, Maria: Your enthusiasm and creativity have made my world brighter.

To my partner in television, Michael Hill: His genius and talent helped us drive the studios crazy. Michael, you're the best!

To Don and Skippy McCoy: Business partners, roping partners, but most of all, true friends.

To Buck Wicall, partner and friend. Powder River, Buck!

To Stephanie Edwards, a very special lady who has sat beside me every New Year's morning for over twenty-five years as we host the Rose Parade.

To Leeza Gibbons: Always there for me, no matter what I need. You're one of the classiest women I know.

To Jerry Perenchio, my only mentor: Thanks for the worldly lessons, my friend.

To Jim Wagner, partner and friend: Thanks for all the laughs.

To Arnold Shapiro: He believed in my television talents before anyone else.

To Jo Ann Berry and Marie Ratzman: What a wonderful contribution you have made to my life.

To Andrea Shrednick: You have sent me down so many roads and helped me get over so many roadblocks. And thanks to you, I have reached my final destination—happiness.

To Mark Mayfield: His honesty and talent helped lead to my success as a speaker. Most of all, Mark, thanks for the friendship.

To Melinda Bachelor and Melody Alexander: They keep my world moving. You guys at FirstClassSpeakers.com are the best.

To Jodee Blanco who walked up to me at a convention in New Orleans and said, "How would you like to write a book?" Well, Jodee, here it is and it's all your fault!

To Glenn Yeffeth who had the guts to publish this project after so many said "no."

To Dave Hull whose Beatle stories were invaluable. He truly was the Fifth Beatle.

To my friend Joe Quasarano, Executive producer of the Rose Parade: He has always fought for me and I am most appreciative.

I would especially like to thank Bill Earl for writing his book about KRLA, *Dream House*. The information inside has been invaluable to me.

To my friends Mike and Virginia Kelly: They were one of the reasons that I was successful in the concert business.

To Deborah Foshee: Your smile and talent have added so much to my life.

To Charlie O'Donnell: Were it not for him, *The Newlywed Game* would not have happened. Charlie has been interwoven with my life for so many years!

My thanks to Arthur Barens, attorney and friend.

And finally a special thanks to my precious daughter-in-law, Susie. Thanks for the beautiful poem, three wonderful grandkids and for always having the ability to understand me. I love you, Susie.

SPECIAL ACKNOWLEDGMENT

Coming from the world of radio, I realize how tough it is to entertain an audience for three or four hours every day without a script, without writers and depending solely on your own imagination to keep the audience entertained. The men and women in this group we call disk jockeys are some of the most creative people I have ever met. Some will veer off onto the wrong path and let poor taste take the place of entertainment, but most are true to their audience and unbelievably talented. It is real tough to walk into a restaurant knowing you have a huge following in your community and no one recognizes who you are, yet the local television weatherman is given the best seat in the house. So, to the disk jockeys of America, my hat's off to you!

The Beatles • Mick Jagger • Cary Grant
Merle Haggard • Dolly Parton • David
Letterman • The Rolling Stones • The
Beach **INTRODUCTION** Leeza
Gibbons • Jerry Lee Lewis • Gene Autry
Roy Rogers • Monty Hall • Roy Orbison
Buddy Hackett • Barbara Mandrell

INTRODUCTION

BOB EUBANKS' LIFE holds true to the rule of thumb that says that the cover of a good book shouldn't give away its content. To find that my friend was a real cowboy was a surprise. Knowing what all Bob's done in his life was intriguing to me. I'm sure readers will find it the same way.

Our lives came together and stayed together for some interesting years. There's one thing everyone will agree upon about Bob Eubanks—you know when you meet him he's a business man and he makes no bones about it, which is the sign of a great business man.

Since our days on the road together, much water has run under the interstates of America. One time we wrestled to the ground and as our eyes met in the dust, Bob said, "Haggard, you're in pretty good shape for a country singer." I took it as a compliment coming from a man who's tussled with some of the most powerful men in the entertainment industry. We've wrestled around some since then, but always on the same side.

This man's life does make for good reading.

What Bob lacks in good looks, he makes up for in talent!

Merle Haggard
June 2004

The Beatles • Mick Jagger • Cary Grant
Merle Haggard • Dolly Parton • David
Letterman • The Rolling Stones • The
Beach Boys ___ner • Leeza
Gibbons • Jerry Lee Lewis • Gene Autry
Roy Rogers • Monty Hall • Roy Orbison
Buddy Hackett • Barbara Mandrell

PROLOGUE

I HAPPEN TO BELIEVE we all have a pot of stew out in front of us. Inside that pot of stew are the ingredients of our lives. Mine are no better than yours and yours are no better than mine, they are just different. This is not an autobiography. It is simply a book about the ingredients of my life—some personal, some business, but mostly about the incredibly interesting people who make up my pot of stew.

I am a man with a limited amount of talent. If anybody has ever made something out of nothing, it's me: I can't sing, God didn't tune me; I can't act, I embarrass my children every time I try; and I have absolutely no aptitude for detail. I do have an active imagination and I love nothing better than to come up with a new idea and nurse it to fruition. Sometimes I win, sometimes I lose, but with God on my side, I never fail.

If you like this book tell a friend you love Bob Eubanks' new book. If you don't like this book, since I'm always mistaken for him anyway, tell a friend you hate Bob Barker's new book.

God bless.

CO-AUTHOR'S NOTE

The Beatles • Mick Jagger • Cary Grant
Merle Haggard • Dolly Parton • David
Letterm ••• • The
Beach Boys • Ike and Tina Turner • Leeza
Gibbons • Jerry •• • Gene Autry
Roy Rogers • Monty Hall • Roy Orbison
Buddy Hackett • Barbara Mandrell

I N THE FALL OF 1985, Bob Eubanks was busy with a number of projects, including a new syndicated version of *The Newlywed Game*. He was
also presenting a live version of the famous show at shopping malls around
the country. Those appearances gave fans in far-flung locations a chance
to see the man himself in action, as well as get a taste of the glamour of a
Hollywood production. When it was announced that *The Newlywed Game*
was coming, excitement was high at the Factoria Mall, a shopping center
in an affluent eastside suburb of Seattle. Mall officials contacted the photo
studio across the street and asked if the photographer would be interested
in shooting the event. Intrigued by the prospect of meeting the man he'd
watched for years on television, he jumped at the opportunity.

An hour or so before the show, the photographer crossed the street
and began taking candids of the contestants, as well as shots of the stage
and growing crowd. A few minutes before show time, the contestants
were shown to a back room where they met Bob and posed for photos
with him.

Afterwards, the contestants sat on folding chairs in a semi-circle
while Bob gave them the run-down on what to expect. As Bob warmed
up his contestants, the photographer kept to the background, discreetly
taking photos—as he had done on hundreds of similar occasions.

Suddenly, Bob turned to the photographer and snapped, "Hey pal,
you're done."

His dismissal was sharp and the embarrassed photographer quickly left
the room, tail between his legs. Although he continued taking photos during the stage presentation, he returned to his studio rattled by the experi-

ence. For years, the photographer recounted how callous Bob Eubanks had been and assured anyone who asked that "Bob Eubanks is a real jerk."

Jump forward fourteen years. The photographer had long since left his studio to pursue his true passion: writing. He moved to Los Angeles, worked as a television writer, sold a couple of movies (that haven't been made yet) and became a successful author. Not long after he co-authored a best-selling memoir about the late Andy Kaufman, the book's publicist phoned. She wanted him to meet with someone whom she enthused had "an amazing story." He was excited until she told him that the "someone" was Bob Eubanks. Concealing his reluctance, and the fact that he and Mr. Eubanks had already met, the photographer-turned-writer agreed to go. Five minutes from the restaurant he nearly canceled, but curiosity got the better of him and he continued on.

The 1999 Bob Eubanks was nothing like the 1985 Bob Eubanks. As the writer listened to Bob, he was surprised and impressed, not only by the fascinating content of his anecdotes, but also by the storyteller. Bob Eubanks, it turned out, was not an ogre, but a warm, sincere man with a marvelous collection of personal tales. At the end of a two-hour lunch the writer was on board, having had a couple of lessons hammered home—that people have bad days...and to be less judgmental. He was also struck by how a few simple words, uttered ungraciously by one man, had created a mythology that had bitterly festered in another man for too many years. How could the photographer have known that Bob had an aversion to photographers? Who knew?

If you haven't guessed by now, the photographer was me. Bob and I first proposed telling his story five years ago and, like many things in Hollywood, it took that long to bring it to fruition. In those intervening years I have come to know Bob well. I took his story on as if it were my own, making it more of a quest than simply another writing gig. With the same zeal I had disparaged Bob, I now found myself championing him. "No, *The Newlywed Game* is just a small part of Bob's story. It's really the history of rock and roll, of country music, of television and even radio. It's an amazing story."

Only after we finished this book did I reveal my long held "secret" to Bob. Now that it's done, the ghosts of the past have been put to rest. I consider Bob Eubanks a friend. Sixty-some years in the making, and five years bringing it to print, it was a story that absolutely needed to be told, and I am proud to have been a part of it.

Matthew Scott Hansen

CONTENTS

The Beatles • Mick Jagger • Cary Grant
Merle Haggard • Dolly Parton • David
Letterman • The Rolling Stones • The
Beach Boys • ------ • Leeza
Gibbons • Jerry Lee Lewis • Gene Autry
Roy Rogers • Monty Hall • Roy Orbison
Buddy Hackett • Barbara Mandrell

OUT CALIFORNIA WAY

THE FACE IN THE MIRROR was sick with terror. Staring back at me was a wide-eyed, twenty-eight-year-old kid in a ridiculous green Brooks Brothers blazer who had no idea what he was doing. A deer in the footlights, in less than five minutes I was to step in front of the cameras to tape my first national television show. My mouth was so dry my tongue felt like shoe leather and in my palms such rivers flowed I feared the ink on my note cards would run, leaving me more in the dark than I already felt. Suddenly, I was sick to my stomach. I got paralyzed as if someone had punched a button.

"Please God," I pleaded, gazing heavenward for comfort but finding only a cracked fluorescent fixture, "let me get through this. Please help me."

I stared at the little logo on my breast pocket with the backward lettering that said *The Newlywed Game.* I was quickly coming to terms with the reality that this was about to be a catastrophe. A few years earlier, having watched me fail miserably at another show, my wife and kids sat me down and bluntly told me to stay in radio, insisting I was just not a natural for television or acting. Now I was seeing myself through their eyes.

I sucked in a series of deep breaths and tried to get a grip. There was a knock at the door. I shook my shoulders to loosen up and opened it. There stood two smiling men in dark suits. I assumed they were ABC execs come to give me some sort of "good luck, Bob" speech. I grinned stupidly, desperate to appear confident.

1

"Hi guys."

"Bob?"

"Yeah." I instinctively extended my hand to shake theirs.

Instead of taking my hand, one of them thrust a large manila envelope at me and their cheery expressions vanished.

"Mr. Eubanks, we're with the Federal Communications Commission and you are hereby ordered to appear before the United States government's anti-payola committee."

The other fed pointed at the envelope in my hand. "That's a federal subpoena. You'd better be there."

And they left. All of us in L.A. radio had been harassed about payola, but I'd never received a federal subpoena. Although I was not guilty of anything, whenever agents of the federal government deliver something like that, you take notice. Their timing could not have been worse. My impulse was to run like hell, head for the stable, get on my horse and ride into the hills until the nightmare passed.

Then the intercom blared, "Bob Eubanks on stage, please."

It's been said that life's pivotal moments come and go quickly. Somehow I reached deep down and got through that first show, although it nearly ended in disaster. Three times in a row I screwed up a simple question about the Seven Dwarves, and each time we had to stop tape while I recovered. Afterward, director Bill Carruthers angrily narrowed his eyes. "Eubanks, give me back your jacket." Then executive producer Chuck Barris came up to me, unable to hide his concern.

"Bobby, loosen up. You've done something I've never seen anybody do before."

"What did I do?"

"You just went a half hour without blinking. Blink a few times for God's sakes. Let 'em know you're not an oil painting."

I was humiliated.

"Okay, Chuck, I'll definitely blink."

As we shot the next set of shows I frequently looked down at the two-word instruction on the note taped to my podium: BLINK, DUMMY. I walked off the stage that afternoon, elated I had faked my way through it all; then I remembered the subpoena waiting in my dressing room and my heart sank. Blowing a TV show was frightening enough, but the nightmare of what might await me was even more terrifying. I had never taken a dime of payola, nor did I know anyone who had, but I did

ABC PUBLICITY PHOTO

Heeeeeere's Bob!

know one thing: with the government, if they want to get you, innocent or not, they will get you.

The Great Depression was barely underway when John Eubanks met Gertrude McClure. Both were from big families. John had seven siblings, Gertrude nine. They fell in love and decided, despite the dismal economy and having no jobs, to get married and start their own family. They then made the biggest decision of their young lives. With employment scarce in their beloved Missouri hill country, they heard that salvation might lay in Michigan, with stories of jobs aplenty in the car factories. With a large group of relatives, they loaded into their cars and caravanned toward what they hoped was prosperity. They landed in Flint but soon found, like the Joads in *The Grapes of Wrath*, that the promises of steady, decent paying work was just an illusion. Gertrude ended up waitressing and John went to barber school. Upon graduation he was qualified to earn a quarter per head, but spent most of his time playing the guitar as he waited for customers. Eight years later, in 1938, John and Gertrude Eubanks had their only child, Robert Leland Eubanks.

Before I was two my folks made another life-changing decision. They had been listening to what they hoped this time were reliable rumors, that the aircraft industry was hiring as a prelude to a war which seemed inevitable. Filled with hope, along with all of my other relatives, they pulled up stakes yet again and optimistically headed for sunny Los Angeles.

When they arrived there were no golf courses, few apartments, and all the swimming pools were in the back yards of rich people. Their big visions deflated, they ended up crammed into a boarding house. My discouraged relatives soon went back home, but my folks hung in there and held their ground.

As the war came, so did the jobs, and my dad got a job at Vultee Aircraft in Downey, so we moved to nearby Bellflower. As a little guy, I was convinced my dad made all of the airplanes in World War II. Meanwhile, Mom stayed home to raise me. I loved my mother very much, but life with her could be hard. Of the two major traumas that I carried from my childhood, the first was the belief I had nearly killed her during childbirth, something that I heard more than once growing up

The second, an event that occurred in 1945, probably changed the way I felt about love and loss for many years. My mother gravely announced she had only a short time to live. She was so convincing that my distraught dad summoned all our relatives from the four corners of the country to say their goodbyes. At seven, the certainty that I was about to lose my mother was nearly unbearable to me. Everyone in the family rushed to her bedside for one last word or embrace. And sure enough, mom died—fifty-three years later at the age of 90.

Some years before she passed away I wrote the hospital where I was born and discovered that my birth had been uneventful. After thousands of dollars and years of therapy, in that one moment I realized that all the guilt I had lugged around for years had been unnecessary. Guilt sucks.

In 1935, Leo Seltzer responded to the pressures and culture of the Depression and invented a thing called Roller Derby, a skate-bound version of the dance marathons that were so popular. The marathons offered broke and hungry teens a chance to test their endurance for a little prize money. By the 40s, Roller Derby had evolved from a way to have fun and make pocket change into an actual sport, a blend of wrestling and skating complete with a circular track, lots of excitement and its own set of stars.

By the time I was ten I was completely turned on by the glamour and action and wanted to be a Roller Derby champ like my heroes Speck Saunders and Red Smart. As with most kids so taken by something, I jumped into it with all I had. I began practicing skating with a nearly fiendish drive. Around this time, my mom decided I should also be in show business and began shopping me around to agents and photographers. I got modeling work almost immediately, despite an errant fang I called my "snaggle tooth." I was soon doing print ads for J.C. Penny and commercials for Pard dog food.

In December of 1948, my folks got a call asking if I was available for a photo shoot on New Year's Day with The Singing Cowboy himself, Gene Autry. While my mom and dad were simply excited, I was on cloud nine. I loved horses as well as anything to do with the cowboy way of life. As far as heroes, Gene Autry was one of my biggest. I credit photographer Shiny Wright, the man who recommended me for the job, for not only introducing me to my idol, but giving me my first big break in the bargain.

On January 1st, 1949, Mom and Dad took me to the studio at CBS where Gene was doing his live radio show. We waited for nine hours but I didn't mind a bit. When Gene finished his broadcast he came over and shook my hand. Then we shot an ad for one of his many holdings, Paddock Clothing Company. He was in and out in no time—but it was one of the biggest moments of my life, and still is. I had been in love with all things western since I could remember. I seemed to have a new fascination with western life each week. If it wasn't cowboys and singers like Gene Autry, Roy Rogers and the Sons of the Pioneers, it was the horses. Since I could talk I had been begging my folks for a horse. Unfortunately it wasn't too practical, given that we lived in a housing tract in Bellflower, but my parents patiently promised me one day I would get my horse. One Christmas Dad managed to scrounge up the money and bought me a Sears mail order saddle. It was such a sweet gesture. They couldn't any more afford a horse than the man in the moon but the saddle seemed to promise that a horse would come some day. A few

One of the biggest days of my life with Gene Autry in 1949.

I hope you can see my snaggle tooth as I model for JC Penny's in 1948.

MOUNTAIN MUSIC

RANCH HANDS—Jim Dove, Larry Lynn, Burton Knudson, and Bob Eubanks (left to right), stand behind guitarist Gene Gilman in recent performance of the Ranch Hands, Clark Junior High instrumental group, that will appear before Montrose-La Crescenta Kiwanis and Crescenta-Canada Rotary in School Week programs slated by the two fraternal organizations. Ranch Hands have entertained CVCC at recent meetings where they were an instant hit. —Ledger Photo

The Valley Ranch Hands, in junior high. The guy on the right is me. I only knew three chords and only in the key of E.

Pard Dogfood Ad.

"My Heroes Have Always
Been Cowboys."
Circa 1943.

years later came my first horse—a little blue roan mare named Ginger.

Despite my schedule being filled with school, riding, skating and earning extra money for the family as a child actor and model, I began to develop a passionate interest in another field: radio. By the time I was about thirteen I knew everything about the top deejays in town, and I also knew that's what I wanted to be. The Big Five at KLAC, including Gene Norman, Peter Potter and Dick Haynes, were my new heroes. Although rhythm and blues was my music back then, by the time I started high school in 1952 Alan Freed, a disc jockey from the East Coast, had christened a new form of music. He called it rock and roll. With the advent of rock and roll I was hooked and set my sights on becoming a rock and roll disc jockey. And I let everyone know it.

When I was seventeen, and after discovering I actually had a knack for skating, I dropped out of Roller Derby school and got into figure skating. Part of my decision was based on the fact I weighed 140 pounds and damn near got killed mixing it up in Roller Derby. Then, when coaches and other sports people started talking about roller skating being accepted as an Olympic sport, I got gold on the brain. Looking back, I wasted a lot of time on roller skating and should have switched to ice skating—at least it had a future. Nevertheless, by the time I was eighteen I had gotten all the way to the Nationals and took fourth place, despite falling seven times in a 3-1/2 minute routine. By the way, around this time I began dating a girl who I thought was my age. She was beautiful and had a body to match. And when I found out she was eleven I dropped her like a hot potato. The next year she began dating forty-six year old Errol Flynn. He died of a heart attack four years later. I told you she was built.

After I graduated from Pasadena High School in 1955, I enrolled at Pasadena City College, less so for the curriculum than the chance to be close to my girlfriend Joyce. When I discovered they had a broadcasting department I signed up for classes, hoping to ditch my high-pitched Mickey Mouse voice and develop a rich baritone like all the big voiced announcers I admired. What I didn't realize until later was that most of them got their big deep voices by inhaling three packs of Viceroys or Chesterfields every day for decades.

While I wanted to be a disc jockey more than anything, and my folks were always supportive of me, they also wanted me to get a job. One day dad came home from his barber shop and announced he'd

Go ahead and laugh! National Championships, Melrose Park Illinios, 1956.

BOB EUBANKS ARCHIVES

talked to a guy who could get me a job at Lockheed. I didn't know what to do. It wasn't radio, but it did pay four bucks an hour, a lot of money at the time for an eighteen-year-old kid. It also would be a big help toward the $85 a month my folks were shelling out for radio school. On my first day I arrived and parked in Lockheed's huge parking lot. It was a beautiful sunny day as I got out of my car and watched the thousands of other employees trudging into the gigantic assembly buildings surrounding Burbank airport. I had a weird feeling this was not what I wanted to do.

I reported to my supervisor and was told my job would be assembling radar racks for Lockheed Electra aircraft. Oh my God! I panicked when I looked over the confusing mass of aluminum framing and multicolored wires and tubes. Somehow they expected me to put it all together. I freaked out even more when I was told I had to buy a bunch of complicated tools to complete my job. I am perhaps the most mechanically challenged human that has ever lived. For years I thought a Phillips screwdriver was milk of magnesia and vodka. Now, somehow, I was to make sense of these alien parts and put them together so they worked. I listened with wide-eyed amazement as this fellow tried to show me how to put these things together. At first all I could think was "how on earth did he learn all this?" Then all I could see in my mind's eye was a Lockheed Electra's panicked flight crew trying to pull their plane up after the radar rack, my radar rack, failed them. Get me out of here!

On the third day when I parked I was so stressed out it took a lot to drag myself out of my car. I joined the massive stream of aerospace ants as we poured across the lot. I tried hard to imagine another week there, let alone a lifetime. Then God sent a message. On my way into the plant a heavyset worker ahead dropped to the ground in front of me. It was so fast I had just enough time to leap over him. When I, along with a number of other workers, tried to revive him we were shocked to find he had clocked out of this life. The second message was pretty clear. This fate—and job—was not for me. So I gathered up my tools—which I shouldn't have owned anyway—went inside and quit. Back home I related the story to my folks then told them I wanted to concentrate on radio school. They gave it their blessing, and I joke to this day that Lockheed was my last real job.

I'd gotten about all I could from Pasadena City College's broadcasting department and Joyce had dumped me (her mother told her I'd never amount to anything), so I scraped together the money and enrolled at the Don Martin School of Broadcasting in Hollywood. I was told the course generally took nine months. Taking home my course materials the first day, I fantasized that in less than a year I would be a working deejay. I set my sights on the big rock and roll stations like KFWB, vowing I would one day work at a place like that. I sat at the desk in my bedroom that night in 1956 and it became an imaginary control console. I cued up non-existent 45s of Elvis and The Platters and pretended to be one of the top rock and roll jocks around, hanging out with musical stars and running from screaming hordes of fans as I jumped into my late model convertible.

Back to reality, I needed a job until I could graduate from broadcasting school. Over the next few days I decided to try a new approach to job seeking: I would get discovered. Everyone had heard the fable of Lana Turner being discovered at Schwab's Drug Store on Sunset (it was actually the Top Hat Café across from Hollywood High on Highland) so, like a jerk, I put a Broadcasting magazine under my arm and strolled up and down Hollywood Boulevard for several days. Talk about naive. To my surprise no one discovered me, although I did get some strange looks. Now that being discovered had not worked I went back to looking for help wanted signs. That got me nothing. A few days later, back at the Don Martin School I saw an ad on a bulletin board. It advertised an opening for an usher's job at the Egyptian Theater.

When Egyptian king Tutankhamen's tomb was discovered in 1922, a craze for all things Egyptian swept the country. That year impresario Sid Grauman and his partner opened the Egyptian Theater. The Egyptian was one of the more prestigious movie houses on Hollywood Boulevard, so when they offered me a job as an usher I happily took it. After all, it was the entertainment business. The theater was playing the special road show version of *Oklahoma*, the first film to be shot in the dazzling wide-screen 70-millimeter format called Todd-AO.

At that time it was all the thing to put big movies in theaters and give them extended runs, the likes of which you'd never see today in our era of instant gratification and overnight box office numbers. Of course you didn't have the huge variety of entertainment media that you do now, and a special film like *Oklahoma* could play for a couple of years before being replaced. The Egyptian had even been remodeled and the screen redesigned with a curve just to accommodate the film's special format. It was the talk of the town, and as an usher I was on the front line, decked out in my heavy wool uniform and goofy hat, opening limo doors for the likes of Gary Cooper, Elizabeth Taylor, Debbie Reynolds and Eddie Fisher (although the last three did not come together.)

I also stood in the lobby hawking souvenir programs at the top of my lungs. My sales pitch was sort of racy for the time, "*Oklahoma* programs! Souvenir programs! Read all about 'The Girl Who Can't Say No!'" I sold them for fifty cents and put a dime of that in my pocket. I made some decent money but paid for it in embarrassment when I'd see a cute girl from my high school looking at me like I was some kind of weirdo. One of my other duties had not been in my official job description when I'd been hired. About a week or so after I started my manager decided he could trust me. He called me to his office one day and handed me fifty bucks.

"Take this over to a place at the corner of Hollywood and Ivar. See a guy named Jimmy and give it to him."

I took the money and walked down the block. Jimmy, it turned out, was a little sleazeball of a guy and a bookie. From that day on my manager would regularly hand me cash and I'd go see Jimmy. I put up with that job for nearly two years, suffering through *Oklahoma* (a very extended engagement) twice a day for nearly that entire time. While I endured my sentence at the Egyptian I kept active in skating and continued my radio school.

After the *Oklahoma* run, I was ordered to clean the marquee and our section of sidewalk. Once or twice a day the walk in front of the theater would become littered with leaves from the rubber trees. I didn't mind sweeping the leaves, but that big tall sign scared me. Now, I'm really afraid of heights, and because of that I tried to avoid it, but my boss tapped me because he and I were the only male employees and he refused to send a girl up the ladder. The ladder was at least fifteen feet tall and, to make it worse, was on wheels. My technique was to wipe a foot or two of the marquee and then slowly pull myself inch by inch to the next section. At the top of that ladder I felt the slightest movement would literally cause me to eat the big one. I remember looking down the long sign and grimly looking at all of the letters of the film we were now playing—*The Bridge on the River Kwai*—and how I would have to avoid knocking them out of place.

While I was carefully wiping off every inch of the marquee, five young guys, probably in their early twenties, came down the boulevard. Neither they nor I could know they were about to change my life. Spying the hapless jerk in a tacky uniform way up that wheeled ladder, the temptation was too great. As they walked by, their ringleader nonchalantly elbowed the ladder, sending me wheeling down the sidewalk, clinging for dear life and screaming at the top of my lungs. When I came to a stop I quickly climbed down and hugged Mother Earth. Shaking from head to toes with anger and fear, I rolled the ladder back and climbed up to complete my job.

About ten minutes later the five jerks returned. This time I locked eyes with the ringleader until they got below me. Just as he reached for the ladder, I sprang into action. Remembering a move I'd seen in the movie *Mister Roberts*, I hooked my feet around the outside of the ladder and slid down to meet this guy face to face. He gave me a cocky smile so I grabbed my broom and, as he turned to run, I creamed him across the back of the head, sending him ass-over-apple cart. As luck would have it, the moment I whacked him my manager stepped from the box office.

"Eubanks! You're fired!"

"You can't fire me!"

"I can and I just did."

"No you can't because I quit."

And I did. Two exceptional feelings of satisfaction came from that moment. The first was immediate as I laid into that clown with my broom, and the other came forty-three years later when I had the enormous honor of receiving a star on the famous Hollywood Walk of Fame for my work in radio. And guess where my star is? Just about the same place I bashed that bonehead with my broom. Ain't life wonderful?

Meanwhile, I was now two years and three months into Don Martin's nine month course, mainly because I was still skating and going to the national championships. When the nationals rolled around each year I'd have to quit radio school to get ready for them, further delaying my completion of the course. Losing my job at the Egyptian turned out to be a good thing as it got me out of my comfort zone and made me look at my future. And I was also so sick of the theme to *The Bridge on the River Kwai* I thought I would throw up. I decided it was time to get serious about my radio career and finally get that first class radio license.

Back then, the FCC required that all radio stations have a "first phone" on duty at all times the station was being operated. A first phone was radio slang for someone who possessed a First Class Radiotelephone Operator's License. During the daytime at any given radio station there would usually be a first phone on duty anyway, adjusting things and making repairs, but at night, overnights and on weekends station managers didn't often have the luxury of a high paid engineer hanging around twiddling his thumbs. They got around the rule by hiring jocks with a first phone. The upshot was you essentially had to qualify as an engineer just to do the time, temperature and play Bo Diddley records.

It seemed unfair to a twenty-year-old with zero aptitude for such weird things. The test required nothing short of an engineering degree, with questions ranging into scientific voodoo such as phasing the towers, impedance, wattage and worse, actually completing schematic drawings of electrical circuits. The saving grace was that the good folks

One of the biggest days of my career. My Star on the Hollywood Walk of Fame.

at Don Martin knew all the test questions and most of your training was spent memorizing the answers. Despite this advantage I still flunked the exam twice. For my third attempt I drove to downtown L.A. and filed into a big old dark and dreary government building. I took my seat in a colorless hall with hundreds of other aspiring DJs and engineers and promised myself this time I'm gonna pass this sucker.

Nearing the end of the test I began to feel a huge sense of relief that I was home free. I knew almost every question—they were like old friends. And then I saw the last two questions and knew I was in trouble. They were ringers, questions I'd never seen in any Don Martin class. I felt sick to my stomach. The questions were "draw schematics of these circuits." What? Finish off these circuits? Were they nuts? How about the answer to the meaning of life? Suddenly, nerves must have kicked in as I had the painful urge to use the bathroom. Frustrated, I took my test sheet up to the examiner and asked to be excused. I went into a stall, did my business, then just sat there with my head in my hands.

I was gathering my strength to possibly face a third failure when a miracle happened. I turned my head and couldn't believe my eyes. On the wall of that toilet stall, along with girls' phone numbers, someone had drawn those two circuits. And labeled them. I thanked the bathroom angel that had given me the gift, pulled a pen out of my shirt pocket, copied the drawings on my hand, and raced back to the hall. Completing my test, I left with the confidence that the third time would truly be the charm. It was. A few weeks later I got the word: I could now operate a radio station. A whole new world had just opened to me, even though I didn't know a bolt from a volt.

Within a few years of the end of World War II, the radio business braced for the rise of FM. Clearly superior to AM in its sound quality, it was seen as the coming thing. Unfortunately for FM radio and its proponents, consumers didn't see the need to spend an extra five or ten bucks for a radio with dual bands. And it was a rare car radio in the '50s that had an FM scale because all of the big radio stations were AM. So all through the '50s and much of the '60s people listened to AM and were happy. Only when people started looking for higher quality in their broadcast music in the late '60s and early '70s did FM begin to gain a foothold.

I began tying up loose ends in my old life and preparing for a new direction. Skating had given way to my new passion, radio, and I set out to find a job. I got two offers, and the better one was from KWTO in Springfield, Missouri. They offered me the incredible sum of $400 a month to be an on-air personality. I made plans to go to Missouri, a place where my family had roots and one I had been visiting nearly every summer since I was a kid. The job was a great opportunity for me, except for one thing. As I sat on the end of my bed, my bags packed, my '55 Chevy gassed and ready to go, I asked myself, "Wait a minute, dummy, why are you leaving the market everyone wants to be in?" I gritted my teeth, made the call to Missouri, and said thanks but no thanks. Then I called the station manager who had made the other offer.

The Beatles • Mick Jagger • Cary Grant
Merle Haggard • Dolly Parton • David
Letterman • The Rolling Stones • The
Beach Boys • Tina Turner • Leeza
Gibbons • Jerry Lee Lewis • Gene Autry
Roy Rogers • Monty Hall • Roy Orbison
Buddy Hackett • Barbara Mandrell

AND NOBODY CALLED

THE RECEPTIONIST AT DON MARTIN was a guy named Dick Moreland. Moreland's other job was at KACY, in Port Hueneme. The second job tip came from Moreland when he told me about an opening there. He was working weekends and told me they needed an all-night deejay. Even though KACY was in Southern California, prior to applying I had never heard the station because its signal didn't reach that far. Fifty miles up Highway 101 from L.A. in the small coastal community of Port Hueneme, KACY was billed as the number one station in Port Hueneme. That wasn't too tough a claim since it was the only station in Port Hueneme. While the big L.A. stations like KMPC had serious power—up to fifty thousand watts—KACY had a mouse-like two-fifty. With the Pacific on one side, and mountain ranges on the other, I used to joke that two hundred of those watts went into the ocean and the remaining fifty covered the cemetery next door.

In addition to being underpowered, KACY really wasn't much to look at. In the middle of an orange grove, it was a shabby little cinder block building hunkered between two huge transmitter towers. With few windows, it featured a decorative porch that appeared to be an architectural afterthought. When I first pulled up on the long asphalt driveway, it looked like the perfect setting for a horror movie. I pictured the undead rising from their graves around 3 A.M. to grab the unsuspecting deejay.

My salary was set at $320 a month, and for that I was assigned the shift that's always lowest on the rung, the graveyard (no pun intended) from midnight to eight. But it didn't matter because I was now officially a Rock and Roll Disc Jockey. My first night on the air I arrived early and got the lay of the place. The station was divided into two rooms, a very modest office area with a few metal desks, and the control board, situated in front of the large picture window that looked onto the driveway. At night a couple of gooseneck desk lamps lit the console and nearby record rack. In the other room was the transmitter, news teletype and a work bench illuminated by a glaring fluorescent light. However humble it was, my dream had come true.

I memorized every move made by Chuck, the deejay before me, as he operated the control board. I had never worked this board before, but my training at Don Martin had given me confidence and the hundreds of hours playing deejay in my car and bedroom were culminating in this moment. I knew I was as good as this guy Chuck. Since the records were so short back then, two to three minutes—just long enough to fit on a 45—as soon as his shift ended I leaped into his seat and got ready to utter my first words on radio. While his last song wound down, I put a record on the other turntable and cued it up. As the song faded, I slowly slid the pot on the control board to open the microphone. I took a deep breath and let it out quietly.

"It's four minutes to six and fifty-seven degrees in Lancaster." Then I let the record spin and my career as a deejay had begun. I was filled with pride that my opening lines were totally cool. Then Chuck burst into laughter. I turned just in time to see him fall against the wall in hysterics.

"What's so damn funny?" I asked indignantly.

When he managed to catch his breath he gasped, "What the hell did you say?"

Now I was worried. I shook my head. "I, uh . . . "

"You said four minutes to six and fifty-seven in Lancaster?"

"Yeah."

"It's four after twelve and our signal doesn't get halfway to Lancaster."

I looked at the microphone, my new enemy. "Oh shit."

Chuck laughed again and headed toward the door. He saw I was frozen and pointed to the turntable. "Song's almost up. Good luck, hotshot."

Aside from that first goof, my time at KACY was productive, and I learned a lot about the radio business. And it was a great time to be in radio. Prior to my coming on board, KACY's format was what would now be called Adult Contemporary, with a playlist of artists like Andy Williams, Perry Como and Johnny Mathis. Soon after I came on board they changed their format and now were playing the "wilder" stuff, acts from the new and exciting world of rock and roll like Elvis, The Platters and Danny and the Juniors. The world was changing and so was the music. After settling in for a few months, I decided to do what all big-time rock deejays did: I would have a record giveaway contest. I wanted to do everything the big guys did so I came up with the perfect, original plan: an album giveaway. I went to the manager with my proposal. The station got plenty of free records, so two albums would be nothing in the bigger scheme to gauge my incredible success. I asked him for two albums.

"Forget it. We don't have any albums to spare."

I was stunned and hurt he would turn me down. "C'mon, man, it's only two albums."

"No. What's the point? Why do you need a contest?" He looked back down at his Broadcasting magazine. Every deejay had a contest and I couldn't believe he didn't understand that. When he looked back up he saw me standing my ground. He sighed. "Alright, if you want to run a contest, go ahead. But you'll have to find the albums yourself."

Determined, I went to Pal's Record store in Canoga Park and invested eight dollars of my salary in two albums and started running promos for The Great Album Giveaway that evening. Over the next two weeks, I probably promoted my giant album extravaganza 300 times. I mentioned it between nearly every song, that come Tuesday after next, at 2 A.M., those albums would belong to two lucky listeners. I pictured their cars racing down our long driveway as they hurried to get first pick of the albums.

After two weeks of plugging the giveaway it was finally time. I sailed through the news at 1:59, cleared all two phone lines, and reminded listeners of my number. Since I hadn't really thought out how my contest would actually work, when the time came I simply blurted out that I would give both albums to the first person who called. I meant to say "the first two listeners" but it just came out that way. I put on The Coasters singing "Charlie Brown" and felt a tingle go up my spine. I sat back and watched for the buttons on the phone to light up. And guess what? Nobody called.

The song finished and I gave out my phone number again. Then I checked to see if my microphone was open. I played another song. And still nobody called. Slightly panicked, I climbed under and behind the console, double checking all the connections to the board and the microphone. They seemed fine, although had there actually been a problem, despite my first class license, I wouldn't have had a clue. But there didn't seem to be anything wrong. I played the next few songs and a sickening feeling came over me that I was just a guy sitting in an orange grove talking to himself and his undead friends nearby. I realized with a dark smile that the residents of the nearby cemetery were probably the only members of my loyal audience. Because . . . to my dismay . . . nobody called. So I made up a name, proudly announced the "winner," and took the albums home.

The contest depressed me. I realized my job consisted of sitting in the middle of an orange grove in the dead of night and talking to myself. I decided I had to escape overnights. Although it would take years until I concluded I was simply a competent "time and temp" jock, and not one of the wild men or "boss jocks" who would rise to stardom in the '60s on their sheer radio talent, I did develop a talent for making up commercials on the fly. I would open the commercial log (where the sales staff indicated which advertiser was to receive a commercial and when) and it would often say something like "commercial for Wagon Wheel Lumber (see Yellow Pages)." I would then ad-lib a commercial using the information from their yellow page ad. To this day, if asked, I can talk for exactly thirty or sixty seconds, no more, no less. I also learned to "cold read" the news, that is, picking five minutes of copy off the teletype and reading it for the first time, on the air, as if I'd already practiced it several times.

And there were other lessons to be learned about radio, some of them less practical than philosophical. Several months after the album giveaway failure I was once again reminded of my mortality when the transmitter went out for five hours and, unbeknownst to me, I chattered away the whole time, not even reaching my fans in the graveyard. No one noticed, not even the station manager or staff.

You would think hanging out in the middle of some orange trees in 1959 in Port Hueneme, California, between midnight and 8 A.M. was always deadly dull, but it wasn't. The control room had a big window just inches from the board that looked out toward the driveway. At night, with no exterior lights, it was just a black frame. Fog would often roll in from the nearby Pacific, giving it a lonely and creepy atmosphere. One night I was listening to The Fleetwoods wind down "Come Softly to Me" and turned to cue up a record on the other turntable. As I looked out the window six inches away I found myself face to face with a grizzled, bearded mug peering in at me. It scared the shit out of me. I ran to the front door and double checked that it was locked. Later, I found out he was just one of my faithful audience. Albeit, like my friends in the cemetery, he had no radio, he was one of the many Boxcar Willies who had set up camp less than a hundred yards away. The railroad passed nearby and hobos had established a small community on the other side of the cemetery. Even though they couldn't hear me, I felt a bond with these homeless men as we were all stuck in that foggy orange grove together.

KACY's general manager, Jack, was a hard-ass ex-Marine and a real bully. The whole staff was scared to death of the guy. Although he never really picked on me, the same could not be said of some of the other jocks. One morning I left work, jumped on the 101 and was driving home. I flipped on the station to see how the jock after me was doing and heard that awful ka-chook ka-chook ka-chook as the needle skipped at the end of a record track. It went on for a while, so fearing something had happened to him, I turned around. I pulled down the driveway, slammed on my brakes and rushed into the station. On the control room floor I found the other jock, bleeding from the mouth and half dazed. Our station and the sales and management office were about five minutes apart. Apparently, the jock said something our manager didn't agree with and the manager came over, beat the living crap out of him, then casually went back to the sales office as if they'd talked about the weather.

Jack also had two hard and fast rules: Never play two album cuts back to back and never, under any circumstances, "play those goddamn Hi-Lo's." I didn't understand the latter. The Hi-Lo's were a popular and talented vocal quartet. And though I didn't see the harm in playing two records in tandem—called a segue in radio—I tried to stick to his warning. The problem was that sometimes nature called at 3 A.M. and two minutes and twenty seconds wasn't enough to . . . ahem, finish business. Once at 4 A.M. I broke his rule and, lo and behold, the phone rang thirty seconds later.

"I told you, no two songs back to back!" he screamed.

Did the man sleep? I wasn't the only guy on radio with this problem. Many stations at that time had the no segue rule and it wasn't until Marty Robbins recorded and released "El Paso" that jocks around the country breathed a sigh of relief. "El Paso" was a bountiful four minutes and twenty-two seconds, giving all of us just enough time to accomplish any immediate bodily functions. I would crank up the monitors in the control room, put on "El Paso," race into the other room, ripping off the news from the teletype as I passed, and head to the bathroom to rehearse the news, all the while keeping my ear on Marty's voice. Near the end of the song he sings about a deep burning pain in his side. When Marty got that deep burning pain, done or not, I had to wipe, flush and run. More than a few times I read the news with my pants around my ankles.

Marty Robbins was the savior for many '50s radio jocks. A fellow radio man once observed that more "girls got laid and deejays used the bathroom to 'El Paso' than any other song in history." I don't know if that's true, but for deejays in the '60s, the long songs were the Beatles' "Hey Jude" and Led Zeppelin's classic, "Stairway To Heaven." By the '70s, the rise of Album Oriented Rock (AOR) and FM stations gave air staffs a number of extended cuts such as Pink Floyd's "The Wall" and Lynyrd Skynyrd's "Free Bird." Nowadays, so few people say anything on radio that taking a bathroom break is no big deal.

After nearly a year working the all night shift I was getting tired of the grind and the loneliness. The straw that broke the deejay's back happened one morning about 4 A.M. I was having trouble keeping my eyes open when two headlights came barreling down the driveway. For a moment I thought the car was going to keep going, taking me and my board with it. Then I heard squealing tires and a very pregnant woman leaped from the car and started banging on the front door. She was sobbing hysterically.

"Help! You've got to help me! My husband's gonna kill me!"

That got my attention. I glanced outside for the husband then turned to her.

"Okay, tell me what's going on."

"My husband," she wailed, "he's gonna kill me! He threw me outta our double wide." Then she added, "And he's gotta shotgun."

"Oh boy. Alright, he may want to kill you, but he's not going to kill me."

I ran out and cut the lights in her car, then came back, locked the door and turned out the lights. As my song wound down I fumbled in the dark for another and got it on the turntable. I realized I was also in danger of playing two songs back to back. As the highway patrol dispatcher came on the phone, I watched the tone arm winding toward the end of the 45. I threw another record on the other turntable and cued it with one hand.

"Could you hold a sec?" I asked the dispatcher. Then I got right on top of the microphone and whispered, "That was The Crests with 'Sixteen Candles.' It's 4:17 and you're listening to Port Hueneme's number one station, KACY." I turned back to the phone. "Okay, sorry. Uh huh, yeah, she says he has a gun, a shotgun."

So here I was, in an isolated radio station in the middle of the night, crawling around the floor with a pregnant woman whose drunk husband was after her with a shotgun. Thank God the cavalry was coming.

At that moment I was only slightly more afraid of being shot than I was of having my manager call and scream at me for playing two records in a row. Fifteen minutes later the CHP arrived and found the guy, drunk as a skunk and staggering around the grove about fifty yards from the station. And yes, he did have a shotgun. The next day I confronted my ex-Marine hard-ass manager with a demand, "I want better hours or I'm outta here."

Apparently he liked my contribution to the station because he immediately moved me to the far more civilized 6 A.M. to noon shift and dropped my old overnight shift because it wasn't profitable. No longer a mole, I became reacquainted with the sun. But the new shift brought a different challenge to my life, which was getting up at 4:30 A.M. Going to work at midnight was one thing, but getting up in the middle of the night was downright unnatural. To maximize my time in bed I soon created a very tight schedule to get to work.

Leaving my house in Canoga Park at five sharp, I would drive out the 101 and descend from the mountains past Thousand Oaks into the little farming community of Camarillo. At the Associated Truck Stop I would pull my little VW between the Peterbuilts and KWs at precisely 5:45. Running inside, I would wave to a sweet, toothless old waitress named Minnie who would have my standard breakfast—a hamburger patty and two eggs over easy—hot and on the plate. I would barely sit down, shoveling it all down in less than five minutes. Zooming out of the parking lot, my next hurdle was a bit dicier. The northbound train crossed the tracks near the station between 5:58 and 6:01 A.M. Either way I was late for work if I stopped to wait for the train to pass. Usually I had a good margin of safety, fifty yards or so, but sometimes the second I cleared the tracks, I'd look in my rearview mirror and see a blurred train. The engineers always blew their horn. I wasn't sure if they were saying hi or telling me to get the hell out of their way. Later, I found out that MPs patrolling the nearby base routinely took bets whether or not the crazy deejay in the VW Bug would beat the train. Years later my son, Corey, would be considered one of the world's best stunt drivers. Maybe it's in his genes.

As the morning jock it was my duty to turn on the transmitter and let it warm up before I began broadcasting. The prescribed warm up time was half an hour, but I often gave the old war horse less than two minutes to cough and spit and clear its throat before it was rock and roll time. Opening the station in the morning was always pretty creepy, what with the fog shrouding the orange grove and cemetery and the sleeping hoboes that looked like cadavers under the big oak. When I would open the front door I would quickly slide inside and lock it to keep any bogey men from getting their clutches on me. Then I would inch down the wall to the back room like a blind man because the idiot who wired the place thought it would be a great idea to place the light switch farthest from the door.

One morning I was doing my Helen Keller routine on my way to the switch. I heard the news machine clacking away and used that as a reference as I moved along the wall. As I reached for the switch my elbow hit something and a gunshot shook me to my core. Then a spine chilling scream welled up from the blackness and I could feel the claws of some inhuman demon ripping at my chest. I was in the middle of a full blown horror movie and nearly peed in my pants. I found the switch, flipped it and expected to be face to face with some hideous apparition bent on having my soul. It was in fact a terrified little black cat who had been locked in all night and was now backed into a corner and hissing wildly. The "gunshot" was the Yellow Pages hitting the floor. Crisis averted, the cat and I finally settled down and soon became friends.

Several months after I switched to mornings, KACY began to come out of its coma. Our brute of a GM was replaced by a great guy named Glen Lockheart. In the world of small town radio Glen may have been the most creative manager I've ever known. Glen believed in creating excitement, and he did, with one contest or giveaway after another. Not too many months after Glen's arrival, our boast of being number one in Port Hueneme (an inside joke around the station) was replaced by being able to say we were actually number one in Ventura County. It was a substantial claim. Pretty soon the mood around the place changed from that of prison camp to nut house, with each of us trying to out-practical-joke the next guy.

Our afternoon jock was a guy who called himself Jack Sands. DJs have always changed their names to reflect whatever they thought sounded cool, so I don't know if that was his real name or not, but one day he announced he was holding a contest to test his listenership.

"Folks," he said to his audience, "I want you to help me out. Go find some sand, good old garden variety beach sand, from the kids' sandbox, sand in your garden, whatever. Put it in an envelope and send it so me, Jack Sands, here at the station."

It was a wacky idea and I was pulling for him to succeed, but he had the same results as my first big album giveaway. My buddy Dick Moreland (now the program manager) and I felt bad that Jack's sand gimmick went bust, so Dick and I came up with a plan to cheer him up. For a rock jock in small market radio, reading the news was always a chance to show off one's inner Walter Cronkite. In the middle of his newscast, Jack was informing greater Ventura County about the Pope's illness. Looking out the window, he was momentarily distracted when he saw a dump truck backing toward the station, the ding ding ding of its back-up indicator loud enough to be heard over the air. When the driver raised the dumper, Jack stumbled. But when a yard of sand WHOOSHED out all over the porch, he stopped in mid-sentence and abandoned the mike. I thought it was hilarious until Moreland hit me up for half of the cost of the dump truck. Then Glen Lockheart insisted we have it removed, which took another chunk out of my modest salary.

Several days later the remnants of the sand joke nearly caused a catastrophe. Things were fairly loose at KACY and one of the salesmen doubled as the newscaster for the all-important local noon news. This guy was also pretty slick with the ladies and seemed to have them all over Ventura County, which often made him late in delivering his newscast. Other than having your equipment fail, nothing pisses off a jock more than having the next guy late for his shift, or in this case, newscast.

At one minute to noon this guy was nowhere in sight so I angrily ripped a sheet of stories off the wire and got ready to fill in for him. I sat down a few seconds to noon and waited for the commercial to end. Then I heard the high-pitched whine of an engine coming closer. Just as I started the newscast I looked down the driveway and saw our Romeo make the turn from Pleasant Valley Road onto our driveway at about sixty. His little Austin-Healy Sprite hurtled toward me and for a moment it seemed he wasn't going to stop. I stiffened, ready to leap from the console. Then he hit the brakes... but nothing happened because the sand from our prank was still all over the road. He smacked into that goofy front porch and it collapsed onto him and what was left of his Sprite. I went to music and ran outside. I pushed the porch roof off him and he sat up, looking around, a bit dazed. Then he brushed the debris off his tie and reached up to adjust his dusty toupee.

"Shee-ittt, Bobby! What happened?"

Dick Moreland was also quite the joker. One morning I was in a hurry to read the news and tore off a three foot length of paper from the news wire. With no time to trim it down I quickly circled the pieces I wanted and began reading over the air. A few seconds into my newscast I smelled smoke and looked down. Moreland had lit the bottom of the printout and the flames were climbing toward my hands. I calmly kept reading despite the flames inching up the sheet. Pretty soon I was sounding like an auctioneer, reading the last minute or so of copy in about twenty seconds. I finished with nothing but a pile of ash on my console.

It was during my time at KACY that the concert bug hit me. That disease stayed with me for many years and I only have Dick Moreland to blame for infecting me. One day after my shift, Moreland took me aside.

"Bob, "he said, "let's put on a concert." I gave him a "you're insane" look. He handed me a 45. It was "Too Much Tequila" by the Champs.

"How popular is that song?" he asked me.

It had come out a year or two earlier but we probably got more requests for it than any other single song. I knew the Champs featured a Latin sax player named Chuck Rio and a lot of our audience was Latin.

"It's pretty popular. You're saying we can book the Champs?"

Suddenly my wheels were turning.

Dick Moreland and I presented the Champs. It was the first concert I ever produced. No wonder we didn't make any money—tickets were a buck and a half!

"I'm telling you, we can make more money in one night than we do with the station in a month."

By then I was making about $400 and that certainly intrigued me.

"You can book them?"

Moreland nodded. "Think of this market. We'd make a killing."

Maybe he wasn't so insane. In the next week Moreland proved he was good for his word and got the Champs booked. We reserved an outdoor venue in nearby Oxnard and were in business. The station kicked in advertising and we ran off a bunch of posters, plastering them all over town. By the day of the concert Moreland and I each had invested about six months' salary in the event. Although I was slightly nervous when we opened the ticket office, within 30 minutes I was a wreck because we had sold a grand total of 20 tickets. Our sure thing was starting to look like a sure disaster. However, within the next hour we had accumulated a crowd of about 200. Unfortunately, some of them included members of the Oxnard police department who had entered to "keep an eye on things." As the Champs played, the mayor confronted us about the music.

"This trash is permeating every home in the entire city," he said, his angry face beet red. "Turn it down or we'll shut you down!"

We asked the Champs to turn down their amps for their final songs and they happily obliged. Despite the lack of turnout, the concert was great. The mayor also didn't know that everyone there was witness to a little musical history. It wouldn't be significant for another ten years or so, but two of the band members, a couple of Central Texas kids named Jimmy Seals and Dash Crofts, would become superstars with hits like "Summer Breeze" and "Diamond Girl." After the band was paid and we did the accounting, Dick Moreland and I had lost around $3,000. It put a big hurt on our bank accounts but there was no turning back: we were officially rock and roll promoters.

IT'S NOW OR NEVER

WITH THE CHAMPS CONCERT DISASTER still stinging, I took a step back and sized up my life. I was tired of sitting in an orange grove and talking to transients and dead people. I was ready to move up, and there was only one place to be and that was L.A. A new station in town had everyone excited. In 1941, a broadcast license was given to a station in Pasadena with the call letters KPAS and the frequency of 1110 AM. Its primary market was the farming communities between Pasadena and El Monte.

In 1945, it became a country station, and to avoid confusion with the old format and rural market, the decision was made to change its call letters to KXLA. Along with the name change they got a power boost to ten thousand watts. During those days they boasted shows hosted by future legends Rex Allen and Tennessee Ernie Ford and even soon-to-be car sales mogul Cal Worthington. I remember going down to KXLA in 1949 to watch Cliffie Stone doing his live show "Dinner Bell Roundup." No one had any inkling at that time of the battle that would begin brewing a decade later between KXLA's predecessor and cross-town rival KFWB in a format that didn't yet exist. I would be in the middle of it and, in the end, partly responsible for deciding its outcome.

On January 1, 1958, KFWB switched to the hot "Top 40" format to service the growing baby boomers who were tired of listening to their folks' music. Soon, kids had an exciting place on the dial to enjoy Ricky Nelson, Elvis and groups like the Dell-Vikings and the Everly Brothers. KFWB also began scouring the country for top personalities to push their format. Back then stations lived and died on their air staff lineup and KFWB had one of the best, assembling what would be known as the "Seven Swingin' Gentlemen."

In no time, KFWB was the hottest station in town and that got the attention of two Canadian brothers, Don and Jack Kent Cooke. Don also happened to have American citizenship. That last distinction was extremely important as no foreigner was allowed ownership or management of an FCC license or licensed facility. According to U.S. law, the airwaves are owned by the American public and merely licensed to stations, so it was illegal for anyone but an American citizen to operate a station.

In addition to wanting a station in Los Angeles, the Cooke brothers also understood that legal wrinkle so they bought KXLA's transmitter and equipment and made Don the official owner. In 1959 the Cookes petitioned the FCC to change the call sign to reflect the new station's market, which was the entire Los Angeles basin. Then they shelved the country format and quietly prepared for war with KFWB. Their new station, now called KRLA, was the beginning of a dynasty. By 1960, word had gotten out and KRLA was the hot new rock and roll station that had jocks all over the country sending in their tapes.

I mentioned to my dad that I wanted to redo my demo tape with the hopes of getting a better job. I told him we didn't have the facilities at KACY to do it right. Aside from that, I didn't want KACY to know I was looking for another job. Dad said he cut the hair of an engineer at KRLA and volunteered to ask the man if I could come in some evening and work on my tape. A few weeks later the session was arranged and I drove over to Pasadena in the middle of the night to the KRLA studio. Located in the Huntington Sheraton Hotel, KRLA was what I had envisioned big time radio looked like. It had a formal lobby with mix and match sofas. The tables were covered in neatly stacked magazines of the broadcast trade. It smelled of leather and smoke and success. The place had changed somewhat since I had been in the audience eleven years earlier but I had gotten so used to Kay-Cee I was no doubt wide-eyed for a few minutes until we got down to working on my tape.

I returned to my morning shift at KACY but couldn't get KRLA out of my head. I was counting the days when KRLA's Program Director, Herb Hyman, would find my tape among the hundreds on his desk, recognize my talent, and summon me immediately. I never got the call. A few months went by and I finally decided to just go over to KRLA and hang out. My son Corey often says that "Luck is opportunity and talent meeting each other." I'm still not sure I have that much of the latter but on that day I sure had enough of the former to make up for it.

Sitting in the lobby, flipping absent-mindedly through a magazine, I was half hoping to catch a glimpse of one of the big time jocks like Jimmy O'Neill or Sam Riddle. Suddenly the conference room door burst open and out poured the jackpot—every jock at KRLA. I had happened upon a meeting of the air staff and heard them all grumbling about who would take the shift of the overnight man, Frank Pollack. It seems Pollack had serious back trouble and no one wanted the duty of working their own shift then staying up all night to do Pollack's. Like a scene out of a movie I leaped into Program Director Herb Hyman's path and, cupping my hand over my ear, I intoned in my richest, most impressive Don Martin radio voice, "Hi there. I am a disk jockey."

Apparently Herb's back was against the wall because he actually paused and sized me up.

"You belong to the union?"

"No," I said confidently, "but I will by this afternoon."

"You have any experience?"

"Two years at KACY, overnights and mornings."

"Never heard of it. Kay-zee?"

"Kay-cee. In Port Hueneme."

Herb took another long look at the skinny brash kid standing in front of him.

"Okay. Join the union. You're on tonight. But only tonight."

I floated out on a cloud. I felt like the batboy given the chance to bat fifth for the Yankees. I borrowed $320, paid the union, then showed up for work about fifteen hours later. My shift was about to start and I entered the studio, taking the seat of the outgoing deejay. I settled in behind the impressive console and looked through the glass to the engineer fussing with the bank of equipment. I turned to the other panel of glass that opened onto the lobby and some of the kids sitting on the sofas waiting to get a glance at one of the jocks at work—in this case, me. Right then I knew I would have a very hard time going back to KACY. How're ya gonna keep 'em down on the farm after they've seen Paree?

My first shift at KRLA was uneventful and I assumed that when it was finished so was my big shot at stardom. I went back to my morning job at KACY, but the next day got a miraculous call from Herb Hyman.

When I first became one of the KRLA Eleven-Ten Men in 1960.

It was short and sweet. He liked what I had done and offered me a weekend slot, my dream come true. Now I was working mornings at KACY and weekends at KRLA. After a week or so I made a big decision and quit KACY with the hope I could fill the next full time job to open up at KRLA. I didn't have long to wait. My previous benefactor from that first night, Frank Pollack, a rock and roll disk jockey who hated rock and roll, had really bad back problems and finally quit, leaving an opening. There was a short contest among the air staff to get the shift and I won. I was the newest, full time deejay at L.A.'s second most powerful top 40 radio station. I was twenty-two years old and one of the "Eleven-Ten Men."

After I got to know Herb I pitched him on hiring my pal, Dick Moreland from KACY, to fill my weekend slot. He did and Dick was at KRLA for several years, eventually becoming Program Director. Later, Bill Keffury came over from KACY, and he, in turn, brought Jim Steck from there to read news. No one would have guessed that my hiring at KRLA

PUBLICITY PHOTO SERVICE

Proud to be an Eleven-Ten Man. KRLA circa 1961.

would soon turn a little 250 watt station in Port Hueneme, California, into the farm club for one of radio's most influential stations.

What I also didn't know was that my new station was in serious trouble.

Apparently the Cooke brothers, in their acquisition of the station, had committed a number of blunders and outright deceptions and had gotten the FCC after them. The first problem came from the original promos used by the station when they changed their call letters. The station was physically based in Pasadena, but the transmitter was in El Monte. While the FCC did not require that a station identify itself by its transmitter location, you were required, at the very least, to mention the city you were in. For instance, the on-air IDs should have said "KRLA, El Monte." Even "KRLA, Pasadena" would have been acceptable. The Cookes had promos created that said "KRLA, Los Angeles" because, face it, it sounded a heck of a lot more impressive. That was strike one with the feds.

The next debacle was "The Golden Key" contest.

During the format change between KXLA and KRLA, the station began running its new playlist of Top 40 hits, but had yet to introduce its new staff of exciting air personalities. To kick off that big event on September 3, 1959, when both the improved air staff and shiny new 50,000 watt transmitter would be unveiled, a lucky listener would solve a series of clues and find the "Golden Key" that would "switch on the station" and make the symbolic transition. The object of the big quest, the Golden Key, was advertised to be hidden somewhere in the Los Angeles basin. Once the contest got underway several problems surfaced. One, there was no Golden Key. Two, with no Golden Key it follows that what does not exist cannot be hidden. Three, the clues that were given over the air were literally fake, made up just to fill the spots. With thousands of listeners scouring all of SoCal for the mythical Golden Key, I'm sure they would have been furious had they known they were on a snipe hunt.

A day before the contest was to end, the Cookes finally decided to come up with a key and hide it at Marineland. They handed out some easy clues, making it simple for the listeners to find. It was also a convenient way out of their little dilemma. But when word got out that the contest had been badly conceived, and even more poorly executed, the FCC started investigating. The last straw settled into place with the "Find Perry Allen Contest."

With their goal of assembling a young, exciting group of young jocks that was closer in age to their target audience than KFWB's "old fogies" air staff, the Cookes cast about the country for youthful and exciting deejays. They set their sights on Perry Allen, an announcer with WKBW in Buffalo. They made a deal to hire Allen and devised a contest that would give a listener a chunk of cash if they walked up to Perry Allen—who by the implication was somewhere on the streets of Southern California—and asked him, "Are you Perry Allen, the newest member of the ever-lovin' Eleven-Ten men?"

If the person in question turned out to be Perry Allen, the observant listener would receive $10,000 from KRLA. In 1959 a new Cadillac could be had for less than $5,000, so people took the contest very seriously, asking just about everyone if they were "Perry Allen, the newest member of the ever-lovin' Eleven-Ten men?" The problem was Perry Allen was still in Buffalo on WKBW, finishing his commitment there. Someone at KFWB got wind of that technicality and sent two guys to

Buffalo. During a break in his show, Allen was told two men wanted to see him. He went out to greet them, expecting they were on a goodwill mission from KRLA. One of them said, "Call your new boss Jack Kent Cooke and tell him he owes KFWB ten thousand dollars." But they made lemonade from a sack of lemons when they went on the air and announced "Even KFWB listens to KRLA." That really pissed them off.

Then an angry Jack Kent Cooke compounded his first mistake with an even bigger one: fighting KFWB over the ten grand. With his involvement in that brouhaha he suddenly became visible to the FCC. Combined with the other improprieties, it was now apparent to the FCC that the "Canadian" brother was running the show so they stepped up their investigation. What they discovered, on top of the phony contests and a guy from the Great White North pulling the strings of an American radio station, was perhaps even more shocking to them.

Written logs are kept of everything a station sends out over the air, from commercials to public service announcements to what songs were played. The logs are sacrosanct and must, according to the FCC, be meticulously documented. What the feds found out was that KRLA had been phonying their logs. Because of the station's agricultural heritage in servicing El Monte, after it made the format change it was still required to run a specific number of farm reports, as well as some religious programming, usually shuffled off to early Sunday mornings when few were supposedly listening.

What was actually happening was that songs by artists like Dion and the Belmonts and Ritchie Valens were being logged as crop reports or uplifting religious messages. When the FCC unraveled that little "secret" they flipped. The next thing Jack and Don Cooke knew they no longer had a broadcast license and subsequently lost ownership of the station. So for years, including my entire stay at the station, which was 1960 to 1967, KRLA was owned by the federal government. Until the dispute was settled years later, all profits from the station were donated to the USC Broadcast Department and funneled to public broadcasting. For seven years I literally worked at the best funded non-profit station in the world and the American public owned one of the hottest rock stations around.

It was weird. The government appointed a guy named Larry Webb to administer the station until the legal mess with the Cookes could be satisfied. Like clockwork, early each week we would receive a telegram from the FCC informing us we could continue operating for that week only. Few listeners had any idea of the situation, or that they were part owners in the station, however small their interest. Ironically, the government ended up having to pay the Cookes about $900,000 a year for the rental of the transmitter, which the Cookes owned. That yearly figure was just about what they had paid for the entire station in the first place. At one time, Jack Kent Cooke, among his many other acquisitions, owned the L.A. Kings hockey team and the world famous Lakers. He also built the Forum in Inglewood by doing something that was way ahead of its time, but common now: selling the advertising rights.

Once I had gotten acclimated to KRLA, I became aware of the influence the station had over "The Land of Eleven-Ten." Picture a balmy summer evening, sitting at a stoplight on Sunset or Ventura Boulevard in your '59 Chevy, and through the open windows of the cars next to you would come the sounds of KRLA's signature jingle. The station promoted itself heavily, and with the cash and reach to back up the contests you'd see KRLA signs and banners everywhere, put up by our listeners with the hope of winning money from us. Christmastime saw our stickers and banners in a surprising percentage of the homes and businesses you'd pass on the street. They were all looking for the KRLA Santa Claus to come and make someone's Yuletide a rich one. On Valentine's Day the station ran a "Most Creative Valentine" contest. We got thousands of entries, including a two-ton concrete heart.

The station turned their jocks into stars, with a constant stream of personal appearances. On top of that, we all had our pictures constantly circulating in all manner of promotions for the station. Soon people began to recognize me. It was exciting, yet a little strange at first. We also had many adoring fans, some bordering on obsession. A few years later, musicians would start referring to such zealous fans as groupies.

KRLA's entrance was up some stairs, with only one way in and out. The kids who couldn't fit in the lobby would hang out on those steps at least eighteen hours a day, hoping to catch sight of one of their idols, or better, talk to them and get an autograph. Television news woman Kathleen Sullivan told me years later she had been one of those kids waiting on the steps. It was all harmless fun . . . usually.

Dick Biondi, who came on board in 1963 to do nine to midnight, asked me years later if I remembered a long-haired guy who was a lot older than the rest of the kids and used to sit on the steps and hold court. Though the fellow was small in stature, he had intense eyes and a street demeanor that had the girls hanging all over him. I told Dick I didn't remember him. He played a guitar and Dick said of the few times he heard the guy he wasn't bad. Apparently he also wrote songs but no one at the station stopped to listen. Had they done so they might have taken heed.

"His name," Dick told me, "was Charlie...Charlie Manson."

There were other encounters at KRLA that weren't ominous but certainly could be weird. Deejays have always gotten calls from female listeners who, although sounding quite sexy on the phone, were often lonely women who would have trouble getting a date with a sighted person. An exception walked into the station one night and asked to speak to me privately. She was very attractive, and when I looked through the glass my first instinct was to tell the receptionist to let her in. Then she started in on this crazy rant about how I was sending her subliminal messages over the air and needed to stop immediately. When asked to leave she became agitated and I finally had to call security from the adjoining Huntington Hotel.

Another nut became a long term affliction for me. I started getting letters from a Long Beach woman who promised me all sorts of graphic sexual favors and worked suggestive song titles into her text, like "I'd like to 'Sugar Shack' up with you." She signed them "Boo Boo Baby." Pretty soon my Boo Boo Baby letters became the talk of the station and I got ribbed by all the other jocks. There was no way to keep them hidden because they'd fill the station with the stench of her awful perfume. Boo Boo Baby was very persistent, but I tried to ignore her advances. Eventually, apparently out of frustration over not having answered her, she sent me something that was guaranteed to get my attention: a Polaroid of her buck naked with those same song titles written all over her pale, flabby body.

As the years passed, Boo Boo sent me at least one letter a week at KRLA until I added *The Newlywed Game* to my schedule in 1966. Then the nut began addressing the letters "care of ABC." But when I got a call from ABC's fan mail department telling me she had crossed the line, I had to put the brakes on Boo Boo Baby. She wrote that she was going to have a baby and that the father was not her husband, but rather, me. That she and I had never met posed a problem for her claim, but I assumed her husband would not take the news well, reasoning that any-one stupid enough to marry Boo Boo was stupid enough to believe her.

I called the Long Beach Police. To my surprise Boo Boo Baby turned out to be a housewife with children in high school. Her husband was a successful businessman with no knowledge of her secret obsession. Af-ter their investigation the Boo Boo Baby era in my life came to a blessed end. But then Edith of Bridgeport, Connecticut, seemed to take the baton. Not long after beginning hosting duties on *The Newlywed Game*, Edith began sending me telegrams. She literally sent one five days a week for three years, without fail. Her plea was simple: meet her at a local bar in Bridgeport. Finally Western Union quit showing up. I guess Edith found someone else to drink with.

While on the air at KRLA I did engage in interactions with people who were far more interesting and rewarding than Boo Boo and Edith. All of the jocks experienced an assortment of people coming through the studio to visit them, from record company reps to individual artists hawking their wares, all trying to get us to give their product some air-play. One young record promoter in particular stood out and we struck up a friendship. He was an Italian-American kid in his late twenties who grew up in Detroit.

He and I used to sit and talk for hours about music and our dreams for the future. He'd experienced a few successes writing songs for oth-ers, but was trying hard to break in as a singer in his own right. He had just started working under producer Phil Spector and was hopeful that big things awaited him. He was getting paid $200 a week to push his catalog of songs.

Not many months after we met he told me he'd started dating a girl he was crazy about and mentioned she could also sing. He brought her by and the first thing I noticed was that she was taller than he was. She was also very young, maybe seventeen. But despite the hair hanging down over her face and her delicate age, she had a charisma that was inescapable. From then on I never saw him without her. The night he introduced me to his girlfriend, Cherilyn LaPierre, he told me they were going places and he had big plans. It turns out that my friend, Sonny Bono, was right.

Despite the occasional odd encounter and desperate groupies, we had a lot of fun at KRLA. The air staff consisted of a wildly creative and relatively uninhibited group of guys. Someone on the staff usually had some sort of a practical joke going. Our news director, Bill McMillan, took himself way too seriously, which made him a natural target. When McMillan bought a new Thunderbird he kept bragging about what a great car it was and what a great guy he was for buying it. One of the guys in the news department, Cecil Tuck, had too much of Bill's T-Bird talk and decided to take him down a notch or two. One morning while McMillan was busy inside the station, Cecil went out to the parking lot and, with the help of welder buddy, affixed a metal whistle inside the grill of McMillan's new T-Bird. As soon as McMillan jumped into his T-Bird, turned onto Oak Knoll and hit thirty-five, it sounded like the police were trying to pull him over. McMillan wore out three Ford dealers before someone discovered that whistle.

Newsman Jim Steck loved to rifle through everyone's mailboxes in search of really good party invitations. Although he was on the staff, he wasn't a jock and didn't get the highly sought after invites to "A list" parties. When the air staff got tired of his scavenging we played a joke on him. We phonied up a really fancy looking invitation to a party allegedly hosted by Frank Sinatra. Steck took the bait, went to the "party," and realized he'd been had. He never pilfered the mailboxes again.

In the fall of 1960, KRLA did something no one had ever done in the radio business: they traded one jock for another with a different radio station. Perry Allen was not that happy at KRLA and wanted to move from a Top 40 station to one that played what was called Middle Of the Road, or MOR. Meanwhile, across town a rising young star named Wink Martindale worked at MOR station KHJ. Already host of KTLA television's local dance show, *POP Dance Party*, broadcast from the recently renovated Pacific Ocean Park in Santa Monica, Wink wanted to move to Top 40. So KRLA sent Perry Allen to KHJ, who in turn gave them Wink Martindale. It was probably the first and only time that ever happened in the history of radio.

Wink settled into the 6 A.M. to 9 A.M. shift. The only complaint I ever had about Wink was that about twice a month he would oversleep, forcing me, the overnight guy, to cover for him until he arrived. I would fume but I still liked Wink. About six months after he arrived, he decided to move over to KFWB. His much coveted morning spot was then thrown to the whims of our listeners when a contest was announced

With my early mentor, Wink Martindale.

giving them a chance to vote for his successor from the rest of the KRLA staff. I won. That move gave me a decent jump in salary, especially for a twenty-three-year-old kid in 1961, to $12,000 a year.

Despite having modeled and skated in front of audiences since I was a child, as well as having performed as a deejay, I always worried my career might some day require me to appear on live television. My fear was I would falter and just not come across. Fortunately, at least at that point in my life, I'd never had to. During Wink's run at KRLA he would occasionally have other jocks on his *POP Dance Party*. One time he invited me to come on. It was my first television appearance and I was extremely nervous. Though comfortable behind the microphone in the safe confines of the studio, the idea of thousands of people (who I couldn't see) watching my every move intimidated the hell out of me.

On Wink's show I felt wooden, stiff as a board. And my own self-consciousness was further reinforced by watching how easy Wink made it look. He was totally in command of his show and the audience, and

I could feel the waves of confidence coming off him—something I just couldn't summon in myself. After the show I went home, counting my blessings all the way, delighted I wasn't forced to do that every day. Therefore, I was surprised when Wink and the producers started inviting me back regularly. After a while I became comfortable on camera and developed friendships with the executive producer, Al Burton, and the associate producer, Arnold Shapiro. Arnold went on to great success, producing many shows, including the Emmy and Oscar-winning documentary *Scared Straight*, *Rescue 911* and CBS's *Big Brother*.

Less than a year later, probably sometime in early 1962, after deciding *POP Dance Party* might be hindering his chances at a national TV career, Wink left the show. When he did, he suggested me as his successor. I guess Al and Arnold liked what they had seen because I was contacted and offered the hosting job. Despite my concerns over being alone in front of the camera, I accepted. My salary was $56 to host the ninety-minute live show.

The Pacific Ocean Park complex was pretty impressive. Created in 1956 to rival Disneyland, the twenty-eight-acre ocean side park featured all sorts of amusement rides and activities. Thousands of visitors would flock to the park every day so it was easy to get kids for our audience. I inherited the show as well as the sponsor, Formula 42 Lemonized Cream Shampoo. Right off the bat, I felt tension from some of the others who had been with the show during Wink's reign. The regular dancers were Wink loyalists and most of them gave me the cold shoulder. Wink was also much beloved by the television audience and I found it hard to connect with them, both with my live audience and the kids at home. Our ratings started to drop almost immediately.

I was also increasingly self conscious and found myself very uncomfortable on camera. The ghost of Wink haunted me from the get-go. I was asked to host an album sponsored by Formula 42 Shampoo. Wink had a million-selling hit called "Deck of Cards" in 1957 and someone thought I might be able to bottle some of that lightning by doing my own album. I've always felt the cover photo made me look like a Basset Hound. Unlike Wink, I did not perform, but the record featured decent covers of hit songs by a local band, the Pastel Six (more about them later). I still have a copy of the album but have completely forgotten what's on it.

Soon after I took over it was decided to move the show away from

POP Dance party with Frankie Avalon.

POP Dance party featuring the fabulous Lettermen. (Note my greasy hair!)

On the set of POP Dance Party.

One of my musical heroes, Roy Orbison, on the set of POP Dance Party.

Santa Monica and Pacific Ocean Park. I don't know if the perception was that the park was bordered by a seedy section of town, but we took the show to the Long Beach Auditorium. We were only down there for a short time, but one night Ketty Lester was to appear and sing her hit "Love Letters." For various technical reasons (mostly money) our artists would lip-synch their performances while we played their record. Our sound man was in the truck outside the auditorium and when I introduced Ketty, she held her microphone to her mouth and began to belt out what could be described charitably as singing with a mouthful of molasses. Our stalwart sound man had put her 45 on the turntable and to Ketty's complete humiliation, inadvertently set it on 33-1/3. The moaning sound that ushered forth gave the impression she was in the process of expiring. To make the whole incident even worse, the NAACP contacted the production company and accused them of having the "orchestra" play off tune. The potential for such screw ups often made live television far more interesting—and nerve wracking—behind the scenes than what you would actually see at home.

Not long after the Ketty incident we moved to our permanent home at the Pickwick Recreation Center in Burbank. Now we were called the *Pickwick Dance Party*. That's when things went from bad to worse. Because of its location, the Pickwick Rec Center was much harder to control for live television than either Pacific Ocean Park or the Long Beach Auditorium. Kids were always walking across the background and flipping off the camera. One time it happened during one of my Formula 42 spots and, although it was entirely out of my control, I got an earful over it.

Finally, the producers rethought their choice of me as host after an incident that turned out to be the low point for me. Right in the middle of doing a commercial (live television was always a crapshoot) a kid outside the park blindly tossed an egg high in the air and it came down right on top of my head as I was in the middle of a Formula 42 Shampoo commercial. The egg-doo didn't help to ingratiate me with Formula 42's ad agency, McManus, Johns & Adams, and they probably saw it as a bad omen. Their account exec, Harmon "Oscar" Nelson, met me in the lobby at KTLA and gave me the news I was out of a job (at least on that show—I still had several other jobs). I remember walking out of that lobby with tears streaming down my cheeks. (Incidentally, legend has it that when Oscar Nelson was married to Bette Davis, the actress stepped

Arnold Shapiro (far right) with a member of the Southern California Plymouth dealers. The local CBS station wouldn't let me host Scholar Quiz because I was a Rock and Roll Disk Jockey. So I did the commercials! So there!

up to the podium at the Academy Awards and remarked that the backside of the little statue she had just gotten for 1938's *Jezebel* looked like that of her husband Oscar—hence the nickname of that most famous of awards.)

I went home and told my family I had been fired and they sat me down and lovingly expressed their deepest wishes that I never again think about doing television and to stick with radio. I reluctantly agreed, but kept the hope alive that some day in the future I would overcome my problems and demonstrate to everyone I could actually shine as the host of a television show.

Meanwhile, *Pickwick Dance Party* continued on with a new host, a young actor named Joby Baker. He lasted about three weeks and then I got a call from Al Burton asking me to come back. Apparently Formula 42's ad agency was willing to forget both the egging and my limited ad-libbing skills. I honestly cannot remember if I returned briefly or not.

Maybe a year or two after that, Arnold Shapiro approached me with an idea for a high school quiz show. He asked me to host it and I agreed. But when he took the package to Leon Drew, the manager at CBS's affiliate, KNXT, Drew liked everything except me.

"I don't want some rock and roll disk jockey in our halls," he said stiffly.

Drew agreed to produce Arnold's show but said he would substitute me with their staff announcer, John Condan. When Arnold told me this I was furious. Then I thought about it and realized I actually had some muscles to flex and came up with a way to visit a little irony on Mr. Leon Drew. I made some calls and discovered that the show's sponsor was to going to be the Southern California Plymouth dealers. I then made myself available to them (for a reasonable fee) and became their on-camera spokesman. And so for the three years the quiz show was in production, Leon Drew was constantly reminded that the face that paid for his show was that rock and roll disc jockey.

The Beatles • Mick Jagger • Cary Grant
Merle Hagg... ...ton • David
Letterman • The Rolling Stones • The
Beach Boys ...ner • Leeza
Gibbons • Jerry Lee Lewis • Gene Autry
Roy Rogers • Monty Hall • Roy Orbison
Buddy Hackett • Barbara Mandrell

TWISTIN' THE NIGHT AWAY

ONE OF THE THINGS THAT STRUCK ME after I'd been at KRLA for a while was how talented the other jocks were. Although people seemed to like me and what I offered, I always felt I needed something else to make me stand out. I knew I was competent but my gut told me I needed some kind of an edge to make me more attractive to management. Despite the fiasco with the Champs concert I wanted to promote some more concerts and, with the backing of KRLA, I felt I had a much better chance at success in L.A. than in Port Hueneme. Fortunately my radio shift only required three hours a day so I had plenty of time for other possibilities.

In 1962 there were few specific places for underage kids to congregate and go dancing, so armories, high schools and various meeting halls filled that need. A weekend in Southern California saw hundreds of such dances featuring live music. At that time there was no shortage of bands to book. As a jock at such a popular station I knew I could practically have my pick of local acts. I decided to team up with a guy named Eddie Davis. I would line up the acts and Eddie would find the venue and make the arrangements.

At the time I took it for granted, but looking back it's almost laughable how much talent surrounded me. In any given week I might book the Bobby Fuller Four, Jimmy Rogers and Dick and Dee Dee to play different schools all over the basin. I usually paid $175 a gig and they were happy to get it, not because it was such great money, but because they were currying favor with an Eleven Ten Man who could play their music.

We put on a dance at the Rainbow Gardens in Pomona one night featuring a new act from Hawthorne. They played a genre that had been around a few years called surf music. The kings of surf music then were Dick Dale & His Del-Tones. Dick had carved out a small empire on Balboa Island in Newport harbor and drew huge crowds. The problem with Dick Dale was no one could book him. I heard his dad managed him and controlled him pretty tightly. Still a big draw more than forty years later, you'll recognize Dick's razor edged guitar theme "Miserlou" as the musical signature of Quentin Tarantino's *Pulp Fiction*.

This other group had only been a band for about a year but I knew they were building a following. They had one hit so far, a song called "Surfin'." Although it only charted at around 75, "Surfin'" showed lots of promise. I thought their music was really special, with terrific harmonies and lyrics that spoke of cars and girls and surfing. Yet as much as I liked their music I felt their name was a real drawback. Despite that, I felt they had a shot at the big time and wanted to book them.

There were five guys in the group, three of whom were brothers, one a cousin. Their dad, like Dick Dale, managed them. Murray Wilson was a middle-aged man with horn-rimmed glasses who looked more like an aerospace engineer than a song writer and surf band manager. I sat down with Murray at a table near the stage. When the group took a quick break after tearing the crowd up with a surf song, I leaned over to Murray.

"So they really love to surf. Who's the best?"

"None of 'em," he said curtly. "Only Denny," he said, indicating the drummer, one of his sons. "He's the only one who surfs."

I looked at Murray. "You're kidding me?"

He explained further. "They know a lot of kids who surf. It's all image, the whole beach thing. You don't have to surf to sing about it, do you?"

I shrugged. "I guess not." That brought me to my only complaint. "I'm not so sure about their name. Have you thought about any others?"

Murray shook his head. "We tried some others, like The Pendletones, but changed it. Russ Regan over at Era Records came up with the name. I think The Beach Boys is fine. We're sticking with it."

Turns out he was right. A week later I saw the cover of *Time* magazine and it featured a Chevy "woody" with a surfboard on the roof cruising the streets of Kansas City. The article talked about the popularity of surf music and how the Beach Boys were at the forefront. I vowed never to make any more name change suggestions.

During my years at KRLA I was lucky to work with some of the best jocks who ever sat in front of a microphone. We were all pretty young back then and no one had the sense that many on that KRLA staff in the early to mid-'60s would one day be considered radio legends. When I started in 1960 I was in awe of these great air personalities like Jimmy O'Neill, Frosty Harris, Bob Cole and Sam Riddle. When Bob Cole left not long after I came on, I made a bid for his noon to three shift. Instead, they hired a guy named Roger Christian. Roger stayed at the station for about a year and then went over to KFWB. Roger was also a very talented song writer, co-writing the Jan and Dean hits "The Little Old Lady From Pasadena," and "Dead Man's Curve" in 1964. Roger also teamed with Beach Boy Brian Wilson in 1963 and 1964 to provide the lyrics to many of their best known songs. Brian, who knew even less about cars than surfing, needed a guy who was familiar with the nuances of power shifts and riding the clutch. Together they wrote such classics as "Shut Down," "Cherry Cherry Coupe" and even the tribute to land speed record holder, Craig Breedlove in "Spirit of America."

Early in 1963, KRLA added some new air staff, including two men who would go on to qualify as legends, "Emperor" Bob Hudson and Casey Kasem. Casey came in for the noon to three shift, with Bob taking the morning slot while I moved to 6 P.M. to 9 P.M. Bob Hudson was a big, hard-drinking guy with a wicked wit and a habit of crazy antics that sometimes got him in trouble. Hudson grabbed big ratings from the start because of his outrageous approach. I swear the guy would say anything, and sometimes he did. The station was located a block away from South Hudson Avenue, and as soon as Hudson discovered that fact he capitalized on it. Pretty soon he had gullible listeners believing the street had been named in his honor.

My favorite Hudson story is the time he went to a Laker/Celtics playoff game and the Lakers lost. The next morning Emperor Hudson went on the air complaining bitterly about the officiating. A few minutes into his broadcast he had worked himself into a lather and began claiming the game was fixed. Once he was wound up he ranted the entire three hours about the "fixed" game. When he walked out of the booth at 9 A.M. he had a surprise waiting for him. Greeting him were attorneys from the Lakers, the Celtics and the NBA. Before lunch time the lawyers had drafted an apology that Hudson was to read on his show every fifteen minutes for the next two weeks! His face turned purple every time he had to read that apology.

Casey Kasem was the opposite of Hudson: a calm, soft-spoken man with no vices that I knew of. With all the crazies at the station at that time, Casey was a breath of fresh air and a true professional without the huge ego many of our air staff lugged around. To everyone's dismay he actually prepared for his show. He also didn't engage in most of the antics and silliness that went on at the station. Everyone respected him tremendously, even the irrepressible Hudson who, for some reason unbeknownst to anyone but Casey, did anything Casey told him to do.

Whenever Casey needed someone to fill in on his TV show he usually came to me and I was honored. We got along great until one day when I subbed for him. His trademark sign-off was "Keep your feet on the ground and keep reaching for the stars." Being the smartass I am I couldn't help but mess with his famous line. At the close of the show I uttered in my best Casey impression, "Keep your feet in the stars and keep reaching for the ground." Casey was not amused and never asked me to fill in for him again. Casey's American Top 40 was a radio staple for years, and though he's passed on the torch, it remains one of the most popular syndicated shows on the medium. He was inducted into the Radio Hall of Fame in 1992. Casey long ago forgave me for brutalizing his sign-off and was there to congratulate me when I received my star on Hollywood Boulevard in 1999.

By 1963 our station had become a force in radio, enough so to attract top personalities from around the country. One of them, working at Chicago powerhouse WLS, was a young superstar named Dick Biondi. KRLA set their sights on him and he was hired. Dick took the shift after mine, the nine to midnight. During his first stint at KRLA (he did about six months or so and then left, but came back in 1965 for about two years) Dick created the Dick Biondi Road Show, a showcase that brought new acts to high schools all over Southern California. Dick was inducted into the Radio Hall of Fame in 1998.

When Biondi quit the first time in the fall of 1963, a fellow was brought in to replace him who, in my opinion, had more impact on L.A. radio than anyone before or after him. Dave Hull was a high energy jock who came to us from a station in Florida and quickly made his mark.

When Dave was at WONE in Dayton, Ohio, a listener wrote to him and said she couldn't stand "all the hullabaloo," presumably from the combination of Dave's personality and the music he played. He looked it up in *Webster's Dictionary,* where it was defined as a "clamorous noise or disturbance, an uproar," and thought that fit him to a T; so he reinvented Dave Hull and became The Hullabalooer. When the Beatle invasion began, The Hullabalooer became the unofficial "fifth Beatle," but much more on Dave later. Today, the Hullabalooer lives out in Palm Springs and does an afternoon show on KWXY. I still consider him the greatest living authority on the Beatles.

Another character who was committed to the KRLA asylum in 1964 was Charlie O'Donnell, or Charlie "O" as he was known. Charlie took the nine to noon, right after Hudson, until the Emperor got fired for insubordination and left for KBLA in 1966, and at that time assumed Hudson's morning shift. Charlie was the original announcer on *American Bandstand* and has handled announcing duties on many shows including *The Dating Game, The Newlywed Game, The Gong Show, The Joker's Wild* and *Tic Tac Dough.* Charlie was the original announcer on *Wheel of Fortune* and has held that position most of the three decades the show has been on.

In 1913, the American Society of Composers, Authors & Publishers, known as ASCAP, was founded. ASCAP's job was to account for all uses of singers' and songwriters' creations and to protect them from exploitation. The mentality for protecting artists came about when, nearly fifty years after the fact, it was revealed that beloved American songwriter Stephen Foster had died penniless in 1864. ASCAP did, and still does, require licensing money from any entity that plays people's songs, from radio stations to night clubs to the roadside café with a single juke box.

For the next three decades, ASCAP worked great for mainstream artist members, but in 1940 another organization called Broadcast Music Incorporated, or BMI, was formed to service what was considered "alternative" forms of music, like jazz and blues. ASCAP didn't take BMI seriously until the '50s when BMI began grabbing up artists that ASCAP wouldn't touch, in the burgeoning jazz and blues fields as well as that new sound called rock and roll. By 1960 the stuffed shirts at ASCAP had enough of the rapidly growing upstarts and cried foul. They couldn't believe that deejays would be playing certain songs over and over without some secret form of compensation. How could anyone have such passion for this completely uncivilized form of "music?" There must be something fishy going on, like paying people to play your record. It was dubbed payola, a hybrid of the words "pay" and "Victrola," for the old style record players. Prior to that, paying deejays or stations to play your song was accepted, but commercial bribery, which ASCAP was claiming this actually was, was not. There was also blood in the water from the recent quiz show scandals, during which it was discovered contestants had been given game show answers in advance.

Politicians, and those pulling their strings, were seeing corruption everywhere and caused hearings to be held by the House Oversight Committee. Not unlike the McCarthy hearings, suddenly every deejay was suspect, particularly rock jocks. Were people taking money to play songs? I'm sure they were, but I never knew anyone who admitted to it, and most jocks, like members of a close fraternity, told each other everything. Was it wrong? Grocery and retail stores to this day receive money and perks from vendors to improve their shelf position. Is that wrong? It's business.

Among the prominent deejays paraded before the committee, Alan Freed and Dick Clark were probably in the deepest grease. Essentially, Freed wouldn't say he was sorry and Dick used a combination of reason and an explanation of how he had divested himself of all his musical interests. Freed got a minor conviction in 1962 (his sentence was suspended and he paid a $300 fine) but it ruined his career, and Dick got a mild slap on the wrist. The example of Freed cast a pall over the entire industry. The feds were now on the trail of anyone who had taken money to play records and would continue to do so for several years to come.

One of the big changes the payola scare ushered into radio was how songs were selected for airplay. Prior to payola, every station's deejays would get together and pick from a list of hits or new songs that were being considered. It was a democratic process that resulted from many sources the jocks drew from, including feedback from listeners on their personal feelings about each song. The problem with that system, at least how management saw it in relation to their fear of possible abuses, was that they had no control and the jocks had too much control. It was far harder to keep an eye on your whole air staff than it was to have one person making all the creative decisions. Hence, the duties of the music or program director were increased to picking all the music. From that point on, that is the early '60s, jocks had less and less say in which songs they played and eventually were playing strictly off a list created by program directors, known as PDs.

With that much power over what went over the air, PDs grew in their stature and were soon the principal targets in the cross-hairs of record companies. By the early '80s and the rise of New Wave and alternative rock and other formats, PDs had achieved enormous power and the more successful ones were being hired as consultants for dozens or more stations to provide their winning formats. Today, PDs are practically the only ones left in radio, with big conglomerates owning chains of hundreds of stations in markets all over the country. These stations are often serviced by satellite from a central facility by deejays who simply back-announce three or four songs in a row. If you're listening to the radio in, say, Grand Forks, North Dakota, or Dodge City, Kansas, your "local" deejay could very well be sitting in an air conditioned studio in Valencia, California. I heard a story recently about someone calling their town's radio station to give them critical information to be released during a community emergency only to find their "station" was actually located three states over.

Payola had KRLA management shaking in their shoes. Among many warnings, we were told to stay the hell away from a restaurant called Martoni's down on Cahuenga between Sunset and Hollywood because it was a well known hangout for record promoters. The word was this: don't be seen with any of those people outside the station.

I did receive what might have been regarded as a type of payola, but at the time I had no idea what it was. *The Adventures of Ozzie & Harriet* had been a big hit since its inception as a radio show in 1944. In 1950 it made the leap to television on the Dumont network and a year later found its home for the next fifteen years at ABC. Former bandleader Ozzie Nelson was a very canny businessman, and in an episode in the fall of 1956 showed younger son Ricky forming a rock and roll band. About six months later Ricky's group debuted a version of Fats Domino's "I'm Walkin'" and it, along with another song, "A Teenager's Romance," became a big hit. Ozzie was nearly fifty years ahead of *American Idol* in horizontally integrating products from one medium (television) into another (music) and making a killing. Ricky's talent and good looks, along with his weekly TV exposure, made him a heartthrob for millions of teenage girls.

As deejays at KRLA we were able to help Ricky in our own small

Do I look like the owner of a bicycle shop? On the set of *Ozzie & Harriet* during my first acting attempt.

ways. Soon I had Ozzie phoning me. I had been told by some of the other jocks that Ozzie would hire some of us for small roles in the hopes that we would be favorable toward Ricky and play his songs. Ozzie never, ever asked me or, as far as I know, any of the other deejays, to play any of Ricky's records. It was so subtle, I did not put two and two together until much later when I realized our TV parts almost always coincided with the release of a new song by Ricky. A few years later I was watching myself in a rerun of the show and it dawned on me that Ozzie had hired me to play the owner of a bicycle shop.

I've been on a lot of sets in my time and the set of *The Adventures of Ozzie & Harriet* was one of the most relaxed and pleasant I'd ever seen. Ozzie was very laid back but quite purposeful. Though a calm man, his eyes told you he always knew exactly what was going to happen next. He admitted to me he was not the most natural actor and told me his secret for staying focused: he kept a coin in his hand all the time the cameras rolled. Somehow that coin kept him thinking about the scene at hand and not the thousand other details of his busy life. To keep the kids and crew relaxed there was a basketball hoop set to one side of the stage. I enjoyed a few games with Ricky and David and some of the other kids and crew members between takes. All in all it was an enjoyable experience and one of the most creative forms of payola I'd ever heard of. I find it ironic that today record promoters pay radio stations and conglomerates monthly fees to get their records played. In our time we would have been in big trouble for such a thing.

In 1960 Chubby Checker created a national phenomenon on *American Bandstand* when he sang his blockbuster hit, "The Twist." Less than a year later, a night club in New York called Joey Dee's Peppermint Lounge became the epicenter of that phenomena when people began twisting the night away. The Peppermint Lounge soon became known around the civilized world as the place it was all happening. People have said the Peppermint Lounge was the first disco. When the Peppermint Lounge's house band, Joey Dee & The Starliters released their 1962 song, "Peppermint Twist," it became a huge hit and immortalized its namesake club. (Incidentally, many people do not know this, but movie tough guy Joe Pesci was a guitarist for the Starliters during that time.)

With the huge success of the Peppermint Lounge, I began to visualize a way to move my dance business in a new direction. The high schools and armories had served me well and I had developed a relationship with many rising stars like the Righteous Brothers and the Beach Boys. I decided I would start a dance club for teenagers. But when I looked into it I found the laws were strict. Any place allowing anyone under 18 to dance was required to serve food. Not wanting to get into the full blown restaurant business just so kids could dance, I seized on the next best alternative: a club for kids 18 to 25; old enough that I didn't have to open a restaurant, but young enough that I didn't really need a liquor license. The rationale was that if a guy had to choose between girls and booze he'd take the girls.

I hooked up with three partners, my good friend Mickey Brown and brothers Roy and Stan Bannister, to help shoulder the investment. Soon we were looking for the right location. Down on the far east end of Ventura Boulevard, in North Hollywood, was an old club. Probably dating from the '20s, it had been a well known strip joint at one time and was now known as The Larry Potter Supper Club. A drab windowless façade, it wasn't much to look at but had lots of room and, aside from lousy parking, was in a great location. We made a deal with the owners to lease it and kicked in $2500 each. Cleaning the place up was a chore. Deep in the bowels of the club, in a warren of odd, dank little rooms with troll-sized doors, among the piles of old papers we found appearance contracts with famous strippers like Lili St. Cyr. On the first very long day of cleaning we all walked out itching like crazy. We quickly realized we were covered with fleas. A few days later, after a good defleaing, the four of us went down to the courthouse to register our business. When we got there we realized we had not selected a name. Given that the Peppermint Lounge had inspired us, we had been toying with some sort of variation on that. Ernest Evans had the same idea when he reinvented himself in the shadow of Fats Domino. His new alter ego, Chubby Checker, went on to become The King of the Twist. With peppermint in mind I suggested something with the word cinnamon. As the waiting line advanced toward the business recorder's window we realized The Cinnamon Lounge didn't sound quite right, but we had no good alternatives or variations. When the clerk asked what the name of the club would be one of us just blurted out "Cinnamon Cinder." What the word cinder had to do with anything I don't know, but alliteration was big then so the name stuck.

Since we were modeling ourselves after the Peppermint Lounge, we needed a house band. Unlike today, many of the bigger touring acts of the time didn't travel with a large entourage of musicians, but rather relied heavily on the house bands of different venues to back them up. We found a group of young musicians who had been playing together for a few years. They had a lively, fun sound and called themselves The Pastel Six.

We got the place cleaned, remodeled, put in a dance floor and prepared to open our doors. I called Murray Wilson and asked him if we

BOB EUBANKS ARCHIVES

North Hollywood Cinnamon Cinder circa 1963.

could book his kids. I had been paying the Beach Boys $175 for the armories and high schools but Murray wanted more.

"Three seventy five," he told me.

"Wow!" I gasped. "I don't know, Murray, I'm not sure I can make money at that price."

"You'll make money," he said. "The boys are going through the roof. They're about to go national. I can't take less; sorry."

I made the deal with Murray Wilson and set the Beach Boys as the act that would open the Cinnamon Cinder. Our cover charge was set at a buck fifty and a Coke from the bar would cost you thirty cents. I bought advertising on KRLA (I didn't get a deal) and we prepared for the big opening. With a capacity of a little over 400 we did the math and figured if we could fill the place every night we could make some money. Any less and we'd be hurting financially inside of a month. Our Tuesday opening night was rousing. The Beach Boys drew a full crowd, and when we closed the doors that night we congratulated each other and knew we had a hit. Wednesday night we had eighty people. Thursday we had forty-four. By the close of business that evening we were already worrying about going under. I had weathered the loss from the Oxnard concert a few years earlier, and, despite my making decent money between the station and the dances, losing another $2500 would really hurt.

By Friday afternoon we knew it was make it or break it time. By about seven o'clock a few kids began lining up. Within an hour they were winding down the block. We breathed a sigh of relief. When we opened the doors the place filled to the brim and we were turning kids away all night. Anyone who was a teenager during those years will remember the famous dress code from all clubs: no Levis or capris, please!"

Once the club was open all we had to do was buy acts. I turned to the local groups who had done so well when I was doing the high school dances. People like the Righteous Brothers and Jan and Dean sang their hearts out and helped to make the club a success. I made a little more money with them than the Beach Boys because I only paid them $150 each for their performances. Now that the Cinnamon Cinder was up and running and making a little bit of money we just needed some great promotion to keep it going.

About six months after we opened the North Hollywood Cinder, we noticed that many of our club goers were coming up from the south, particularly the Long Beach area. We decided the best way to serve them would be to open a club down there, which we did.

One of the people I had befriended in the business was Russ Regan, a record promoter who would become the president of Uni Records and later the president of Twentieth Century Fox Records. Russ was also a songwriter and had written a couple of novelty hits, including "The Happy Reindeer" which became a Christmas classic for many years. As I mentioned, he also came up with the Beach Boys' name. Not long after we opened Russ suggested he write a song for the club. My attitude was "sure, knock yourself out," and I promptly forgot about it. A few weeks later I stopped by the club before my shift at KRLA and saw Russ working with the Pastel Six. They were practicing a number I was not familiar with. Whatever they were playing, the band didn't seem too enthused.

"What's up?" I asked Russ.

"I wrote that song for you. I'm trying to sell the band on it."

"You actually wrote the song?"

"Yeah. 'Peppermint Twist' was a huge hit. It put the Peppermint Lounge on the map."

"I know, Russ."

"Well, like I said, I wrote one for the Cinnamon Cinder."

"Great," I said, "let's hear it."

Russ and the band rehearsed a few lines then fired up a full rendition. When the Pastel's band leader, Bob Toten, hit the chorus and intoned in his deep southern drawl, "It's a verrry nahce dahyance..." I cringed. I slapped Russ on the back, thanked him and the band, and got in my car to head to KRLA. On the way I thought "Oh man, that's a real piece of crap!" Not long after that The Pastel Six recorded "The Cinnamon Cinder" and released it. It didn't take long before "The Cinnamon Cinder" went to number 17 in the country and really put us on the map. All over the country—thanks to Russ Regan—what was essentially a two-minute commercial for Cinnamon Cinder was now running thousands of times a day. Once Cinnamon Cinder became a national name, some people started hearing Elvis's 1962 hit "Return To Sender" as "Return to Cinder." Who was I to talk them out of it?

Barry Friedman, our PR guy, came up with another great idea to get us some more national publicity. You cannot overestimate the impact the Twist had on popular culture during that time. Barry sought to capitalize on that fad by staging a Twist contest—for elephants. We held the contest at the Cinder in North Hollywood and every local television news outlet, as well as a host of newspapers, showed up to cover our pachyderm dance contest. Once again, we managed to get loads of free publicity for the Cinnamon Cinder.

Later that year I realized I was spread pretty thin between my radio job and running what was becoming a chain of nightclubs. I needed more help, and that came in the form of a cute eighteen-year-old kid who had just relocated from Long Island. Teri Brown was already working in the record business for a guy named Irwin Zucker. He was paying her a buck an hour. But despite her lack of decent compensation, Teri had a lot to offer. She was smart, poised, had a great sense of humor and kept brilliantly cool under pressure. And Teri really knew the music business—her dad was a record exec and her uncle was the legendary band leader Les Brown.

I paid her a little more than Irwin Zucker and she soon proved herself invaluable. She took a lot of pressure off me by jumping into the breach and mostly taking over arranging for all the acts. Wednesday nights were slower than weekends so we came up with the idea of calling Wednesdays "Talent Night" and booking our headlining acts for those nights. What that meant for our acts was that they would get to play Long Beach at nine then shuttle all the way up to North Hollywood to put on a midnight show. Weekends were a gimme for business, and on those nights the Pastel Six was all we needed to keep lines running down Ventura Boulevard. But those midweek slumps required acts like the Beach Boys, Jerry Lee Lewis and the Righteous Brothers to fill the house. In no time Teri seemed like an old hand, not only at booking the acts and keeping track of the schedules for two clubs. She was also terrific at seeing to the needs of the artists. In many cases she played the role of chauffeur, ferrying the musicians between the two clubs.

Sometimes the acts would drive themselves, but if they were from out of town often either I or Teri would give them a lift. One of our favorite acts couldn't drive himself if he'd wanted to, partly because he was thirteen. Little Stevie Wonder always put on a fabulous show and packed them in. But he was even more fun shuttling between the clubs because of his sense of humor. One time Teri borrowed my new '63 Pontiac Bonneville convertible to bring Stevie up from Long Beach and whacked into a curb. A frantic Teri began wondering how she was going to explain the damage to me.

Always unflappable, Stevie chimed in from the back seat, "Oh, don't worry, Teri. Just tell Bob I was driving."

Stevie entertained me with a story of how he and his friends laughed their heads off when his neighbors saw a nine-year-old blind kid riding a bicycle. I used to kid Stevie I had only one club and I was just driving him around the block for an hour. In 1982 I was sitting in Rubens on Cahuenga in North Hollywood. I heard a big commotion in the room next to me, with the crowd hooting and hollering and cheering. I just had to see what was going on. When I peeked around the corner I saw Stevie, now in his early thirties, taking the stage. Encouraged by the audience, he decided to perform on the spur of the moment. We all watched Stevie perform a terrific set and afterward I left a note with his entourage saying hello and congratulating him. A few minutes later one of his people escorted him to my table where he graciously thanked me for helping him in the early days of his career.

One of my favorite acts to play the Cinder was a local group who had recently relocated from East St. Louis. Originally establishing themselves as an electrifying R&B band, due in large part to their incredible lead singer, they were trying hard to break into the ranks of pop music hit makers. Consequently, The Ike and Tina Turner Review toured relentlessly. One evening Ike and I were talking just before their set and he confided, "Tina and I aren't makin' any money on these shows."

I paid them $1150 a night for the two shows, one at North Hollywood, then down in Long Beach. That much money was very good in 1963. "I don't understand, Ike. What's the problem?"

"I got eleven musicians on my payroll. I can't afford to not have good people. So when you split it up, Tina and I aren't gettin' a dime. But it's okay 'cause I just want to keep the band going."

I felt bad but couldn't justify giving them more. Ike never complained again. I had heard rumors about Ike's terrible temper but had never seen it. That said, I was still a bit fearful of him and, had he threatened me that night, I just might have coughed up another couple hundred. What kept them going was the non-stop touring and proceeds from the records they recorded. Already big stars in the U.K., they had recorded a few hits, but on the R&B charts. The Ikettes, the three women backing up Tina, had produced a hit in 1962 called "I'm Blue (The Gong-Gong Song)." The money from the song helped buy their tour bus, which Ike had named the Gong Gong Bus.

Tina was the consummate pro yet also had a devilish twinkle in her eye and liked to gently kid me. I had been getting complaints from the L.A.P.D. about so-called "dirty dancing" violations, where performers and even patrons were being watched by undercover cops to make sure they didn't do anything lewd or immoral. In retrospect it was all pretty ridiculous but the cops could make sure you lost your license if they got rubbed the wrong way so I had to take it seriously. After the first few times I saw her act and her amazing gyrations, as much as I loved her energy, I was afraid the nervous cops might shut us down because of her. So I took her aside and asked her to tone it down a bit.

She smiled and put her hand on my arm. "Oh honey, don't worry, it'll be fine."

She went on stage, and for the first number or two she was cool. Then she started a song, looked over at me and winked. Then she lit up the stage with the most incredible high-energy performance you've ever seen. She was all over the stage, shaking and singing, and the crowd went crazy. I suppose if there were any cops in the audience on that night they were probably as riveted as anyone else by the magnetic show. Whether that performance had anything to do with it I don't know, but I never heard a police complaint again. There were many who said Tina Turner was the hardest working woman in show biz, and after what I saw I never doubted that. She's also one of the nicest.

One night as they waited to go on, I walked into the kitchen to see how they were doing. Tina sat at the end of one of the steel food prep counters applying her makeup. A few steps away, spread out on the concrete steps leading out the back door were Ike and most of the musicians, chatting and warming up. Ike and I struck up a conversation and it came around to his aspirations for seeing his band go to the top. Many years later I heard a story about Ike and Phil Spector and how their relationship got started.

Phil Spector was the hottest producer in music at the time. Ike had approached Spector with a proposition. With a seemingly endless supply of hits and a track record of turning unknown acts into stars, Spector was the dream producer of any up and coming act. Ike told Spector he thought Tina was ready to make the next big career move and wanted Phil to produce her records. Spector invited them over to his West Hollywood home to talk. When they arrived they were told to wait for Spector, who was "busy" but would be right with them. After waiting more than an hour, the naturally impatient Ike began wandering around the large home searching for the legendary producer. Upstairs, Ike entered the rec room to find Spector alone, leisurely shooting pool. Ike went berserk, infuriated over the snub.

Apparently the altercation didn't completely dissuade Spector from his interest in Tina because they made up and went on to work together. A few years after that conversation with Ike, Phil produced Tina's first big breakout hit, "River Deep, Mountain High" and they had a string of huge successes after that.

About a year before I opened the Cinder I came to realize that being a big time jock required a cultivated look. We weren't movie stars, but being a deejay in L.A. meant you had to look like one. My increased salary allowed me to upgrade both my car and my wardrobe, but I hadn't found the right hairstyle. Prior to the '60s, most men kept their hair short and that was that. But postwar influences were allowing men's hair to creep past their collars, and Elvis and Buddy Holly had made the roll and the wave fashionable. One day Tony Orlando came in and his hair was all styled, blow dried and sprayed. It's not like I made it a habit of staring at other men's hair, but it looked great to a guy who was still using Brylcreem. A few days later Wink and a couple of the jocks at the station came in sporting cool hair styles and I asked one of them where he got it cut.

"Jay Sebring. It's the hot spot in town." The salon was named after the founder, Jay Sebring, a slight, handsome guy with a lot of charisma. My dad had cut hair for years so I knew something about barbering. The first time Jay styled my hair I knew he was gifted. He was the first to use hair spray on men and had developed a line of hair care products. He was a pioneer in the field and helped show men of the '60s that flattops and D.A.s were so . . . '50s.

After my first visit to Jay I saw my dad later and I told him where I'd been. My dad was a very proud man and I could see the slightest hint of hurt in his eyes. He had been cutting my hair since I was a toddler. But he also knew times were changing and barbers were becoming "hair stylists."

"What'd it cost?" he asked.

I was almost embarrassed to tell him because he still got two bucks for a haircut. "Fifteen dollars."

He just stood there with his mouth open. "Holy smoke! Fifteen bucks?"

He ran his hand through my hair and narrowed his eyes. "Hmmm."

Dad had never heard of Jay Sebring and knew nothing of his techniques. He asked me a lot of questions and was particularly taken by the fact Jay cut the hair all one length, then used hair spray—on a man's hair! I demonstrated to dad how Jay had turned the brush while blowing my hair. As I described all of Jay's "secrets" I began to see a twinkle in my dad's eyes. It wasn't until the next week when I stopped by his shop in Tujunga that I realized all of dad's curiosity was his version of "reverse engineering." In the window was a sign that brought a smile to my face: Hair Styling—$7.50.

After I had been going to Jay for a while I realized the place served the "A" list of the film and music industry, with regulars like Steve McQueen and Warren Beatty. I convinced our house band, the Pastel Six, to go see Jay. Just as I had been, the band were all Brylcreem guys, but in no time they'd been converted, and within a few months, so had just about every guy standing in line to get into the club on any given night. By then they almost all had that layered "Sebring look."

Though his company continued on, for Jay it all came to a horrific end on a warm evening in August 1969. That night, Jay Sebring, his close friend Sharon Tate and three others were slaughtered in Sharon's Benedict Canyon home by crazed members of the Manson family.

Since the kitchen at the Cinder in North Hollywood wasn't actually being used to prepare food, it often became the rehearsal hall, dressing room, or staff meeting place. We put a ping-pong table in there to keep the bands occupied while they waited to go on. I wasn't a bad player and sometimes if time allowed I'd take on a visiting artist. One night Chuck Berry challenged me to a little tournament then proceeded to whip my butt good.

"Where did you learn to play like that?" I asked.

Chuck nodded. "Hell man, I just spent a couple years learnin' the game at a special ping-pong school."

His people chuckled as I narrowed my eyes, sensing I was being set-up. "A ping pong school? Where was that?"

He grinned. "A place called Leavenworth."

During the time Chuck was in prison, Beach Boy Brian Wilson wrote a big hit with "Surfin USA." It turned out it was the exact melody of Chuck's hit from the '50s, "Sweet Little Sixteen." Chuck eventually was awarded a fairly tidy sum for Brian's "oversight." Perhaps Chuck's stint behind bars left him wary. I would pay Chuck $300 for his shows and, of all the acts I hired, he was the only one who insisted on being paid in cash.

I always tried to fill the Cinder's schedule not only with the hottest acts I could find, but I also strove to give the kids a wide variety. One source that I really wanted to tap was, for the most part, unavailable. As much as I wanted to book Motown acts, it was hard to because founder Berry Gordy rarely let his acts tour. He preferred to have them stay in Detroit and crank out hits. You certainly cannot argue with his results. Once Otis Williams of The Temptations confided to me that all Motown acts were put through an intensive six-month training course in everything from grooming to etiquette to costuming. He likened it to being in the army.

About this time, and maybe a year after my dismissal from *Pickwick Dance Party*, I was offered another show, *Hollywood Dance Time*. Despite my family's warning to stay away from television, I accepted and immediately began hosting the 6:30 P.M. Saturday show for Channel 11. The difference between *Hollywood Dance Time* and *POP* or *Pickwick* was that this was my show, not a Wink Martindale hand-me-down.

The show not only used a set that replicated the Cinnamon Cinder, but also featured my house band from the Cinder, the Pastel Six. Now that I had been at KRLA for some time and was getting to know all the local bands through owning the Cinder, I was much more confident

BOB EUBANKS ARCHIVES

Hollywood Dance Party for Channel 11 in Los Angeles with Cinnamon Cinder Band, the Pastel Six.

than when I was thrown into *POP* or *Pickwick*. Yet another irony: my sponsor was Formula 42 Shampoo.

Back at the Cinder we had been trying to book Jerry Lee Lewis for some time but he was never in town. We finally nailed down a date and offered him $750 for playing both the Long Beach and North Hollywood clubs. For some reason Teri wasn't available to do the driving so I was nominated to ferry Jerry between our clubs. Although Jerry was consuming prodigious amounts of booze during that time we struck up a great conversation that first night and immediately became friends. We talked about rock and roll and where it had been and where it was going, then discussed Jerry's career—where he had been and where he was going. He admitted it had been up and down, but he was hopeful about his future. In the car he was thoughtful and reserved, almost quiet, but when he took the stage he became another person, with fire in his eyes, leaping around and pounding those 88 keys like a man possessed.

One day I was standing backstage at KTTV waiting to go on the air when an older gentleman happened by. We greeted each other and struck up a conversation. He had a European accent and was very interested in how my show was doing. Then he proceeded to tell me how he thought television in general was going down the tubes, no pun intended. He spoke with authority and I was impressed, but had no idea what his function was at the station as I had never seen him before. Turned out the man who had introduced himself as John Kluge was the owner of the station, and not just that one. A modest investment in a Maryland radio station less than twenty years before had snowballed. A few years before I met him Mr. Kluge had formed Metromedia which, among its holdings, included Channel 11. He later sold his broadcast empire to media magnate Rupert Murdoch. In 2003, *Forbes* listed 89-year-old John Kluge as one of the richest men in America.

In the spring of 1963, jock Sam Riddle left us for KFWB and that's when I was moved to his 6 P.M. to 9 P.M. slot. Wanting something new and fresh to kick off my move, I came up with an idea that gave my audience a chance to be directly involved in my show. I called it Teen Toppers and the idea was that every night a different high school would give me a list of their favorite songs and I would play them. Student representatives at the chosen school would poll the student body and send me the results. Kids tuned in to hear what other schools' lists featured, all the while itching to get recognition for their own school. It created a friendly rivalry and was a lot of fun.

Yet the show was not always free of errors. One time I referred to Placentia High School as Placenta High School—something I'm sure the kids of that school had heard before from competing schools. Another time my show producer Vaughn Filkinns left me a sheet of paper that said the principal of one of the high schools was Mr. Ball, and in a hand written note below it wrote "first name Harry, I presume." I didn't pick up on the joke and called the man Harry Ball for the whole hour. Finally, some kid from the school called and told me "I don't think the guy's first name is Harry." Yeah, I fell for it. Despite the occasional screw up, the personalization feature made my show a big hit, and for the first time in the station's history, we beat KFWB—if only in my time period.

The Beatles • Mick Jagger • Cary Grant
Merle Haggard • Dolly Parton • David
Letterma ... es • The
Beach Boys • Ike and Tina Turner • Leeza
Gibbons • Je ... • Gene Autry
Roy Rogers • Monty Hall • Roy Orbison
Buddy Hackett • Barbara Mandrell

EIGHT DAYS A WEEK

ATE IN THE SUMMER OF 1962, four young Englishmen entered a recording studio in northwest London and began assembling a series of recordings that would change the face of music. The studio was in a converted, two-story 19th century building named after the thoroughfare on which it was located, Abbey Road in St. John's Wood. The young men called themselves the Beatles, a tribute to Buddy Holly's Crickets. By the fall of that year, as their music began taking the U.K. by storm, word had gotten across the Pond that something special was happening.

At KRLA we were tapped into the music scene. The jocks and all the musicians and music producers who visited us daily were talking about this new sound coming out of England. I'll be the first to admit I was never good at picking a hit. I've always been pretty good at making the right business moves and trying to work harder if not smarter than the next guy, but the strength of one song over another generally eluded me. Yet when I first heard a Beatles' song (I think it was "Please Please Me") I knew it was a fresh, new and exciting sound. Although I had been buying brilliant acts like the Beach Boys and the Righteous Brothers for several years, even to my ear the Beatles represented an entirely new direction in popular music, and the moment I heard them my wheels began turning as to how I might capitalize on that.

The Beatles' star was rising during the spring and summer of 1963, but KRLA's was not. KRLA was still considered a powerhouse, but KFWB had been beating us in the ratings since I had been there, and there was talk of a shake up, or worse. Perhaps the fact we were a "government owned, non-profit" station kept heads from rolling a bit longer, but something had to give. Management fixed their sights on KFWB and we would beat them or else. I'm proud to say I played a part in what happened next at KRLA.

January 18, 1964, saw the first U.S. charting of Beatles' songs, "I Want To Hold Your Hand" and its flipside, "I Saw Her Standing There." The reaction was unprecedented, with "I Want To Hold Your Hand" shooting to number one immediately. It would be the first of twenty-one number one hits for the quartet over the next six years they were together. The request lines at radio stations across the country were suddenly flooded with calls for these extraordinary rockers; Elvis and the Beach Boys had disappeared from the face of the earth. Even old hands in radio, guys who had been around in Elvis's and Sinatra's heyday, had never seen anything remotely like it. Beatlemania was building, and being so close to popular music every one of us at KRLA could feel a change coming in our industry. We all knew history was in the making, that what we were seeing was really big, but we would not realize how big until the perspective of years to come.

Around this time, Dick Moreland, our program director and my old buddy from KACY, brought Dave Hull into his office. He handed Dave a copy of the Beatles' latest 45.

"We think these guys are going to be a phenomenon. I want you to be the president of the Beatles fan club."

In 1962 while in Columbus, Ohio, Dave had taken one look at the Beatles picture on special radio station release of "Love Me Do" and thought they looked scruffy. He gave them zero chance of success.

"Why me?" he asked.

"Because you're the perfect guy. Just get into it, you'll be great!"

"If I'm going to be the president, I also want to be the vice president, speaker of the house and sergeant at arms."

"No problem."

"And I do anything I want."

"Okay."

"I mean anything."

"Okay."

On Sunday, February 9th, 1964, Ed Sullivan did indeed put on a really "big shew" when he introduced "those plucky lads from Liverpool, the Beatles!" According to Nielsen ratings, somewhere around 70 million American citizens were sitting in front of their tellys watching John, Paul, George and Ringo belt out five songs in two short sets. I was one of them. The electricity in the *Ed Sullivan* theater that night came through my television and struck me like lightning. I watched the screaming girls and studied those four kids performing. They were excellent musicians, calm, assured, and their dress and appearance were unique, a style that I could feel would be instantly trendsetting. As they finished their last song, "I Want To Hold Your Hand," I stood up and paced the house. My head was spinning with ideas as to how I might do something with this group. What that was I wasn't sure.

A few days later I would find out. The Beatles organization put out the word they were planning a U.S. tour in August and September. Excited, I grabbed the phone and made a few calls. I found out that they had not yet committed to play Los Angeles. Right then I decided I would find a way to book them and bring them to town. Although I was a small fish in the pond of talent buyers, I had a sense of destiny I could not explain. All I knew was that I was going to bring the Beatles to Los Angeles.

Meanwhile, the new president of the Beatles fan club in L.A., Dave Hull, had embraced his new position with gusto.

"There is absolutely no truth to the rumor Ringo has cancer" was the first "rumor" he "scotched" on the air as the new president. Dave began creating a series of rumors and then "dismissing" them as false. Then he put his talents to work finding other items of interest.

As Dave was stirring up the fans, my phone calls to secure the Beatles revealed the first hurdles. Julie Steddom-Smith, a friend and agent with General Artists Corporation, a national powerhouse booking agency, told me GAC was the agency handling the Beatles for their US tour.

"Can I get them?" I asked her.

"No decision's been made," she said, "But anyone making an offer has to send a wire and offer a guarantee."

"How much?" I knew that huge acts like Frank Sinatra could command as much as a $10,000 guarantee. I was hoping it wouldn't be that much because raising it would be difficult, given I made $12,000 a year.

"Twenty five thousand."

I gulped.

"And," she continued, "that's against 60 percent of the gross over $50,000."

I double-gulped. I also knew that even if I managed to come up with the twenty-five grand I would still be standing in a long line of fellow talent buyers to win the deal. Lou Robin was the big talent buyer in town, regularly lining up the top acts. I didn't know that he had already passed on them, citing that he would "never pay that much for anyone." He would later end up with the San Diego date for the Beatles, and, ironically, was the only promoter on the Beatles tour to lose money. Julie confided that fellow GAC agent Danny Cleary was at that moment fighting to get the Beatles for his client, Shelly Davis, owner of the Crescendo and Interlude nightclubs.

Julie assured me she would fight to get me the date, Sunday, August 23, 1964.

"The only problem," she told me, "is that it might be hard convincing them since you've never put on a concert on this scale."

The truth was, other than the hundred and forty odd people who attended The Champs performance in Oxnard, I had never put on an actual concert. But I had to keep her confidence up as I felt it would telegraph to whomever she was lobbying to get me the gig.

"That's true, Julie, but I've been hiring bands and booking club dates for years. I've never had a problem. You know me, if I say I can do it, I'll do it."

Later she called back with new information.

"The Beatles will only play the Hollywood Bowl. You'll have to get the Bowl locked down before you get the Beatles."

Perched on the south slope of the Cahuenga Pass, a canyon connecting Hollywood and the San Fernando Valley, the Hollywood Bowl was and still is the premier venue in Los Angeles. One of the largest and most picturesque natural amphitheaters in the world, the Hollywood Bowl was opened in 1922 and has seen some of the greatest musical acts of its time. With around 18,000 seats it was also, by several magnitudes, the biggest event I had ever arranged.

Rather than be intimidated, I told Julie to keep fighting for me at GAC and I would deal with the Bowl. The first phone call I made was to Kenny Hahn, the County Supervisor for Los Angeles County and a man who knew everyone in town. His son, Jim, is the current mayor of Los Angeles. I had met Kenny at a funeral and after some brief chit chat told him my situation and asked if he could help me with the Board of Directors. He said he would see what he could do and get back to me.

Dave Hull, the Hullabalooer in the center, with Derek Taylor, the Beatles' Press Officer, Hollywood Bowl, 1964.

As I fought to bring the band to town, Beatlemania continued to build in America. Ed Sullivan helped fuel the fire by bringing the Beatles on his show an unprecedented three weeks in a row. While I went about my business on the air and running the Cinder, my stomach churned as I thought about all the others who were doing exactly what I was doing: trying to get the Beatles. I even heard rumors that among my fellow jocks was yet another person vying to get them. KRLA's Program Director Rebel Foster had connections and was supposedly in the hunt for the Fab Four. As the man who picked the music for such an influential Los Angeles radio station I figured the Beatles might not want to say no to him.

As I nervously awaited Kenny Hahn's return call I decided to settle the ugly possibility of Reb Foster taking the Beatles away. I spoke to my partner, Mickey Brown, and we agreed to minimize our risk with Foster. I went to Reb and made an agreement that if he booked them he'd split it with us, and if we booked them we'd do the same. Part of the deal was including his relative (a cousin, I think), a guy named Bill Utley. What I did not know was that neither the Beatles nor GAC were remotely considering Reb Foster as the promoter for the concert date. Clearly, it was one of the dumbest things I ever did in business and the first in a series of mistakes I made in organizing this concert. A few days later Kenny Hahn called me.

"Bob, if you have the Beatles," he exclaimed triumphantly, "you've got the Bowl."

I was happy and grateful that Kenny had managed to convince the very conservative Board to allow this "rock 'n' roll" concert, but now I had a new dilemma. I didn't have the Beatles. I called Julie and told her to give GAC the full court press and nail down the group for me. A nervous few days passed and she called back.

"You've got them." God bless Julie Steddom-Smith—she'd done it. Then came her next words and I cringed slightly. "If you've got the Bowl, you've got the Beatles."

Only I didn't. Have either, that is. I quickly decided the only way to settle this was to get everyone to agree to everything. The best way to do that was to get them all on a conference call. I did, they did and twenty-six-year-old Bob Eubanks had just landed the Beatles at the Hollywood Bowl. The negotiation for GAC was handled by Jerry Perenchio, then an agent. Jerry later became my agent and much later, a billionaire media mogul as chairman and CEO of Spanish language network, Univision. I credit Jerry not only with being a good friend, but also for becoming one of my few mentors in the world of show business. We concluded our deal in late February, which left me with what seemed to be a couple months worth of work to complete over the next few weeks.

My first order of business—now that I had opened my big mouth and locked down the concert of the year, if not the decade—was how to pay for it. I was making decent money for 1964, but $25,000 cold cash was a staggering sum for me. I decided to appeal to my bank. Security Pacific was one of the most prestigious banks in Southern California, so I expected something like this would be normal business for them. I went to my home branch at Topanga and Ventura and found the manager. I politely told him I had some business for him and asked that we sit down. When we did, I plainly stated exactly what I needed.

"You want to what, Mr. Eubanks?" was his incredulous response. In the vernacular of the time, I suddenly recognized this man as a "total square." Though he seemed to have zero idea, or interest in, who the

Beatles were, he did seem interested in what mental condition prompted me to visit him.

As he stared at me I repeated, "I need to borrow the money to put up a guarantee for a concert I'm promoting." I handed him an envelope my accountant had prepared. "You'll find my financial statements are in good order. I would use my home as primary collateral."

Without bothering to look in the envelope he pompously leaned back in his overstuffed leather chair, steepled his fingers and addressed me like he was trying to communicate with a rhesus monkey.

"Mr. Eubanks, Security Pacific Bank is a lending institution, not some fly-by-night street corner loan shark. The bank does not get involved in musical concerts or such things as 'entertainment' schemes. We take great care to place our customers' monies in prudent investment opportunities like homes and stable businesses. What you are proposing is, quite frankly, extremely naive. Good day."

He sat forward and picked up some paperwork, effectively dismissing me. I was in and out in about four minutes. I left, shaken and feeling like I had asked for money to get a heroin fix. But I was also mad and more determined than ever. As I walked to my car I thought about that stuffed-shirt banker blowing me off and said to myself, you'll be sorry, buddy, you'll be sorry.

Feeling a bit desperate I remembered a small store front bank not too far from my home in nearby Woodland Hills. Something told me to try them. But Transworld Bank sure wasn't Security Pacific. Decidedly less formal, I stepped into what amounted to a lobby and had to walk around a motorcycle that was dripping oil onto the linoleum tile. I suddenly had doubts about the whole project, sort of an *Ohmigod, it's come to this* kind of revelation. I approached a teller. She saw me eyeing the leaking motorcycle.

"Oh that. We just repoed it. What can I do for you?"

"I'd like to speak to your manager."

She nodded toward a middle-aged woman seated at a desk in the corner. She looked friendly and casually authoritative, and had an air about her that said maybe she'd listen to me. I walked over and held out my hand.

"Hi, my name is Bob Eubanks."

She looked up, smiled and took my hand. "Liz Miller. You look familiar. Aren't you on TV? I think my son watches your show."

I was hoping her son hadn't seen my disastrous *Dance Party*, or worse, the egging at *Pickwick*. *You're the egg on the head guy. No loan for you!*

"What can I do for you, Mr. Eubanks?"

"I need to borrow some money against my home."

"Sure," she said, gesturing for me to sit. "And what's the reason? Remodeling? Purchasing a car maybe?"

"No, I need to pay a guarantee to a musical group. I'm a concert promoter."

She was intrigued. "Mmhmm. And how much do you need?"

I braced for impact. "Twenty-five thousand dollars."

To her credit, Liz Miller didn't blink. "Must be some musical group, huh?"

"They're called the Beatles. They're English."

"Oh, sure, I know them. My son's their biggest fan."

I was quickly becoming a big fan of her son. She took out an application.

"Well, Mr. Eubanks, I'll need to get some information from you."

A half hour later, when I walked out of Transworld Bank, Mickey and I were fully funded promoters.

Now that I had secured the Beatles for Los Angeles, and given that I was the 6 to 9 P.M. jock at KRLA, we immediately became the official Beatles station. I cannot overemphasize the power that group had in the music industry at that time. Everything was Beatles. If you didn't worship a particular Beatle you had any one of three others to obsess over. The media picked up on the craze and we got reams of free press. Dave Hull, now president of the Beatles fan club, began referring to himself as the fifth Beatle. There were many people billed as the "fifth Beatle" over the years, but Dave was probably the most ardent of them all.

One thing that baffled people, from station management to the Beatles organization, was how Dave managed to get the Beatles' home phone numbers and addresses. No one might have noticed had he not given them out over the air. Soon the Fab Four were being driven nuts by the effects of this relentless fan/jock/stalker in L.A. Dave recently revealed his secret to me and it was more like something former *Washington Post* reporters Woodward and Bernstein might have experienced during the Nixon days.

In February of 1964, Dave was working his nine to midnight shift

1964 Hollywood Bowl Beatles contract, signed by Brian Epstein.

BOB EUBANKS ARCHIVES

and got a phone call. An anonymous man told him that the Beatles would be at LAX the next morning at a specific gate and time. Dave tried to get more information but the caller hung up. Dave went home and forgot about it. The next morning he got up and remembered the call. He looked at the clock. The caller said the Beatles were allegedly arriving in about an hour. Dave figured it was a hoax, but then knew he would kick himself if it turned out to be true. He grabbed his tape recorder and jumped in his car. At the airport Dave went to the gate and waited. Just when he was getting ready to leave, chalking it up as a cruel joke, a plane arrived. He asked one of the airline employees if the Beatles were on the plane. These were certainly gentler times and the woman happily looked on the manifest for him.

"Yes. Two of them at least."

Dave held up his recorder to bolster his credibility. "I'm with KRLA and I'm here to interview them."

With that she let him get on the plane. Stepping into first class he recognized John Lennon, sitting with his wife Cynthia, and George Harrison, with girlfriend Patti Boyd. After speaking to the pair, who were charming and happy to answer his questions, Dave was accosted by their angry manager, Brian Epstein. Despite being told to get off the plane, an undaunted Dave tarried to ask George a few more questions. Dave came away with a respect for Lennon and Harrison, but maybe even more importantly, the reluctant president of the Southern California Beatles fan club was now a big fan himself.

From that first mysterious phone call tipping him off about the Beatles at LAX, Dave began receiving such calls with all sorts of tantalizing information, particularly for the president of the Beatles fan club. Dave was receiving gold nuggets like the Beatles' home phone numbers, their addresses and other bits of guarded trivia. Not sure the phone numbers were accurate, Dave took a fly one day and called the number attributed to George Harrison. He figured he had developed a rapport with the Beatles' lead guitarist during their interview and if by some chance he actually got him on the phone he'd have something to say. But he expected it to be a phony lead. Instead, an older woman's voice answered. She had a charming Liverpudlian lilt.

"Hello?"

"Hi, this is Dave Hull, the Hullabalooer with KRLA eleven ten radio in Los Angeles. Who am I speaking to?"

"Louise Harrison."

"And you are ... ?"

"Yes, George's mother."

Dave had struck pay dirt. Louise Harrison turned out to be a godsend for Dave. One of the sweetest, most giving ladies he had ever met, Louise became Dave's "inside man" with the Beatles. He repeated to her the other numbers he had been given and she carefully went over them and made slight corrections like prefixes and so on and literally presented Dave with the Rosetta Stone for all things Beatle. When Dave had a question or wanted to confirm something he would just give Louise a call and she would help him out. Even after he gave out their personal information to his Beatle-hungry fans Louise still cordially took Dave's calls and answered his questions.

Then it was Capitol Records' turn to be infuriated when Dave secretly obtained a copy of a not-yet-released Beatles record. He took it back to Pasadena and immediately began playing it on his show. That gave Capitol fits. And so from early 1964 on, Dave somehow managed to obtain the latest Beatles records, sometimes weeks before they were officially released. This not only made Capitol crazy, but also Brian Epstein and KFWB. Dave was being accused by KFWB of all sorts of skullduggery, that is, until they offered him a job right after the 1964 concert (which he turned down). The truth was a man in Capitol's pressing plant was a big fan of Dave's show and would grab one of the first records off the presses, put it in his jacket and smuggle it out of the plant. He would then get the record to Dave who, of course, ran with it. The man never asked for a dime and Dave always considered his early jump on everyone else as a public service to his listeners. Largely because of the Hullabalooer's risk-taking, pretty soon KRLA caught up with, then surpassed KFWB in the ratings. Dave's "early" releases kept coming to him regularly until mid to late 1966.

But that was nothing compared to his biggest stunt, which nearly got him arrested. When the Beatles did their 1964 concert, Dave and our newsman Jim Steck were at the airport seeing the Beatles off to their next destination, Denver. Station manager John Barrett had assigned Dave and Jim to get as many interviews with the band members and entourage as they could. When the Beatles' jet was sitting on the tarmac waiting to be buttoned up and given clearance to go, for a moment there was no one around the plane. As Dave and Jim looked up at the portable stairway against the plane Jim glanced conspiratorially at Dave.

"C'mon, let's go."

"What? Are you nuts? Isn't that a federal crime?"

"I don't know," said Jim as he headed up the stairs. Dave followed.

The administrative staff recognized them, saw their recorder and let them on, assuming they had official business. Jim and Dave found seats among the other members of the press (those officially on the flight) and made themselves comfortable. No one in their group was allowed forward into the first class area where the Beatles and management were. Once they were airborne Jim reached in his pocket.

"I've got about fifty cents. You?"

Dave rifled his pockets. "Eight bucks."

Once they landed in Denver they deplaned and milled around wait-

KRLA Reunion—the pretty lady is Wink's wife Sandy, who used to be my secretary.

ing for the Beatles to come down the stairs at the other end of the plane. Ringo was the first to see them. He looked surprised and impressed, knowing they were not part of their traveling entourage.

"Damn Dave, you got here awfully quickly."

Roadie Neil Aspinall freaked out when he recognized them and summoned press secretary Derek Taylor, who blanched when he saw the pair of stowaways.

"This could be a royal mess. We must put you on the manifest straight away."

The only guy who could "phony up" the manifest was Epstein himself. Derek took them to Epstein's hotel suite where he was sprawled on the couch, exhausted, with a drink in hand. When he saw them he was furious.

"How in the bloody hell did you get on that plane?"

They told him but it didn't seem to calm him down.

Derek calmly said, "Brian, we have to put them on the flight manifest."

Epstein stared balefully at them both for a long moment then picked up a pen and paper.

"How do you spell your names?"

After all that, Dave had the brass to ask for backstage passes to that night's concert, which Epstein grudgingly approved. Then they went to the hotel lobby and called their boss John Barrett.

"We're in Denver," said Jim, "and we need money."

When he told Barrett of their little trip Barrett immediately wired them the princely sum of fifty bucks to the hotel's Western Union office. The station also bought them plane tickets home.

Our first problem with the Beatles concert occurred when setting the ticket prices. We had to order tickets and place advertising so we needed to settle on which seats would go for how much. The Beatles organization told GAC to tell me the boys were adamant that the most expensive ticket not exceed seven dollars. I cringed when I heard this as I was hoping to get around ten. After the excitement of making the deal, I figured out our expenses, and after including their forty percent cut, I was suddenly worried that there was a possibility we might not make money. With the limited ticket prices that could be a very real scenario.

We set the prices at $3, $4, $5, $6 and $7. When we started making plans for the ticket sales, the Hollywood Bowl's box office manager, Bill Murphy, was very blasé about the whole thing. We told him we were concerned the extraordinary demand might give them and their ticket agents around town a real run for the money. Murphy had heard we were new to this scale of concert and treated us accordingly.

"Don't worry, we can deal with anything that's thrown at us. We've had Frank Sinatra here a number of times. We can handle your Beatles."

"We've heard from other venues that the crowds for tickets are huge," I cautioned.

Teri spoke up. "What if we sell out in one day?"

"One day?" Murphy chuckled at the amateurs. "No way. That absolutely won't happen. If you're lucky we'll sell through by the end of the week. I've heard this group is popular so that just might happen."

KRLA spent $2500 and bought a full page ad in the *LA Times* announcing that tickets for the August 23rd concert would go on sale at 9:30 A.M. on Saturday, April 25, 1964. The night before the tickets went on sale hundreds of kids camped out along Highland Avenue and the entrance to the Bowl, not to mention their many other ticket agencies around the LA basin. I was hoping that the Bowl's Bill Murphy would be wrong and that they could handle selling all those tickets in one day.

We had been running our company—Hoopla Promotions we were calling it for the time being—out of the den of Teri Brown's parents' home in Sherman Oaks. The morning the ad hit we got a panicked phone call from Bill Murphy, our skeptical box office manager.

"We're flooded here! This may sell out a lot sooner than I'd planned!"

Murphy had repeatedly warned us it would be impossible for them to sell 18,000 tickets in one day. Although they were using regional offices of the Auto Club of Southern California and Mutual Ticket Agencies (this was before computers and Ticketmaster) Murphy now told me he was beginning to fear being overwhelmed. What I think he really feared was the unknown because the Bowl's box office had never seen anything before (or since) generate such a frenzy among fans. I sent Teri down to report back. She called from a pay phone to tell me that the lines of kids snaked down Highland and half way to Hollywood Boulevard, about half a mile south. She described seeing a limousine creeping along the curb, with the chauffeur patiently keeping an eye on several kids as they moved along in line. Curious, she went over and introduced herself. The chauffeur was pleasant.

"I'm Ellis Dean, Nat Cole's driver."

He gestured toward the children, the eldest of whom, a cute fourteen-year-old, shook Teri's hand.

"I'm Natalie, Natalie Cole. And this is my brother Kelly and my friends."

Teri thanked her and wished them well. Three and a half hours after the tickets went on sale I got a call from the Bowl box office. Bill Murphy sounded like he'd been running a marathon.

"We're sold out!"

I was shocked. I had hoped we'd sell out in a few days but wasn't expecting it in a few hours. I was very glad but now I had to consider the possibility of booking a second show. Given how fast the tickets sold through, a second performance the next day seemed to be a guarantee. I called the Bowl back and they said Monday, August 24 was available. I called GAC and they told me the Beatles were also free. I put pressure on GAC to get the Beatles to agree to a second date. There was only one thing standing between me and that possibility: Brian Epstein. With a background in managing a branch of his family's chain of music stores, Brian Epstein had discovered the Beatles and carefully molded their image over a period of several years. He was considered hard nosed and sometimes very difficult to deal with. I was warned of this when GAC advised me it would be my job to talk to Epstein personally and convince him to extend the Beatles for one more day in L.A. I was given his phone number and cautioned to phone him only at 11 A.M. his time. Since there is an eight hour time difference between London and Los Angeles I had to get up at 3 A.M. to make the call.

The first morning I rang and a lady with a clipped British accent and haughty attitude informed me, "Mr. Epstein cannot speak with you today. Would you please call back tomorrow?" When this charade went on for several days I got fed up with her blowing me off. I was producing the biggest concert of their tour and the guy wouldn't talk to me. I just didn't understand Epstein's thought processes: I was trying to make the guy some money.

Getting nowhere fast with the Brits, I decided to call Jim Lee, a friend who managed singer Chris Montez. Jim had set up Chris's European tour during which the Beatles opened for him. Jim knew Epstein so I hatched a plan. I made Jim an offer.

"If you can get Epstein to go for a second date I'll cut you in on the action."

I was beginning to worry I was potentially cutting the income pie with so many people Mickey and I might not have any left for ourselves. I really didn't want to end up homeless but I did what I thought was best at the time.

I was learning. I told Jim I would buy him a ticket to London where he could personally reason with the reclusive Epstein. I also began to understand how important this second show was to me. Being new to the large scale concert business I had already made another critical mistake: I didn't hold back enough tickets. For a big demand, extreme visibility event like this I should have held back at least a few hundred tickets for the record companies, celebrities and the press. Why celebrities? Because they might not only be able to do something for you one day, they also add to the glitz and energy of the show. You're only as good (or bad) as your last deed in Hollywood and I wanted everyone to look as favorably as possible on this so that I might stay in this business. As to the press, I needed them to review the concert and give me ink that I couldn't buy at any cost. With all the tickets from the first concert gone I realized the second show was my only way to fill that gap. Epstein never got back to me, but he did finally meet with Jim Lee. During their meeting he told Jim he would not agree to a second concert because he was afraid it wouldn't sell out. Apparently Epstein had absolutely no clue as to the power his four boys wielded over American teens.

I was approached by a local Chrysler/Plymouth dealer who made me an intriguing offer. He would give me a new Plymouth Barracuda if I would get a picture of the Beatles alighting from it. That was going to be a chore since the car only had two doors, but I figured for a new car I'd give it a try. If we had time I'd ask the band to pose by the car.

Meanwhile, two people I didn't know were about to cause me some severe headaches. Bob Crane, later Hogan of *Hogan Heroes*, was a deejay at KNX. For some reason he began telling his listeners one morning that he had it on good authority there were counterfeit tickets being distributed by some evil-doer. This "news" created a massive panic and spurred thousands of phone calls to practically every one and every thing associated with me. It took a while to settle that ugly rumor down.

Then Walter Winchell announced in his column in the *L.A. Times* that there "would definitely be a second concert at the Hollywood Bowl." This was enough to drive me crazy, given this was all exacerbated by Mr. Epstein's antics. The phones rang off the hook, with everyone trying to find out about the alleged second concert. The old guys who ran the Hollywood Bowl's box office went nuts and called me in a panic. I decided the best way to put a stop to it all was to phone Mr. Winchell and set everyone straight with a retraction.

I called his office in New York and they told me he was at the Ambassador Hotel in Los Angeles. They gave me his room number so I called. I was patched through to his room and after a few rings I heard that famous gruff voice.

"Yeah."

"Mr. Winchell, this is Bob Eubanks. Before I get into why I called I just wanted to tell you what an inspiration you were to me and my family during the war. We used to sit around the radio and listen to your broadcasts from London and it meant a lot to us and I've always wanted to tell you how much I appreciate you."

"Yeah . . . " he said, impatiently.

"Anyway, Mr. Winchell, you said in your column there would be a second Beatles show. I'm the promoter of the concert and I wanted to tell you that there will be no second show at the Bowl."

There was a slight pause, then Winchell barked, "Go fuck yourself," and slammed the phone down. I sat there in shock as the man who had meant so much to me in my childhood had just burst my bubble.

TICKET TO RIDE

AS AUGUST DREW CLOSER, and the Bowl date loomed, there were countless details to work out. The Beatles management had many requests (or demands), and I also had to arrange security for the Bowl, as well as plan how to get the band in and out of the venue. That was proving to be a bit scary because we were hearing stories of the group being swarmed by hundreds or even thousands of screaming girls and the Bowl's layout presented sort of a dead end alley for us, so to speak. To complicate matters, GAC told me the Beatles had received all sorts of cooperation from the New York Police Department, such as escorts, security and the like, but when I went to the L.A.P.D. and presented my demands for freebies they essentially told me to stuff it. They said they would not use taxpayers' resources to support some "rock and roll group." If we wanted the same level of service as in New York we'd have to pay for it. This infuriated GAC, particularly their New York office. I never let GAC know it, but I agreed with the L.A.P.D.'s position. It was the Beatles' party and I felt they should cover their own costs.

The entrance to the Hollywood Bowl is located on Highland Avenue on the edge of a lightly populated part of town just above the bustle of Hollywood. The problem was there was literally just one way in and one way out. With no back way to draw upon we would have to get very clever in how to move the band in and out. The only way that made sense was to use several decoys. We began making plans and many phone calls.

The Beatles arrived in Los Angeles that Sunday morning fresh from a concert in Vancouver, B.C. Dave Hull and I, along with some others, met them at the gate. Along with the group were a number of their entourage, including their road managers Neil Aspinall and Mal Evans, Derek Taylor, their press officer/publicist, and the impossible-to-get-on-the-phone Brian Epstein. We were all pretty young I guess, but Epstein's appearance surprised me. He was more than three years older than I, but looked like a schoolboy. I chose to put the pettiness of our earlier dealings aside and we were cordial with each other. I was surprised at how unintimidating he was in person.

The next day, Mickey and lawyer Tom Nast accompanied me to a bungalow on the grounds of the Beverly Hills Hotel to meet with Epstein. When we got there, Epstein was in the bathroom. When he came out one of the first things we noticed was his fly was open. As Nast shook his hand he couldn't help but remark, "That's quite an entrance, Brian." Fortunately for us Epstein's open fly set the tone of the meeting because he was so flustered by the incident he uncharacteristically acquiesced to everything we asked for. In person, Epstein was pleasant, though not the overly charming man I'd been led to believe.

For some reason during their three day stay in L.A. Teri Brown was drafted to drive Brian around. Although he was only about six years older he insisted she call him "Mr. Epstein." They spent several hours together, with her driving him all over Hollywood and Beverly Hills. The most amusing part of their little journey was that instead of an impressive car, as you would expect such a visiting dignitary to be transported in, they rode around in Teri's little Ford Falcon with a torn headliner. To this day, Teri is mightily impressed that the often imperious Mr. Epstein never mentioned it. Another thing I found interesting about Epstein was that almost every time I asked him something concerning the band he would say "ask John." Although he was the band's manager, this told me a lot about the hierarchy of the Beatles organization. Brian may have been the manager but John was the boss.

The Beatles organization had made arrangements for the band and their entourage to stay at a mansion in Bel Air on St. Pierre Road. I never visited them there but I understand they whiled the time away reading and playing Monopoly, a game they were apparently obsessed with. According to Derek Taylor's book, *Fifty Years Adrift*, the boys had gotten used to living in hotel rooms and were suddenly presented with a home the likes of which they'd seen only in movies. A lavish estate on two acres, the place was marble and mirrors and terraces and featured

Every time I would ask Beatles Manager Brian Epstein a question, he would say, "Ask John."

a secluded pool. I discovered years later that despite their wild success they were not yet mega wealthy. Derek pointed out in his book that although the Beatles were making money hand over fist they hadn't really seen as much as most people would have thought. Their tour money was being held in escrow for tax reasons and their record money was paid out maybe twice a year. They had only had hits for maybe a year or so and it takes a long time for royalties to be paid. What money they had probably came from advances.

A few hours before the 5 P.M. press conference at the Cinder in North Hollywood, I left the club and made the five-minute drive up Cahuenga to the Bowl. The place was already a madhouse. Hundreds, if not thousands of kids were lined up waiting for the gates to open. I walked down the line, saying hi and greeting the kids. They were the most starry eyed and focused group of kids I'd ever seen. I thought to myself if someone could only bottle that form of control it would sell like crazy to parents.

Beatle press conference, Cinnamon Cinder, 1964.

1964 Beatles press conference, Cinnamon Cinder.

BOB EUBANKS ARCHIVES

Handling a situation at the Beatles press conference 1964.

As soon as I got back up to the gate two institutional buses emblazoned with "L.A. Marshal" pulled up. A big marshal swaggered over to me.

"You Eubanks?"

"Yes."

"We're with the marshal's office. Where do you want us?"

I was told the L.A.P.D. would be stepping up coverage in the area but the marshal's involvement was news to me.

"I'm sorry. Who told you guys to come down here?"

"I believe it was Mr. Hahn. We're here to protect the neighbors in the hills."

Kenny Hahn never mentioned this little detail. I smelled a problem.

"So the county's providing this service?"

"No. My men are off duty. They're being paid by the organizers of the event."

I narrowed my eyes. "That's me."

The man shook my hand. "We'll try and give you your money's worth." And with that he turned and started shouting orders. I stood there and watched my hundred newest "employees" climb off the buses and disperse into the hills around the Bowl. I felt slightly sick that at the end of the day Mickey and I might be owing money.

After the band rested, a couple of limousines brought them and their entourage to the Cinder for the press conference. The place was an utter zoo. The door on Ventura Boulevard was clogged and we had a number of people trying to screen out anyone other than the press and those who had permission to be there. The limos arrived and we routed them down the parking ramp on the west side of the building. The one with the Beatles inside stopped in front of the back door and the boys jumped out, racing from the clutches of screaming girls who had stormed our "skirmish line" and gotten through. They ran up the same steps the Beach Boys had sat on warming up on many occasions, and waited in the kitchen until we could clear a path to the stage for them.

I believe the legal capacity of the club was something like 440, but that afternoon I swear we had 800 people in there. The press conference got going a little after its scheduled time, and it took a while to quiet the crowd. I had the band seated in front of the stage, at floor level, and I was on the stage with a microphone trying to maintain some semblance of order. The Beatles seemed a little groggy, and it took a while to get the conference in gear. Finally someone asked a question, first by pointing out that a psychologist in Seattle (they had just played there) had condemned the Beatles as being detrimental to young people. Then they asked if the Beatles thought they were detrimental to young people. The boys looked puzzled, probably trying to figure out why someone would ask such a stupid question. Many of the questions were trivial and silly, but the Beatles remained poised, smoking cigarettes, whispering asides to each other and just trying to get through it.

At the end of the press conference we rushed them to their waiting limos. Screaming girls jammed the driveway and the sidewalk in front of the club. They had been waiting outside for their beloved Beatles to appear. When the boys leaped into the limo the cry went up to storm them. I told the limo drivers to punch the gas and the limos shot up the driveway and burst onto Ventura Boulevard—totally blind—and made left turns so hard the tires smoked. We were so damn lucky as Ventura is one of the busiest streets in L.A. For a few seconds I could see the next day's headline: Bob Eubanks Kills Beatles In Limo Crash. Or worse, Beatle Limos Run Over Fans.

Getting them into the Bowl turned out to be fairly simple, but we knew getting them out was going to require brilliant planning, perfect execution and possibly a miracle. The Bowl is laid out with a central driveway coming up the hill from Highland and either continuing on up to a parking lot above the Bowl or turning left and ending behind the band shell. There was literally no back or side way into the facility. The famously picturesque band shell was a huge half-funnel shaped structure with dressing rooms just behind it. (It was demolished in the summer of 2003 to make way for a bigger band shell). A roadway passing under the dressing area provided access to the facilities under the band stand.

We had several plans and backup plans, but our first worked just fine. We sent the band in their limos right up the drive and safely to the back door of the band shell. I breathed a sigh of relief when the Fab Four were delivered, unscathed, to their dressing rooms. A rider in their contract specified they wanted "an adequate sound system, clean towels, a case of Coca-Cola and a TV"—a long way from the demands rock stars soon began making. I gave them everything but the TV. I told them they could get their own TV.

Waiting backstage, the boys hosted a small queue of celebrities waiting to say hello. The small dressing rooms had a few chairs and barely room for clothes hangers and a place to sit in front of the mirror. The combination of the warm night air and cigarette smoke also made it pretty stuffy inside. John and Lauren Bacall were having a deep chat when I leaned in and interrupted, asking John if he would like to meet Debbie Reynolds. He and Bacall looked at each other for a moment then Lennon shook his head. To this day that has bothered me because Debbie is one the kindest, most genuine people you could ever meet.

The opening act was the Bill Black Combo, popular musicians who had been with Elvis for years. Rumor has it that the Bill Black Combo paid someone $10,000 to secure a place on the tour. Jackie DeShannon was on the bill after the Bill Black Combo. As soon as Jackie DeShannon finished her last number I assembled most of the KRLA staff and we came out and introduced the Beatles. The station had quickly become Beatles Central and every jock was involved in promoting the concert in one way or another, so I felt it was only fitting we all share in the glory. The mixed screams and cheers from the crowd of nearly 18,000 was so loud you couldn't hear someone if they were yelling right in your ear. Prior to their taking the stage, I went to John.

"I'm worried about what the crowd is going to do. If you could, please don't say 'This is our last number.'"

John shook his head. "I can't do that. But we will try and get out off the stage as quickly as possible."

When the Beatles walked onto the stage at 9:22 P.M. I would have sworn you could feel that one explosion of enthusiasm all the way down in Long Beach. The boys opened with "Twist and Shout" which led into "You Can't Do That." Back then the Bowl had a shallow reflecting pool in front of the stage. I had extra security in front just waiting for some young girl, overwhelmed by acute Beatlemania, to fall in while trying to leap across it. Surprisingly, that didn't happen until just after the concert. The noise of the screams was deafening and I know for a fact that even fans sitting in the first few rows did not really hear the group. They played a short set, about thirty minutes, but it was truly historic. From "A Hard Day's Night," they finished their performance with "Long Tall Sally," bowed and—true to John's word—they waved and raced off the stage. This was the critical moment for me. What would happen in the next three to five minutes would either make or break me as a concert promoter.

First, we had an assemblage of limos waiting right outside the area directly behind the dressing rooms. As fans poured down the side aisles toward that area, they were going to create sort of a pincer effect and surround the group. As the limos started to move, kids surrounded them, even climbing onto their roofs. As the limos staggered through the crowd, it looked for a moment as if they would be crushed by what was now (in the course of less than five minutes) several hundred kids.

Had the Beatles been in those limos it would have been a terrible risk. Now that Plymouth Barracuda, supplied by the dealer in hopes I would get him a photo of the Beatles using his car, was going to come in handy. The Beatles raced out a side door and there waiting for them was not a plush limo but that 1964 white Plymouth Barracuda. Jammed like four sardines in a tin, the Beatles hunkered down and were driven sedately out of the Bowl. They reached a Standard gas station down on Sunset about a mile away and switched to a limo. The photographer who was supposed to capture the Fab Four alighting from the Barracuda either wasn't quick enough or the boys were onto him because the photo showed only their backs. When the car dealer saw the photo he refused to give me the car.

The next day, Monday, a charity event benefiting the Hemophilia Society was hosted for the Beatles and interested celebs. The garden soiree

If I could have gotten a front view of the Beatles with the car, the car would have been mine. Too bad!

was held at the home of the mother-in-law of Alan Livingston, president of Capitol Records. Lots of stars bought tickets for $25 each and brought their kids. Given the fascination with the Beatles came mostly from teens and preteens, some of the guests seemed unlikely since they arrived without any children. Famous movie tough guy Edward G. Robinson showed up, as did comic legends Jack Benny and Groucho Marx, who quipped to news reporters he was there to "get drunk." Lloyd Bridges showed up with some of his kids, including fourteen-year-old Jeff. Other luminaries at the gathering were Jack Palance, Rock Hudson, Jack Lemmon, Shelly Winters, Eva Marie Saint, columnist Hedda Hopper and Mrs. Dean Martin and her kids, among them, future singing star and teen heartthrob, Dino.

The event was designed to give each participant a chance to say hello to the Fab Four and get a photo with them. Two of the most important guests at the event, Derek Taylor and Brian Epstein, were stopped at the entrance to the party by overzealous security guards. They were allowed to come in only when one of their people inside, a man named Hal York, vouched for them. Ironically, Hal York was just a very ambitious fan who had ingratiated himself with Epstein and had actually been allowed to accompany them on the tour. The fund raiser was a smash and the Beatles went back to their mansion that Monday evening, charged up and ready to have some fun.

During the Sunday press conference, when asked which Hollywood celebrity they most wanted to meet, Paul responded, "Jayne Mansfield." Apparently word got back to the famously voluptuous actress and she extended the Beatles an invitation to meet with her privately. After some wrangling over locations and whether photographers would be present (she wanted them, they didn't) the Beatles finally arranged to party with her at a very non-private place, the Whiskey-A-Go-Go on the Sunset Strip.

Interestingly, the guy who started it all, Paul, didn't attend. Earlier that evening, Paul and Derek had gone to Burt Lancaster's mansion to watch *A Shot In the Dark*, the latest Peter Sellers's Pink Panther film. I guess Paul was tired from laughing so much. Though I was not there I heard an amusing and true anecdote. Upon their meeting Jayne tousled John's hair and asked, "Is it real?" Whereupon the wickedly quick John Lennon fixed on Ms. Mansfield's abundant cleavage and quipped, "Are those real?"

Prior to the concert, Capitol Records came to me and asked if they could record the concert. Because I had the lease to the building (for that night) they could not record without my permission. I agreed on one condition: that I be allowed to write the liner notes for the album. (For those of you who don't remember, in the '60s there were no CDs or cassettes, so albums were only on 12" vinyl records and they all had dust jackets that often included notes about the recording.) The story I heard was the Beatles were unhappy with their performance and refused to let Capitol release the recording. In 1977 when Capitol and the Beatles finally decided to release the Beatles at the Bowl album, they came to me and said that the Beatles long time producer, George Martin, wanted to write the liner notes. With my thirteen-year-old agreement in hand I said, "Fine, but get out your checkbook." And they did.

After shelling out the $25,000 guarantee, with the additional gate receipts, I paid the Beatles a total of $58,000—all for a half hour's worth of work. A pretty significant payday in any era. On the other hand, after the dust finally settled and we paid the Beatles and everyone else associated with the concert, Mickey and I ended up splitting $4,000 with

Reb Foster and Bill Utley. For all my trouble I had pocketed a thousand bucks. A pretty pathetic payday in any era. I looked on the bright side and saw it as not losing our house.

As soon as everyone had been paid I sat back and replayed the whole thing in my head. Given all of the headaches, hard work, near disasters and costly mistakes, I swore to myself I would never go through it again. So for a day or two in September of 1964 I was depressed and out of the concert business forever. Then a few days later I remembered I'd booked an up and coming group called the Rolling Stones and that getting out of that contract wouldn't be easy.

They say many women describe childbirth as exquisitely painful and during labor swear they will never repeat the anguish. Yet moments after giving birth they've forgotten all about the pain and are ready to go again. So it was with me and concert promotion. Within a few weeks I was looking forward to the Rolling Stones concert and already negotiating with the Beatles for their 1965 return. I had both feet firmly back in the concert business.

Aside from the Beatles themselves—with whom I really did not have much personal interaction—the face of the group for me was really Derek Taylor. A former journalist, Derek wrote such rave reviews in the U.K. about the Beatles in 1963 it caught the attention of Brian Epstein. About the time the tickets were going on sale for the Bowl concert in April, 1964, Epstein was hiring Derek as his assistant as well as publicist for the band. Derek was a handsome and exceptionally witty fellow. In his early thirties, he was married with four children. When the Beatles arrived in Los Angeles I liked Derek immediately. He was a great help in bridging the gap between what I needed to have done and his hard-headed and standoffish boss Epstein.

Not long after the concert, we formed what I believe was the first ever public relations company for rock and roll groups. Although PR companies existed, most were older, stuffier, established firms and I thought younger blood might attract bands looking for a fresh approach. Having operated at the level of successful groups like the Beach Boys for a few years already, I perceived a void in the area of public relations for rock groups. I had seen the Beatles organization create massive hype and wondered if it was not just the Beatles themselves but also really brilliant media manipulation. I wanted to find out. It would be the first such company of its kind. With the success of the Beatles concert still fresh in everyone's minds, I called all of the acts I knew and found the reception good. The Beach Boys were interested and so was one particularly hot local band with a compelling fusion of country, rock and folk music. Although the Byrds had not yet produced a hit I knew they were on the verge. We set up the offices of Prestige Promotions at 6290 Sunset in the Sunset Vine Tower, an impressive office building at the southeast corner of the famed intersection. My partners were Mickey Brown and Cecil Tuck. In February of 1965 we decided Prestige Promotions could use the services of someone who had been in the middle of the greatest musical PR in history. I called Derek Taylor and offered him the job of running Prestige Promotions. When we talked salary I told him we could only pay $215 a week, which he agreed to. When he arrived with his family I helped him secure a rental house up in Nichols Canyon for $250 a month. I negotiated the rent with the owner, an out of work actor named Charlie Stewart who proceeded to tell me the people he "hated the most were disk jockeys." Despite the man's rudeness Derek and his family needed a place to live so I forked over the $500 deposit to get them in the door. Anything English was the rage so I got Derek's 4-1/2-year-old son Gerard a job with the station doing promotional spots. That sweet little boy with his veddy British accent immediately created a sensation with fans and soon he had his own local fan club.

I really liked Derek but felt he never could acclimate himself to "doing business," as he saw it, in the "American Way." I think when he perceived his job to be intruding on his personal relationships, or not appearing to be simply unbridled fun, he lost his momentum. He had an entirely different philosophy as to how one conducted business affairs, and it did not include the "naked ambition" us Yanks seemed to exhibit. Almost as soon as I hired him we had signed the Byrds and the San Francisco band the Beau Brummels. Later we would represent the Beach Boys and Paul Revere and the Raiders.

Not long after he came on board, we sent Derek and Dave Hull to the Bahamas to interview the Beatles while they were filming *Help!* Derek arrived feeling like an outsider with a tape recorder in hand, yet that was what his job was at that moment. I understand the Beatles felt a bit awkward with him at first, since Derek was showing up as a journalist again and not as one of the inner circle, and the magic he had felt as such had mostly vanished. But the interviews he and Dave brought back were great and we packaged them to sell to radio stations around the country. We placed an ad in *Billboard* and expected the orders to pour in. To my astonishment we got no takers. Ironically, many years later Dave Hull put some of those interviews up for auction online and sold them within minutes for $25,000.

Discouraged by his humiliation at having to become just another bloodsucking journalist in the eyes of the Beatles, as well as the shock of his initial efforts going for naught, Derek didn't last long with Prestige Promotions. A former accountant named Eddie Tickner, and his partner, Jim Dickson, a former musician, had formed a publishing company, then a management firm, and Derek went to work for them, taking the Byrds and the Beau Brummels with him.

BLOWIN' IN THE WIND

The Beatles • Mick Jagger • Cary Grant
Merle Haggard • Dolly Parton • David
Letterman • The Rolling Stones • The
Beach Boys • Ike and Tina Turner • Leeza
Gibbons • Jerry Lee Lewis • Gene Autry
Roy Rogers • Monty Hall • Roy Orbison
Buddy Hackett • Barbara Mandrell

HAVING DODGED A BULLET with the Beatles concert, my partners and I decided to open a third Cinnamon Cinder in Alhambra, a community just south of Pasadena. The idea was to service the growing populations in the San Gabriel Valley. Now with three clubs the Cinnamon Cinder was supporting itself. Success tends to breed success and I found more and more people were asking me to franchise the Cinnamon Cinder name. The truth was it probably made sense to trade on the name. While we did set up clubs in San Bernardino, San Diego and Fresno (they all failed), I was just too busy to sit down and try and figure out the complicated structure of a national franchise. The Cinders were not only achieving increasing name recognition nationwide, but many of the acts we helped get started, groups like the Beach Boys, Jan and Dean, Chris Montez and the Righteous Brothers, were creating hits songs and beginning to draw the national spotlight.

The British invasion was in full swing by late 1964 and one of the bands that everyone was talking about was the Rolling Stones. Although they hadn't yet produced any top 40 hits in the U.S. their music was getting released, and it was just a matter of time before they struck gold with a smash hit. They had a vastly different sound than the Beatles. Whereas the Beatles had a slick, almost packaged pop sound that had hugely widespread appeal, the Rolling Stones had a gritty, soulful, almost angry sound; they performed a lot of rhythm and blues covers. Many kids thought the Stones were a Black act until they finally saw their pictures.

The Stones were picking up steam and I felt lucky I had nailed them

It used to be a strip club but we made the Cinnamon Cinder the coolest place in town.

down for a concert date. We were quickly becoming one of the top concert promotion companies in Southern California. With our success with the Beatles many people were watching to see what we did next. When I was offered the Stones I jumped. Buying them back then wasn't hard because they were on a relentless tour schedule. They were set to be in our area in November so we set the date for November 1, after clearing the Long Beach Auditorium as the venue. The Auditorium had 4,000 seats so we negotiated a deal with the Stones for a flat $4500, meaning we paid that only and no percentage of the gate.

I heard rumors that the Stones could be difficult. They had a reputation for partying as hard as they worked. And they worked hard. Their tour schedule between 1964 and 1965 would have almost no holes in it for rest and relaxation. We put the tickets up for sale and they sold out immediately. I could have kicked myself for not booking the 13,000 seat Long Beach Arena, because any time tickets sell out in one day you can pretty much count on doing at least double your business with ease.

The concert was on a Sunday afternoon, and I arrived at the Auditorium a few hours before show time. The Stones were already in their dressing rooms when I walked in. In the first room was Brian Jones, alone, practicing on his guitar. My first reaction was utter surprise, maybe even dismay. Having bought many acts by then, I was used to clean cut artists like the Righteous Brothers, the Beach Boys or the Beatles. The Stones were a whole new breed for me. Brian's brown suit was sweat stained and badly wrinkled and his fingernails were dirty. His hair was also much longer and bushier than the Beatles.

In the adjoining room I met the rest of the group and they looked like they had just gotten off work from the local Richfield gas station, having just changed out of their greasy overalls and into greasy jeans and torn jackets. Like Jones they had very long scruffy hair. I said hello to them as they changed their clothes and couldn't help but notice their legs had blue streaks from dye that had leeched out of their jeans. I guess they'd been living in the same clothes for months. In addition to their shabby appearance the band members were indifferent and cold, and their road crew was uncooperative, but I tried to be friendly with all of them.

When the band took the stage they were transformed. Those raggedy kids that hadn't particularly impressed me had been replaced by a well oiled machine that commanded the stage like none other I had seen, including the Beatles. The Rolling Stones were raw and created a powerful blend of rock and traditional rhythm and blues, offering up something no one had ever heard. In about two songs I came to have an enormous respect for them and acknowledged they were incredibly talented. Their lead singer, that painfully skinny kid, Mick Jagger, strutted the stage like a prowling panther, his moves more sexually charged than a young Elvis, his rich, strong vocals belying his almost fragile body.

The crowd seemed to scream as loud and hard as they did for the Beatles, despite having less than a quarter of the numbers. In the early to mid-'60s it became the custom to throw jelly beans up on the stage. With the Stones that started to change when all manner of items, from the traditional jelly beans and candy to panties and bras began to litter the stage. Near the beginning of the concert a girl's boot landed on stage and I could see Jagger scanning the audience for its source. I could tell during the entire concert it distracted him—it didn't affect his amazing performance, but he was literally waiting for the other "shoe" to drop.

In the middle of the second encore the twin to the first boot flew onto the stage and the relief on Jagger's face was clear.

I had heard that Rolling Stones fans were wilder than Beatles fans, so I cautioned Jagger before the show to get off the stage as soon as their set was over. He ignored my caution and continued taunting the girls in the front rows to come up and join him on stage. It was a tease because the security guards weren't going to let that happen, but it created a lot of overwrought girls who screamed and cried their eyes out to get a touch of Mick's hand. I made a mental note that this crap would have to change if and when we did another concert together. I didn't think that would happen given that I did not get along with the band all that well.

During the Stones brief visit, Teri Brown befriended lead guitarist Brian Jones. Many people do not know this, but it was Jones who founded the group, with Jagger and Keith Richards joining later. A phenomenally talented musician who could play just about anything, Brian also came up with the name and, at least early on, plotted the direction their music would take. But Brian told Teri he felt isolated from the other members of the group. Part of his isolation came from his lack of interest in using drugs, something the other band members embraced with zest. Ironically, he would die of a drug overdose in 1969.

Brian also told Teri he felt alone on the road because of an ongoing feud with Jagger. With Jagger backed up by Richards, and to a lesser extent the other members, that acrimony would keep Brian distanced from the others, except on stage, when they all seemed to come brilliantly together. Brian eventually joined in the drug use to develop some camaraderie, and it killed him.

As deejays at KRLA we were often asked to host various events. With the Rose Bowl game a day or two away, I was asked to MC a Big Ten football banquet at the Hollywood Palladium. Told it would be a star-studded affair, I was excited to host it. When I arrived one of the NCAA officials escorted me to my dressing room. Expecting to have it to myself, I was awed to find Bob Hope, Red Buttons, Pat O'Brien and band leader Les Brown just sitting around the small room chatting. Each was completely deadpan and taking turns telling jokes. I found out that night that comedians hate to laugh at each other's jokes. Hope would start out, "Did you hear the one about..." and get two or three lines into it and Buttons would grumble, "Yeah, I heard that." Then O'Brien started an old chestnut and Les Brown would stop him. In turn, each one would try and get through a joke. I sat with them a whole hour and never heard a complete joke.

On New Year's Eve, 1964, we booked the Righteous Brothers, and because of their growing popularity agreed to pay them the unheard of price of $1250 for the gig. That was a huge leap from the $150 I had been paying them two years before, but with a string of regional hits and a growing fan base those two young men from Orange County were commanding bigger and bigger booking fees. That night as the singers warmed up in the kitchen, Teri sat down with Bobby Hatfield and struck up a conversation. After a few moments Bobby shared something with her.

"We just cut a song this afternoon with Phil Spector."

Across the kitchen, Bill Medley was buttoning up his dress shirt. "We think it's going to be a hit."

"What's it called?" she asked.

"'You've Lost That Lovin' Feeling,'" said Bobby. "Wanna hear some of it?"

Teri nodded enthusiastically. "Of course."

Bill took a deep breath and began to sing a beautiful song about a love gone bad. Bobby jumped in for the refrain. They ended on the refrain and looked to Teri for her reaction.

Her eyes were wide. "I've got goosebumps, guys. You're right, it's fantastic."

Though they didn't sing their new song on stage that night, sure enough, a few weeks later "You've Lost That Lovin' Feeling," filled out in all its glory with Phil Spector's trademark Wall of Sound, rocketed to the top of the charts. It went on to become the most played song in radio history. From that day the Righteous Brothers never looked back. That was also the last time they ever played the Cinder, not because they were too good for us, but as they were now national stars we simply couldn't afford them. I was very happy for them. They were always total gentlemen and two of the nicest men in the business. I was saddened to hear of Bobby's passing in November 2003.

Despite the November 1964 Rolling Stones concert going so well I was slightly surprised when I was offered their May 16, 1965, concert. The band didn't seem to like me and I figured the first concert would be the last and put them out of my mind. When their management offered me the gig I decided three things needed to be different from the last concert. One was size of the venue, the second was beefing up security and finally, it was critical to get the band to cooperate in dealing with the crowd after the show. Having learned my lesson this time I booked them into the Long Beach Arena with its 13,000 seats. The tickets sold out promptly, and I envisioned another great success. Of course their fee had gone up quite a bit since the year before, from $4,500 to $20,000 plus a piece of the gross, but I was happy to pay it given the much larger venue.

They arrived in Los Angeles a few days before the concert to do some interviews and record in the studio. Teri Brown was given some duties of helping them out, driving band members when they needed it and generally seeing to their needs. An interesting little piece of history: in the days before the concert, they went into a local recording studio and laid down the tracks for what would become their first number one hit, "Satisfaction."

The day of the concert I could feel the tension in the growing crowd. An hour before the show some idiot girl climbed way up a drain pipe to get into the building. Fortunately the police rescued her before she broke her neck. I had been warned that the Stones had a type of fan I hadn't seen before, aggressive with an angry edge to them. Over the previous year since the Beatles arrived I began to sense an increased desperation in all the fans. In 1964 they screamed and cried but pretty much remained civil. Not so in 1965. Suddenly the screaming girls who occasionally crushed limos under their sheer mass were now coming after the objects of their obsessions as if they wanted to kill them. I was completely baffled by their seemingly insane behavior.

The Long Beach Arena offered me another problem: escape. The back door was situated so that anyone could gain access to the area. Enough unruly people could create a bottleneck and trap the group. I cringed as I pictured hundreds of crazed fans attacking the Rolling Stones. I didn't want to be the first promoter to have a band torn to pieces by its admirers. I took Mick Jagger aside and gave him a warning, based upon his performance the previous November.

"Please don't tease the girls when you finish. Just get off the stage. We have to get you out of here really fast. Otherwise we may have a big problem."

He assured me he would cooperate. The group took the stage and had a fantastic set. I could tell in the six months since I'd last seen them they had grown a lot, both as musicians and showmen. Jagger was even more confident and strong in the way he sang and controlled the audience. I knew at that moment that if the Beatles had any competition—if there was such a thing as the "best band around"—the Stones were about to give them a run for their money.

The Stones management had arranged for a helicopter to fly them the 40 or so miles back to wherever they were staying. Since the chopper couldn't land anywhere near the Arena, it would do so a few blocks away and the band would be transported from the Arena to the chopper by car. We had a small station wagon inside the building pointed toward the large doors of several loading ramps. The plan was to get them in the car seconds after they finished their set and shoot them down the ramp and to safety. Timing was everything. If they dawdled even a few moments it could give fans enough time to congregate around the ramp—and everyone in the Arena knew exactly where the Stones would be making their exit.

As they played the last few songs of their set the audience took on an ugly tone. I saw girls pushing and scratching each other to get closer to the stage and there was an animal look in their eyes I had never seen at a concert. I eyed my watch and kept looking at the path the group would take from the stage to the escape car, making sure it was clear. When they finished their last number and took their bows I actually felt like we had a chance. Then Jagger did exactly what I'd asked him not to do: he tarried on the stage, taunting the crowd. Probably 4000 girls shrieked their hearts out as Jagger stayed up front, whipping them into a frenzy. Meanwhile, a large portion of the other 9000 members of the audience were exiting the Arena and heading toward the back door.

I stepped to the back of the stage and shouted to the security people to get ready. Meanwhile, Jagger held court on the stage for what seemed like an interminable time.

Finally the crowd swarmed the stage and Jagger and the rest of the band ran toward the back and the awaiting station wagon. We got them inside, but by now the mob awaiting them outside was huge. When the doors to the ramp burst open the sight before me caused my jaw to drop. Not hundreds, but literally thousands of screaming kids, a wall of them, and all that stood between them and the Stones' little station wagon were maybe fifty members of the Long Beach Police Department.

The driver of the car panicked and rolled down the wrong ramp and almost immediately the kids overwhelmed the cop's skirmish line. My heart was in my throat as I watched their car disappear under a mountain of flesh. Somehow they kept the doors closed and no one broke the windows as the station wagon crept through that manic mass of humanity. I watched them roll over a girl's foot and she didn't even blink. One lone cop crouched on top of the car, wielding his baton in vain as dozens of kids surrounded him and jumped up and down on the roof, slowly crushing it. The panicked Stones lay on their backs and put their feet against the caving roof to keep it from smashing them.

The station wagon eventually cleared the crowd and sped away, but it was heavily damaged. I later got a bill for $3200 for the car. The police were probably never the same, and Mick Jagger swore he would never work with me again. He was true to his word and did not.

I believe it was a little later that same year Teri Brown got trapped in a limo with the Dave Clark Five as they tried to exit the same venue. I also promoted that concert and we had arranged a police motorcycle escort to get them out of the Arena. In the melee after the concert, the cop tried to start his bike and it wouldn't kick over. Teri later told me the crowd of thousands caught them, just as they did with the Stones, and she and the members of the band were also forced to lie on the seats and floor of the limo and use their legs as supports to prevent the limo roof from crushing them.

The limo finally pulled away from the crush of the crowd. Climbing a nearby hill, they stopped to remove a tenacious 15-year-old from the roof. The bodyguard got out and tried pulling the screaming kid off the top of the limo. A local man walking his dog happened by, and thinking he was witness to a child being attacked, went up behind the bodyguard and knocked him cold with a right hook. The cycle cop finally got his bike going, arrived, and convinced the citizen he had not just broken up a child abduction. It was pretty crazy, and having learned my lesson with crunched liveries, Dave Clark got the $8,000 bill for the limo.

Despite the near catastrophe, the Rolling Stones concert was a financial success. They appeared on the show *Shindig* a few days later and debuted "Satisfaction." Less than three weeks later they released it as a 45 and it catapulted them into superstardom. Combined with their innovative sound, relentless work ethic and that first of many mega hits, they were suddenly being regarded as nearly equal to the Beatles. But in their case, they were the evil twins, the bad boys of rock, as opposed to the Beatles' squeaky clean image.

The dizzying rush of the preparations and execution of the Beatles concert in August of 1964 had passed but now we were gearing up to bring

BOB EUBANKS ARCHIVES

My one and only picture with the Rolling Stones backstage, 1965.

them back in 1965. We negotiated with the Beatles, GAC and the Bowl, this time coming up with an agreement to do two concerts, August 29 and 30. This time we offered them a flat fee, $45,000 for each concert, with no piece of the gross. This allowed Mickey and me to both cover our costs and know what they would be from the start. Paying them $90,000 seemed like good business on both sides and the deal was made.

By early 1965 another benefit from the Beatles was emerging and the management at KRLA was delighted. In little more than a year the station had gone from number two in the market to eclipsing KFWB and grabbing the bragging rights as to which was *the* station in Southern California. I'd love to take credit for it, but it was also the hard work and tireless promotion of the other jocks, as well as management's smart decision to throw the resources of the station behind our position as "Beatles Central."

A few weeks before the back-to-back Beatles concerts, on Friday, August 13, violence broke out in Watts, an impoverished community in south-central Los Angeles. Partly in response to a routine traffic stop by the CHP, as well as a general perception in the community that the recent national Civil Rights Act of 1964 had been set back by California's Proposition 14 (which the U.S. Supreme court later declared unconstitutional), the incident escalated into a full scale riot. It lasted six days, and more than thirty people died. Someone even threw a Molotov cocktail through KRLA's window but miraculously it didn't ignite. I was worried there might be security problems for the concerts, but by the week following the riots things had calmed down.

The 1964 press conference had certainly been historic, but it had also been sort of a disaster. It was hard to hear anyone, took too long to get going and the questions had been inane at best. This time we were going to hold the conference at Capitol Records' famous headquarters at Hollywood and Vine, and I set a limit on it of twenty-five minutes. Since meeting the Beatles I realized they were very bright, possessed of that droll British wit and didn't suffer fools. With that in mind I hired a UCLA psychologist to ask questions and give the conference an air of intelligence. My idea backfired slightly because the Beatles loved the psychologist's questions so much the press conference ran over an hour and the Beatles were late to the concert.

Aside from the conference running late, this time we were much better organized and got them into the Bowl without any real concerns or close calls. After the concert it was much the same. Paying them the flat fee, and having two concerts back-to-back paid off. After we'd covered all the expenses, Mickey Brown and I actually ended up with more money than the band made—and the split was just between the two of us this time. Oh, those were the good old days. We had also gotten a lot smarter since the first concert. Not only did we make quite a bit more money off the concert itself, we also made a tidy haul by selling KRLA the right to say "KRLA presents the Beatles."

With the sequel to the first Beatles concert a huge success, I had entered a new arena: I was now considered one of the top rock promoters in the business, something that had just sneaked up and replaced my primary career focus as a deejay. Yet I was still doing my show at KRLA, now six days a week.

Meanwhile, Beatlemania had helped transform KRLA into the new powerhouse in L.A. radio. Station management was ecstatic with me; they saw me as the primary reason it had happened. I really felt that success stemmed from a lot of factors and many other people had contributed to the station's turnaround, but if they were going to give me credit I wasn't going to argue. I saw an opportunity to advance my position and sat down and renegotiated my deal with KRLA.

Although I had launched myself into the top level concert business and had been playing with the big boys for a while I was still undervaluing myself and the "hard-ass" deal I made with KRLA was really quite ridiculous in retrospect. I held them up for a $3,000 a year raise, four weeks of vacation and a five day work week. While there were top jocks around the country making $50,000 or $60,000, even a few bringing in as much as $100,000, I was content to make less than twenty. At the time I didn't know such salaries were possible, yet had I known that I probably would not have been able to ask for it. My accomplishment of bringing the Beatles to L.A. and helping make KRLA number one still couldn't overwhelm my own insecurities that told me I was not as talented as the other jocks. Despite my obvious successes I felt I couldn't let up for a moment in finding new ways to make myself valuable to the station.

To add even more to my already very full plate, by late 1964 I had been fielding inquiries about getting other artists into the Bowl. Bob Dylan, a Minnesota kid who in a few short years had made a name for himself as a composer and musician, was available the week after the Beatles date, in early September, 1965. His hit "Like a Rolling Stone" made him a star. Although I didn't know much about him, the buzz around the station was that he had a huge underground following. I agreed to try and line up the Bowl for him. We set the concert date with the Bowl for September 3, 1965. I assumed that having a hit song meant a lot of people would be interested in seeing Dylan. We had sold the Beatles concerts out in a little over three hours so I figured Dylan would at least sell out, if not in several hours. I was wrong. Ticket sales started out slow, and for a while I thought we were going to lose our asses. But in the days prior to the event sales picked up a bit and the evening of the concert we had a decent crowd streaming in. All told, we sold 7,000 of the more than 17,000 available seats that night and actually made a little money, even after paying Dylan $15,000.

Unlike most concert venues that forbid unauthorized food and drink, the Bowl actually encourages patrons to come early and make a picnic of it. Most Bowl patrons bring food and wine, but that evening Dylan's crowd mostly seemed to smoke their dinner. I had never really seen hippies before and this group was quite an education. I saw more buckskin than in a John Ford movie, and the aroma of marijuana blending with musk and patchouli oil created a heady perfume in the summer night air. I watched as the procession of tie-dyed garments, eye popping cleavage and antiwar buttons passed by, and, despite my being the promoter of the concert, I suddenly felt very out of touch. These flower children were probably averaging about half a generation older than the Beatles audience—not too many years younger than I was—yet in my suit and carefully coiffed hair I felt more like Joe Friday than a hip concert promoter.

It was also a very low keyed event compared to other concerts. In fact the crowd was so mellow I regretted spending money on security. The only "demand" Dylan's management had made was that his drummer needed a drum set. We rented a drum set but when it arrived and was set up I realized it was a crappy excuse for a musical instrument and felt guilty we hadn't done better. To my surprise no one complained.

Dylan was an eccentric but was also completely unpretentious and unassuming. Whereas we arranged to have the Beatles arrive and depart in various armored cars and limousines, Dylan drove himself up the hill to the artists' parking lot in a nondescript compact car with a gorgeous blonde next to him. Just before the concert was to start, a guy with about a three-joint buzz staggered up the ramp behind the stage and demanded of the security people that he see Dylan.

He caused such a commotion I was called. I rounded the corner and saw this longhair decked out in shabby clothes with a buckskin jacket under his arm.

"What can I do for you?" I asked him.

"I wanna see Dylan."

Yeah, you and 7,000 other fans, but I kept my patience. "Why?"

He held up the jacket. "I stole his jacket from his dressing room in Seattle and I wanna give it back to him."

The story was too improbable to be made up so I went to Dylan's manager, Albert Grossman. When I relayed the story to him his eyes lit up. The young troublemaker was brought back stage and allowed to hand the jacket directly to Dylan with his profuse apologies. Dylan was very cool about it and the kid was treated like a hero for returning the jacket.

The first half of the concert featured a great acoustic set. The crowd went wild (in their own, laid back way) when each song was announced. I was amazed that this slight, frizzy haired kid who sang through his nose captivated the crowd like he did, but even I could hear the brilliance at times. He took a break after the acoustic set and then the audience could see stage hands setting up the amplifiers. Many in the crowd began to grumble, but pretty soon that turned to boos. I wasn't sure what to make of it, but when Dylan returned with an electric guitar I saw what all the fuss was about. I'm not exaggerating when I say a good half of the audience got up and started making for the exits. I turned to Grossman standing next to me.

"What's going on?"

He shrugged. "Purists. They can't stand electric guitars."

It was one of the strangest exoduses I had ever seen, or ever would see, in my years in music. It didn't bother Dylan a bit that the rats were leaving the ship as he plunged into an energetic electric set. As he got to what seemed to be the last songs of the concert, the crowd began yelling "Like a Rolling Stone!" After enough demands Dylan finally mumbled, "Ah, man, I forgot my G harmonica."

With that about fifteen harmonicas flew onto the stage. At least one must have been a G because Dylan sorted through the harmonicas littering the stage, picked one up and closed with "Like a Rolling Stone." It brought down the house—what there was left of it.

The Beatles • Mick Jagger • Cary Grant
Merle Haggard • Dolly Parton • David
Letterman • The Rolling Stones • The
Beach Boys • Tina Turner • Leeza
Gibbons • Jerry Lee Lewis • Gene Autry
Roy Rogers • Monty Hall • Roy Orbison
Buddy Hackett • Barbara Mandrell

THAT'S THE WAY LOVE GOES

NOT TOO LONG AFTER THE 1965 BEATLES and Dylan concerts we made the decision to shut down the Cinnamon Cinder in North Hollywood. We had opened a Cinder in San Bernardino but it had burned down a week later so maybe that was a sign. Also, the regulations had since changed regarding teens and clubs, and business had dropped off for many other reasons. Though owning it less than a year, we also closed the Alhambra club because it just didn't seem feasible anymore to keep them all going. I was also deeply involved in several other businesses, not to mention having to be at the station five days a week. Mickey and I eventually ended our partnership, sometime in 1967, at least for several years, and he ended up with the Long Beach Cinder as part of the deal. Frankly I was getting tired of working seven days a week and the Cinder had come to represent just one more thing to deal with. Little did I know that getting the Cinder out of my life would be opening the door for a new adventure, one that would change my life.

In the late spring of 1966 KRLA had assembled a basketball team to play the faculties of high schools and local colleges for charity. One night we played the teachers at Cal State Northridge. One of the celebs on my team was Bobby "Boris" Pickett, best known for his novelty hit, "The Monster Mash." Bobby was doing very well as a commercial spokesman so I asked him who his agents were.

He told me, then added, "But the best agents are Abrams-Rubaloff."

"Do you think they'd sign me?" Before Bobby could answer, fellow KRLA jock Charlie O'Donnell erupted into laughter.

"No way, Eubanks. Unless you're a known actor with credits they won't touch you."

That was just the kind of challenge I liked. I held out my hand to O'Donnell.

"Five bucks says I at least sign with them. Whether they get me work is another thing."

Charlie laughed even harder and shook my hand. "You're on."

That was a Wednesday. The next day I called my friend Ned Tanen at Universal. Ned would later run Paramount Pictures. I figured Ned knew pretty much everyone in entertainment.

"Do you know Noel Rubaloff?"

"Sure. We were agents at MCA."

"I'm looking for a commercial agent and Bobby Pickett said this was the guy."

"I'll call him," offered Ned.

Noel Rubaloff agreed to meet with me the next day, a Friday. I went to his office and he greeted me warmly. After we got the usual small talk out of the way, he leaned forward.

"Chuck Barris is casting a new game show called *The Newlywed Game*. I don't know anything about it but they've been talking to ABC, and haven't got an order yet, but I know the brass over there's interested. Now here's the deal: Chuck's talked to everybody in town and he's more or less settled on a host, but I think you'd be perfect. If you're interested I'll call him and try and get you in there."

My original goal had merely been to sign with Abrams-Rubaloff and collect O'Donnell's five bucks. Although I seemed to have less than a snowball's chance, my first thought was not excitement but rather concern: this would only give me another duty in my already full schedule. In addition to KRLA, I also had to deal with the work load of my concert business and our rock PR company. But the meeting also represented a chance—however slight—to host a national television show. I was excited and scared to death. Chuck Barris already had a hit called *The Dating Game* so I knew people took him seriously. This was for real.

"Sure," I said, "I'd love to meet with Chuck Barris."

Noel was right about the hosting spot. Barris had tentatively chosen an actor named Scott Beach, a member of the cutting edge San Francisco based improv group, The Committee. But Noel also somehow knew Barris was still discreetly continuing his search so he must not have

ABC PUBLICITY PHOTO

The darlings of the ABC daytime lineup circa 1966: (l–r) myself, Jim Lange, Allan Ludden, Monty Hall and Tom Kennedy. I wonder if Lange still has those pants!

been too ecstatic about Beach. Noel made a call, talked to Barris and set an appointment for the next morning, a Saturday.

The next day Noel and I drove over to meet with Barris. Walking into Barris's office I knew I was in for something strange when I saw the urinal hanging on the wall. Mostly hidden behind a vast oak desk cluttered with papers and odds and ends, Barris was a small, shy man sporting a shock of curly hair. He was on the phone and waved us in. He later told us the artifacts on his desk were brought to him by his staff from different exotic locations they had visited while chaperoning couples on his hit show *The Dating Game*.

After we had dispensed with the small talk, Barris turned blunt. Looking me over he said, "I gotta tell you, Scott's my first choice to host, but let's see what you can do. Do you mind doing a little run-through?"

I had no idea I would be auditioning. "No, I don't mind," I lied.

"Great. Listen, we'll just have you do a quick run-through for the staff. Okay?"

"Sure."

As we walked toward the door, he added, "Oh, and Paul Picard might be here, too."

Picard, I found out, was the Head of West Coast Programming for ABC. (Picard would eventually be replaced in that position by a young exec named Michael Eisner.) One of Barris's staff, Larry Gottlieb, took me to a room with eight chairs in a row for the contestants. A group of chairs for the audience faced them. Larry gestured toward the contestants' chairs.

"Okay, here's the format: four couples, all newlyweds, married two years or less, will be given two sets of questions by you. First, you'll ask the ladies while the husbands are out of the room, then we bring out the husbands and take the ladies out. Then we put them back together and see if they knew how their spouse answered each question. The winner gets a prize. Simple, huh?"

I nodded, pretending to be enthusiastic, but thought it was the dumbest idea for a show I'd ever heard. Larry started in on a complicated series of instructions and I just glazed over, completely lost. All I could think was "I'm a radio guy so what the hell am I doing here?" I knew Wink Martindale had made the jump to television, and for a while it seemed I was chasing him, matching his career moves with similar ones of my own, but this is where I knew it would end. I also knew that when they hired him for *What's This Song?* in 1964, NBC changed Wink's name to Win. I had a vague fear some such fate awaited my name.

Larry left and after a few minutes ushered in four couples. Noel later told me that after I had gone off with Larry Gottlieb, Barris said that if the audition didn't work out he might hire me to warm up the crowd and be the announcer for Scott Beach. Noel, Barris, Paul Picard and a group of Barris staffers entered and sat down to watch my performance. I was hoping I wasn't about to make a fool of myself. I thought about the five dollar bet with O'Donnell. Since I had not yet signed papers with Noel I knew I would owe O'Donnell if I blew this.

Stoic Paul Picard had his arms crossed in a defiant "show me what ya got, kid" pose. I looked at the couples and my hopes brightened slightly. They were all smiling and seemed ready to have fun. Once I got underway and made it through the first few questions I forgot all about my high-powered audience. Couple number two were Hispanic and the wife was a total pistol. Her hubby had been out all night gambling so she lit into him ruthlessly. It was funny as hell. They really broke the ice. As the moments ticked by I got more and more comfortable and found I was very much at home in bringing out the funniest comments in them.

Within a few minutes I felt like I had been doing the show my whole life. I also understood Barris's brilliance. I had dismissed the idea of the show a few minutes before but now realized the potential it had. I glanced over and saw the staff in stitches, then noticed both Barris and Paul Picard were laughing out loud. I knew I was onto something. Later that day Barris made Noel an offer for me to host his newest show, *The Newlywed Game*. Of course, I first had to sign a contract with Noel to represent me. As I put pen to paper I thought about Charlie O'Donnell and his five dollars I was about to collect. I smiled to myself. We had made the bet on Wednesday and it was now Saturday. Only in Hollywood.

The story goes, two fellows named Nick Nicholson and Roger Muir came up with the idea for *The Newlywed Game*, literally wrote it on a napkin and gave it to ABC. ABC loved the idea, gave it to Barris and offered him some money to develop the show. Development in the entertainment business means that someone comes up with an idea, someone else (usually) pays for a chance to develop that idea, and then people are hired to fine tune it until they have a script and/or a pilot, or in our case, a run-through. ABC decided it wanted to see a full blown run-through of the show, complete with live audience, before it would commit to the next step, a pilot. After that, if we were lucky and they loved the pilot, then it tested well, we would get an order for actual shows.

We began rehearsals for the run-through and I found myself freezing up again. The magic I'd found during the office run-through had vanished and I felt really uncomfortable. As the agonizing days and weeks of rehearsals progressed I was sure Chuck's staff felt they'd made a big mistake with me. But as the day grew near for the real run-through I began to get my legs under me and one day I came in, began my rehearsal, and suddenly it all gelled. Within a few days I was convinced that the magic I had created that first time had returned.

Bill Carruthers was the show's producer, and though he was an imposing figure, a stern general in his Brooks Brothers sport jacket, he showed me a lot of patience and compassion in the early days. I'm sure Carruthers and Barris had their doubts about me at times, but I'm

People will say anything
to win a toaster!

CAPITAL CITIES / ABC PUBLICITY PHOTO

CAPITAL CITIES / ABC PUBLICITY PHOTO

The host with the most—
late 60's.

CAPITAL CITIES / ABC PUBLICITY PHOTO

Newlywed Game in the Late 70's. Would you buy a used car from this guy?

thankful they hung in there with me. I might have stayed in radio had they not looked past my nervous moments and believed in me.

The big day arrived and I drove to 1313 North Vine, the production facility reserved for the run-through. For television producers, one of the nice things about Hollywood is that there has always been an inexhaustible supply of people willing to stand in line to see anything. Out front stood 300 people waiting to get in, but in this case they were not strangers but rather friends and family of Barris employees. When I got inside and prepared to take the stage the nerves returned. I told myself the panic I was feeling would subside as soon as I got in front of the audience, but in the moments before that happened I had second, third and fourth thoughts about what I was doing. Then they called me to go on. I walked out, waved and stepped in front of the podium. A peacefulness came over me and I was suddenly just fine. I don't necessarily believe in precognition, but the fact I would see that podium a lot in the next four decades might have had something to do with that calm. Maybe in some way I knew I was home.

I gazed out at the audience, then at the guys I had to sway: Ed Vane, head of ABC Daytime, and the rest of the ABC suits in the front row. Although this run-through was without cameras, I knew they were the critically important audience. I turned my attention to the couples. Couple number one was a young aspiring actor and comedian named Dom DeLuise and his wife, Carol. The format of *The Newlywed Game* was really not designed for comedians or actors—they have a difficult time being themselves—but Dom DeLuise was very funny and our banter got the audience laughing. I glanced over at Vane with his "Okay, make me laugh" expression and knew the Dom and Bob Show wasn't going to be enough.

Then couple number four came to the rescue. The husband was sort of a macho guy with little sense of humor and his wife was a drop-dead gorgeous blonde. When I asked her "What is your favorite nickname for your husband," she looked blank for a second then, totally deadpan, responded, "Numbnuts." The crowd went crazy and the ABC execs nearly fell out of their seats. With that reaction, radio deejay Bob Eubanks had just made the jump to network television. ABC was so thrilled by our run-through they gave us a production order that night without even asking for a pilot, a move that is rarely done. The show was to be slotted sometime in ABC's daytime schedule. Thank God for Dom and Numbnuts.

VINE STREET THEATRE
SUNDAY MAY 15, 1966 — 7 P.M.

Special Premiere Presentation

of

A NEW TELEVISION SHOW

A CHUCK BARRIS PRODUCTION

in association with ABC-TV

Invitation to the original *The Newlywed Game* run through—Dom who?

* * * *PRODUCTION STAFF* * * *

THE NEWLYWEDS

Danny *and* Terry Howard

Ron *and* Barbara Waranch

Dom *and* Carol De Luise

Denny *and* Cathy Marples

YOUR HOST

Bob Eubanks

ANNOUNCING BY

Scott Beach

FOR CHUCK BARRIS PRODUCTIONS

producer ....Larry Gottlieb

associate producer ....Walt Case

writers ....Jonathan Debin
                                           Mike Metzger

contestant coordinator ....Linda Derman

music director........................Lyn Barris

production assistant ....Joan Thompson

production staff ....Bob Catley
                                              Sue Chalfin
                                       Marianne Giammarino

FOR ABC-TV

design ....George Smith

technical supervision ....Ted Hurley

lighting ....James Kilgore

audio ....Doug Nelson
                                             Jack Black

My first contract was for thirteen weeks at $900 a week. That was nearly three times what I was making at KRLA. (By the way, I loaned my first paycheck to the accountant at KRLA to buy his girlfriend Bonnie a fur coat—and he never paid me back!) In addition to my amazing salary, the contract also called for regular escalations of my salary, all the way to $1650 a week in the fifth year. I couldn't imagine doing the show for five years, let alone one. I was simply hoping to make it through the first taping. The show was to be produced at ABC's facility at Prospect and Talmadge, in Los Feliz, north and east of Hollywood.

The first time I pulled into the parking area I remembered when, as an eleven-year-old, I rode a horse in a live western show starring Rex Bell around that very lot—only then it was dirt. As far as I'd come in those sixteen years, I still had nagging doubts about my abilities. A healthy sense of fear can keep you sharp, on your toes. But what I was feeling was pure panic. The set for *The Newlywed Game* was built and we did more rehearsals. Then the first taping date was booked and the show was set to debut in July, 1966. Barris's original choice for host, Scott Beach, was hired to do the warm-up. At any live taped show in Hollywood, whether it's a sitcom or a game show, the producers hire someone to warm up the audience by telling jokes or funny stories and generally getting them in a festive, jovial mood. On his first day Scott baffled the audience with anti-Vietnam songs. In 1966 Vietnam had really only been on most people's radar for a year or two so the frequent and widespread protests had not yet occurred. Scott's songs only served to depress the studio audience. The next day Scott was let go and Johnny Jacobs was brought in to do warm-up as well as the announcing duties. Johnny was also the warm-up and announcer on *The Dating Game*. One of the best in the business, Johnny was a true artist and perfectionist. Once he came to me after a show and apologized for over-warming my audience, getting them "too high for that particular format." Johnny and I became very good friends and ended up owning two radio stations in northern California together.

When I arrived for work the first day of taping I prayed that the show would go more than one season. I also prayed that the host would last more than one show. The day the very first episode of *The Newlywed Game* was scheduled to debut, Secretary of Defense Robert McNamara decided to give the American public an update on what was going on in Vietnam. CBS and NBC aired McNamara and ABC went with Bob Eubanks. That was Monday, July 11, 1966 and we premiered with a huge 42 share. Today those are Superbowl numbers. The show was off and running.

For the first six months of our run *The Newlywed Game* was shot in black and white, which was customary for daytime shows. In early 1967 ABC made the decision to package us into an hour with *The Dating Game* and put us on Saturday nights. With the nighttime show came another exciting development: color. It sounds funny today, but color was a big deal back then. You could feel the excitement on the set and I remember getting goose bumps when I heard Johnny Jacobs say for the first time, "From Hollywood, *in color*, here come the newlyweds." The daytime version eventually caught up with the night version when both were produced in color.

The Dating Game came on at 7 P.M. and we followed at 7:30. Initially we were up against *The Jackie Gleason Show* on CBS, one of the hottest shows on TV, and a single seasoner called *Maya* on NBC. We did well in our time slot and ABC was happy. Also, with the move to prime time—in addition to doing the day version—the money was getting crazy. With the addition of the evening show my salary doubled overnight.

Although Chuck's favorite child was *The Dating Game*, our ratings were usually a little better. He spent a great deal of his time on that show and we almost never saw him. Chuck seemed to be able to capture exactly what middle America was looking for on television, and his shows continued to be big hits, from ours to *The Gong Show* about ten years later. He rarely gave me any feedback about the show but when he did it was always constructive and almost always right on target. The early Barris programs were some of the first reality shows.

The Newlywed Game was primarily a comedy show, not really a game show in the strictest definition. Prizes were handed out merely to acknowledge someone won and someone lost. People did not come on the show because of the prizes. We purposely kept the prizes to a limited value to preserve the integrity of our contestants. And they would certainly pour their hearts out for a toaster. Had we given away the cars or pricey luxury items that other shows did we would have risked polluting the process by taking the focus off having fun and turning it into a steely eyed contest to land that big prize. Keeping things simple let the show seek its own light-hearted level. When I first began the show, I was very concerned about making mistakes. When I'd blow a line I'd always yell, "Stop tape!" As time went by when I realized that the mistakes could be some of the funniest moments, I actually found myself making mistakes on purpose, and the audience ate it up.

Sometimes the laughs came from sources beyond our control. The studio was on the edge of a residential area and one day, during taping, a Dalmatian wandered in and trotted over to the set. I cracked up and the audience did too, but the laughter doubled when the dog stepped over to the grand prize—a bedroom set—and lifted his leg for all to see.

We had an art director named Sherman Loudermilk. Like many of the people Barris chose to work for him, Sherman was quite a character. He made it known to everyone that during his annual vacation he would travel to Vietnam to work as a soldier of fortune. (Barris himself has claimed to have been a CIA operative during this time.) While shooting a segment we had a cake that was being used as a prop to display one of the small prizes. During the commercial break I kidded Sherman that I'd give him five bucks if he took the cake and threw it in the face of our stage manager, Eddie Dusek. Why did I do that? I was probably bored and more so, I certainly didn't think he'd do it. Almost as soon as I'd issued my challenge Sherman grabbed the cake, walked over to Dusek and hurled it at him. Dusek was too quick and dodged out of the way, but couple number four were sitting right in front of him and took the cake full on. Loudermilk and I caught hell. I was told that the break necessitated by our stunt, as the wardrobe and makeup people de-iced couple number four, cost Chuck $10,000. I never made another bet with Sherman Loudermilk.

Barris's organization was referred to as The Love Company. It was not your typical workplace. It was not uncommon for the employees to congregate in Chuck's office for an impromptu musical jam session. Most played air guitars. Chuck also delighted in tormenting the network suits with his outrageous behavior. When they visited the office Chuck had the entire staff turn out in a parade, complete with uniformed staffers playing band instruments, majorettes, and Chuck as the grand master leading it on a big motorcycle—and this all took place in the office hallway. The network execs tolerated it because Chuck was a hitmaker.

Chuck rarely shaved so between that and his uncombed mop of hair he looked chronically unkempt. He also rubbed his nose all the time (I think it was just a nervous tick) and the word "stuff" was his favorite utility noun. To say Chuck is eccentric is like saying the Pope is devout.

One year Chuck sent me a case of wine with my name on the label—knowing full well I do not drink.

To aid them in selecting which shows were best for reruns, the Barris producers created an in-house rating system for their shows. A rating of 1 indicated a bad show, while a 2.5 was a good and 3 was a great show. The rating system spurred a competition between the shows, with us versus *The Dating Game*. When the rivalry became heated Chuck assumed the rating duty and always gave the Dating Game the best numbers. I heard a rumor that was never confirmed (but talked about a lot) that when Chuck created *The Dating Game* it was actually a "reworking" of an old radio show called *Blind Date*. Aware of *Blind Date* from the get-go, Chuck philosophized that if *Dating Game* was a bomb the issue would simply go away, and if it were a hit he would pay. It was a hit and he allegedly paid $900,000 to the creators of *Blind Date*. All of Chuck's oddness aside, I have nothing but good things to say about him. I will also say that if he was a CIA assassin then I'm Mary Poppins.

I had some surprise answers to my questions over the years, not many, but there were some doozies. I asked a lady what the one thing was that her husband told her not to talk about. She looked around, and as if she were telling only me and the people on the set, not millions at home as well, said, "My husband and my cousin are going to kill my uncle for the insurance." What made it even funnier was when the husband came back and gave the same answer. Either they were putting us on or they were perhaps two of the dumbest criminals ever. They got ten points for being in synch on the murder question and hugged and kissed like they'd just admitted to taking romantic walks in the rain.

Only twice in the history of *The Newlywed Game* did we not air a taped show. Once we caught a couple cheating. They were using a code to match their answers and we caught them. The other incident caused us to change our policy about using people's last names. I asked a wife if her husband ever got a valentine from any woman other than her and she replied, "Marsha Weinstein." We wrote Marsha Weinstein on the answer card. The husband got it wrong and we thought nothing else about it. Then, before we could air the show, we heard from Marsha Weinstein's lawyer. Turns out the husband was flying to New York to marry Marsha Weinstein and met and married his flight attendant instead. Jilted Marsha didn't want to be reminded of that ugly chapter in her life and threatened to sue, so we pulled the episode. From then on we never used a last name.

The Beatles • Mick Jagger • Cary Grant
Merle Haggard • Dolly Parton • David
Letterman • The Rolling Stones • The
Beach Boys **WUNNERFUL** • Leeza
Gibbons • Jerry Lee Lewis • Gene Autry
Roy Rogers • Monty Hall • Roy Orbison
Buddy Hackett • Barbara Mandrell

OW, IN ADDITION TO THE NEWLYWED GAME, I was not only running Prestige Promotions, I was still on the air at KRLA and active in the concert business. And our biggest concert to date was coming up: the Beatles for the third time. But they had outgrown the Hollywood Bowl—realistically, probably in 1964—so I looked around for the biggest place I could find. We thought about the Rose Bowl, with room for around 100,000, but decided on Dodger Stadium. Taking a page out of the Booking the Beatles Manual, I knew that since the band had filled Shea Stadium, and had done well in other large venues, they could probably fill the 45,000 seats of the Dodgers' home field without much trouble. Mickey and I made arrangements to book the stadium.

I worried for a while that John Lennon's infamous comment in March of 1966 that the Beatles were more popular than Jesus would cause lots of problems. Radio stations around the country were banning their records and there were some protests that centered on destroying Beatles records, but most of that died down by the time our August 29 concert rolled around. I read that the Beatles' second Shea Stadium concert, the week before ours, did not sell out, leaving 11,000 seats vacant. Not so with ours. Not only had we sold out the 45,000 tickets, but Dodger owner Walter O'Malley helped by buying the entire second level for his season ticket holders.

The deal with the Beatles was also different from the previous year when we made a straight buy-out. This time Epstein wanted a piece of the action again so we agreed that we would pay them $100,000 against 60% of the gross. Walter O'Malley's largess was not lost on us. We arranged to give the entire centerfield bleacher seats to a group that worked with blind children. The stadium manager, Dick Walsh, was easy to deal with, but was somewhat distracted by another controversy brewing within the team. Their two pitching aces, Sandy Koufax and Don Drysdale, had walked out just before the 1966 season in protest over their salaries. The two men were essentially most of the Dodger's strength and they knew it. In 1965 Drysdale had 23 wins and Koufax had 26. These days if you get 10 wins you are paid in the millions. The pair were asking for $175,000 each, unheard of at the time. They eventually settled (Drysdale for $105,000 and Koufax for $120,000), but the brouhaha kept the Dodgers a little unfocused where we were concerned.

Since the press conference was going to be at the stadium, getting the Beatles in was going to be easy because the crowds had not yet arrived. It was always much tougher bringing popular groups in when the crowd was already there. We brought them into the stadium in an armored car and delivered them to the press club where they would wait until the press conference. As I was walking out, John stopped me.

"We have a party after the concert, so we need to get out of here as soon as possible."

"We'll do the best we can."

The press conference went well, but as expected, John ended up fielding most of the questions, almost all of which centered on his Jesus comment. It was a far cry from that first, disorganized, lightweight press conference at the Cinder just two years earlier. There wasn't that unbridled adulation and gushing curiosity from the press. By now the Beatles were a very well known quantity and, at least in the case of John's comment, not everyone had a reason to like them anymore. The band was also at the end of their tour and looked physically spent.

Dave Hull spent much more time with the band than I did and he recently told me that the Beatles had changed quite a bit by the 1966 concert. He said he was a little disappointed when he hooked up with them because most of that boyish silliness from 1964 had been replaced by a hardness. In those two years the Beatles had become the number one act in the world, even replacing their idol Elvis as the top rock stars of their time. There were rumors of infighting within the group, and of course, they had discovered drugs. Yet some (including members of the Beatles) credit drugs for unlocking great hidden vaults of talent. For whatever reasons, Dave observed they had become different, more distant, and

BOB EUBANKS ARCHIVES

Beatles press conference Capitol Records, 1965.

it saddened him. Dave and I agreed that during the first concert in '64, McCartney and Harrison had been pretty friendly. In '65 it was only McCartney who was still affable. In '66 they were all difficult.

For the first time since I began doing business with them, the Beatles actually expressed fears for their safety. As I mentioned earlier, the crowds had been evolving over the previous few years, and a crowd this size usually had a few nuts. Because of that we planned what I thought was the perfect escape. The stage was constructed at second base and behind it was a tent. In the tent was a Lincoln Continental I had borrowed from a friend at Executive Car Leasing. The plan was for them to go right from the stage to the car and out the centerfield gate before the fans could get to them.

After the press conference, Mickey and I walked the periphery of the huge parking lot to make sure everything was in order before the mayhem began. When we returned to the stadium gate we were stopped by a burly security guard who didn't care who we said we were.

"You're not going in. My orders are no one goes in and that includes you."

We tried to reason with him but he wouldn't budge. We went back and forth for almost ten minutes. Mickey and I were furious when he refused to call his supervisor. I was baffled by his inability to reason out

the situation—what if what we were saying was true? Finally, he grudg-
ing called his supervisor on his walkie-talkie and the situation was resolved in seconds, with a big apology from the supervisor.

My fellow co-emcees, the Eleven-Ten Men, and I introduced the opening acts, the Ronettes and Bobby Hebb. Hebb had a big hit at the time
called "Sunny." Then came the Fab Four and the crowd's pitch went from
frenzied to insane. The show went well, with the Beatles doing their traditional thirty-minute set. The concert was as big a hit as I had expected,
and, like usual, no one could hear the band playing. This really irritated
me because we had been forced to rent a sound system that cost us the
outrageous price (at that time) of $750. Despite the size of the venue and
being outdoors, the only thing amplified were the screams.

The moment it was over the Beatles rushed into the tent behind the
stage, got in the Lincoln and sped out of the stadium. I stepped onto the
stage and confidently announced, "The Beatles have left the stadium."

Suddenly, the crowd began to point and yell and I turned to see the
Beatles' Lincoln come limping back onto the field like a wounded duck.
When the car rounded the corner to leave the stadium, it had been attacked by thousands of kids waiting outside the gate. With the suspen-
sion crushed, the driver did a quick u-turn to escape the mob. We quickly
rushed the Beatles from the broken Lincoln into the dugout to wait for a
replacement vehicle. Someone had let the air out the tires of our armored
car so it was down at the 76 station at the far corner of the lot getting
pumped up. With the crowd coming down onto the field, they were
quickly overwhelming our weak security. We needed to think fast.

Meanwhile, it was the Beatles' turn to be furious. John was particularly angry, venting on both me and Mickey. Mickey can easily handle
himself, so when he and Lennon got in each others' faces I thought they
might come to blows and I pictured the headline: Promoter KOs Beatle.
I got in between them and told Lennon he'd just have to wait, that the
situation was temporarily out of our control. That wasn't good enough
and he persisted in his yelling. That's when I got mad and said, "Okay,
if you want to get out of here, we'll get you out of here." We didn't have
time to wait for the armored car so I remembered there was an ambulance on duty. We had a quick meeting with security and we ordered it
brought around.

"We're taking you out in the ambulance," I told the Beatles. "We're
going to put you in the back and put a sheet over you. So lay still!"

We got them into the ambulance, covered them up, and the ambulance crept down through the parking lot. Mickey and I and a few security guards followed on foot ten or fifteen yards to the sides of the ambulance so as not to call attention to it. But we stayed close in case there was a problem. As the throng tried to find the Beatles, we hoped we could take them out literally right through the middle of them. The ambulance started down toward the 76 station. The crowd began to thin out and we thought we were home free. Then the ambulance driver gunned the engine and took off at a fast clip. About a hundred feet later he hit a speed bump, followed by a horrible crashing sound as we watched the radiator fly from beneath it in a massive spray of sparks. The ambulance came to a screeching halt. The horrendous sound got the attention of the nearby crowd and they all turned and suspiciously eyed the stricken ambulance. At that moment I had a sense of what a surrounded George Custer felt.

Then, just as the Indians began moving toward us, the cavalry arrived. The armored car appeared, lumbering up the hill, just in time to transfer the Beatles into it. Hundreds of screaming girls climbed over the armored car, covering it like a bee hive. A lone security guard stayed on the outside and fended off the manic pack. He was pulled, punched and grabbed every which way. In either an act of self defense or retaliation, he grabbed a young lady by the hair and jerked with all his might—only to have the hair come off in his hands! It took him a moment to realize it was a wig and he had not inadvertently scalped her.

Now the surrounded armored car had the Beatles safely inside, but couldn't move. That's when the second wave of cavalry arrived, and a more motley, but blessed sight I have never seen. The Hell's Angels appeared out of nowhere, choppers rumbling like the hounds of Hell. They efficiently formed a motorized rolling wall around the Beatles' truck and escorted them to safety. For a such a maligned and controversial organization, I certainly owed them my thanks that day.

As the armored car vanished from our sight, Mickey and I exhaled hard from stress and exhaustion. With the deal we'd made with Epstein we ended up paying the Beatles $120,000. After paying the stadium rental and other costs, Mickey and I made a decent profit. Not long after that I sat down and put a pencil on what the individual Beatles probably made. After paying their manager, their agent, the PR firm, opening acts, hotels, airplanes and supporting their entourage, I figured each of the Beatles made less than $4,000. It's no wonder they didn't want to tour anymore.

It was one of my proudest moments in the concert business, when, as the promoter, I made more than the act—in this case, the Beatles.

The Dodger Stadium event was the next to last major concert the Beatles would ever do. Their appearance at San Francisco's Candlestick Park the next evening became their swan song as a touring, live group. A few weeks after our show, John met Yoko Ono in London and George cut off his hair and traveled to India to study under sitar virtuoso Ravi Shankar. It was the end of an era, but it had been an amazing, frustrating, nerve wracking and ultimately incredibly satisfying run. Almost a year to the day of our last concert, on August 27, 1967, Brian Epstein would be found dead in his bed from a drug overdose. I never had any other dealings with the Beatles.

The dissolution of the Cinders was complete by 1967. Looking to do something different, I arrived at an idea to expand my concert business. The business had never been completely formal and for the past few years, despite its success, it had really been a side business. My assistant Teri Brown had moved onward and upward to other projects, so I started looking around for a partner. For some reason, I've always had partners in my business ventures. I'm not sure whether it's lack of confidence in my own abilities or I'm just lazy. I do know that I'm an idea guy—I hate details—and I always look for detail people to round out my talents. Who knows, maybe it's none of those reasons and it's simply that the year of overnights all alone in the KACY graveyard traumatized me and I just hate to be alone.

While working with my friend Dale Sheets at Universal MCA Television, I became very impressed with his assistant, Steve Wolf. Bright and extremely ambitious, Steve was just the kind of guy I was looking for. Steve was also looking to branch out so we came to an agreement and Concert Associates was born. We set up our office on Sunset Boulevard in Hollywood, and it didn't take long for us to become a major force in concert promotion in Southern California. One of the first office decorations we added was a large painting of the Beatles that had been the prize winner at a KRLA art contest. It wasn't long before Steve requested that we move the painting to another room. I asked why, and he said Ringo's eyes followed him, making him uncomfortable. We moved it.

Before Wolf became my business partner, I spent time at his office working out various deals. We were chatting in an elevator at Universal on our way to lunch one day when we were suddenly interrupted by an almighty voice behind us. "Wolf! Get a haircut!"

It was the legendary Lew Wasserman, head of Universal. Wasserman was adamant that his people were dressed and groomed to the nines. The story also goes that Wasserman would literally take anyone's phone call—the catch was you had but 20 seconds to make your case and keep him from hanging up. Wasserman, like many studio moguls, had started out as an agent. If you work in Hollywood you will inevitably come in contact with an agent. Agents are much reviled, but I have met decent people who were agents. I have also come to regard their veracity with some skepticism. Among others, I have been represented by the William Morris Agency a number of times. I have had some good agents there, including Mark Itkin and Steven Konow. I have also had some agents who were, well, not as responsible.

I had signed with a guy at Morris named Charles Barrelli. I had not heard a peep out of him for about five months and called to see what he was doing for me.

"I'm sorry, but Mr. Barrelli has not been with the agency for six months," said the operator. About a week later I received papers from the agency to re-sign as their client. An old joke in Hollywood was that when heiress Patty Hearst disappeared, the reason they couldn't find her was because she had signed with William Morris. I did not re-sign with them.

One of my favorite Morris stories was about their former CEO, Sam Wiesborg. Like anyone who has steered the famous agency, he was a larger than life character, choosing to reside at the Beverly Wilshire Hotel, just blocks from his office. Mike Gursey, a former WMA agent, told me that if Wiseborg asked an agent to go for a walk between Monday and Thursday that agent could probably rest easy. But if the walk were scheduled on a Friday you were probably toast. During the Friday walk Wiesborg would inform you you'd been fired and, on cue, a limo would pull up and whisk him away, leaving the sacked ten-percenter standing on the curb without a job. For some reason, such creative firings rarely happen in other fields.

In the beginning, the energy around the office of Concert Associates was infectious. We had signs on doors designating different departments like the Rock and Roll Department and the Country Music Department. We felt we were going to take over the music promotion business. And while we were busy establishing ourselves by buying the hippest, hottest acts in music, we soon became embroiled in a controversy in what seemed to be the opposite end of that industry.

The Newlywed Game was shot in Studio E at the ABC studios at Prospect and Talmadge. When we weren't in production, the space was used by the *Lawrence Welk Show*. We were also the lead-in for the Welk show on Saturday nights and I had met a few of people associated with the program. The stage manager at *The Newlywed Game* was a guy named Lee Bernhardi, and was married to the youngest of the Lennon Sisters, Janet Lennon. Through Lee I eventually met his wife and the rest of the Lennon Sisters, Dee Dee, Peggy and Kathy. They had been four sweet, wholesome kids when the show began airing nationally in 1955. Ranging in ages from eleven to sixteen, the girls were an immediate hit. By 1968 they were the stars of a cast that featured a huge ensemble of entertainers. Of course, the biggest star of the show was Lawrence Welk himself.

An improbable superstar, Welk was born in 1916 in North Dakota of German immigrants. He did not learn to speak English until he struck out on his own to find his fortune in his early twenties. Welk made a name for himself as a polka bandleader and, after touring the country for years, decided Southern California was the place to settle. By the time *The Newlywed Game* went to Saturday nights, Welk's show was ABC's highest rated variety show. People have made endless jest of Welk's thick accent, wooden manner, corny jokes and style, but there was no doubt among television execs that in the heartland the man was king.

It was also known around ABC, but not to the public, that Lawrence Welk was absurdly tight with a buck—people joked he probably had the first dollar he ever made buried in his wallet. With a cast of forty-two people, his payroll costs were a paltry $9,000 a week! When I heard that number I remembered the news a year or two earlier that the three principals on *Bonanza*, Lorne Greene, Michael Landon and Dan Blocker were each making more than $10,000 a week.

Lee Bernhardi approached me and asked if our company would consider managing the Lennon Sisters. Despite being the stars of his show, Welk was paying the girls union scale—a Dickensian $187.50 each per week—and had been doing so the last thirteen years. Feeling they were worth a lot more money, they screwed up their courage and went to

Welk for a raise. Welk kept such a tight rein over his performers it didn't surprise them when he turned them down, but then he threw them for a loop by encouraging them to find management who could book them outside gigs. Unfortunately for Lawrence Welk, they did.

We soon settled into life with the Lennon Sisters, which was a very active family operation including their dad, Bill—who unofficially managed them—four husbands, a multitude of siblings and other family members, kids, in-laws, neighbors, even pets. Our first move was sure to be seen as complete betrayal by their boss and mentor, the cheapskate Mr. Welk. Steve sat down with execs from ABC and told them we were going to ask Welk to give the girls a raise. That the girls were siccing their "hired muscle" on their German/American benefactor was guaranteed to cause him to go ballistic.

"How much?" asked one of the network suits.

Steve didn't flinch. "A thousand a week. Each."

The demand was like a collective fist in the gut to each of the execs in the room. They knew Welk would blow his cork when he got our demand. He did, and the second thing he did was go to the press, not only telling them the sisters wanted $4,000 a week but making it sound like they each wanted that much. Then he made it clear to all who would listen: nobody on Lawrence Welk's show got paid a thousand bucks a week.

That was true. What was also true was that Lawrence Welk owed many of his cast members large sums for back rehearsal, and the union expected him to pay. One of Welk's main singers quietly informed me he was owed more than $30,000 in back rehearsal pay but was terrified to bring it up because of what Welk might do. The climate around the set was tense. Many of the people on his show took Welk's financial abuse because they were afraid to incur his ire and risk getting fired. And because of the ensemble nature of the *Lawrence Welk Show*, as well as its homespun flavor, many of the entertainers rightly felt they would be unemployable elsewhere.

Not so with the sisters, who had a strong following and were successful recording artists in their own right. They were also the bedrock of the show, much beloved and squeaky clean performers who epitomized the type of family entertainment Welk offered America. Welk knew all of this but still refused to pay up. Wanting to keep the peace on their hit show, the ABC boys stepped in and ponied up the money for the sisters. But to get their money's worth, they threw in the proviso that the Lennons would have to make appearances on variety shows like *The Hol-lywood Palace* and *The Andy Williams Show*. All was well, but only for a few weeks. It must have finally gotten to Welk because he fired them. The sisters were hurt but also relieved to be leaving. They were ready to step out on their own and test the waters without Welk hovering over their shoulders.

As I became more involved with the sisters I also met other cast members in their circle who had tales to tell. Many of them centered on Welk's infamous "cost controls." My friend Eddie Wenrick was hired by Welk to promote the songs in Welk's sizable and highly successful music catalog. Eddie needed a tape recorder to play the tunes he was pitching to record producers. He went to Welk and asked him to spring for one. I would think back then you would be talking about less than fifty bucks. The parsimonious band leader looked at Eddie as if he'd asked for a private helicopter to fly between meetings.

"Eddie, my boy, if you can't sell the tunes by humming them they're not worth selling."

Eddie got very good at humming.

This was the same boss who pulled out all the stops at Christmas by handing out Lawrence Welk calendars to his loyal artists for presents. It was also not uncommon for him to approach cast members with a tray of Yule cookies and magnanimously ask, "You want *a* cookie?" And woe be it to the greedy ones who took two. To coincide with the release of his 1971 memoir, *Wunnerful, Wunnerful*, the Los Angeles city council declared Lawrence Welk Day. When Welk was handed a scroll by the council to commemorate his big day he, in turn, presented the council with one copy of his book with the idea they could pass it around.

Stories of Lawrence Welk are not widely known because the living cast members still revere the man, despite his passing in 1992. Always known as Mr. Welk, even to his closest associates, Welk inspired both loyalty and fear in those he employed. Welk was absolutely literal with his cue cards and apparently would read anything you put in front of him. One night, a new cue card guy, apparently overwhelmed by Welk's benevolence at hiring him, made the mistake of slipping in an extra card at the end of the broadcast. Everything was fine as Welk read his usual "And goodnight everybody and keep a song in your heart," but when he continued, "...And thank you, Mr. Welk." The band leader added, "It's been nice working for you."

Another night, he quickly scanned a card and, mistaking a common Roman numeral for a capital letter from the alphabet, warmly exclaimed to the audience, "And now a medley of tunes from World War eye."

The Lennon Sisters had many stories about their boss and shared them once we became close. Welk's Teutonic dialect often had his "Ts" sounding like "Ds." As the girls prepared to go on for a special Valentine's Day tap dancing number wearing theme costumes featuring large hearts, he introduced them with, "And now the lovely Lennon Sisters...with a heart on." Welk also had a problem differentiating "Ps" and "Bs" so when he warned his staff the "ABC executives will be here today, so everybody pee on your toes," his people got tears in their eyes trying not to crack up.

During the time they were shooting the Welk show on Stage E, neither I nor anyone else was allowed to use the famous Lawrence Welk dressing room. But when Tom Jones signed with ABC to do a weekly variety show in early 1969, *This Is Tom Jones*, all that changed. ABC, desiring to suck up to the Welsh sex symbol, told Welk he would now have to share his dressing room. As soon as Jones settled in he made some additions to the room. Welk walked in one day and found a bed. The arch conservative band leader ran around the set grumbling to anyone who would listen, "Why does he need a bed? Why?"

Then Jones had some boxes delivered to the set. At this point just about anything irregular would have irritated Welk. When he saw the large stack of boxes, Welk noticed the word "fragile" all over them and exploded. Perhaps fearing he was being forced to share his room with yet another artist, in this case some Italian he'd never heard of, he began yelling at producer Jim Hobson, "Chim! Chim! Who is this fellow Frajeely?"

Welk's lack of tact and his occasional naiveté was sometimes replaced with a cold business streak. For many years the lighting director for the *Lawrence Welk Show* was a guy named Truck Crone. Truck told me that when the show was moved from the Prospect and Talmadge studio to the Hollywood Palace the new stage was eleven feet shorter. This posed two major problems. Frustrated, Truck took Welk aside.

"I'm sorry Mr. Welk, but this stage is eleven feet shorter so I can't get the whole band onto it, let alone try and light them."

Welk looked the stage over then yelled to producer Jim Hobson. "Chim, fire eleven feet of musicians."

Despite his shortcomings, Lawrence Welk was also deeply respected and even worshiped by many of those who worked for him. Slyly creative, Welk was also a relentless entrepreneur, always looking to improve his show and make a buck in the process. In 1971 the ABC suits panicked because they didn't think they were reaching the all important youth market and, after sixteen solid years, dropped the still popular *Lawrence Welk Show*. But Welk had the last laugh by turning around and syndicating the show to more than 200 stations. This not only kept his show going but at an even greater profit to himself. Call him corny, but every week Lawrence Welk and his family of performers were invited into living rooms across the country to offer an hour of gentle, homespun diversion. Mr. Welk was an American original.

About a year after they left the Welk show, the Lennon Sisters suffered an almost unimaginable tragedy. In the early '60s, Peggy Lennon, the next to oldest sister, began getting letters from a stranger who treated her as if they were married. The man persisted in stalking her for years, writing letters, showing up when the sisters performed and generally terrorizing Peggy, her sisters and her family. Finally the man was committed to a mental institution and that seemed that. Then, in 1968, he was let out and things got worse.

When the nut was released he was now really riled and wrote to President Johnson to beg him to stop Peggy's impending wedding. The FBI, and supposedly the CIA too, were keeping an eye on him, but apparently not well enough. In the summer of 1969, Steve Wolf was in Denver with the sisters while they were making an appearance, and got a phone call from the FBI. They warned him the lunatic was on the loose and to watch out. The feds had intercepted a letter from him claiming he was in Denver and planned to get to Peggy. The FBI recommended that the sisters lay low until they could find the guy. Alas, the FBI was too late.

A few weeks later, on August 12, 1969, their dad, Bill, was getting ready to leave his job as golf pro at a Marina Del Ray range when he was accosted by the crazed fan. Danny Lennon, oldest brother of the Lennons, walked up and found the two in a heated argument. The man pulled a gun and Bill ran. The man shot him and fled. A few weeks later the man was found in his car, having committed suicide with the same gun he used to kill Bill Lennon. The event decimated the family, and the sisters just didn't have the heart to travel or entertain, so Steve and I quietly let them go.

The Beatles • Mick Jagger • Cary Grant
Merle Haggard • Dolly Parton • David
Letterman • The Rolling Stones • The
Beach Boys • Ike and Tina Turner • Leeza
Gibbons • Jerry Lee Lewis • Gene Autry
Roy Rogers • Monty Hall • Roy Orbison
Buddy Hackett • Barbara Mandrell

THANK GOD I'M A COUNTRY BOY

I N THE COURSE OF MANAGING the Lennon Sisters, Steve and I had the William Morris Agency negotiate their recording contract with Mercury Records. We had been anxious to make the deal because we had arranged for Snuffy Garrett to produce the record. Garrett was the brilliant producer behind Bobby Vee and the Everly Brothers, among many. While dealing with WMA we became particularly impressed with Jim Rissmiller, the young agent handling WMA's end. We were so impressed we decided to steal Jim away from WMA. We made him an offer and he became the newest member of our team.

It was also somewhere during this time period that the reclusive billionaire inventor and film producer Howard Hughes had been contemplating buying ABC. Holed up in his penthouse suite at the Desert Inn in Las Vegas, the famous phobic flipped on *The Newlywed Game*. When it was over he picked up the phone and called his right hand man and former FBI agent Bob Maheu and told him to cancel the deal. Apparently, Howard Hughes was so appalled by what we were doing on our little show it was enough for him to scuttle the deal to acquire the network.

I was slowly tiring of constantly dealing with the insanity of rock groups and all the problems that went with them. Whether it was the screaming fans (and sometimes frighteningly crazed ones), all sorts of overwrought security and later on, drugs, I began to wonder if there wasn't some other area of the musical entertainment business that would be more comfortable to operate in. One of the biggest headaches a promoter has is dealing with backstage. In cities other than Los Angeles you often have people claiming to know a member of the band and you deal with them accordingly. The thing about being in Los Angeles is that the problem multiplies by a factor of twenty because it's also the home of most of the record companies, PR firms, agencies and acts. Consequently you always have someone back there telling you they work for so and so, or they know so and so. Sometimes they really were connected to someone influential (or were influential themselves) so you'd have to be careful.

My favorite line about the crowds backstage comes from Merle Haggard's long time manager Fuzzy Owen, the master of the malapropos and a fount of non-sequiturs and down home sarcasm. One night Fuzzy surveyed the mass of people backstage and yelled to me across the room for all to hear, "If any of these performers get in the way of the backstage people, lemme know and I'll have the performers removed." That thinned out the room real fast. Backstage passes had become sought after by the mid-'60s and very soon roadies got the word to give them to any cute girls. The lack of selectivity by rock groups in their choice of young ladies became such a joke roadies began wearing t-shirts that said, "No head, no backstage pass."

Probably sometime in 1967 I bought Herman's Hermits for a concert at the Anaheim Convention Center. To get the Hermits I had to deal with Premier Talent in New York, owned by the godfather of rock agents, Frank Barcelona. Frank and his assistant, Barbara Skydell, were real pains in the butt and very difficult to deal with. They had all the big English acts which gave them an arrogance that made them impossible to negotiate with. When I called to buy the Hermits they informed me the group had an opening act and I had to take them if I wanted the Hermits. I wasn't thrilled about some up and coming group I'd never heard of. I grudgingly agreed to their opening act to get the Hermits. It turned out to be a good move because the 9000 tickets sold out immediately. Although this other band had not yet claimed a hit on the U.S. charts they had developed a following here.

Even though it was billed as a Herman's Hermits concert, I had been warned the other band could be a little difficult. On the day of the concert I was policing the backstage area because, as with any concert, that's where all the problems were (as the promoter I was responsible if something went wrong or someone's underage daughter fell into misadventure). And, as if on cue, I noticed this opening act's band members smuggling young girls backstage. I had some words with the band and their roadies. At first they argued but eventually accepted my order. I thought the issue was over, but less than fifteen minutes after laying down the law I noticed the drummer hauling his bass drum case across the floor. It was practically making grooves in the concrete. I may not be Charlie Watts but I know a bass drum does not weigh a hundred pounds. I watched the feisty little drummer hauling the load for a moment then turned to one of their roadies.

"What's his name?"

"Keith."

"Keith?" I said in a raised voice. "Just what the hell are you doing?"

He muttered something about "buggering off" so I went over and kicked open the drum case. Some mother's sweet little 15-year-old daughter fell out and gave me an "oops" look.

I turned to Keith. I was pissed off.

"I told you guys I wouldn't put up with this crap."

Now he was pissed at me.

"You can't tell us what to do backstage."

"For this evening this is my backstage. I can tell you to do anything I want."

"Go fuck yourself you sonofabitch."

"This is the last time you will ever work for me."

"Good! We don't want to work with you again, you wanker."

And they didn't—much to my chagrin. The Who became one of the biggest acts of the late '60s and on. Sadly, Keith Moon died of a drug overdose in 1978.

We bought a lot of great acts during that time. I also saw a considerable change in the music between the early to mid-'60s and the late '60s. As the acts matured and new ones came along the music became more serious. I set up a concert for the group Cream, led by the great Eric Clapton. I knew little about the band but as they played their set I could see they represented a new element in rock music. I remember thinking "these guys are not only great musicians; their music is really sophisticated." I had the same reaction to Jimi Hendrix. Yet while I thought his music and skills were amazing, I found the burning and destroying of his instruments—like the Who—wasteful and unnecessary. Hendrix also represented the new rock artist, brilliantly talented but living a hyped up, drug-laced lifestyle. In their worst nightmares, the acts of four or five years before could never have imagined such a drop into the abyss, yet many of them (those who survived) were now embracing the fast lane with gusto. I saw rock music changing, becoming harder, tighter and edgier, and I was becoming less and less comfortable with it. By the time Led Zeppelin broke onto the scene the loss of innocence was complete, the '60s were over and, I thought, so was my career as a rock promoter. I was ready for some changes.

With *The Newlywed Game* paying me a very good salary I felt I could finally take a breath. We could tape a year's worth of shows in 35 days so I had time to relax for the first time in my life. Approaching thirty, by most accounts I was pretty successful. I had always worked so hard because of a fear of failure in everything I did. And, after nearly ten years, the radio business was no longer as fun as it once was. So, with murmurs of petty jealousy over my good fortune always in the background at the station, I gave my notice at KRLA and walked away in 1967. I had no regrets. I had enjoyed my time there but things had changed. KHJ, with their new boss radio format, was kicking KRLA's ass. But on top of that, since joining the station seven years before I had become a concert promoter, club owner and now the host of a national television show. Clearly, my career had evolved quite a bit. And the station's staff that had been so much fun in the early days was mostly gone, on to other stations, other careers. It was time to move on. And with the closing of the Cinders my life had changed quite a bit. I was settling into my routine on *The Newlywed Game* and for the first time in my life I slowed down enough to inhale a deep breath and really taking stock of my blessings.

Even though I was out of the Cinders and KRLA I've never been one to kick back and do nothing. My home was in a lovely town called Calabasas, a former Chumash Indian settlement. Today, Calabasas is considered upscale and chichi, but back then it was just a sleepy little western town on the outskirts of civilization. Although cars and pickup trucks had replaced horseback as the primary form of transportation, horses were still the number one recreational ride. My kids would often ride their horses over to the famous Sagebrush Cantina, one of Calabasas's favorite eateries. I met two guys, Buck Wicall, who had experience in the retail trade, and neighbor and roping buddy Don McCoy, who was in the heavy equipment business. The three of us shared a love of horses and thought a western store would be great thing for Calabasas. Very

THANK GOD I'M A COUNTRY BOY

soon after, we opened the Calabasas Saddlery.

At first it was fun, driving down to my store and talking with prospective customers. It was a pleasant place to hang out. That first November we owned the Saddlery I had just finished taping *The Newlywed Game* Christmas show and was eying the huge Christmas tree that was part of the set. I thought it would look good in the store, despite being property of the studio. I enlisted a stage hand, Pat Donaroma, to help me carry it out to my truck.

"I'll help," he said, "but if I see security I'm outta there."

We began hauling the enormous decorated tree out to my pickup. Just as we got within ten feet of the truck a security guard rounded the corner and came toward us in a menacing way. Pat dropped his end.

"See you, prick," he said as he turned and slowly slithered away, leaving me to hang alone.

The guard sauntered up with this sour look on his face. I simply smiled and asked, "Hey, could you help me load this tree into my truck?"

He smiled back, "Sure," and happily obliged. I looked over and saw Donaroma peering around the stage door like Kilroy, his eyes wide.

As much as I loved the Saddlery, it didn't take long before being in one place all the time started getting to me. The store also didn't do the type of business we needed it to. One problem none of us foresaw was the amount of cash that got tied up in inventory. We carried some nice things but having five or ten of each hat and pair of boots in ten or fifteen sizes really added up. Eventually our inventory exceeded $100,000 which was a lot of money back then. Soon we were $40,000 in debt, so in 1969 we bailed out. I'm glad to see the Calabasas Saddlery is still there to this day. Retail just wasn't for me.

Not long after Jim Rissmiller joined Concert Associates I started to do a lot of soul searching. I was having concerns about the music business and felt I was nearing the point where I wanted to leave. It's funny how when you open yourself up to things the universe often accommodates you. Around this time Steve and I got a call from Dick St. John at Filmways Corporation. Dick told us they were interested in acquiring Concert Associates. Steve, Jim and I reached an agreement that I would sell my interest in the company in return for Filmways stock and, if I decided to return in the future, they would take me back.

Now, other than *The Newlywed Game*, I was really free. I'd been able to sell the company and cash in on all my efforts to build it into something. (Over the next several years my stock in Filmways looked pretty solid, especially when Filmways expanded their operation. I hung onto the stock, hoping it would eventually go up and really pay off. Ten years later, in 1979, they merged with financially troubled low-budget film giant AIP. It briefly looked like a good fit and that the recombined company would thrive. Then the company made an even bigger jump when they became part of Orion Pictures a year or two later. Unfortunately, Orion had even bigger financial problems than AIP and it all fell apart around 1983, leaving my stock worthless.)

The arrangement of the sale of Concert Associates included my leaving in return for the stock, but secured Steve and Jim's positions with the company. My arrangement with Steve and Jim had been if and when I wanted to come back they would have a place for me. The problems with Filmways didn't affect Concert Associates and in the meanwhile Steve and Jim turned the company into a force in Southern California rock promotion.

Shortly after leaving Concert Associates I was approached by a young man named Larry Valen. Larry had done a tour in Vietnam and was currently a page on *The Newlywed Game*. He asked if I knew anyone in the music business. Music was his passion and he wanted a shot at a role in the industry. I called Wolf and Rissmiller and Larry was in. He stayed at the company for years and eventually ended up running Universal Concerts, booking all of the dates for the Universal Amphitheater. Larry now runs the concert division for the world famous House of Blues in Hollywood.

By 1970 the sale of the concert business was a distant memory and I was now occupied taping *The Newlywed Game* only a small portion of the year. Since I didn't have to be in the city too often I decided to move the family farther up the coast where we had a little breathing room. The kids were older and sons Trace and Corey had since traded their interest in horses for motorcycles, while daughter Theresa was deeply involved with horses, so we needed a place for them to cut loose. I found what I considered heaven on earth in a town called Santa Ynez, amidst the scenic wine country above Santa Barbara. Many years later, Michael Jackson would buy a plot of land nearby and call it Neverland Ranch.

The man who owned the ranch I fell in love with had it on the market for $130,000. As much as I wanted it I still told him he was nuts to ask that much and offered him $120,000. He took it. What I got was twenty acres of gorgeous rolling hills, with seemingly miles of rustic fences, barns, stables, riding arena and two houses. It was my version of the Ponderosa. I had loved riding horses since I was a kid and this place gave me a chance to be a gentleman rancher. I settled into a routine of riding and roping.

After taking a few years off from the high energy world of music promotion I was feeling restless. I guess I'm just one of those people who needs five or ten things going at once. I decided I'd recharged my batteries enough, had my brush with retail, worked the ranch and now it was time to get back to work, so to speak. I contacted Steve Wolf and Jim Rissmiller and reminded them of our agreement that they would let me come back. They offered to let me start a country music division, but, to my surprise, would not bring me back as partner in the entire business.

Since I had left Steve and Jim had turned Concert Associates into something far beyond what it had been. Now known as Wolf Rissmiller Concerts, their company was becoming the top talent buyer and concert promoter around. Steve and Jim felt they had done all the work and that letting me come back as a full partner would not be good business. While I understood their reasoning, I have always honored my word and was disappointed they did not honor theirs.

I've had my share of stalkers and weirdoes and even threats in my time, but fortunately none of them ever proved tragic for me. Although I live my life freely I always keep an eye out for the guy or gal with that off kilter look in their eye that says "I'm probably nuts so watch out." In addition to the random crazy fan, I am also now a believer in never putting your name on a very visible company because all you're asking for is trouble. I believe that was what proved fatal for Steve Wolf.

Sometime in the mid-'70s, he and Rissmiller put on a concert. Afterward, Steve retired for the evening to his isolated Mulholland Drive home high above the city. When your name is on 18,000 tickets for a single concert, and someone with a criminal mind calculates that number times the twenty dollar face value, they might be under the crazy impression you take that money home with you. I think that was the mind-set of the two young punks who broke into Steve's home that night. After giving them what money he had, Steve pressed the button to open the security gate to allow them to leave. As they were walking out the door, almost as an afterthought, one of them turned and shot Steve point blank in the chest. His last words were, "Why did you do that?" Steve's murder extinguished one of the brightest lights in show business. Had he lived I am convinced Steve Wolf would have become the head of a studio or major record company.

When I couldn't make a deal with Wolf and Rissmiller to take me back I immediately made plans to start another promotion company. I soon teamed up with my old partner, Mickey Brown, my former employee Teri Brown, as well as new partners Jim Wagner and Michael Davenport, to form Concert Express. Our primary focus was going to be country music. Soon we set up our first concert, with Buffy St. Marie, the former folk singer who had just made the switch to country music.

The notion behind Concert Express was that our team would use all of our experience in rock and roll promotion to introduce that style of promotion to country music. That was a time when country music was in the grip of the good ol' boy network out of Nashville and the artists were not well served. To make matters worse, country artists had no good options if they didn't think they were getting a fair shake from their management and promoters. The country singers back then were often victims of poor promotion, mediocre management and wildly inconsistent treatment from city to city. I thought there might be a demand for our expertise. Jim, an experienced country music agent, was installed as the head of American Management, the agency division of our venture. Michael would put together the national concerts and Teri would work her magic in PR and artist relations, while Mickey and I would hold it all together. All the pieces were in place and we had high hopes we could make a dent.

When we brought Teri in, she in turn brought her clients, including her good friend Phil Everly, half of the famous Everly Brothers. Phil was looking for management and wanted to establish a separate career, as well as continue working with his brother Don. Although successful performers, Don and Phil got along like oil and water. Just booking the Everly Brothers could be a real chore given the layers of people involved. Don had a manager, Jack Daly, and Phil was represented by Teri through us. On top of that, the Everly Brothers were represented by Danny Weiner at the agency IFA. In order for a client to book a date they would call Danny, who would call Jack Daly, who would call Don, then Danny would call Teri who would call Phil. Of course, everyone had to agree or the date didn't happen. It was the most convoluted, ridiculous situation I had ever seen in my years of booking acts. Especially given that they were brothers.

I'm happy to say that the Everly Brothers have put their differences aside, are now getting along and have only one manager. I'm convinced that if they had found the right manager early on, like Ken Kragen, the man who took Kenny Rogers from an over the hill artist to a major country act and movie star, the Everly Brothers could have reached real stardom in their later careers. I always felt the Everly Brothers never reached their true potential. As an aside, the Everly's dad, Ike Everly, was the inventor of a finger picking style of guitar playing which was later made popular by Merle Travis and Chet Atkins.

Although country would be our focus, rock music was what we knew and we weren't going to turn acts down because we needed to make money. But getting back into concert promotions was harder than I expected. In my three year absence things had changed a lot. Despite what happened to Hendrix, Jim Morrison and Janis Joplin, drug use among artists had lost no momentum and, on the other front, sometimes concert goers got out of hand. I often thought about the tragedy at the Stones concert in Altamont in 1969 when the Hell's Angels were hired as security and a young man got killed. When I resumed the promotion business I was always worried something like that might happen, that a concert I had organized and was responsible for would get out of control and someone would get hurt—or worse.

In late 1973 we had bought the group War to play the Flamingo Hotel in Las Vegas. Their opening act was Captain Beyond, a band formed with guys from Iron Butterfly, Johnny Winter's group and Deep Purple. The actual concert was inside, but we made our biggest mistake by putting the portable bathroom facilities outside the venue. We would have used one of Las Vegas's many civic venues but, at least at that time, the City of Las Vegas required promoters to deposit, in an escrow account, the estimated gross of the concert. They had been stung by some shifty operators and were only trying to protect themselves, but for a legitimate promoter like myself such a requirement was just nuts. Looking for private venues, the casinos were the second biggest game in town as far as audience capacity.

The Flamingo was not a huge arena, offering room for around 2000 people. The problem arose when people "needed" to use the restrooms. Because the portable toilets were outside, they were allowed to exit the venue and then were let back in when they showed their ticket stub. Instead of legitimately using the facilities, many people were trading stubs and giving them to others outside and soon our crowd had grown to nearly 4000. The police threw their hands up and, had we encountered any problems at all, we would have been in big trouble. The concert degenerated into one huge pot party. I took Teri aside as the crowd thinned out afterward and made a pronouncement.

"We will never do another show where we can't put our families in the front row."

It was then I decided to cut back on rock promotion and move toward another area.

The Beatles • Mick Jagger • Cary Grant
Merle Ha   • David
Letterman • The Rolling Stones • The
Beach B   Leeza
Gibb   Autry
Roy Ro   bison
Buddy Hackett • Barbara Mandrell

LOVE'S NOT WORTH A DIME UNLESS IT'S FREE

I BELIEVE MY LOVE OF COUNTRY MUSIC is in my DNA. My folks were from the hills of southwestern Missouri. My mother was born in a little town not too far from the Arkansas border called Crane. Dad's home town, Jenkins, is too small to even make it onto a map. They were raised on country music. When the Depression kicked the pins out from under them, most of the hillbillies migrated north, looking for opportunities in the industrialized cities. Later, many headed out to California's breadbasket, the Central Valley, seeking a chance to pick or harvest something for decent wages. They took their music with them.

My dad and my Uncle Marv used to sit for hours in front of the Victrola listening to 78s of Bob Wills and the Texas Playboys, Kitty Wells, Roy Acuff and just about everyone in the Grand Ole Opry. Like most American families in the '40s and early '50s, until television took over, Saturday nights would find us gathered around the radio or record player. In our case it was always country music.

I remember a meeting with an executive at Capitol Records in 1965 about the upcoming Beatles concert. Once we got business out of the way we chatted about other things. He was very knowledgeable about music, so out of the blue I asked him who he thought the next country superstar would be. Without any hesitation he answered, "Merle Haggard." I was familiar with Haggard's music but never saw him as the next big thing. I filed that information in the back of my brain and began listening to his music more intently over the next few years. In 1970 he was named Entertainer of the Year by the Country Music Association.

During his career Merle has compiled a string of hits unmatched by any other country entertainer.

I decided I was tired of promoting only rock and hatched a plan to begin promoting the kind of music I'd always loved. I put out feelers and immediately ruffled some feathers. While country music didn't have rock's cachet or paydays, the people promoting country wanted to keep it to themselves. During that time the promotion of country music was handled by a core group of agents and promoters who knew each other and did not like outsiders from either coast. I was told that it was a very tight good ol' boy network and breaking in was pretty much impossible. I had also been warned by more than a few people who cared for my welfare that I might encounter some ugliness if I tried. Nevertheless, I flew out to Nashville to get the lay of the land and make some contacts. The first night I was there the phone rang about 1 A.M. in my room at the Airport Hilton.

"Hello?"

"This Bob Eubanks?" came a gravelly, unfriendly male voice with a deep southern drawl.

"Yes, who's this?"

"This is the person tellin' you to gitcher Hollywood ass back where you belong. Go home and stay outta the south. Understand, Mr. Hollywood?"

"I think so."

Then he hung up.

I got the point. I decided a more subversive approach might be better: don't beat 'em, join 'em. I would stay on the West Coast for the time being, but if I could get in tight with one of the top acts in country music I would no longer be seen as a "Hollywood" outsider. I called Merle Haggard's office and arranged a meeting with Fuzzy Owen, Haggard's manager. Fuzzy told me to come down to the Anaheim Convention Center and meet with him and Merle. The idea was not to talk any business, just to say hello. I wanted to see what kind of guys they were and they certainly wanted to see who I was.

To create a game plan for him I had done some research on Merle Haggard. His parents had migrated from Muskogee, Oklahoma, and ended up in the Bakersfield suburb of Oildale. The legend in this case was true: Merle was literally born in a converted railroad boxcar on

April 6, 1937. His dad died when Merle was young and he became quite a handful. A committed delinquent, Merle was in and out of more than a dozen institutions until he got into real trouble and ended up going to prison for nearly three years. Merle also lived in many hobo jungles around the country, experiencing more life by 25 than most people do by 75. I won't detail Hag's life here—there are several very good books on the subject, including those by the man himself—but suffice it to say, when Merle writes a song it comes from the heart and many hard miles. Although my plan was not to discuss business with Fuzzy and Merle at that first meeting, I had formulated an idea that just might get Merle to sign with me. Although country artists did not generate the types of paydays rock stars did back then, they toured constantly, and I figured what they didn't do in sheer dollars they could make up in volume. I also felt they would pose far less headaches and risks. Rock stars wanted specific types of limos, luxurious suites and exotic catering. Country stars, on the other hand, simply wanted a relatively clean place to change and were happy with good promotion.

At our first meeting Merle was quiet and intense, with a stoic face—at least for that first meeting—that could beat anyone at poker. He was sizing me up and kept a reserved attitude. We only spent half an hour or so together, but just before he went on stage he seemed to warm up to me a bit. Just the opposite in temperament was Merle's manager.

Charles "Fuzzy" Owen was truly a character and was one of the few people Merle trusted implicitly. An Arkansas native, Fuzzy settled in Bakersfield in 1949 and began playing country music in local clubs, particularly the famed Blackboard Café. With many refugees from the Dust Bowl in the '30s and '40s importing their music to California, Bakersfield soon became an important hub in the development of modern country music. Fuzzy teamed up with his cousin Lewis Talley and opened a tiny recording studio and a publishing company to go with it. In 1953 Fuzzy and Buck Owens' estranged wife Bonnie recorded "A Dear John Letter," a song written by Hillbilly Barton. Fuzzy and Lewis liked the song so much they made a deal with Barton: the rights to the song in trade for Lewis's 1947 Kaiser. Not long after that, "A Dear John Letter" was recorded by Ferlin Husky and Jean Shepard and became a number one hit. With that Fuzzy and Lewis were on their way.

They opened a bigger studio and, in the early '60s, made the acquaintance of a local kid who had just finished a stretch in San Quentin for a bungled, drunken robbery. Merle Haggard played the local clubs and Fuzzy was soon performing with the young ex-con. Fuzzy appeared regularly on a local television show and asked Merle to join him. He liked Merle's style and eventually convinced him to record. From that time on he managed Merle. From the day they met, Fuzzy has believed in Merle more than Merle believed in himself.

Fuzzy often overshadowed everyone else in Merle's crew, including Merle, as far as being the biggest character, but there were other contenders for the crown. Lewis Talley not only drove Merle's bus but also entertained him while they were on the road. To give you an idea of Lewis's sense of humor, he named his band Lewis Talley and the Whackers. Lewis could keep you laughing twenty-four hours a day. One of my favorite Lewis stories concerns his dog, Brownie Doodle-ums. In the '60s, Lewis was playing bass at the Blackboard. Early one morning after getting off work he knocked back a few drinks, went home and landed in bed about 6 A.M. Moments later, the police pounded on the door. They told him that his dog had been killing chickens and they issued him a leash law citation.

After the police left, as Lewis crawled back in the sack he noticed Brownie Doodle-ums safely snuggled under the bed. As Lewis put it, "Goddamn, Brownie hasn't been killing any chickens, he's right here!" Later that day, Lewis went down to the courthouse, pleaded innocent on behalf of Brownie Doodle-ums, and demanded a jury trial. Lewis then went on about his business. On the day of the trial, Lewis was in L.A. with Merle who was recording an album at Capitol Records. The trial date plumb slipped Lewis's mind.

Flash to an evening a few days later. Lewis was coming out of the Blackboard with one of his favorite dumplins (Lewis called every girl a dumplin') when two Bakersfield cops approached and informed him he'd not only missed his trial date, but because of that, a bench warrant for his arrest had been issued. Lewis pleaded with the officers that he and the dumplin' be allowed to follow them to the station in their own car and clear things up, but the officers were unmoved.

As they put Lewis into the back of the cruiser, he came face to face with the cops' other partner. A big German Shepherd warily eyed Lewis as he tried sliding past his fearsome seat mate. Then the cops, in their haste to get Lewis to the pokey, slammed the car door on the dog's tail. That dog went berserk and lunged at what he figured was the source of his pain, the felon sitting next to him. Lewis pasted himself against the opposite door while the trapped tail kept the canine's slobbering jaws mere inches from his face. Then the cops opened the door and the dog was all over Lewis. As they rolled around in the back seat, Lewis said he grabbed everything he could to make the dog feel good. By the time they got to the jail, he and that old dog were not only best friends, but he had manually straightened out its tail. It was a typical Lewis Talley adventure.

Years after I had gotten to know Fuzzy Owen, I heard a story that epitomized him—not his taste in music, but his stubbornness. Singer and songwriter Tommy Collins was fishing with Fuzzy at Hag's home on the Kern River. Tommy kept trying to pitch Fuzzy on a new song he'd just written, but Fuzzy would allow nothing to interrupt his fishing. So Tommy tried a new tact. He wrestled Fuzzy to the ground, jammed a knee in his chest and proceeded to sing. After a few bars an angry Fuzzy pushed him off.

"Goddammit Tommy, that's the biggest piece o' shit I ever heard. Who cares about some damn flower? Now lemme git back to my fishing!"

Tanya Tucker, then Helen Reddy, would soon prove Fuzzy wildly wrong on that count. Tanya first made "Delta Dawn" a hit in 1972, and a year later Reddy went to number one with it. But aside from a few lapses, Fuzzy's ability to spot a hit has been impeccable.

Another trait that's always amused me about Fuzzy is his ability to twist words to suit the situation. Long ago I started calling them "Fuzzy-isms."

"I bet I've seen a hundred things and this is one of 'em." In discussing country stars Homer and Jethro, Fuzzy observed, "If I was one of 'em I'd wanna be the other." On the hookers that inhabited so many truck stops, Fuzzy opined, "Love's not worth a dime unless it's free." And in commenting on a girl's dental work, he said, "She could eat an apple through a picket fence." Fuzzy and I have also had an odd, long running argument regarding, of all things, weight gain or loss. He has said "you gotta eat a pound to gain a pound," or "you gotta shit a pound to lose a pound." I've tried putting books about nutrition in his face or talking about carbs and protein and metabolism but he would have none of that mumbo jumbo.

He is definitely his own man. Fuzzy was always very picky about his wardrobe which, oddly enough, came mostly from truck stops. And he seemed to exist on an exclusive diet of Dr. Pepper and candy bars. Another eccentricity was his absolute belief in the existence of flying saucers. I ended up covering many miles on tour with Hag and Fuzzy over the years, and it was not uncommon for Fuzzy to stop the busses in the middle of the night, in Nowhere, Wyoming, or the middle of New Mexico so he could set up his telescope and scan the heavens for UFOs.

That first meeting at the Anaheim Convention Center began a ten-year business relationship and a lifelong friendship. It also may have portended things to come. Merle and I chatted while he smoked a cigarette, waiting to go on. When they called him, his cigarette hand dropped to his side and he ran out on stage. A second later I smelled something burning and it wasn't just a cigarette. Somehow Merle's cigarette had ignited the crotch of my pants and my black and white herringbone slacks were ablaze. As the flames leaped down my legs like a cannon fuse I hopped around screaming for water. Someone put out the fire but one pant leg was half gone and my leg was singed.

Fuzzy told me he and Merle would be at the upcoming Academy of Country Music Awards show in Bakersfield a few weeks later. Teri Brown and I arranged to meet them after the show. We drove up to Bakersfield, all ready to make a deal. When we pulled up to the facility where the show was to be held, the entire audience was waiting outside. Someone had phoned in a bomb threat and the place was complete pandemonium. Teri and I made our way through the crowd.

The alarm was eventually called off and the show was spectacular. I stood and watched in awe as Merle Haggard performed one number one hit after another—probably twenty or so. As he closed the show I knew I had to be in business with this man. I was so moved that I felt promoting him was more of a religious calling than a business venture.

When we arrived at the artist's lounge, Merle and Fuzzy and some of the band members were sitting around winding down after the show. On top of the bomb scare Merle had also received some recent death threats and his entourage was on full alert. As we walked in one of his people pulled out a big revolver and, without saying anything, calmly set it on the table. Maybe it was to reinforce the position that neither they nor Merle would be intimidated—or perhaps it was the most overtly hostile negotiating ploy I'd ever seen. Merle saw my surprised expression.

Hag and me, Hollywood Bowl soundcheck.

MICHAEL OCHS ARCHIVES

"I will not be threatened."

I whispered to Teri, "I don't believe this. We're getting out of rock music to avoid drugs and now we've got guns."

But I came to talk business, and although Merle was a little wary both he and Fuzzy knew I had done well for the acts I bought. I'm sure they were hoping I might be able to make their lives a little easier. I jumped right in with my pitch.

"How much are you making a show?"

"Five thousand," said Merle.

"What if I could promise you a hundred dates a year?"

"We can do that ourselves," said Fuzzy.

"I know. But what you don't have is consistency. Every place you go you deal with a different guy, and I don't need to tell you there are some pretty flaky promoters out there."

Merle and Fuzzy looked at each other. I had done my homework and was right on target.

"Okay," said Fuzzy, "but there are some dates we do ourselves."

Fuzzy had deals with Harrah's in Reno and Lake Tahoe and a few others that they would keep to themselves, but I was free to start booking him. My promise of consistency was very important to them and I knew it. There were a lot of carny types and hustlers working the country music concert circuit back then. As a country artist on the road you didn't know from one town to the next how good or bad your accommodations might be or how much a particular promoter would actually spend to get the word out. For the hundred dates I would arrange at least Fuzzy and Merle would be getting what they expected. When I walked away from that meeting I was officially in business with The Poet of the Common Man.

As a performer, Merle Haggard is a genius, a massive talent who stands out in a field of great artists. Like me, Merle has seen more than his share of failure, but that's what makes his music so brilliant. As I got to know the man I realized how uncomfortable he was in his own skin. One of the coping mechanisms Merle developed early on was assuming other people's identities. Perhaps it was his way of dealing with his hard scrabble first years. One of his early roles was that of the renegade, the lawbreaker. Then he went straight and his new role was that of the entertainer. Then, not satisfied to be Merle Haggard the entertainer, he started assuming the identities of other artists he admired.

His first homage, if you will, was to country giant Lefty Frizzell. Merle idolized Frizzell, a trailblazing yet deeply troubled country star who was about ten years ahead of Merle. He began to talk like Lefty, sing like Lefty, and after seeing Lefty in concert, made the commitment to take on Lefty's complete persona. I found out later that Merle included a Lefty Frizzell song on every album he released during that period with the intent it would help Lefty financially. Before Lefty died in 1975, Merle had moved on to an obsession with another artist who died four years before Merle was born.

Known as The Singing Brakeman and the Blue Yodeler, Jimmie Rodgers was the first person inducted into the Country Music Hall of Fame. He is considered the father of country music. Hag's father was a railroad man, as was Rodgers' father, and before he became a music star, Rodgers himself spent years working on the railroads of America. Hag loved railroads and their history and lore. He became fascinated with Rodgers' background and music and released an album of Rodgers' songs. Around that time he took on Rodgers' persona, while losing himself in the new role.

Several years before I met Merle, he and his wife Bonnie went to see the film Bonnie and Clyde. Apparently the experience set him off in a new round of emulation. He immediately began dressing like Warren Beatty's Clyde Barrow and once again became someone other than Merle Haggard. He wrote and recorded "The Legend of Bonnie and Clyde" and it sold a million copies. It was quite strange to watch a man who was idolized by millions assume the identity of other people.

When I joined the Haggard tour Merle's attention was focused on becoming Bob Wills. One of the pioneers of country music, Wills is credited with creating and popularizing country swing. Wills played what might be described as a country version of big band music. Hag was soon dressing, acting and playing like his new hero. To be even more authentic in his tribute to Wills, Hag went out and hired a couple of Wills' former band members, Tiny Moore and Eldon Shamblin, two remarkably talented musicians from the early days of country. Additionally, whether he did it in preparation to become Wills, or became fascinated with Wills during the process, Merle taught himself to play the fiddle, Wills' instrument of choice.

Merle also found an eleven-year-old boy named Tiger Bell who played the fiddle like a child possessed. Merle loved to play fiddle duets with the kid but I worried about what Tiger might be seeing on a tour bus full of colorful country boys. Merle's transformation into Bob Wills got so serious that during concerts the fans would yell at Merle to play his own hits and he would ignore them and continue playing Wills' songs. But like all his other living testimonials, he would eventually return to being Merle Haggard.

Merle has always been a tough one to figure out. He has written heart touching lyrics and created innumerable memorable melodies. His body of work would rival any of the great poets of antiquity in its expression of pain, love and a life lived on the brink. Yet many years ago, Merle told me in a moment of vulnerability that he considered himself both a lousy father and husband. To this day, Merle and I speak often and I feel he has finally come to terms with himself and his roles, not only as an artist, but as a man, husband and father. He has a new wife and family he truly loves, and I believe that time has mellowed him considerably. He's finally been able to put aside the hurt of his early life and accept himself. As they say, you can't really love others until you love yourself.

In the ten years we did business together Merle and I never had a cross word. I suppose we trusted each other, and in our business that's saying a lot. He knew I would never cheat him out of a cent, and I knew he would always deliver for me and not let me down. In those ten years he only missed two concerts.

Those two dates, which were back to back, made the national news. The afternoon before a concert in Denver, he and his bus driver, Dean Holloway, walked up to me in the Holiday Inn.

"I'm gonna go get me a fiddle," announced Merle.

"Okay, " I said, "I'll see you tonight."

I did not see him again for two weeks. Merle Haggard just disappeared off the face of the earth. That night I had to step out on the stage to face 5,000 people waiting to see Merle and give them the bad news. I told them the truth, that Merle was AWOL and we had no idea where he was. There was a murmur of concern but nobody headed for the doors. I continued by telling them we had a great show that night including Marty Robbins and Cajun fiddler Doug Kershaw. At the end of my spiel I offered to give them their money back. Perhaps ten people took me up on the offer. The show was terrific and I ended up making more money than usual because I didn't have to pay Merle his fee.

The next day we headed for Salt Lake City for a concert at the Salt Palace, but there was still no sign of our star. By this time the national media had picked up on the story and someone spotted Merle (pretty hard to hide a 40-foot tour bus). Turns out Merle and then wife Leona Williams had a spat, she took off and Merle went to find her. The Salt Palace concert went as smoothly as the Denver show, and Merle never missed another show.

One time we were doing a concert in Kinston, North Carolina. The venue was a high school auditorium and the local promoter, Ralph Lee, who had a Carolina accent thicker than biscuit gravy, made a request.

"Ah wanna innerduce Muhl Haggahd."

"You go ahead and intro the opening acts, Ralph," I said, "but I'll introduce Merle."

"Nosuh. This is mah shew, ah'll innerduce Muhl Haggahd."

I told Merle, who wasn't too happy.

"Okay, he can do it, but he's gotta say exactly what you tell him."

I went back to Ralph.

"Okay, here's the deal, you've got to say 'Here he is, the Poet of the Common Man, Merle Haggard.'"

Ralph nodded. "Ah'll do it."

When it came time to bring Merle on, Ralph proudly took the stage and grabbed the mike. "Well here he is, the poor 'n' common man, Muhl Haggahd."

Merle looked over at me, rolled his eyes and ran out on stage.

Merle was notorious for doing short shows and would often indulge himself. Unlike some performers who would go on stage in an iron lung before they'd let the fans down, if Merle didn't feel like giving his all, he wouldn't. Not to say Merle didn't care about his fans, he just never allowed himself to feel they owned a piece of him. At a Willie Nelson picnic one night in Austin, Texas, Merle proved that he really could say no to them. I went on stage and introduced Merle and his band the Strangers to about 10,000 drunk-as-a-skunk music lovers. I listened to the music for a few moments then headed back to the tour bus. Not thirty seconds later Merle came running past me.

"Hag! Where the hell are you going?"

He stopped and held up his hands. "Aw hell, they're all drunk. They won't even know I'm gone."

I watched him jog on ahead to the bus, my jaw hanging wide open. The funny thing was, he was right. They didn't notice.

Merle's habit of doing short shows got so bad I actually put a big clock on the stage.

"Hag, when the big hand gets to 12 you can leave. Until then, keep singing."

He followed my instructions and never again left the stage too early.

Merle Haggard has been an enigma to me since we met. Although I spent ten years off and on with him on the road, I believe I got to know him better after we quit doing business and were just a couple of guys talking. Merle could be moody and unpredictable, yet his lyrics tell you who he really is. In his song "Holding Things Together" Merle's words are so poignant one would never believe they were written by a man who professed to being a bad father. In the song, a father speaks to the absent mother of his daughter, pleading for her to return. He even goes so far as to sign her name to a birthday gift to protect the feelings of their little girl.

In "Mama Tried" Merle tells the wrenching story of how, despite his mother's love and steadfast efforts to save him, he still ended up doing life in prison without parole at 21 years of age. In "I Take A Lot Of Pride In What I Am" Merle talks about the lessons he learned in America's hobo jungles and how they helped make him the man he is. Something I would love to do before I die would be to produce Merle's life story as a feature film.

In 1973 Bill Carruthers, my original producer on *The Newlywed Game*, was working for the Nixon White House. Carruthers called me and said that President Nixon was inviting Merle to perform at the White House for his wife Pat's birthday. When I called Hag and told him about the invitation he got very excited and immediately began making preparations for the performance.

Before we were allowed to come to the White House there were background checks and lots of red tape to deal with. The FBI took the names and social security numbers of everyone who walked through the door. We sat back and waited for the bomb to drop. The reason? Here you had a fun-loving, wild-ass band led by a convicted felon (although the year before, Ronald Reagan, in his capacity as governor of California, gave Merle a full pardon). I held out little hope they would be approved by anyone short of the National Association of Bong Manufacturers. To my complete surprise the only hitch was an artistic one.

In the course of the approval process we were required to submit to the FBI the list of songs and accompanying lyrics to be performed that night. The legendary Osborne Brothers, Sonny and Bobby, were on tour with Merle and would also be singing at the White House. One of the signature pieces the two bluegrass stars had on their list was the old classic "Ruby." The FBI, being the musically astute organization they are, mistook the song for Kenny Rogers' "Ruby," a painful story of a disabled Vietnam vet whose wife cheats on him because he can't satisfy her. They told us they would "deal with the issue" when we arrived.

We left Fort Worth and arrived in Washington, D.C. on March 16th. Although that was the actual date of Pat Nixon's birthday, the party was not scheduled until the next day, St. Patrick's Day. We were picked up by a military bus and transported to our hotel. To get "Ruby" approved for the next evening's performance the Osbornes were required to submit the lyrics to the FBI agents to prove it would not embarrass the White House. When the feds realized the Osborne's "Ruby" was not Kenny's "Ruby" it got the green light.

The next morning Merle and his mother had breakfast with Pat Nixon and I had breakfast with Nixon's special administrative assistant, Stephen Bull. Not long into our meal, Stephen had to excuse himself because the president had called a very important staff meeting. I later found out the meeting centered on a rather dicey subject to the Nixon White House: Watergate. I know now that during that time Nixon and his closest advisors were so concerned about the political damage from the burglaries of the DNC office in the Watergate Hotel complex and psychiatrist Daniel Ellsberg's office, they had sunk to discussing who they could pay off. It was this conspiracy of cover up and denial that brought down Nixon's presidency seventeen months later.

After breakfast Merle did something that members of that White House staff talk about even to this day. Before entertainers performed at the famous residence they usually rehearsed in private, and that only consisted of a sound check and warm up. When Merle saw how much the staff loved him, he made arrangements for them to attend the rehearsal. Then he bowled them over by playing not one or two songs, but his entire set.

That evening the East Room glowed in warm light, the full length portrait of George Washington looking down on us. This was the same space Union troops used as a war room and where mourners met a few years later to pay tribute to Abraham Lincoln. Nearly a hundred years later it was where the casket of John F. Kennedy lay in state. Tastefully elegant, the room evoked a feeling of great power and stability, particularly given that it was filled with some of the biggest movers and shakers on the Hill.

Merle had written a poem for Pat Nixon which Teri had beautifully produced for presentation to her. With lovely hand-printed calligraphy on rich parchment, the poem and the attached note really touched Mrs. Nixon. Merle and the Osborne Brothers performed flawlessly and—despite the usual gravity and decorum of the East Room—they brought down the House. I had to smile at the image of Henry Kissinger clapping enthusiastically as Merle finished "Okie From Muskogee" and a large American flag appeared behind the band.

After the performance we all joined a reception line and met the Nixons. Because it was Saint Patrick's Day the president wore a green bow tie with his black tuxedo and the First Lady wore a stunning green dress. As we made our way toward the president and first lady a Nixon staffer offered to give Teri Brown a tour of the Oval Office. She spent the entire time playing chase around the president's desk, fending off his advances.

After the reception line the real party began, and let me tell you, it was more like Animal House than the White House. Servers carried trays brimming with cocktails as they moved about the crowd, dispensing their wares. Soon the atmosphere was quite lively. At one point Nixon's two top advisors, his chief-of-staff Bob Haldeman and domestic counsel John Ehrlichman, took me aside.

Haldeman looked around to make sure we weren't overheard and lowered his voice. "What would you do to change the president's image?"

I had many conflicting pictures flash through my mind—a playful Nixon saying "sock it to me" on *Laugh-In* countered by his sweaty, five o'clock shadow during the Kennedy debate. Then I had visions of Ike playing golf, JFK sailing, Johnson at his ranch.

"You never see him doing anything real. He's always the president, never just a normal guy. I want to see him play golf or something."

Haldeman and Ehrlichman looked at each other as if I'd given them the answer to the meaning of life. They seemed genuinely surprised. I'm sure they were in the throes of trying to enhance their boss's public face, given the unfolding events they were dealing with. A little over a month after our trip to the White House, Haldeman, Ehrlichman, along with Nixon accuser John Dean, all resigned.

That night the Nixons did the unprecedented by opening up the entire White House, including the residential wing, to all the party-goers. Usually access to that area is highly restricted but, for that one evening, all bets were off. The only room we were forbidden to enter was Trisha's because she was sick with a cold.

It was an amazing sight, Merle and his slightly inebriated musicians rubbing elbows with Washington's finest, who, I might add were a bit in the tank themselves. One well-known senator staggered over to me, draped an arm over my shoulder and slurred, "You're probably a nice guy, but I don't watch your stupid show."

I smiled. "That's okay, senator."

"I'm telling you, it's the stupidest show I've ever seen."

At the White House in 1973 with President and Mrs. Nixon. Merle Haggard performed for the First Lady's birthday.

I am very proud to have received this thank you note from the President. It was an evening I will never forget.

THE WHITE HOUSE
WASHINGTON

March 27, 1973

Dear Mr. Eubanks:

All of the guests at the "Evening at the White House" on March 17 enjoyed the splendid program of musical entertainment which was offered that evening. Mrs. Nixon and I want you to know how much we appreciate all that you, and your assistant, Teri Brown, did to help insure that the program would be such a success.

With our thanks and very best wishes,

Sincerely,

Richard Nixon

Mr. Bob Eubanks
c/o Concert Express
Suite 240
9100 Sunset Boulevard
Los Angeles, California 90069

"That's okay, senator."

Then he stepped back, trying to focus his eyes and began, "I remember this one time when..." and proceeded to recite about five episodes of *The Newlywed Game* to me. When he was done I shook his hand and quipped, "God, senator, I sure am glad you don't watch the show!"

The party continued fast and furious until around 3 A.M. That was one occasion when I was very glad I don't drink.

The next morning the military bus came to pick us up at 7 sharp. A very hung over and grouchy crew of musicians met it. As we made our way to Dulles Airport, some of the band members began taunting the Coast Guard driver for being so cautious and strictly adhering to the speed limit. The driver took it for a while but soon I could see steam coming from his ears.

"Okay, you want to get there faster?" he asked. "Fine," and pulled a three-foot stick from under the seat. Wedging the stick against the gas pedal and jamming it under the dash, the bus took off like a cruise missile. With the throttle taken care of, all the bus driver had to do was lean back, put his feet up on the dash and steer. The rampaging bus careened in and out of traffic with luggage and clothes flying everywhere and hillbillies upchucking left and right. We arrived at Dulles in such record time that Don Markham, Hag's sax player, green in hue and legs wobbly, summed it up, "Goddamn, that was like the fuckin' Poseidon Adventure."

Our motley crew straggled though the airport on our way to the gate to catch the plane to San Antonio. Dragging my luggage behind me, I was un-aware I'd forgotten to zip up my dirty clothes compartment and left a trail of underwear in my wake. It seemed a fitting end to our White House visit.

One year to the day after our appearance at the White House, the new Grand Ole Opry building opened in Nashville. Although President Nixon was embroiled in the Watergate scandal he agreed to make an appearance at the opening. I called Sonny Osborne and asked if he was going to attend. The Osborne Brothers were members of the Grand Ole Opry, and though they were not appearing that night Sonny wanted to go and said we would be able to get backstage.

When Sonny and I arrived that evening President Nixon was on stage with Roy Acuff. We ran into Stephen Bull backstage and reminisced about the previous year's party. While we were talking Nixon came off stage and approached us. He acknowledged Bull then turned to us with a big smile and an outstretched hand. "Sonny, Bob, how are you?" I was impressed that it had been a year yet he remembered our names as if we'd seen him only the day before. I later marveled at the fact he remembered us but not those 18-1/2 minutes on that infamous tape. In the '90s when I was hosting the TNN show Prime Time Country I had the Osbornes on as guests. Sonny and I were laughing about being backstage with Nixon at the Opry when he admitted he'd been packing a gun that night. God love those country boys!

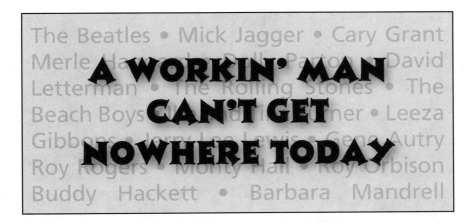

A WORKIN' MAN CAN'T GET NOWHERE TODAY

The Beatles • Mick Jagger • Cary Grant
Merle Haggard • Dolly Parton • David
Letterman • The Rolling Stones • The
Beach Boys • Tina Turner • Leeza
Gibbons • Jerry Lee Lewis • Gene Autry
Roy Rogers • Monty Hall • Roy Orbison
Buddy Hackett • Barbara Mandrell

ONCE WHEN I WAS LOOKING for an act to open for Haggard I thought about my old friend, The Killer, Jerry Lee Lewis. I heard Jerry was still hitting the sauce pretty hard, but he was an electric performer and I thought the match with Hag would be perfect. Since we had last worked together I also heard Jerry had really mastered the destruction of his pianos. He had gotten in the habit of smashing his pianos into heaps, sometimes before his set was supposed to end. Whether he stood on them and kicked them or set them on fire, I was concerned I might be obligated to pay for a piano, which at that time was about $6500 for a top quality concert grand. I came up with a plan.

In the intervening years since I'd last employed him, Jerry's fee had ballooned from the $750 I paid him to play the Cinders to $7500 to open for Hag. Just before the show I went into his dressing room to say hello. Then I pulled out an envelope and handed it to him.

"What's this?"

"Your paycheck. It's a thousand bucks."

He narrowed his eyes. "The hell it is. You're payin' me seventy-five hundred."

"The piano's worth sixty-five hundred. I don't give a shit what you do with it, smash it, blow it up, take a chainsaw to it for all I care. But if it's in one piece at the end of the night you'll get the balance. Fair enough?"

He glared at me, but didn't disagree. When he left the stage later the piano was unscathed, and I gave him the balance of his money. That was our arrangement from then on. I was pretty comfortable with Jerry, and

The 'Killer' and me with country music star, Jody Miller, at Anaheim Convention Center circa 1970.

one night while playing Thibodeaux, Louisiana, I asked him a pointed question.

"You still drinking?"

Perhaps I was the wrong person to ask since I have never been a drinker. It's not that I have a personal problem with anyone having a drink, I was just never interested.

Jerry bristled. "Hell yes. So what?"

His answer was so defiant there wasn't much point in taking it any further. If he drank, he drank, and there didn't seem much I could do about it at that point.

"Okay, just wondering," I said and walked away, imagining what possible disaster the night might bring.

Carlton Haney was a major country music promoter and a real character. He booked a concert with Jerry Lee Lewis and Fats Domino, and when the artists arrived they discovered that Carlton had overlooked a moderately important detail: he had failed to rent a piano. Facing the two fuming piano players, Carlton gritted his teeth. "Fellers, ah don' unnerstan' the prollem. Whin ah hayer George Jones, he allus bring his own git-tar."

When "Whispering Bill" Anderson sang his hit "Where Have All Our Heroes Gone?" he wanted a huge American flag on stage as a backdrop. Put out at having to find a big flag, Carlton was overheard grousing, "The nex' thin' Anderson'll want'll be eleven wounded vet-rans in the front row."

Another Carlton Haney story told to me by Sonny involved a concert the Osborne Brothers did for Carlton. When it came time to settle up with the band, Carlton pulled out his check book. As he was scribbling out a check, something set Sonny's radar off.

"Carlton, this check ain't gonna bounce, is it?"

Carlton paused and looked up at Sonny with genuine concern. Then he quietly folded up the check book and took out another. "Oh, maybe ah should wraht y'all a check outta this account ovah heah."

Fuzzy Owen told me a couple of Carlton Haney stories. One time, Merle Haggard and his band sped through the night 700 miles to get to Philly only to find out the concert Carlton booked had one big problem: Carlton had forgotten to advertise it. Consequently, the house was completely empty, which infuriated Merle. When Carlton called Fuzzy Owen to book more dates, Fuzzy told him in no uncertain terms that Merle would never work for him again. Carlton blew his cork.

"Y'all tell Merle Haggard he's a sum-bitch!"

Fuzzy did—on tape. Unbeknownst to Carlton, Fuzzy had a tape recorder ready to record such an outburst. Fuzzy played it for Merle who became furious and confronted Carlton over the phone.

"Carlton, did you call me a son-of-a-bitch?" asked Merle.

"Oh nosuh, Merle Haggard, I woun't call you a sumbitch."

"Well I got you calling me a son-of-a-bitch right here on tape!"

Carlton, ever cool, gave a classic response. "Merle Haggard, if that tape say anythin' other'n what ahhm tellin' you rayht now, then that tape's lyin'."

In spite of himself, Carlton Haney has been a major force in country music and his Bluegrass Festivals helped to both discover and further the careers of many artists.

I watched a show recently on CMT about the greatest male country music entertainers of all time and was stunned that they omitted Marty Robbins. In my opinion, Marty Robbins should be near the top of any list of all-time country music stars. Ironically, one of Marty's pet peeves was the Country Music Association's designation of "Entertainer of the Year." He felt it was completely politicized and reflected who sold the most albums, not who worked the hardest. Not to take anything away from them, but when people like Willie Nelson, Loretta Lynn and Ricky Skaggs won it really made him mad.

"How in the world could an artist become entertainer of the year when all he does is stand up there and sing number one hits?"

Marty had that old school sense of work ethic and felt the winner should be the person who bled the most for their fans.

Born into poverty in 1925 in the Phoenix suburb of Glendale, Marty Robbins soon developed a love for country music. Like myself, he was nearly obsessed with Gene Autry and would spend his Saturdays at the local theater watching his hero and memorizing his music. He did a tour of duty in the South Pacific in WWII, then came back and, by 1951, had a recording contract with CBS Records. Marty was one of the most successful musicians in entertainment, country or otherwise, with a staggering eighty-three top 40 hits in his thirty-year career. Songs like "Singing the Blues" and "Don't Worry" made him a star, and some of them, like "El Paso," crossed from the country charts to pop music.

For several years I put him together with Merle Haggard as a concert package and the pairing worked brilliantly—at least on stage. Although Merle idolized Marty, sometimes Marty could be cold to Merle, yet Merle overlooked it. The two of them got along fine on the road, partly because they almost never saw each other. The Sons of the Pioneers would open the show, then Marty would close the first half, followed by Merle who would close the show. Although Marty was the senior star, he liked his position of closing the first half. Generally, the act who ends the show is considered the headliner.

Kicking off the first half were The Sons of the Pioneers. The Sons of the Pioneers were founded in 1933 by Bob Nolan, Tim Spencer and Roy Rogers, and had seen many, many personnel changes over the years. They had a seasoned, high energy act that always brought the house down and guaranteed them a standing ovation. Following the Pioneers soon began to demoralize Marty because he felt he either wouldn't be able to meet the audience's expectations, or he'd have a stroke trying to compete with them.

One night after the show in Phoenix he called a meeting. The two of us went into a dressing room and shut the door.

"I'm workin' my ass off. I want to drop the Pioneers," said Marty. "They're killin' me."

This was a difficult moment because I had loved the Sons of the Pioneers since I was probably five years old. In addition to that, I had a contract with them. Now I was facing a future Country Hall of Famer who wanted me to fire yet another future Country Hall of Fame act because they were too good. I suspected the reason for this revolt was because much of his act was comprised of former Sons of the Pioneers hits.

"No. No, I can't do that," I said firmly.

Marty looked surprised. I'm sure he left the meeting feeling a bit disgruntled, but he never said another word about the Sons of the Pioneers. He apparently took up the challenge because he immediately stepped up the energy in his act and from then on regularly brought the crowds to their feet.

Marty Robbins was a creative giant. He was also one of the strangest people I ever worked with. He often did things to either test you or piss you off. I've always tried to be a peacemaker so it's hard for me to understand the mentality of people who go out of their way to create trouble.

He loved messing with people and things, in particular, the Grand Ole Opry, a hallowed institution for many. For Marty it was just another target. When he was in Nashville he would play the Opry, always closing the show. At the end of the broadcast, Ernest Tubb did a live remote from his nearby record shop, making the timing critical. Marty knew this yet almost always went long in his set, knowing it would eat into Ernest's show.

Another time while we were on tour, Merle asked if we would roll a carpet over the stage because some of the venues had bad acoustics and it seemed to help the sound. It became our standard set dressing until Marty complained.

One night after a show he grabbed my arm and shook his head. "I can't stand that carpet. It makes me dizzy when I close my eyes."

"Dizzy? How does a carpet make you dizzy."

"It just does. Get rid of it." There was that mischievous "I'm going to give you shit whether you like it or not" twinkle in his eyes I had become used to by then.

This demand would pose a problem since Marty always closed the first half of the show after the Sons of the Pioneers did their set. After he left the stage, the crew would quickly set up Merle's equipment and he would close the show. Both the Sons of the Pioneers and Merle liked the carpet, so placating Marty would have required removing and replacing all of the equipment on stage twice in one evening. And Marty knew it. So instead of literally taking away the carpet, I decided to address Marty's "dizziness" problem. I instructed our sound man, Charlie Burns, to cut a hole about three feet in diameter right where Marty stood at the microphone.

The next night he was waiting in the wings and noticed the carpet was still there.

"Shit, what'd I tell you?" he asked challengingly. I put my hand on his shoulder and pointed across the stage to the hole in the carpet.

"Right there, Marty. I had 'em cut a hole out for you. It's bare stage for three feet in every direction. You won't get dizzy anymore."

He scowled at me and did the show from his hole. Afterwards he grudgingly told me to "put back the carpet."

Marty could also be very moody. One night in Las Cruces, New Mexico, Marty was in a snit for some reason and decided to alienate the audience. He was quite practiced at pissing people off and in no time they booed him off the stage.

We put on a concert at the Hollywood Bowl featuring country veterans Charlie McCoy and Roger Miller, with Marty closing the first half and Hag closing the show. I knew Marty was bothered by the fact that most of the crowd was there to see Merle. Marty was older and had been a star longer, but at that time Merle's star was burning brighter, and it didn't sit well with Marty. He also knew Merle looked up to him, so it was just that much harder for Marty to swallow having someone pass him whom he almost considered a protégé.

And Merle really did put Marty on a pedestal. Over the years together, Hag had not only cultivated an amazingly good impersonation of Marty, but also named his first born son after him. Before the Bowl show began, Merle approached me.

"Do you think Marty would come out and join me singing 'Today I Started Loving You Again?'"

That song had been one of Merle's biggest hits, selling more than a million copies. Merle was very proud of it, particularly the fact that Marty had thought enough of the song to record it on one of his own

Merle Haggard leaving the stage after a standing ovation at the Hollywood Bowl.

MICHAEL OCHS ARCHIVES.COM

albums. Merle almost sounded like a child as he asked the question, and I knew it meant a lot to him.

"I'm sure he will, Merle. I'll go ask him."

I went to Marty's dressing room. When I entered I could feel a strange energy that I had come to know. An uncomfortable disconnect would often come over Marty and he would become distant, almost sullen. Anyone who knew him understood you might as well save your breath, but I forged ahead because it was mere moments to show time and Merle really wanted this.

"Marty? Merle would really like it if you would join him during his set and sing 'Today I Started Loving You Again.'"

He didn't look at me for a moment, then he turned, his eyes cold.

"Nah. I don't wanna do that."

I paused, debating whether to press Merle's case. Then I left without

Backstage at the Hollowood Bowl with Marty Robbins.

saying anything. I understood that Marty was just that way and Merle would just have to deal with it. I found Merle and my face told him what my words were about to.

"Hag? Marty...he said no. Sorry."

Despite his tough exterior Merle Haggard is a very sensitive man. I saw his eyes tear up. I was angry with Marty for being so callous to a man who worshiped him, a fellow artist who had more than paid his dues, and then asked for this small courtesy.

One thing that always surprised me about Marty was his lack of self confidence. For a guy who spent so much time either in control or trying to exert it, he had a shockingly low estimation of his own worth. The best example of that came from a story my friend and partner Jim Wagner told me. Jim had booked Marty for a series of dates for $10,000 per show. At that time, Marty's going price was $3,500 to $5,000 per show. When Jim told Marty about his bounty, rather than thank him,

Marty cancelled the appearances, telling Jim he just didn't think he was worth that much. I don't think Marty ever appreciated his talents as an entertainer. I also think those formative years watching Gene Autry planted in Marty's head he should be in the movies and not on stage as a singer.

The people around Marty were very protective of him. In the two years I handled the Robbins/Haggard tour I was only on his bus a couple of times. If I needed to talk to Marty I would usually go to long-time friends and fellow band members Bobby Sykes or Don Martin and they would set something up with him. In the time I worked with him, Marty and I had heated words on only one occasion. In Pine Bluff, Arkansas, a girl got backstage to see one of the band members. Marty threw the girl out then angrily confronted me.

"What the hell you doin' letting somebody backstage?"

I stood toe to toe with him and fired right back.

"Your band member brought her back here, not me, so back off!"

He did. He apologized and that was the last of that issue.

My times touring with the bands were lots of fun. We shared meals, stories, jokes and a lot of pot limit poker. One night I checked into a motel and was situated next to one of Marty's musician's rooms. All was quiet until I heard an unholy moaning which soon elevated to a high pitched scream of pain. I picked up the phone and dialed the police. When they got to the motel they discovered that the cries were those of ecstasy, not mayhem. The next day the band member read me the riot act, claiming he was only having a little fun with a local girl. The two of us were the tour's running joke for several days.

I got to know Hag far better than I did Marty, but I did see enough of Marty to develop opinions about him as a complicated man and as a country superstar. When he took the stage and was in the mood, he was one of the most powerful, gifted entertainers to grace those fortunate enough to be in his presence. Marty Robbins left us far too soon.

While I was on the road with Marty and Hag, one of the funniest and most mischievous pranks I ever heard of was told to me by Fuzzy. It concerned Stew Carnell and legendary rodeo cowboy Casey Tibbs. Stew was Johnny Cash's agent and would also book Hag the rare times when I didn't. One night in Reno, Nevada, after a number of hours of heavy drinking, Stew and Casey staggered into the parking lot of the MGM

Hotel and happened to see two identical U-Haul trailers parked side by side. The two soused pranksters couldn't resist. As hammered as they were they managed to unhook each trailer from their vehicles and then rehook each to the other car. I cannot imagine the look on the drivers' faces when they got home and swung open the doors to their trailers only to find nothing that belonged to them.

My country music buddies all had endless stories about the many characters in the business, but few subjects were as colorful as Alvin "Junior" Samples. Truly a good ol' boy, legend had it that the rotund Junior had many of his front teeth removed to appear more rurally authentic to his audiences. He had been a stock car racer, champion bass fisherman and expert harmonica player, but most knew him from his down home humor on Hee Haw. Plucked by the Hee Haw producers from the backwoods of Georgia, Junior had developed a local reputation as a guy who could tell a tall and hilarious tale. Junior had a rollicking sense of what was funny despite little formal education.

When he was first brought out to Hollywood, Junior was given the nickel tour of the main CBS facility down on Fairfax. When a distinguished exec in a dark blue suit happened by and acknowledged them, the PR guy turned to Junior.

"Junior," he began, suddenly not remembering the exec's name, "this is our vice president."

Junior's eyes widened as he clasped the man's hand in his big mitts and pumped his arm furiously.

"Mr. Agnew, it's a real honor to meet you, sir!" he gushed.

My favorite Samples story—and I hope it's true—has become legend in Nashville circles. After Junior died of a heart attack in 1983, it was often told as a warm remembrance of the sweetly naive bear of a man. Prior to his discovery by Hollywood, Junior had never been on an airplane. The Hee Haw producers arranged to fly him from Atlanta to Nashville and, as the reservation agent printed his ticket, Junior looked over the dizzying array of flight information.

"What time does my plane take off?"

"Eleven oh five," she answered.

Junior nodded, unaware that Atlanta was on Eastern time while Nashville was on Central time, an hour's difference.

"And what time do I git there?"

"Eleven oh seven."

Junior was doing some alarming math in his head as the agent reached to hand him the ticket. He stepped back.

"No, I don't want that ticket."

"Why? It's paid for."

"I just wanna go somewhere," he said with a sense of awe, "…and watch that sumbitch take off."

One evening, sometime around 1973 or so, Merle's wife Bonnie Owens and I got to talking on the tour bus. She was telling stories about Merle's years spent as a hobo and his troubles as a younger man. Merle came over and sat down. He told me about the time he fought some fellow hobos over a can of peas and feared he would lose his life over it. He regaled us with many stories, some of which I can't repeat.

In his late teens, Merle and a buddy needed some cash, so they hatched a plan to rob the local service station. They noticed that the lock that secured the place at night was left on the lube rack during the day. When the attendants weren't looking they surreptitiously replaced the lock with one that looked just like it. That night they simply used their key, opened their lock and made off with the dough.

On another occasion, Merle had just escaped from a youth institution near Barstow and was trying to hitchhike his way to freedom. As he walked down the rural road a highway patrol car happened by in the opposite direction. When the patrolmen began to turn around Merle didn't wait for an invitation to be captured and hightailed it to a potato shed, burying himself under the spuds. Within moments the place was crawling with law enforcement. Pretty soon he figured out from heated conversations that a local girl had been raped and he was their prime suspect! Terrified, Merle laid low for hours until darkness fell and he could climb out from under all those potatoes. Later, at a service station, he found out they caught the rapist.

Merle did not like to fly home at the end of a tour. No matter how far from home the tour ended, Merle firmly insisted on taking the bus back. He said he hated to fly commercially because something strange always happened and he was worried that strange could easily become tragic. I would cajole him but he resisted the easy way home. I argued that flying would get him home quickly and flying first class was a heck of a lot cheaper than chartering a plane. Finally, after much coercion I convinced him to fly to L.A. from Birmingham, Alabama.

We had just reached cruising altitude when I noticed Merle tense up and his eyes get wide. I looked down the aisle and saw a guy taking off his clothes. The crazy man announced to the flight crew that he was going to run so fast he would exit the back end of the airplane. He was wrestled to the floor but Merle never flew with me again on a commercial airline. Every time there was an opportunity to fly or drive I would always say, "Aw, c'mon, Hag. Fly home with me. Nothin'll happen," to which he would give me this baleful stare as if to say, "don't even think about it."

I always found the relationship celebrities have with airplanes to be interesting. Today the use of private jets has increased tremendously over what it was twenty-five years ago. I fly a lot and, unless someone is offering otherwise, take commercial flights. I've seen some sights in my years of air travel. One morning at the Philadelphia airport years ago, I was waiting to board a plane to Los Angeles when two huge motorcycle cops parted the crowd like the Red Sea and escorted Nancy Sinatra to the gate. She had been performing at Resorts International in Atlantic City with her famous dad. After a delay while the cops got Nancy and her entourage aboard, the commoners were allowed on. When I finally boarded I had to laugh—after all that fuss, Sinatra and her gang were all sitting in coach. As my rodeo cowboy buddies say, "If you're gonna run with the big dogs you can't pee like a puppy."

Another time I was waiting with the horde to board a United flight out of Chicago. The special services lady from the airline made a big to-do about boarding Marlo Thomas before anyone else. When the rest of us climbed on we saw Marlo Thomas sitting in first class, the menu covering her face. I always wondered: why not just get on last instead of making such a scene?

I was on another flight home one evening and looked over the seat to see who was making a commotion.

"Don't you know who I am?" demanded a strident, high-pitched voice. "I'm Burt Ward, Robin on Batman!"

It had been years since his show had been in its first run, but that was immaterial—he was acting like a complete jackass. After listening to him berate the poor flight attendant, I finally got tired of his rantings about being Robin the Boy Wonder. I stood up and noticed he was a rather diminutive fellow for having such a big mouth.

"Who the hell cares?"

Enraged, he got in my face and turned bright red. "Mind your own business!"

He was practically hysterical.

"I'm making it my business. Now shut up and sit down."

I should have known better than to mess with a man who wears tights. There were the divas and the dolts, but I also had many pleasant experiences while flying. One of my most memorable occurred on a red eye between New York and L.A. I was seated next to a beautiful African-American lady for six hours, and in that time we solved the problems of the world. I knew she was a celebrity but just couldn't place her and didn't want to embarrass her or myself by asking who she was. We talked about show business and world events and even about our families. She was like finding a long lost friend as we hit it off like we'd known each other for years. Just before we landed my brain came into alignment and I recognized Cicely Tyson, the star of many wonderful television and film productions.

DREAMS DO COME TRUE

The Beatles • Mick Jagger • Cary Grant
Merle Haggard • Dolly Parton • David
Letterman • The Rolling Stones • The
Beach Boys • Ike and Tina Turner • Leeza
Gibbons • Jerry Lee Lewis • Gene Autry
Roy Rogers • Monty Hall • Roy Orbison
Buddy Hackett • Barbara Mandrell

ONCE I HAD GOTTEN CONCERT EXPRESS established by signing Merle Haggard and Marty Robbins, I felt it was time to branch
out. Those two acts gave me a lot of clout, and despite the locked door
to the good ol' boy club of Nashville, I was beginning to show other
country artists there was a reasonable alternative. I looked around for
other artists we could buy, and there were several I felt had great talent
and popularity who were on the upward curve of their careers.

Porter Wagoner was a Missouri boy who'd made it big in country. His
career really took off in 1955 when he signed his first record deal with
RCA. Between that year and 1956 he was a regular on ABC's Ozark Jubilee, broadcast out of Springfield, Missouri. In 1957 he joined the Grand
Ole Opry and never looked back. Three years later he went back to television with the syndicated Porter Wagoner Show, which lasted twenty-
one years. Fellow Ozark Jubilee alum Norma Jean Beasley joined Porter
on his new show and became his partner for many duets. Dropping her
last name, she was known simply as Norma Jean to her many adoring
fans. When she decided to get married in 1967 and cut back her schedule, Porter searched for a replacement and settled on a talented 21-year-
old entertainer from Locust Ridge, Tennessee.

Only three years out of high school, the woman stepping in to fill
Norma Jean's shoes was already a rising country star. Bleached blonde
and very pretty, she was just five feet tall, but that was often overlooked
because she was almost absurdly endowed. Yet her beauty and ample
bosom seemed to fade into the background when she opened her mouth
and began to sing. When that angelic and soulful soprano poured forth,

she sure got your attention. On top of that, she was also an extraordinarily gifted songwriter. Porter seemed to have hit the jackpot with his new star, but at first the fans hated Dolly Parton because she wasn't Norma Jean. They soon warmed up to Dolly and she became both Porter's protégé and partner on stage.

I had heard the rumors about Norma Jean and Porter, and when he took on Dolly the rumors flew about them as well. Whether any were true I didn't care, but I had heard from good sources that Porter was almost obsessively protective of Dolly. Dolly had gotten married in 1966 to her long time sweetheart Carl Dean (they're still married), so I assumed Porter was just trying to keep someone from stealing Dolly away. When I met them in 1972, Dolly was on her way to becoming a superstar, yet, regardless of where Dolly might be going, I was interested in being in business with both of them.

Notwithstanding my continued chilly reception in Nashville, I now had a leg up in the world of country music as the promoter of Merle and Marty, but needed more artists to really cement our company's future. I called Porter's agent Tandy Rice and he agreed to hear me out. I had a feeling he would talk to me because, West Coast guy or not, word had gotten around that Merle and Fuzzy Owen were happy campers.

Tandy was a larger-than-life character with big hair and a bigger drawl. Before we actually got down to business I began to see through all that country boy charm and understood I was dealing with a very shrewd operator. As we moved to the meat and potatoes of our discussion I sensed his reluctance. I wasn't sure if he'd gotten the word to stay away from me and was just curious or if I actually had a chance. I'd since gotten the hang of promoting country talent and knew the artist and manager's sore point was almost always the consistency issue. What they really wanted was one honest promoter who would consistently deliver good quality and quantity. I decided a ballsy move was required to either flush him out or end it right there.

"How much is Porter making per live show?"

Tandy leveled his gaze. "At least thirty-five hundred. But I have to tell you, Bob, he's got very few dates available. Just a handful at best."

"A handful, huh?"

"Yessir. At best."

"How many dates would Porter have available if I wrote him a check for $350,000 for 100 dates in the next twelve months?"

Tandy gasped so hard he began choking like a Model T Ford on a cold morning. When he recovered he fumbled though Porter's schedule and, lo and behold, it looked a lot more favorable for me than it had five minutes before.

"Well you know what?" he allowed, "I think we could find a hundred dates in the next year, given the circumstances."

And so began a very interesting new chapter in my life. My partners Mickey Brown and Jim Wagner and I now owned the exclusive rights to the live concert dates for the Porter Wagoner Show with Dolly Parton. The package was a dream come true. Porter Wagoner had a large and loyal following, owned his own sound system, had his own opening act and, best of all, had this delicious blonde who sang and wrote like no one I'd ever heard.

When I met Dolly I was immediately charmed. She was pure country and, despite her success, had her feet solidly on the ground. The first conversation I had with her was typically down to earth. She mentioned something about having to watch her weight all the time and I complained that my weight had crept up a little recently. She smiled and chided me, "You know Bob, it's not the 'taters that makes you fat, it's what you put on the 'taters."

Our first concert together made me wonder if it would also be our last. I had screwed up and booked them on Superbowl Sunday 1973 into Bluefield, West Virginia, a lovely little place in the southwestern Appalachians. We had advertised the hell out of the concert but failed to take into account the biggest sporting event of the year. It was looking like we'd get maybe fifty people, and I guessed Tandy and Porter would be pretty unhappy. We ended up with several hundred stalwart fans, but Porter and Dolly put on a show with such energy and enthusiasm you'd have thought they were playing the Superbowl halftime show. Turns out Porter understood it was a tough day to pull anyone away from the TV and was thrilled. After the show, Porter and Dolly did their usual autograph session. I will never forget the lady who led her son up to the table to introduce him to her idol.

"Looky here, Porter. He looks jess lak you, don't he?"

The kid was six foot two, in an old, wrinkled sequined suit that looked like it came out of the dumpster at the Opry, and sported a blonde coif styled like an ocean wave. When he opened his mouth his vapid grin revealed all three or four of his teeth. The look on Porter's face was worth a million bucks. Porter bit his lip and smiled as best he could. "Yep, he sure does."

Porter and I became pretty good friends soon after we began the tour. As a gesture of his regard he presented me with a Martin D-28 guitar he'd used on Ozark Jubilee. I still have that guitar, although I'm sure there was a time, not too long after he gave it to me, that he would have liked to have taken me and that D-28 and shoved it where the sun don't shine.

As I mentioned, Porter was protective of Dolly. Let me go a bit further and say he was wildly jealous of her. It was so bad I even had a meeting with my staff and warned them not to show Dolly too much attention. It was a shame because, being such a warm people-person, I'm sure there were times Dolly felt lonely because no one was talking to her. And since Dolly was also technically my client, it was awkward because I knew Porter did not approve of us speaking. The only times we had any substantive conversations was when Porter was on stage.

One night while Porter was doing a solo song for the crowd at the Long Beach Auditorium I was sitting in a room backstage. I looked up to see Dolly enter, a subdued, perhaps even sad look on face. I realized she was keeping a careful ear on Porter's song.

"I want to leave Porter. I'm scared o' what he might do, but I want you to manage me." I was literally speechless. On the one hand, Porter Wagoner represented a very sizable investment to us: $350,000. On the other hand, Dolly Parton was only making $500 a night. Yet all indications were she was about to become a megastar. I finally managed to recover enough to say something.

"I would like nothing better than to manage your career, but I need some time to think this over. This is kind of a . . . surprise."

"I know, I'm sorry," she said very sincerely, "but I've got to do this. I'm just scared what Porter might do to himself if I leave him."

"Okay, listen, let's just take this in small steps. You guys have been together for five years, we aren't going to solve this in the next ten minutes. Let me figure out what to do."

Over the weeks that followed, Dolly and I had conversations about how we might break her away. I kept cautioning her to keep cool, but I soon learned that once Dolly gets an idea in her head there's absolutely no turning back. I tried to reason with her that she was not only singing with a country music legend and appearing on his television show, she was also gaining popularity by the week. The problem was that by 1972, Dolly was, by all measures, bigger than Porter. (Dolly was actually inducted into the Country Music Hall of Fame three years before Porter, in 1999.) She knew that, and it made her situation with Porter all the more tense.

During the tour I went back to Los Angeles for a month to tape *The Newlywed Game* and left Mickey Brown with Porter and Dolly. Late one night I got a panicked call from Mickey, and he related the events of that evening. Porter and Dolly had gone out to dinner in El Dorado, Arkansas, and during the meal Dolly broke the news to Porter she was leaving him, and that Mickey and I were going to manage her from now on as a solo act. Porter went ballistic and, after a long heated argument, stormed off. Mickey was calling to tell me we were out of business with Porter Wagoner and in business with Dolly Parton. The fat was in the fire now. Porter was furious with me and bad-mouthed me every chance he got. I felt bad but didn't have much choice. I would gladly have continued promoting his concerts but he wouldn't have it. He and I didn't talk again until the late '90s when we made up and became friends again while I was hosting the television show *Primetime Country* on TNN.

Once Dolly made the break she gathered her family around her. Her extended family was quite large and there was a great deal of talent among them. Dolly can come across as a sweet little country girl from "the holler," but she's extremely smart and very decisive. Understanding she needed a group to accompany her, she immediately put together The Traveling Family Band, consisting of some members of her family, and then she handed the job of band leader to her brother Randy.

Perhaps another reason Porter was infuriated was because Dolly poached his road manager and steel guitar player, Don Warden, and installed him as her road manager. Don is still Dolly's road manager. Then Dolly appointed her Uncle Louie to sell souvenirs and programs and offer Dolly advice. Although we provided the overall management and promotion, the move away from Porter was entirely orchestrated by Dolly Parton.

With the exception of Don Warden, Dolly's entourage, from musicians to road people, were mostly relatives or friends out of her home town of Sevierville, Tennessee. They were earnest, hardworking folks, but unfortunately didn't know squat about the music business. This caused many problems, because I had to walk that tightrope between properly managing Dolly's career and trying to contend with the helpful, but often misguided, suggestions about what she should do next.

The first thing I did was put her on the Merle Haggard concert tour. I wanted to give her the experience of performing before big crowds in big buildings in some of America's biggest cities. If she were to become a superstar she needed to get used to five or ten or twenty thousand people. It didn't take her long at all and she was playing the big houses as easily as she sang to those hundred people in Bluefield, West Virginia. Dolly was incredible on stage. It was quite a sight to see that sweet, reserved little country girl take control of thousands of people and entertain them until they were completely wrung out.

Around the same time I signed Porter and Dolly, I also signed another promising artist, Barbara Mandrell. While Dolly's true strength was her writing, Barbara's emphasis was on her stage presence. Barbara did not write music and, as far as I know, never has, but she was an amazing musician, demonstrating her proficiency on something like half a dozen instruments. When we made our management arrangement Barbara was playing 300 dates a year and making $1250 a day. Our goal was to raise her price, get her some television exposure, and overall, raise her career to the next level.

The big problem I ran into right off the bat was her dad, Irby Mandrell. He ran the show and ruled over Barbara and the rest of the group with an iron hand. Irby understood the need for professional management but found it difficult to relinquish any control to me. Irby also played rhythm guitar (unamplified on stage, for some reason), along with Barbara's pretty sister Irlene sitting in on the drums—and dressed in a man's suit. He was also a strict disciplinarian, even banning blue jeans on the tour bus. Irby and I both had strengths and weaknesses, yet while I held my tongue about his, he was quick to point out mine.

In contrast, Barbara's husband, Ken Dudney was a terrific guy. Ken had been Barbara's drummer and, after doing a stretch in the Navy, came back with his pilot's wings. He and Barbara got married in 1967. Later, Ken flew the private jet for the Governor of Tennessee. He also took care of their little boy while Barbara was on the road and handled all of her business affairs. Ken is a classy guy and never interfered with me in my duties as a manager. They're still married to this day. I'm a big Ken Dudney fan and know how hard it must have been to be married to a rising superstar.

I wish Irby had been as accommodating as his son-in-law. Another problem in my management of Barbara was that I had no say in the

Bob and Barbara
Mandrell shortly
after we signed her
to management.
Who has the
most hair?

music she recorded. Managers are often consulted in this so they can exert some influence and plot a career direction for their artist. Billy Sherrill, Barbara's producer at Columbia Records, hated managers so much he wouldn't even allow me in the studio. Sherrill's strong track record—he had produced major hits for artists like George Jones and Tammy Wynette—made it hard for me to criticize him.

Barbara and I parted ways after about a year. She signed with Dick Blake, another concert promoter out of Nashville. Blake did a really good job for Barbara and I believe it was he who helped get her a network television show in 1980. One of the things about female country artists in the '60s and '70s was that they did not sell tickets nearly as well as their male counterparts. In fact, they often had to be packaged with male stars to get the best bookings—Loretta Lynn with Conway Twitty, Dolly Parton with Kenny Rogers, Tammy Wynette with George Jones. As talented as Barbara was, until she got her own TV show, it was tough for her to sell out concerts. Today, things have changed so much. Now you have female superstars from Shania Twain and Faith Hill to The Dixie Chicks and The Judds, all of whom are box office heavyweights in their own right.

It was 1972 and our management company was flourishing. We were producing almost all of Merle Haggard's concerts as well as managing the careers of Dolly Parton and Barbara Mandrell. During this time new, hot acts were popping up left and right, and I always had my eyes open. I was driving to the office one morning and noticed a sign on the back of a taxi advertising a new album from Twentieth Century Records by a guy named Tony Cole. Not too many months before, our next door neighbor on Sunset, David Geffen, had signed a group called the Eagles who had just brought out two big hits back to back, "Take It Easy" and "Witchy Woman." Just prior to those big hits, John Hartman, who worked with Geffen, offered us the Eagles as an opening act for Merle. When I took the proposal to Hag he declined, instead opting for Emmylou Harris, who had just formed a band with Elvis's former band members and had what was considered a hot act.

Knowing nothing about Tony Cole I called my buddy Russ Regan who was then president of Twentieth Century Records.

"Rusty, who the hell is this Tony Cole?"

"You gotta hear this guy. And he's looking for U.S. management."

I hurried over to Russ's office and we listened to Tony's album. A Brit, Cole and his manager in the U.K. were searching for a partner in the States. I thought the album was really cool and got excited about taking Tony Cole on as a client. Russ phoned Tony's manager in London and did a big build up of me and my company and how we would be great management for Tony. The manager was all excited, but then threw a wrench into the promising machine we were building.

"I'd love for you to take on Tony," he began, "but I need you to take on another artist I've just signed. She's from Australia and she's fabulous. She's blonde, drop dead beautiful and sings like…well, she's absolutely super!"

As soon as I heard about this other singer I got cold feet. With her one decent hit from 1971, which I had heard and was not overly impressed by, I didn't really know anything else about her. A potentially promising artist, she was not yet a star. I figured I had women who were already stars—and both were blondes—so I didn't need to take on someone I would have to develop. I passed on Tony Cole because I didn't want the other singer. Tony Cole never became a star, but the other singer did—a very, very big one. To this day, I have to laugh that I passed on Olivia Newton-John.

Although Dolly Parton was miraculous, her Traveling Family Band was less than stellar. But whatever they lacked, Dolly more than made up for. Despite a few minor problems things seemed to be going well. Guitar great Chet Atkins, also an exec at RCA Records, was well aware of Dolly's potential, and his company was frothing at the mouth to sign her. It was around this time that I noticed Dolly's attitude toward me shift. It was subtle at first, not returning a smile, a coolness—things that telegraph a problem.

Around this time Dolly released "Jolene" and it became her first number one hit. She had hits in the past but the popularity of "Jolene" crossed out of country into mainstream and seemed to cement her position as one of country's biggest stars. I thought we would now really take off, and despite her distance from me, I figured success would heal any rifts. At the Country Music Awards Show in 1974, she came to me and her face told me there was something wrong.

"I can't take it anymore. The pressure the Nashville people are putting on me is more than I can handle 'cause I have a West Coast manager."

I understood her dilemma. I had been getting threats and pressure since I began approaching country artists. I couldn't get people at RCA to return my calls, and there seemed to be a real hostility toward anyone who wasn't southern, or specifically, out of Nashville. It wasn't Dolly's fault. She had to live and work in that world and did not yet have the clout that would have allowed her to do what she wanted. In the end I kissed her cheek, wished her well, and figured that was the end of that.

About a year later I got a call from Dolly. She was in town. "Can we meet?" she asked. "I'm at the Beverly Hilton. There's somethin' I want to talk to you about."

I was happy to meet with her and when I saw her face she beamed and we hugged. It was very different from the previous year.

"I've signed with RCA—you probably knew that."

I nodded.

"And I got this big shiny new bus that the record company gave me, but things are not going like I planned. I don't know what it is. I'm workin' my hind end off but I can't seem to break out to where I want to be."

"And where's that? From where I am you seem to be doing great."

"Yeah, I know, I guess I should be happy, but I want more. I want to be more than just a country singer. I want to act and sing and write—I even got an idea for a children's show."

She showed me a tape of the show idea she wanted to pitch. It involved her playing a character named Little Dolly she'd developed on the Porter Wagoner Show. It was apparent Dolly Parton was full of good ideas and not content to simply enjoy her bounty in the country music business. I had known she was destined for greatness but it was interesting to see how such greatness comes about. Here she sat, more or less on top of the world of country music, yet she wanted to spread her wings, work even harder and tackle fields she knew little about. I had no doubt at that moment Dolly could succeed in anything she chose to do. Then she dropped the bomb on me.

"I want to make a change. Would you be interested in managing me again?"

I didn't know what to say. I knew her status had changed since we called it quits the last time, but I was concerned that the same forces might be working against us again.

"Let me think about it, okay? Give me twenty-four hours. I'll give you an answer tomorrow."

She nodded and patted my hand. "Okay, thanks."

I went home and talked it over with my wife Irma. Managing Dolly was going to be very time-consuming. Between the travel and intimacy of handling a rising superstar, it would have been more than my marriage could take at that point. I was already spending a lot of time with Merle Haggard on the road and this would guarantee me being gone all the time. After discussing it with Irma I recognized how important it was to us that I stay as close to home as possible. I certainly would have made a lot of money with Dolly, but I had been fortunate as well as careful with my money, so that was not really a factor.

I called Dolly the next day and arranged a meeting. When we got together I didn't waste any time. I told her I had decided not to get involved in her career again and hoped she understood. She almost seemed relieved. The day before she had mentioned she was going to have dinner with Mac Davis, and during that dinner he had encouraged her to sign with Katz, Gallin & Cleary. They managed Mac as well as the Osmond Brothers. I had gone into our meeting prepared to suggest the same firm to her. Danny Cleary was an agent at GAC when I dealt with him during the Beatle days and I thought he and his partners would really take care of Dolly. It turned out that Sandy Gallin did a terrific job for Dolly. They formed a production company, he produced her television show and they did some movies together. Under Sandy's guidance Dolly achieved her goal of climbing to the top of the entertainment business.

A few years later I was shooting *The Newlywed Game* at Sunset Gower Studios and I heard Dolly was rehearsing next door at the S.I.R rehearsal studio. When I walked in she stopped the music. Coming down off the stage, she gave me a big hug, then looked me in the eye and said, "No matter what, I will always love you and appreciate what you did for me."

Then something strange happened. In 1980, when Michael Hill and I were producing *The Tony Tennille Show*, we had a number of A-list celebrities lined up to do the show. When the hit film *Nine To Five* came out in late 1980 we booked Dolly's co-stars, Jane Fonda and Lily Tomlin. Yet when our bookers tried Dolly's management people they turned us down. I was surprised and a bit hurt but assumed there was a good reason. Over the next few years, I appeared at Resorts International in Atlantic City, and if I saw Dolly was going to be performing around the same time I would always leave her a note that I'm sure was delivered to her. I never received a response. I was puzzled why she seemed to be freezing me out but kept trying.

In the mid-'90s I was invited by Jack and Sherry Herschend to go to Dollywood, Dolly's theme park in Pigeon Forge, Tennessee. Jack and Sherry were, and still are, Dolly's partners in Dollywood. Sherry knew that Dolly and I went way back and she thought it might be fun for me to surprise her. We took a private plane from Branson, Missouri, and I was very excited to see her. I felt whatever weirdness that existed was behind us. I have always taken pride in being part of Dolly's early career. Sherry and I were standing backstage outside her dressing room when Dolly came out. With a startled look on her face, she managed, "Oh, hi Bob," and walked away. Sherry was stunned and embarrassed for me. I was absolutely mortified as well as deeply hurt. To this day I am completely perplexed by her reaction. What happened? I have a theory.

While backstage at the Tennille show I told Jane Fonda what I thought of the way Porter treated Dolly early on and how I didn't agree with it. I think Fonda may have passed that on to her. What I told Fonda was relatively innocuous—as a matter of fact I was standing up for Dolly—but celebrities guard their privacy and you never know what will set them off when someone divulges what they consider a confidence. Regardless, there are no excuses and I should have kept my opinion to myself. If that is the case, then Dolly, I apologize—please forgive me. If that is not the reason, then Dolly what the hell happened?

A bit of country lore I did not mention earlier was that when Norma Jean left Porter Wagoner's act, and before he hired Dolly, there had been another young singer brought in briefly to fill the void. The young woman, a beautician by trade, was offered $50 per show on a ten-day tour covering Alabama and Georgia, but was required to provide her own transportation. She jumped at the chance, and she and her aunt tailed Porter's entourage through the two states in their little Volkswagen.

Less than ten years later I was in San Jose standing at the door to the huge Golden Eagle motor coach owned by this woman. Having since traded in her Volkswagen, she had also become one of country music's biggest stars. Tammy Wynette and her husband, the legendary George Jones, sat inside waiting to meet their new promoter, and I was pretty nervous. This was our first concert together and I hoped to prove to them that they had made the right decision in trusting me. I had heard that Tammy and George, unlike many artists, including Merle Haggard, did not have separate buses for their entourage, but packed their band and backup singers into one big happy bus.

My butterflies vanished when I walked aboard and was met by smiles and a very casual atmosphere. The interior was decorated in a Spanish style—from the drapes and upholstery to the wrought iron lamps. Tammy sat in a breakfast booth with backup singer and seamstress Patsy Sledd. Both had their hair in rollers. Jones sat nearby eyeing me. They immediately began asking about ticket sales. I've met few acts who didn't want to know in advance what kind of house they'd be facing. No one wants to perform to a half empty venue.

"Tonight looks good and in general the tour's ticket sales are pretty strong. I don't see any weak dates."

They both looked relieved. The tour turned out to be trouble free.

George wasn't drinking, the crowds were responsive, and I became friends with both of them. I had heard the rumors about George's wild behavior but never saw any of that during our time together. I also saw the real love he and Tammy shared, as well as the unbounded respect for each other's talent. I was backstage during a concert and saw Tammy and Patsy holding microphones and talking up a storm. George was on stage, and at the appropriate moments they would cease their conversation mid sentence, hold up the mikes and sing harmony. It was a dazzling display of focus, timing and talent. But Tammy was not always so unflappable. Early one morning they stopped at a truck stop for a bathroom and coffee break. When it came time to depart, the bus driver broke the road rules and didn't do a head count. Fifty miles down the road a state trooper pulled the bus over and informed them that a very irritated Tammy Wynette was still at the truck stop. I heard the air on that bus was a little thick for a few days until Tammy cooled off.

Tammy was a very classy woman, elegantly simple, not at all flashy. On a trip to Nashville, they invited me out to their home for dinner. Tammy did the cooking and served up a delicious meal of roast beef, mashed potatoes and green beans. After dinner we sat around and George played songs from their latest session while Tammy served coffee. It was like going over to anyone else's home for dinner, except these two were country music superstars. I could see the pride and love in George's eyes when Tammy spoke, and it was clear she also adored him. So it was particularly hard to believe the frightful stories a few years later of their acrimonious break-up.

George apparently really liked me because one night after a concert he gave me one of his guitars, a beautiful Martin D-35. He didn't give me a case with it, so flying in from Tucson I happily paid full fare for an extra seat to protect my prize possession. To this day that guitar sits next to the Martin D-28 from Porter Wagoner.

I lost touch with George and Tammy, and not long after that their world fell apart. I wasn't around them during the time of their separation and divorce, but what I do know is that they were always very good to me and I loved them both. I ran into Tammy several times after she married her former record producer George Richey. She seemed happy, but that fire in her eyes when she had been with George Jones just wasn't there anymore. Every time I saw Tammy after that she seemed to be slipping farther and farther away, as if the life force was ebbing from

her. Several years later I was visiting with her backstage at the Greek
Theater and I asked her, "Are you happy?"

"Yeah," she said softly, looking into the distance, "I love Richey."
Then she looked back to me. "But I'll never love anyone like Jones."

The last time I saw her was in Branson, Missouri, and I was surprised
to see how thin and drawn she was. She also looked tired and worn out,
as if she had just let go. The sparkle that had made her Tammy Wynette
was gone. Not too long after that, in April, 1998, she passed away. A
mere 55, controversy swirled surrounding her untimely death. Country
music—and the world—lost a real treasure on that day. Despite her extraordinary success, Tammy was plagued for many years by hardships
and heartache, from the poverty of her early years, to turbulent marriages, financial woes and finally, poor health. Perhaps that was why
her music had such power, because her songs were haunting cries from
deep within.

I have seen George from time to time, and have gotten to know his
wife, Nancy. In fact, it was Nancy, when I was hosting *Prime Time Country* for TNN, who rallied the George Jones Fan Club to keep me on as
permanent host. It turned out TNN wanted a younger guy. I'm happy to
see George's life seems to have settled down, and despite a horrendous
car crash in 1999, "The Possum" is still going strong. And God can he
sing!

One of the people I teamed up with to promote concerts was Willie
Leopold. I met Willie when he was working for Seattle's Concerts West.
He had produced concerts for Elvis, The Moody Blues, Led Zeppelin
and John Denver, so when we became friends I saw an opportunity to
add some more talent to my team. Our deal made me the financier while
Willie did most of the legwork. We were soon producing concerts for
Bread, Styx and some major R&B acts. I was having some personal conflict at that time. Then my marriage to Irma was troubled, and looking
back I realize how many things I did that now seem self-destructive.
When they started to show in my business life, sometimes people said
things. Willie and I had started the company but initially I (consciously
or not) dragged my feet on making some decisions and I think it might
have cost us.

Willie finally came to me and said, "We can't make money in the concert business if we don't book concerts." We had just lost $30,000 a few

days earlier on an act in Houston called Bootsie's Rubber Band. Willie was right and that's when I made a renewed commitment to him and to our business. Willie and I had a good partnership and there was never a wrinkle until one day he said he needed $15,000.

"Bob," he said, with complete candor, "I've got a family. I've got to live."

I understood and Willie and I continued to produce concerts. Seventeen years later, Willie and I had long since amicably parted company and he was doing very well, so I sent him a note and reminded him of the loan. Several days later I got a check for $15,000 in the mail. Those are the kinds of things that restore your faith in humanity. Willie now manages the career of Melissa Etheridge.

Willie told me a very funny story about his young son. In the late '70s, the inquisitive lad was attending a school for gifted children in Pasadena. As Willie drove him to school one morning, the child turned to him and asked, "Daddy? What's a whore?"

A slightly rattled Willie composed himself and carefully went through book, chapter and verse explaining exactly how ladies of the evening sell their bodies, stressing, of course, what a degrading occupation it was. When he was satisfied he had done his parental duty and handled a potentially unpleasant situation, Willie concluded with, "So why did you ask?"

Having just been given a lot to chew on, the little boy paused for a moment, then turned to his dad. "I saw there was going to be this horror show on TV Saturday night and I didn't know what it meant."

Willie and I were trying to get a break and one day we thought we'd found it. Willie had a big smile on his face when I walked into his office. He told me we had just been offered three Barry Manilow dates. Manilow was very hot so we knew this amounted to three home runs. The only potential problem we saw was, that in addition to Fresno and Anaheim, which were fine, Manilow was also going to play San Francisco, a territory essentially owned by impresario Bill Graham. Bill had become a force to be reckoned with in the '60s and had firmly established San Francisco as his territory. In the mid-'60s, Graham took an old former dance hall and roller rink called the Fillmore and turned it into the core of an entertainment empire. Everyone in the business knew that if you tried to put on a concert in the Bay areas without his approval or participation he would put up a free concert at the same time and bury you. I called him.

"Bill, I've got Manilow for three dates. Would you be interested in co-producing the San Francisco date with us?"

He laughed. "Hell no. Manilow's a giant pain in the ass. He's all yours. But if you want to bring him on up it's okay with me."

Notwithstanding Graham's assessment of Barry Manilow, we were excited to have the dates and booked him into the beautiful Opera House in downtown San Francisco. As we expected, all three dates sold out immediately and Willie and I were counting our money. Little did we know how accurate Graham had been about Manilow and what problems he would cause us.

A half hour before the doors opened for the San Francisco show, Manilow walked out on the stage with a sour look on his face. I had heard his sound check had not gone well and someone warned me he was on the warpath. As he surveyed the Opera House he shook his head like a captain deciding whether to take his ship into choppy waters.

"I'm not going on."

I did a double take. "I beg your pardon?"

"I'm not going on. The front row is too close to the stage. It won't work for me."

I had a slightly panicked meeting with his manager and road manager and they said he wasn't joking. I quickly gathered the usher staff and ordered that the front row be reconfigured. The doors opened a half hour late and I breathed a sigh of relief when none of the fans mutinied.

It's always dangerous to open the doors late when you have a mob of kids outside. Sometimes it's catastrophic. Several years later at a Who concert in Cincinnati, the promoters horribly botched their crowd management by opening the doors late to a concert that featured what was then called "festival seating," another name for first come, first served. When the doors were finally flung open, the mad rush to get closest to the stage resulted in a horrific tangle and fatal crush of people. Eleven kids were killed and scores of fans were injured.

Another problem promoters had with rock acts in the '70s was their prima donna attitudes, along with their money and time-wasting ego trips. Once I promoted a concert for Donovan. It was a pretty large venue, and just before the concert was to start, Donovan's father approached me. He was an aging hippy in a florid print caftan.

"You'll have to turn the air conditioning off." I looked at him like he was insane. With thousands of kids inside the Anaheim Convention Center, the heat would have been unbearable with no air moving. I just stared at him.

"Donovan can hear the air conditioner. That's why you have to shut it off." I shook my head. "Nine thousand kids in here and you say he can hear the air conditioner? No way, pal." I walked away.

Often, many acts would order everyone out of the building during their sound checks—and that usually included the building manager and his staff. It was incredibly arrogant and inconvenienced many people, but the self-absorbed musicians just didn't care. I found it ridiculous that these egomaniacs had buildings cleared just so they could test their microphones. These sound checks often caused the doors to be opened late and that always had me worried about crowd control. (The latest bit of ego gone wild I've heard in recent years is that certain artists, when rehearsing with a symphony orchestra, have forbidden the musicians from making eye contact with them. Build a bridge and get over it!)

Although the Fresno date went fine, Willie and I noticed how unhappy Manilow's crew was. They gossiped incessantly about him and you could see how uncomfortable and downright afraid they were. I've always maintained you can tell the quality of an executive by the people around them, and for Manilow that did not say a lot about him. As a musician I respected him, but if he was trying to lead by example he was a miserable failure.

The next night in Anaheim looked like it would be a good concert. I was very familiar with the Convention Center and we had sold 9,000 seats. Because the Convention Center was an oval, when the performer came out, some of the audience on the edges would get a look at their back. Manilow took one look at it and had a fit. He walked onto the stage and ordered us to move every person who would have a view of his back when he made the fifty-foot walk from the wings to center stage. Someone determined there were 276 offending patrons.

I told Manilow and his management there was nothing we could do. Manilow disagreed, contending that if he wanted it it would happen.

"What the hell do you want me to do?" I asked. "Have 276 people stand around and wait until you get on stage?"

"Yes," he said.

This really pissed me off and we got into a screaming match. I'm usually a calm guy but something about his arrogance just set me off. Maybe it was acceding to the silly demands of high maintenance rock stars over the years, I don't know, but I laid into him. In the end, I calmed down and allowed his management to direct the ushers to take those 276 paying fans out of their seats until the star made his entrance. Once Manilow was on stage, the poor folks were shown back to their seats. It was absolutely ridiculous. After that concert Willie and I vowed never to deal with Mr. Manilow again.

In the concert business, concert buyers also have to kiss the butts of the agents, because it's the agents who assign the promoter different acts. They tend to treat promoters like second class citizens, often acting with arrogance because they know you really need them. I also know for a fact that there are agents who have been bought off by promoters. Another worry is that if you piss off an agent who reps big names it can cost you, because they'll tend to cut you off. That happened to me and Willie one time.

We bought the band Journey from the agency ICM for three dates and turned around and spent $17,000 to promote the concert. Then the band cancelled. On top of that they didn't even pay us back for the advertising. We never made a stink with ICM because we were afraid they would pull the plug on us and not sell us any dates for other big artists they represented. So if you ever see Journey tell them they still owe me $17,000!

In the fall of 1974 I got a call to audition for host of a new game show that had what sounded to be one of the best hooks I'd ever heard of. It was called *The Diamond Head Game* and was to be shot in Hawaii. The set was to be poolside at a hotel and the background was the breathtaking scenery of Hawaii. The hook, as the producers boasted, was that the set designer was God. My agent, Noel Rubaloff, offered to arrange the audition, then warned me,

"I'll set this up, but I don't think you should get involved with these guys."

"Why not?"

"Ed Fishman and Randy Freer, these guys were cue card holders. They've had one semi-successful show (called *Dealer's Choice* and shot in Las Vegas), but that's it. Bob, I really don't know if they know what they're doing."

"I'll take my chances, Noel. I can always say no."

I went over to the offices of their production company, Fishman-Freer, and got a tour of the mocked-up set they'd created. Laid out on the floor of the hallway and offices were large cutouts representing the islands of Hawaii. So far it looked pretty silly and the briefing I received left me wondering about their sanity.

"Okay, Bob," began one of the associate producers, "you'll ask the contestants questions, and for each new set of questions, you'll jump to the next island."

"Jump?"

"Yes."

"Literally jump?" I asked, not sure I'd heard it right.

"Yes, literally jump. Then you'll...."

"You want me to physically leap from island to island?" I was trying to picture myself bounding like a gazelle, on national television, across a set of multi-colored plywood islands.

"Why can't I just walk between them?"

"Because... there's water between them. The Pacific Ocean."

"Well, not on the set, surely."

The young associate producer was looking taxed. "No, of course not. The water's figurative."

"Figurative water...."

"Yes, figurative water."

"Can I figuratively jump?"

"No, I'm sorry. You have to jump." Then, as if offering me good news, he said, "But only one island at a time. You'll be asking questions between jumps."

I gave up. "Oh, sure, in that case...."

Bill Hart of Columbia Television and Wes Harris of NBC's owned and operated stations showed up for the audition and were standing nearby. I turned to them and they seemed as skeptical as I was. I thought the idea and execution seemed like a fiasco waiting to happen. We did a run-through and I was absolutely certain my lack of enthusiasm showed through. On the drive home I was torn between missing out on a potential opportunity and relief that I didn't get it. I figured I would never hear from them again. A few days later Noel called and, to my utter shock, told me I'd been offered the hosting job. He said they had actually gotten a thirteen-week commitment from NBC for both day and night time airings. Against Noel's recommendation to walk away, I considered the money, which was pretty decent. After talking it over for a few minutes I made up my mind.

"Noel," I said, "I'm going to Hawaii."

The first glitch surfaced a few days later when the producers told me I was to have a co-host, a very pretty brunette named Jane Nelson. The problem was Jane Nelson was known as a model. She had been the model on several shows over the previous few years, including Fishman and Freers' other show *Dealer's Choice*, a Barris show called *Treasure Hunt*, and a *Newlywed Game* "tribute," *The Neighbors*. One thing I learned years before, in Hollywood you have to protect your position because that's all you've got. Once someone starts chipping away at where you are you can begin a downward slide that is exceptionally hard to counteract. Although the last iteration of *The Newlywed Game* had ended the year before, I was only thirty-six years old and looking forward to many more years in the business. It wasn't that I didn't respect or like Jane, it wasn't personal at all, but I couldn't accept her as an equal without hurting myself. I put my foot down. I told the producers that Jane would either be the model or she'd be the sole host of the show. The Jane issue went away very fast and she was set as the model, that is, my "Vanna." I found out later that Jane and producer Ed Fishman were an item. They eventually got married, had kids and are still together.

We flew to Hawaii to begin production and drove to the hotel where the show would be shot. The first thing I noticed was that the hotel was at the opposite end of the island from the actual Diamond Head, which is a few miles southeast of Honolulu and dominates the skyline on Waikiki Beach. We were in Kuhuku, on the north end or windward side of the island. It was also the tough part of the island of Oahu, a gang ridden "bush" enclave where haoles (a.k.a. howlies, a.k.a. Caucasians) were not particularly welcome. When we checked in we were warned not to leave the grounds of the hotel at night. One of our young assistants, Riley Carsey, the son of future mega TV producer Marcy Carsey, went to a Laundromat with his girlfriend wearing a T-shirt that proclaimed "Hurray for Haole-wood!" and was accosted by local thugs. Had it not been for the intervention of an old local woman he probably would have been beaten to a pulp.

I had mistakenly assumed that because we were going to tape the show on Oahu we would have the activities and sights of Honolulu at our fingertips. What we had was Kuhuku and it was depressing. I went to a local movie theater a few days after I arrived and noticed rats crawling across exposed pipes overhead. I kept bracing for Willard to drop into my popcorn. At 3:30 one afternoon I saw two local girls screaming at each other. It escalated to hair pulling, then ended up in a full scale punch-fest, with several men required to pull them apart. And that was just the hotel lobby.

Nowhere was safe. I was in the bar one night and watched a huge, drunken local try to bully his way in, only to be stopped by the equally gigantic bouncer. They had words and the drunk left. But not for long. He went out to his car, got his gun, came back and ended the discussion with a bang. The cops took the murderer away and the hotel began looking for another doorman. It was a lovely, restful place.

I had a talk with the hotel manager and asked him why a Vegas hotel chain would buy a hotel in Hawaii. A seasoned hotel pro, the manager told me his chain made their acquisition expecting gambling to be approved on the islands. Legal gambling to this day has never been approved in the state. Had his chain done their homework they would have found that Hawaii's vice was tightly controlled by a mix of ethnic crime bosses. All gambling, prostitution, numbers, drugs and even the "enforcement" of laws regarding the aforementioned were in the grip of organized crime, and there was no way they were going to relinquish any of that to a pack of haole casino owners.

A day before we were to begin production I happened by an interesting scene. Ed Fishman was at a table near the set and was arguing with the man sitting across from him. Fishman was screaming and pounding the table. The other man was completely calm. Perhaps the pair of 350-pound Samoans standing behind him with their arms crossed had something to do with his demeanor. Turns out the man was the rep from the local stage hand's union. He won the dispute.

One of the biggest problems we had with the show was finding contestants. In L.A. you have an endless pool of people, given the population and constant stream of tourists. In Hawaii, particularly the north side of Oahu, finding people was no easy task. To make matters worse, our show burned through a massive number of contestants because we taped six shows a day and needed eight people per show. Finding 48 people per day taxed our contestant coordinator, Richard Clark. An Aussie, Richard was a flamboyant guy who wore yellow platform shoes.

Yours truly with the lovely Jane Nelson on the *Diamond Head Game*.

The Money Volcano on the *Diamond Head Game*.

He was hilarious and never seemed to let anything get him down. Richard worked very hard to find people, and when he couldn't find enough tourists (our preferred contestant), he would accost locals at stores, restaurants and even on the street and convince them to come on the show. Years later, Richard worked with me in Branson and Nashville on a live game show. He's still one of my closest friends—I was honored to be the best man at his wedding.

On the first day of the shoot I walked out the back of the hotel to the set and came upon a very odd scene. All of the members of the production, from tech guys to the producers, were standing solemnly around the pool, heads bowed, while a Catholic priest in a Hawaiian shirt and clerical collar blessed our production. I found out that none of the locals would work until the set was blessed. It's too bad NBC didn't send a mid-level exec to include a blessing of future ratings. When the priest was done, a local shaman gave it the official Hawaiian blessing. The blessing was probably a good thing because earlier that morning our producers, Fishman and Freer, had been thrown from a catamaran and nearly died. I guess the gods were warning them. Perhaps the gods had an inkling how bad the show was going to be and took a shot at putting Fishman and Freer out of their future misery.

The show was shot outside by the hotel pool. The set consisted of four islands (there are actually eight islands in the chain, though only six are open to tourists) and the "Money Volcano." The game began with two contestants standing on each island. After answering a series of questions, one contestant from each island would be eliminated leaving a representative from that island to go to the next round. Then the four island representatives would alternate answering questions and "climb Diamond Head." Actually, it was only three steps, but whoever remained, after the others were eliminated by wrong answers, got a chance to enter the Money Volcano.

Announcements repeatedly promised that the Money Volcano was a place "Where there is a fortune in cash and prizes!" The Money Volcano was actually a big plexiglass box that looked like an oversized phone booth. In it was fifty thousand bucks in various denominations of bills and slips of paper with prizes written on them. Once inside the Money Volcano, the contestant would have fifteen seconds to grab as many bills and prize slips as they could. The complication was a large fan underneath the booth whipping the paper around like a tornado. The Money Volcano also posed one problem to the producers that no one ever considered. As soon as you opened the door, the constant breezes pool side would snatch dozens of bills and sail them into the sky. During our run the producers lost at least $1500 getting people in and out of that stupid booth.

For contestants inside the Money Volcano, despite having hundreds of "opportunities" whirling around you, it was still pretty hard to grab any of the slips or bills. Another problem was that, mixed in with the various denominations of bills, there were also a sizable number of two-dollar bills which might later present a setback for the contestant. Once they'd managed to hang on to as many bills and prize slips as they could in the fifteen seconds, the producers would then take the slips and bills and separate five from the pile. These would represent the contestant's five chances at either more cash, a $5,000 prize package (a trip or furniture) and possibly an exciting grand prize. As I turned each bill or slip over, the first three bills were worth $100 and the slips represented prizes. The fourth slip or bill was the prize package, and the fifth was the grand prize. The contestant could stop at any time and decide to keep their cash and prizes, because if I turned the next one over, and it was a two-dollar bill, they would lose everything.

It was a tough system but the producers knew it severely limited the number of grand prizes they might have to award. With hundreds of bills in the Volcano they were pretty confident that a prize slip with a really valuable prize would not be grabbed, and if so, a two-dollar bill would very likely end up in the pile before it. And if it didn't, it was perhaps more likely a contestant would chicken out before it was drawn. So confident were they that they went out and dropped 40,000 bucks on a new Mercedes as the grand prize. Such a lavish prize gave the show more credibility, and the producers were pretty certain that their "investment" would never have to be paid out. Forty grand was a huge risk for them in 1975—in many parts of the country you could buy a helluva house for that much.

They printed a special bill with a picture of the Mercedes, threw it in with the rest of the bills, then crossed their fingers. The grand prize was ballyhooed on the show teasers and the taping day arrived where the Merc was the big prize. The first contestant to have shot at the car was a guy in a goofy safari outfit. Safari Guy went into the Money Volcano and came out with his wad of bills. A production assistant straightened the pile and got it ready to hand to me after the commercial. During the commercial break, just before I was to count out Safari Guy's five bills and slips, I was taken aside by one of the producers. He looked stricken.

"What's wrong," I asked.

"He's got the damn car. The car slip, it's in his pile."

We looked discreetly over at Safari Guy. He seemed completely oblivious to what that special little colored slip at the bottom of his pile represented. I couldn't believe the luck.

"No shit?"

My producer looked at me like I was about to carry a state secret behind enemy lines.

"Whatever you do," he said through clenched teeth, "do not let him have that car!"

I went back over to Safari Guy and we came out of the break. I picked up the pile of bills and pulled out the first one, hoping the guy would win at least a hundred or two before he froze up. On the first pull he won a hundred.

"Okay, you've won a hundred dollars. Are you sure you want to take another chance and risk losing it?"

The guy looked into the audience, presumably to find his wife. He nodded. I pulled out the next bill and he won another hundred. I looked off camera and saw Fishman and Freer both visibly rattled.

"You're up two hundred dollars. Why don't you quit now while you're ahead?"

Safari Guy stayed the course. "No, I'll go for it."

I pulled out the next bill, now hoping for the producer's sake it would be a two. Safari Guy won another hundred. Now he was in line for the $5,000 prize suite. Truth was, that was full retail. The producers, with endorsements and discounts likely paid a whole lot less than five large for that prize.

"You've won 300. Are you willing to take a chance and lose it all?"

He nodded vigorously. "I want to go on."

The producers held up a hastily scrawled sign that Safari Guy couldn't see. It instructed me to offer him a new kitchen. I did and he still wanted to go on. Another sign quickly came up.

"Okay, I will offer you, on top of the new kitchen, a brand new bedroom set!"

The audience shrieked their approval. But Safari Guy was steadfast. "No, I'll keep going. Let's see what it is."

One bad actor with two great actors—Jerry House and Ron Kuhlman during the shooting of *The Brady Brides* for NBC.

NBC PUBLICITY PHOTO

I pulled out the slip and it was NOT a two-dollar bill. The man had just won the $5,000 prize and was one piece of paper away from costing the producers a very expensive car. I looked over at Fishman and Freer and could see they were ready for defibrillators. They held up another sign. I looked Safari Guy in the eye and oozed as much compassion for him as I could muster. "I really don't want to see you lose everything. I'll tell you what, just to make it interesting, I'm prepared to give you the kitchen and the bedroom set. But on top of that, I'll even throw in all the money you have in your hand!"

The crowd went crazy and now the guy was squirming. It was a tough decision. For him, he could still lose it all. He didn't know he really couldn't lose.

His lips tensed and he looked to the audience. He sighed, then he slowly shook his head. "I'll go for it." I knew Fishman and Freer would survive the loss of the car, but now it was a test of wills. I had to see

NBC PUBLICITY PHOTO

My kids told me never to act, but I tried it anyway. On the set of *Rip Tide* with Gene Rayburn, Thom Bray, Perry King and Joe Penny.

what this guy would do. A shakily held up sign gave me my final card to play. I paused for effect.

"We're down to it now. With this next piece of paper you will either win the car . . . or lose all your money, the bedroom set, the kitchen, and all that cash, all together worth many, many thousands of dollars. Okay, one last chance. I'm authorized to give you one more thing . . . not only all the other prizes and the money in your hand, we will give you an entire living room suite!"

The audience screamed at him to "Take it! Take it!" I watched him scan the crowd for the green light from wifey. If she nodded yes we were screwed. It was a lot to risk, and he had no idea the car was at the bottom of the pile. He would have to be completely nuts to go for it. He made eye contact with his wife but I couldn't tell what the verdict was. He opened his mouth.

"I'll go for it!"

Shit.

Fishman and Freer slumped as if the doctor had just given them a week to live. I pulled the slip and that 40,000-dollar Mercedes-Benz was driven away by the first contestant to vie for it.

We shot six shows a day and every day, without fail, it would rain about noon. Rain in Hawaii is pretty gentle and like clockwork. Despite the rain, we never broke stride in shooting. The only thing that initially jeopardized our production schedule was not a natural occurrence. Before we began production we noticed that during run-throughs, every fifteen minutes or so, big helicopters churned past from the military base on top of the island. Ed Fishman went to a cocktail party the day before production began and met a General Brooks, the man in charge of the helicopters. Ed asked him if he could reroute the choppers, which Brooks gladly agreed to do. On the first day of taping, a huge transport chopper began flying in circles nearby, obliterating our audio. Fishman went berserk, grabbed the phone by the pool and got Brooks on the horn. Within minutes, almost like magic, the big chopper made a hasty exit.

After taping thirteen weeks of shows (which only took a few weeks) the format was revamped to cut the number of contestants to six and reduce the dollar value of the prizes. I knew it was the beginning of the end. Fishman and Freer were losing money at a prodigious rate and had to trim the fat. Unfortunately, the show was doomed from the start, mainly because it was a weak concept. They eventually went into panic mode and decided we should tape even more shows in a shorter time frame and knock the prizes down to the bare minimum.

One of the prizes was a "trip" to Marina Del Rey, a lovely upscale community just a few miles south of LAX. I put quotes around the word trip because, given that we were in Hawaii, and while the prize included hotel, dinners and a limo, when our announcer Jim Thompson rattled off what was included, as he got to the last three words he dropped his voice and threw away "airfare not included" faster than an auctioneer. Now our prizes were sounding like some time share scam.

In a dying gasp to save money, Fishman and Freer had us taping fifty-six shows in eight days, up from our normal forty-eight. They also made short shrift of the Days of Mercedes. In the end the most lavish prizes were sets of decorator bricks. By September of that same year, *The Diamond Head Game* sank slowly into the Pacific. Fishman and Freer nearly lost their asses and *The Diamond Head Game* almost ruined the careers of Columbia's Bill Hart and NBC's Wes Harris. As for me, I was already on to my next show.

The Beatles • Mick Jagger • Cary Grant
Merle Haggard • Dolly Parton • David
Letterman • The Rolling Stones • The
Beach Boys • Ike and Tina Turner • Leeza
Gibbons • Jerry Lewis • Gene Autry
Roy Rogers • Monty Hall • Roy Orbison
Buddy Hackett • Barbara Mandrell

THE GREATEST

ON MARCH 8, 1971, a prize fight was held at Madison Square Garden. No ordinary contest, this one was billed by its promoters as The Fight of the Century. It pitted reigning heavyweight champ Joe Frazier against arguably the greatest boxer of all time, Muhammad Ali. There had been an enormous amount of controversy surrounding the fight, starting in 1967 when Ali protested the war in Vietnam and refused to be inducted into the Army. He was subsequently stripped of his title and given a five-year sentence. Although his conviction was overturned by the Supreme Court in 1970, his title was gone. Meanwhile, Ali's childhood friend, Jimmy Ellis, had taken the title away from Jerry Quarry in 1968, only to lose it to Frazier in the fifth round of their title bout in February 1970. From that day the showdown between Frazier and Ali was on.

Just before that first fight in 1971, Ali had predicted Frazier would go down in six. Instead, Frazier showed what he was made of and went the full fifteen rounds, retaining his title by a decision. In 1973, Frazier lost that title in Jamaica to a young boxer named George Foreman. With that defeat, any Ali/Frazier rematch lost a bit of its sparkle since it was no longer for the title. But the pride of two great pugilists was a heady inducement, and fans were transfixed when Frazier and Ali met for the second time. Having recovered his chops after the four-year layoff, this time Ali was the one who took it by a decision.

In late October, 1974, Ali was in Kinshasa, Zaire, for the "Rumble in the Jungle," where he would face the heavyweight champ of the world, George Foreman, in an attempt to take back his title. In workouts prior to the fight, the hulking Foreman was observed laying jackhammer blows on a heavy bag. Speculation raged that Ali was over the hill and his younger and stronger opponent just might devastate him. But once in the ring, Ali's experience shone through. By allowing his opponent to deplete his energy by raining relentless ineffectual body blows, Ali out-strategized the powerful Foreman. After patiently waiting until the younger man wore himself out, Ali went to work. In the eighth round, Ali sent the exhausted Foreman to the canvas, took back the title that had been stripped seven years before and set the stage for a rematch with Frazier. And this time the title was on the line.

The first Ali/Frazier fight in 1971 was historical from another standpoint. Prior to it, boxing promoters employed closed-circuit television to bring fights to small venues like movie theaters and banquet halls. Jerry Perenchio had a bigger vision and was the first to bid seven figures for the closed-circuit rights to a fight. His grand scheme was to forget the little venues and to put the fights into big houses, like arenas and stadiums. In the cities or territories where he didn't promote the fight he sold the rights to local promoters. I knew that Jerry had not only teamed up with Norman Lear to syndicate Lear's wildly successful TV shows, like *All In The Family*, but they had also formed a partnership to finance other ventures. I called in 1975 to see if they would be interested in setting up a concert promotion wing with me. Jerry countered my proposition by asking if I would like to be involved in promoting the upcoming Ali/Frazier fight to be held in the Philippines. They were actively trying to secure the closed-circuit rights to the third fight and the offer was too good to pass by.

Because of some of the key players involved, the Nation of Islam's Herbert Muhammad, and the irrepressible Don King, the behind-the-scenes sparring was almost as compelling as the main fight itself. The wrestling match between King and Muhammad over control of Ali was intense, and I was to see glimpses of it, as well as the stakes involved. Initially, Jerry made a deal with Herbert Muhammad for the full closed-circuit rights to the fight. He dispatched a friend named Zack to Chicago to deliver a check in the amount of seven figures to Muhammad. When Zack arrived at O'Hare he was met by one of Muhammad's men. When he tried to hand over the sizable check he was told the rights had been sold to Don King, but Jerry and Lear could have the rights to four states: California, Nevada, Texas and Louisiana. They had little choice but to take the new deal.

Such an epic fight needed a title, so it was dubbed "The Thrilla in Manila." Given that it was in a foreign country, complete with a huge time difference—a whole different day, not to mention spread over three times zones in U.S. venues—our work was cut out for us. Jerry had a great team, including his business affairs man, Alan Horne. Alan had also owned a chain of karate schools. He went on to form the extremely successful Castle Rock Entertainment, then became chairman and CEO of Warner Bros. Perenchio also hired famous odds maker Jimmy "The Greek" Snyder as our PR guy. We immediately began booking large venues for the fight. As was Jerry's custom, in cities where we would not be presenting the match, we sold the rights to other promoters.

Soon after we began arranging telecast locations, I got a call from Jerry.

"Whatever you do, don't book this thing into the Forum."

The Forum in Inglewood was a large arena and would have been perfect. But there was one problem—it was owned by Jack Kent Cooke. Jerry and Cooke had a long term feud going and Jerry refused to do business with him. I'm not sure what had caused the bad blood between them but I believe it had to do with bidding for other rights. I followed Jerry's lead and concentrated on places like the L.A. Sports Arena and the Universal Amphitheater. But Cooke was pretty crafty and began advertising that the fight would indeed be at the Forum. At first, Jerry was furious that Cooke would try and slide one in like that. But in the end, Jerry capitulated, seeing the value of going with a large place that would easily fill up versus holding on to an old grudge with his Canadian nemesis.

One of our biggest coups—booking the Louisiana Superdome—almost didn't happen. The Superdome was brand new and had not yet had a closed-circuit fight. The Superdome people agreed to the date, but then told us we had to clear it with officials of the State of Louisiana who, in turn, informed us we were required to have a Louisiana boxing license. Obviously we didn't have time to apply and go through all the red tape so the alternative was to partner with a local who had one. The problem was that the only guy who had one happened to be in prison. So our partner in Louisiana for the Thrilla in Manila was a convict. Once the deal was done, someone warned us that Superdome security was so porous we should expect at least 5,000 people to sneak in—and they did.

Given what a legend Ali has since become, it might be hard to believe that it was actually hard to get publicity for the fight. Jimmy The Greek wasn't much help and we were trying to devise ways to get some ink in the press. It was decided that since the fight was 8,000 miles away we would hold a local event, a workout for both fighters. We set up a public workout at the Plaza near the Century City shopping mall. Ali checked into the Century Plaza Hotel with his entourage, taking an entire floor. On the afternoon of the workouts Jerry came by the Plaza and said, "Let's take a ride."

We drove up into the hills above Sunset and arrived at the home of former football great, Jim Brown. Inside was Brown, a small man from Ali's camp, and, to my surprise, George Foreman. The subject of the meeting turned out to be an exploration of the possibility of another Foreman/Ali fight. I knew that there was no love lost between Jerry and Don King and I quickly realized there was no one there representing King's interests. At the end it was agreed that the meeting was to be kept quiet from anyone who wasn't there.

A few hours later I went to Ali's suite at the Plaza for another meeting. There, in the background, was the small man from the earlier meeting at Jim Brown's. When he saw me he looked stricken and began to sweat profusely. Apparently he didn't know I had anything to do with Ali. As the meeting progressed he sidled up to me.

"If you tell anyone I was at that meeting," he whispered, "they'll kill me."

Needless to say I told no one and the proposed fight never happened. The Thrilla in Manila took place on October 1, 1975, and was a success. Jerry and Lear made some money and I got a real education, not only in large event promotion, but also in running such an event many times zones away and, in particular, dealing with the strange world called boxing. Oh, and perhaps my biggest thrill was that I got Muhammad Ali's autograph, which I treasure to this day.

Some years before we promoted the Thrilla in Manila, I met a guy named Howard Rose, a fledgling agent at Perenchio Artists. A protégé of Jerry Perenchio, Howard walked, talked and dressed like Jerry and even went so far as to obtain Jerry's old phone number. During the planning for the fight, Jerry hooked me back up with Howard, who had since moved into artist management. Howard had discovered a young English singer and piano player down at the Troubadour in 1970 and signed him. Within a few years, Elton John was one of the biggest acts in pop music.

From the time I met Howard Rose I thought he was arrogant, but since he worked for Jerry Perenchio I tolerated him and always treated him graciously. When Howard offered us an Elton John date I was slightly surprised. I suppose my being in business with his mentor swayed his decision. The date was set for October 2, 1975, in Las Vegas at the Convention Center. What would later prove to be a problem was that Elton's contract required all seats in the house to be reserved, yet the Convention Center had never done a reserved seat concert. Prior to this concert you either bought an upstairs ticket or a downstairs ticket. We assumed the management of the facility would brief all of their people on the new wrinkle.

When the tickets went on sale they sold through quickly and we chalked up what we thought would be a big win. About three o'clock on the day of the concert I was standing in front of the Convention Center speaking to someone about a last minute detail when a teenage kid came up and asked me a question that collapsed my world.

"Mr. Eubanks? Excuse me, but which of these tickets is real?"

The kid handed me two tickets for the same seat. I felt dizzy. About five hours to show time and I had just been made aware of a counterfeit ticket scam. Fake tickets are like cockroaches: if you see one you can assume there are hundreds, if not thousands more. This scenario is what every concert promoter fears. In a festival seating situation it would be possible to allow some fakes to get by without undue strain on the facility. In this case, with all reserved seats, there was zero margin for error.

After closely examining the tickets we were amazed at what good fakes they were, but there was a tiny difference: the letters of the seat locations on the real tickets were raised slightly, and by rubbing your finger across them you could feel the difference. We immediately had a meeting with the facility staff and instructed them to carefully rub each ticket before accepting it. The crowd began pouring in. As the place filled up one of Elton's PR guys, a pipsqueak of a man, announced to me and the event staff that he would not allow anyone to take pictures during the performance and that we would be confiscating cameras. I told him that he was "one brick shy of a load" and that we would do no such thing. So he proceeded to mount a one-man campaign to banish all cameras from the house. As he went off to grab people's cameras, another minor disaster was in the making. The event staff—not used to the reserved seating concept—got things tangled up. After a promoter's rendition of a Chinese Fire Drill that went on for nearly two hours, we finally got everyone into their assigned seats. In addition, we confiscated several hundred phony tickets. Pretty soon the Convention Center was smelling more like a Pot Smokers Convention than an Elton John concert. As we neared the final few moments to show time I breathed a sigh of relief that disaster had been averted.

Meanwhile, Elton's PR guy was roaming the crowd of 9,000, trying to confiscate cameras and not having much luck. As the concert got underway he returned to Elton's dressing room, disheveled and flustered after being shoved around by angry patrons who were not going to let some snippy little twerp grab their cameras. After composing himself he emerged from Elton's dressing room with a new bomb:

"Elton won't come out of his dressing room if he sees a policeman in uniform."

"You've gotta be kidding me!" was my reply. "Would you repeat that?"

"Elton hates cops and doesn't want to see any police uniforms when he comes out. If he does he'll stay in his dressing room."

As standard concert security I had arranged with the Las Vegas Police Department to provide a number of off-duty officers to work the event. Of course they were wearing uniforms because a uniformed presence can stop most problems before they start. I had not only gotten to know some of them before the concert, but had also heard the L.V.P.D. had some pretty good ol' cowboys on the force, so I was fairly sure they weren't going to take shit from anyone. I thought about it for two seconds and followed the PR guy back into Elton's dressing room.

"Here are your two choices," I announced to everyone in the room. "You get the cops in uniform...or cops nude. Either way they stay." I figured neither Elton nor his management wanted him upstaged by naked law enforcement officers. The PR guy and Elton huddled in the corner with tennis star Billie Jean King, who was part of the entourage. There was a great deal of hand waving, but the concert went on with clothed cops. For all of our headaches we made a grand total of $5200. Oh, and the counterfeit ticket perpetrators were nabbed—turns out they were some U.N.L.V. students who might have had promising careers in the graphic arts had they not been arrested for forgery.

The beauty of shooting game shows is that you can produce a whole season in a month or so. So when we were coming to the end of what would be the only season of *The Diamond Head Game*, I was already casting about for something to replace it in my schedule. One day I got a call from Steve Friedman. We worked together on *The Newlywed Game* in the early '70s. Friedman told me he was involved in putting together a new game show with Bill Naud. I didn't know much about Naud, although I heard he had directed some films in the '60s. One he did in 1966, called *Hot Rod Hullabaloo*, was the first film for four-time Oscar nominated actress Marsha Mason.

I went to their production office in Toluca Lake and the first thing I noticed was that Friedman was spouting all sorts of New Age-speak. When I met Naud I realized why. Naud was one of the most unusual men I have ever met. He epitomized the clichéd Californian, a person not only at one with the cosmos, but who actually had a mantra and knew kundalini from fettuccine. It's not as kooky now, but then he was seen as a bit "out there."

The concept for the show included two contestants and six celebrity panelists. I would read the first line of a rhyming phrase and the contestants would write down a line they felt matched up with it. For instance, if the line I read ended in the word "play" then they might write down a sentence that finished the rhyme using the word "okay" or "day." Each contestant would choose a celebrity "poet" to finish the line. If the celeb's line matched theirs they got a point; if it matched their opponent's line, that person scored. Three points won them the round and $250. Winning two rounds gave them the match and the chance to move to the grand prize round. For the grand prize the contestant picked one of the celebrities as a partner. I would give the contestant a two-line rhyme and they would write down three possible rhyming words to end it. They would then have thirty seconds to repeat the couplet as many times as they could, during which time their celebrity partner would start winging out rhyming words. If the celeb got one of the contestants' choices, the player got $1,000. Two words were worth $2,000 and all three words gave them the full $5,000 grand prize. *Rhyme and Reason* was essentially a clone of the time tested *Match Game*.

The format allowed the celebs many chances to flash their wit and get lots of laughs. It helped having a lively cast of panelists. Comedian Nipsey Russell was our sole regular panelist, with semi-regular celebri-

Rhyme and Reason—Love the sideburns!

During the shooting of *Rhyme and Reason* pilot, from left to right panel includes Nipsey Russell, Lee Meriwether, Richard Dawson and Jaye P. Morgan.

One of thirteen cashmere sweaters Mark Goodson bought for me to host *Trivia Trap*.

ABC PUBLICITY PHOTO

ties such as Pat Harrington, Jr., Shari Lewis, Jaye P. Morgan, M*A*S*H's Jamie Farr and Laugh-In alums, actor Charlie Brill, his wife, actress Mitzi McCall, and JoAnne Worley.

We did a run-through for ABC at a church in the Valley which went well. To get us into production, Naud brought in pros I had worked with, like producer Walt Case and director John Dorsey, both from *The Newlywed Game*. When we began production, the first day's audience didn't respond like we had hoped. They were lackluster and didn't laugh at the right moments. We weren't sure what the problem was. This was when Naud proposed one of his odder solutions. Many people in the entertainment business are creative, but also very pragmatic. During our impromptu conference about our audience problem, Naud spoke up.

"I'll go sit down in the studio and work on the audience."

Dorsey looked puzzled. "Sorry?"

"I'll go work on them now."

"But Bill . . . nobody's there."

"Exactly. That's the best time to work on them. Their vibe was wrong. The vibe in the room must be wrong."

"Vibe?" repeated the ever pragmatic Walt Case.

"Yes. I'll go into the studio, sit in the middle and meditate on it. It'll take care of any bad attitudes so they won't return."

Case and Dorsey looked at each other, then at me. I shrugged it off as Naud headed for the studio. Who knows if what he did had any effect, but I can say that the audiences from that point on were great. The show debuted July 7, 1975, and lasted almost exactly a year to the day. On the last day, to use a term Naud might have, there was a really odd vibe in the studio. So much so that as the credits were rolling on the final episode, the celebrity panelists spontaneously began wrecking the set. At first they simply knocked things over, like my podium. But then Charlie, Mitzi, Jaye P. and Pat Harrington really got into it and started tearing things to pieces, ripping up carpet and smashing stuff like drunken fans after a World Cup. I wonder if our theme song, a game show version of metal head/bow hunter Ted Nugent's "Journey To The Center Of Your Mind," might have had some subliminal influence on that.

The way I heard it, the reason our show was cancelled was that Michael Brockman, who was the head of daytime television for ABC, had always taken care of Mark Goodson, the dean of American game show producers. It was well known in the business that if two shows were competing, and one was produced by Goodson, his company always got preferential treatment. Less well known was the fact Goodson hated *Rhyme and Reason* because he thought it was a rip-off of *Match Game*, one of his shows. Furthermore, what really pissed him off was the fact that Richard Dawson, one of his regular panelists on *Match Game*, had done our pilot. When *Rhyme and Reason* was picked up and did bigger numbers than the slower paced *Match Game*, Goodson was furious. About a year later Goodson developed *Family Feud*, which ABC really wanted. The way I heard the story was that Goodson told Brockman he could have *Feud* only if he axed *Rhyme*. So he did, and Dawson had a new job. Of course *Family Feud* has become one of the most successful game shows of all time, a staple for the network and syndication for most of the last twenty-eight years.

For years I could never get an audition with Goodson because he hated Barris as well as despised *Rhyme and Reason*. One night I was at LAX waiting for a plane and ran into Goodson's attorney. I expressed my desire to be able to audition for Goodson. That meeting was fortuitous because a few weeks later I was hired by Mark to do his new show, *Trivia Trap*. The game "Trivial Pursuit" was huge at the time so the Goodson Company developed a show along its lines. Unfortunately, the show had a major hole Goodson refused to acknowledge. In the final bonus round a contestant had to eliminate three wrong answers to get to the right answer. What we all pointed out to him was that if the audience and/or the contestant knew the final answer, getting to the final reveal was a moot point. After the show was cancelled, Goodson took the show to the American Film Institute to do a focus group. The people at AFI told him the same thing we had been saying all along.

One last thing about Mark Goodson. When he hired me for Trivia Trap, I asked him what I should wear. He said, "I'll take care of that." He asked my size and I forgot about it until the day we taped. There, in my dressing room, were thirteen cashmere sweaters from Fred Segal's men's store in Beverly Hills. I loved working for Mark Goodson.

The Beatles • Mick Jagger • Cary Grant
Merle Haggard • Dolly Parton • David
Letterman • The **76**ing Stones • The
Beach Boys • Ike and Tina Turner • Leeza
Gibbons • **TROMBONES** ne Autry
Roy Rogers • Monty Hall • Roy Orbison
Buddy Hackett • Barbara Mandrell

I N LATE 1946, Gene Autry appeared in Hollywood's traditional Christmas Parade. Except for three years during the war, the parade had been a staple of the community since 1928. As the Singing Cowboy rode his horse down Hollywood Boulevard, he heard the children squealing, "Here comes Santa Claus! Here comes Santa Claus!" Gene went home, a melody in his head, along with the opening lyrics provided by the children, and the Christmas classic "Here Comes Santa Claus" was born. Two years later the parade was broadcast for the first time on television.

The parade is a huge draw for Hollywood and features some of its biggest stars. Like the Hollywood sign, the parade was conceived to help boost real estate sales. Of course real estate in Hollywood sold out long ago, but the event remains. The parade is quite lively, with marching bands, classic cars, equestrian teams and, of course, floats. The floats are sponsored by local organizations and corporations, and I was always amused that Fredericks of Hollywood appropriately sponsored the American Lung Association float. The only requirement is that there must be a celebrity on board each float.

A number of people have hosted the parade's telecast. In 1976, when the parade's producers at KTLA were looking for a new host, they came to me. Since I had hosted that year's Rose Parade for the first time, KTLA figured I had some experience doing a parade and would be perfect for the job. They made me an offer, I countered and they choked. We finally worked it out that they would pay me the same I was getting for the Rose Parade.

The Hollywood Chamber of Commerce sponsors the parade and the executive director and honorary mayor of Hollywood, Johnny Grant, is a friend. Johnny was the guy who set the wheels in motion to get me my star on the Walk of Fame. A lovely guy and a real gentleman, Johnny submits parade entrants to the network, which then selects who gets in—and who doesn't. One year, an all gay marching band applied. When the conservative network boys in the Mid-West got wind of the gay musicians they rejected their application. John had the unenviable duty of telling the band they were out. But not to be thwarted, the band simply went away, came back with a new "closeted" name and was allowed in. I can only imagine the look on those network execs faces when the Great American Yankee band came marching by—with the acronym "G.A.Y." boldly stenciled on their tubas.

I was teamed up with actress and former Miss America Lee Meriwether as co-hosts. We did our first telecast together in November, 1977. Over the years we had a lot of things happen that weren't supposed to, and many of them were pretty funny. The famous Crystal Cathedral had a float promoting their spectacular "Glory of Christmas" pageant. The float had an additional feature—an angel suspended from a cable who was supposed to "fly" across Sunset Boulevard as the float motored by underneath. When the time came, my friend, KTLA's parade producer and director Joe Quasarano, said, "Go!"

When the angel missed her cue, Joe yelled into his mike, "Go! Go! Push her!"

The angel crew didn't have the rigging quite right and when they finally got her going, she only went part way down the cable, then only haltingly, and proceeded to flip upside down. With her dress over her head, the audience saw a bit more of the angel than they had bargained for.

Lee was easily flustered by anything that seemed improper. Once, some idiot tossed what appeared to be a spool of thread into the parade's path. A horse got tangled up, panicked, jumped into the crowd, and injured someone. While they were trying to get things back in order, the procession ground to a halt. Parked right in front of us was a high school marching band. Given that they now had the cameras to themselves, the drum major filled the time by performing all manner of amazing antics. As we watched and commented something became pretty clear to both of us, so I wrote Lee a note. "The drum major's fly is open." She blushed,

Lee Meriwether and I during the taping of the Hollywood Christmas Parade.

HCOC / B. LAWRENCE

and shot me a look: Do NOT mention it!!! As soon as the parade got going again, Lee breathed a sigh of relief that I had not commented on the open "barn door." That's when I struck.

"Did you notice the drum major's fly was open?"

Lee turned eight shades of crimson and began to stutter. She couldn't even finish her sentence. I sat there with a contented smile on my face and took a long pause before introducing the next entry. By far, Lee's worst gaffe came when actress Markie Post, star of Night Court, rolled by in a convertible. Lee was supposed to say, "Here's Markie Post, former game show contestant coordinator," a reference to a previous job held by Ms. Post. What Lee said was...well, something else.

Just as she got out "Here's Markie Post, former game show cont..."

the director spoke over her earpiece, causing her to interrupt what she was saying. Unfortunately, she only got out the first syllable of the word contestant, just enough to sound like she had called Markie a four-letter obscenity. The speakers from our broadcast booth were aimed at the parade, and when Markie heard herself described as the "c" word, and by the former Miss America, the look on her face would have topped the mother of all blooper reels. I was absolutely aghast and scribbled a note advising her what had just happened and she laughed, thinking I was joking. But when the calls began streaming in the shit hit the fan. You can imagine Lee's utter embarrassment when KTLA had to issue telegrams to more than 200 affiliates asking them to remove the faux pas. Every year after that, when we would have our pre-parade meeting, to Lee's further embarrassment her tape would be played to huge laughs.

Lee and I had a joke that she knew the stars and I knew their horses. We had a really good rapport and I enjoyed working with her. In August of 1989, KTLA had a party for the sales staff. Prior to the party, the decision had been made to replace Lee. Unfortunately, someone screwed up and invited her to the party. When she arrived to a sea of red faces, some tactless soul dropped the bomb, saying Lee wasn't supposed to be invited because she was going to be fired. It was handled very badly, and Lee was not only crushed but humiliated to boot. I had no early knowledge of her firing and wished that someone had actually thought through how they were going to dismiss her. I am very sorry it was so terribly mishandled.

My new co-host was Leeza Gibbons. Leeza is always a joy to work with, is wickedly funny, never loses her cool, and has also been a very loyal friend. I was a candidate for an Emmy lifetime achievement award, up against local broadcast legend, Dr. George Fischbeck, and a board was convened to hear arguments as to who deserved it. While Leeza and Joe Quasarano waited to give testimony about me, they sat through the presentation for Dr. George and listened to people gush about the elderly TV weatherman and personality. When someone brought up Dr. George's feeble physical condition, particularly his bad heart, Leeza sensed a shift in the board's sympathy. She turned to Joe and, deadly serious, whispered, "Does Bob have any diseases I don't know about?" Fortunately, I did not, but unfortunately, I lost out to Dr. George.

In the early nineties while we were getting ready to broadcast a parade, Leeza and I were approached by Ed McMahon. He was very excited. "When my car passes you, I'm going to have them stop so I can propose to my girlfriend on national television." We thought it was a nice idea so we waited for Ed's car to stop. Then Ed got on one knee in the cramped back of the convertible, proposed as advertised, and we wished them well. And after all that they never did get married.

Eventually, KTLA lost its contract to do the parade, and the party, for us, ended. Now the parade is not shown nationally, but rather over an L.A. station. The only thing I really miss is spending two hours each year sitting next to Leeza Gibbons. Oh, and I miss the money, too.

The Pasadena Tournament of Roses includes, among many festivities, the Rose Bowl and the Rose Parade. I've been doing the Rose Parade every year since 1976. For the ten years prior to my coming on board, Dick Enberg performed the duties. When Enberg was offered a contract with NBC the Rose Parade's producers approached me to host the telecast. It's the granddaddy of all parades. Each year the floats are more spectacular and the parade seems to get bigger and better. There's usually a flyby of some amazing military aircraft, and around a million people line the parade route. It's a lot of fun and very exciting. But of all the floats and marching bands and participants, my heart still belongs to the equestrian units. On New Year's Day, 2004, Stephanie Edwards and I celebrated hosting the Rose Parade telecast for our 25th year together. It was my 28th year doing the show. I am also proud to say that Steph and I have won three Emmys for our coverage of the parade.

Despite being a nationally televised event, and huge business for Pasadena, the Tournament of Roses is an entirely home grown product. Administered by an executive board, it is made up of local people. That most of those people run the gamut from rich to outrageously rich is purely incidental. The people of Pasadena and neighboring San Marino include many captains of industry and lots and lots of old money. To their credit, the event organizers do almost all of the work, including the worst job of all, cleaning up after the horses that make their way down the parade route. I always found it amusing to see a guy cleaning up after Clydesdales, knowing he was probably the CEO of some major company or the heir of an empire builder.

One thing that happens when you get a lot of people together (especially powerful people), is that politics inevitably emerge. The parade has been run for over 100 years and has evolved into a very well oiled

With my Rose Parade partner Stephane Edwards, my dear friend Leeza Gibbons, the Honorary Mayor of Hollywood, Johnny Grant, and my long-time buddy Charlie O'Donnell.

My buddy Stephanie Edwards the day I received my Star on the Hollywood Walk of Fame.

At the Hollywood Christmas Parade with Jimmy Stewart and my co-host, Lee Meriwether.

Miss America never looked better. Myself and Lee Meriwether celebrating the 52nd Annual Hollywood Christmas Parade.

HCOC / B.LAWRENCE

HCOC / B.LAWRENCE

At the Hollywood Christmas Parade with one of my lifetime heroes, Gene Autry.

Promo shot for the Hollywood Christmas Parade with the Grand Marshall, Bob Hope.

HCOC / B.LAWRENCE

machine, complete with severe restrictions, rules and penalties for all participants. If your float breaks down the fine is a cool five grand. The floats must also conform to many design restrictions (including the famous one that anything visible must be made of plant or organic material). Just as extreme is the schedule. One float builder, who had been making floats for the parade for many years, arrived a paltry four minutes late with his floats. He was informed his floats would not be judged. He lost his clients over the flap and never fully recovered from it.

Sometimes the forces at work against the float builders have nothing to do with tournament regulations. One year the floats were nearing completion in the hectic week before the parade. One of the floats featured Missy Piggy and Kermit the frog. To keep an eye on their creations, the people at Henson's company flew a representative out to inspect the float. When the flamboyant little man was taken to the facility where the float was being constructed, he almost had a heart attack.

"Ohmigod!" he shrieked.

"What? What?" asked the panicked float builder.

"You have Kermit playing the banjo with his right hand!"

"Yeah . . . ."

"Everyone knows Kermit is left-handed!"

The float builder apparently did not know that Kermit had a left-handed fan club. The man stared at the nearly completed float not knowing what to do. Then the Henson rep dropped the big bomb. As the crew was applying the zillions of predominantly orange flower petals and crushed botanicals, the rep stormed around the float.

"And everyone knows . . . Miss Piggy HATES orange!"

The float was fixed.

One year Shirley Temple was grand marshal. I went to an equestrian event that was part of the parade and she was there. I was shocked to see she was a heavier chain smoker than any of the guys I ever met in radio. Roy Rogers had grand marshal duties another year, and when the parade went long—and his bladder couldn't take it anymore—he peed into his boot. The world may be changing around us, and although the floats get bigger and better each year, the Rose Parade remains the same, wholesome American institution it has been for over a hundred years.

The promotion and management of artists is an odd business. One of my neighbors in Calabasas, Marty Paich, was a brilliant composer and conductor. He had been the musical conductor on the Glen Campbell show and had produced giants like Ella Fitzgerald and Ray Charles. He went on to conduct scores for many films, including *Dave*, *Pretty Woman* and *The Fugitive*. Marty called and told me his son David had formed a band and was looking for management. According to Marty, David must have inherited his talent because he went on and on about how good he was. David had been making money as a session musician and had formed a group with some other young guys who, again according to Marty, were pretty capable musicians. I told him I was out of the management business but said I would think about what he should do and get back to him. I called my partner Willie Leopold, and we decided Marty should hook his son's band up with the firm of Fitzgerald Hartley.

Though a fairly new company, Larry Fitzgerald and Mark Hartley had a proven record as managers. While at other agencies they had handled artists like Paul McCartney, the Beach Boys, Chicago and Billy Joel. I figured if they signed the newcomers, Marty's son and his buddies would be getting very good representation. Willie called Larry Fitzgerald, told him about the group and asked him if he would at least talk to them. He did and signed them immediately.

Not too long after, in late 1978, the five guys in the band wrote and recorded a song called "Hold The Line." It shot straight up the charts. Toto, as they called themselves, went on to produce a string of hits, including "Rosanna" and "Africa," and became one of the supergroups of the '80s. The punch line to this story is—in the No Good Deed Goes Unpunished Department—after their first hit we called Fitzgerald Hartley and asked to book them for a few dates. They referred us to Toto's agent. The agent flatly informed us that only promoters who had previously dealt with Fitzgerald Hartley would be allowed to book dates for the band. Since we had not dealt with them (in their new Fitzgerald Hartley incarnation) we were left Toto-less. Hey, shit happens.

In that same Unpunished Department I have one more story that comes to mind. When Michael Hill and I were doing *The Tennille Show* he and Walt Case went to a comedy club in Hollywood in search of bright new talent. That night they watched a young comedian do a killer set and came back and raved about him. We immediately booked him for the show. Arsenio Hall did such a great job for us we soon had him back for a second appearance. Years later, when *The Newlywed*

Game was about to return, I called the booker on Arsenio's talk show to get me on to plug it. Turns out their booker was the same one we'd had on *The Tennille Show*. Assuming it would be a slam dunk I was surprised and hurt when I was told I was "not a big enough star" for his night time talk show.

In the late 70s Willie Leopold and I started producing concerts with a company called Crystal Lief Productions. Crystal Lief was run by a very bright young man named Paul Richardson. Since the concert business was very territorial, we often teamed up with promoters who had carved out certain areas, and Paul had established himself in secondary markets like Albuquerque, El Paso and Las Vegas. I liked the secondary markets because the grosses were about the same as the larger markets but the expenses were usually quite a bit lower. Another good thing about smaller markets was that the kids were usually a little bit behind the rest of the world so you could book acts whose popularity may have peaked in the major markets. During that time we were booking a lot of hot acts, including Black Sabbath, Emerson, Lake and Palmer, Fleetwood Mac and the Electric Light Orchestra.

Around 1975 I had hired a young lady named Kim Heier. In the office was an IBM Selectric typewriter that, rugged as it was, Kim managed to break she typed so fast and so furiously. I have never seen anyone type like that. One day I walked in and thought the air conditioner was on—it was just Kim typing. Kim became kind of a miracle worker, performing many duties for me, but her true calling turned out to be settling the box office after concerts.

Settling up after a concert used to be more of an art form than business. Nowadays the big acts all have CPAs who come into the box office and go over everything, but in those days it was the road manager versus the promoter. It consisted of reconciling all the expenses on both sides, that is, the acts and the promoter. After we each submitted our expenses (including the guarantee for the performer) the profit was determined once we knew how much pie was left to cut up. We knew the acts padded their expenses with a lot of phony entries, and admittedly our expenses often had a bit of pork, but in the end it was the way the game was played and everyone usually went home happy.

Kim was our secret weapon in settling the box. There is a lot of give and take and Kim came across as cute and sexy, but she was a formidable opponent. She always struck a hard bargain but no one complained because she did it with such flair and charm. I guess Paul Richardson was even smarter than I first pegged him because he eventually married Kim.

Long before the days when computers and CPAs settled concerts, promoters would sit down with the management of the venue and count all the unsold tickets. The building would then issue the promoter a check. The more tickets left over the smaller the check from the building. The unsold tickets were appropriately called deadwood. One night my partner Mickey Brown was in El Dorado, Arkansas, counting the deadwood. All of the tickets were red. As he counted tickets he suddenly noticed some of those red tickets weren't even from our show. He turned to the box office manager.

"What the hell's going on?"

He just shrugged. "I guess you caught me. So what're you gonna do 'bout it?"

This was right in the middle of good ol' boy country. "Nothing." And that was that.

Concert promotion in the south can be very...interesting. One evening just before a Merle Haggard concert in Monroe, Louisiana, a uniformed police officer strolled in with four other people. There was something not quite right about his expression.

"Can I help you?" I asked.

"Yes. I'm part of the security for the show."

"And who are these people?"

"These are my neighbors."

"Do they have tickets?"

"They don't need tickets."

"Well," I said, "I'm sorry, but they will need tickets."

He smiled. "Not if the show is to go on."

I stared at them for a moment. What could I do? "Have a seat, folks."

In 1978 I was doing a mall show in Paramus, New Jersey, when a young man named Fred Wostbrock approached me and handed me one of the oddest yet most touching gifts I had ever received. It was a collage of my entire career. Such devotion could have been creepy had it been anyone else, but this young man had a quality that was very endearing and I immediately knew he was just terribly enthusiastic and not a nut. It turns out Fred was the ultimate game show aficionado and collected

With my agent Fred
Westbrook and
Charlie O'Donnell
at my Walk of Fame
presentation.

everything he could lay his hands on about game shows. He even went
on to write three books about game shows that are considered by most
to be the definitive books on the subject. Fred also went on to become
my agent. And he has represented me with more passion than anyone
I've ever had.

One of the many things I like about Fred is that he takes it personally
when he doesn't get you the job. Fred and I have a handshake arrangement and his loyalty and talent are incredible. Another thing I admire
about him is that, unlike many agents, he shows a great deal of creativity and drive. While many agents are simply order takers who don't even

try or give up when they encounter a little resistance, Fred comes up with ideas that he translates into work for his clients. Not long ago he knew Jessica Simpson and her husband, Nick Lachey, were becoming popular and read they were going to do a variety show. He made some calls and the next thing I knew he had me booked onto their ABC special. It's thinking like that which has kept me a very busy guy.

I am very grateful for Fred's obsession with game shows. He has not only made many of my biggest deals, he's always available for any friendly advice or counsel. I also owe him a big thank you because many of the photos in this book come from his massive archives. Agents are a dime a dozen, but truly great, dedicated agents like Fred Wostbrock are extremely rare.

Most of the work Fred has lined up for me has been great, but there is one exception and I'll say right off the bat it wasn't Fred's fault. Fred called and said Fox Television was doing an animated show and one of the episodes was a doing a take-off on *The Newlywed Game.*

"All you have to do is ask that famous question 'Where's the strangest place you've ever made whoopee?'" Fred told me. "It's easy money if you're free this afternoon."

I was game and didn't mind poking a little fun at myself so I said sure. That afternoon when I got to the studio they handed me a check and contract and pointed me to the recording booth. Then they handed me the script. My line was pretty simple. "Joseph, where's the strangest place you and Mary have ever made whoopee?" I did the line a few times, gave them some good takes and left. As I was driving down the Ventura freeway suddenly it was like God smacked me upside the head. "Hey stupid! Joseph? Mary?" They were doing a takeoff on the birth of Christ. I had to draw the line.

I got off the first exit and headed back to the studio. I walked in, handed them back the check and their contract, thanked them, and walked out. When the show aired it still had the question but at least it wasn't my voice.

Most people who aren't in the business don't realize how hard it is to find a good agent. Agents understand that (most) clients live and die by what they do for them so it becomes the case of the tail wagging the dog. Even though the agent works for you, technically, as the client you're always waiting to hear what the agent has done for you—or hasn't done.

There's a famous joke everyone who's ever had an agent can relate to. It speaks volumes about how everyone with an agent can get so morbidly obsessed about getting attention from them. The police phoned an actor and gave him the horrific news that, for some reason his agent had come to his home, murdered his wife and burned his house to the ground. The stunned actor's response was, "MY agent came to MY house?" That says it all.

UNDER THE BOARDWALK

I N 1979, I GOT A PHONE CALL from a raspy-voiced little lady in Philadelphia introducing herself as Charlene Trichon. After some preliminary talk, like how she got my number, she got down to business.

"My husband had an idea and I think it would be a great one."

I patiently braced myself.

"I do PR for two local malls. We think you should do *The Newlywed Game* live at our shopping centers."

"What?"

"Would you be interested?"

Do it live? I had no idea what she was talking about. *The Newlywed Game* was a television program.

"I think you're crazy, lady. Do *The Newlywed Game* at a shopping mall? It's a TV show."

"Yes, exactly. It'll be just like TV only without the cameras. It'll work. We'll get an audience, that's not a problem. People will definitely come out to see you."

Now that I'd had ten seconds to ponder it I started to think it might not be so nuts after all. Charlene was very persuasive and, within a few minutes, took me from utter skepticism to actually warming up to the idea. By the end of the call we had an agreement. I would do shows at her two malls in Allentown and Harrisburg, Pennsylvania. Charlene's idea was simple but very smart. Her theory was that of all the people outside of L.A. who couldn't be part of a television audience, many would spark to the idea of being in one in their home town. The only

229

difference was that there would be no cameras. Shopping malls had thousands of customers per day and, according to Charlene, such an event would be a big draw. I thought it just might work.

Charlene flew me out. When we met she reminded me of Joan Rivers, not only in her appearance, but also her go-getter attitude. She came across as a ball of fire, perhaps the most dynamic and aggressive salesperson I have ever met. I was a nervous wreck the afternoon of the first show. The mall had spent a lot of money on advertising and, as the show approached, I was worried that no one would come. I worried unnecessarily. When I walked out onto the stage I was greeted by 5,000 yelling and screaming fans. I was really quite surprised by the turnout and immediately knew we were on to something. The show went great and everyone laughed their heads off. I also laughed—all the way to the bank. At $3,600 for a half hour's work the shows turned out to be some of the easiest money I have ever made. Charlene made a believer out of me.

We knew we were onto to something so Charlene and I made an agreement that she would begin booking me in shopping malls around the country. Over the next seven or eight years she booked me everywhere from Louisiana to California, from the Pacific Northwest to Florida. By 1988 I had played more than 500 malls, bringing *The Newlywed Game* to hundreds of thousands of people. I also became close friends with Charlene and her husband, Larry, and we remain so to this day.

Early on, we set up a system for playing malls that worked for the entire run. Charlene and I would fly to the destination and Dave Kemler, the man responsible for all of the physical elements of the show, would accompany us on the ground. Dave, a hematologist by trade, brought the set and sound system. He always managed to find time away from his real job to assist us in the shows and was so dedicated he once drove from Philly all the way to Denver just to do one show.

Larry Trichon was in the parking lot business in Philadelphia and the nature of that industry brought him in contact with some rather colorful people. In the early spring of 1980, Charlene and Larry invited me to the funeral of a prominent Philadelphia businessman. Although I couldn't attend, I later found out that the dearly departed was none other than Angelo Bruno, boss of the Philadelphia crime family. Known as "The Gentle Don," until his consigliere Anthony "Tony Bananas" Caponigro ordered his "retirement," Bruno's brother-in-law Peter Maggio

BOB EUBANKS ARCHIVE

If you say Bob Eubanks will be at the mall tonight, five people would show up. But Bob Eubanks and *The Newlywed Game*, 5,000 people show up!

had been a friend of Larry and Charlene's. Charlene and Larry told me that a number of uninvited guests also were in attendance—members of the FBI.

When Charlene was booking me into Resorts International in Atlantic City, she and Larry invited me to lunch with Maggio. Only after the lunch did I later discovered that Mr. Maggio was a high ranking "officer" in Mr. Bruno's "firm."

But I had a clue during lunch. Maggio pointed his fork at me, and in his raspy voice stated, "I dunno how you get those stupid people to say all those stupid things on your show."

I smiled.

"Ahh, Peter, if you and your wife were on the show, I could get you to say those same stupid things."

He fixed me with his steely eyes. "Lemme tell ya somethin'. Five gran' juries haven't been able to make me talk. What the fuck makes you think you can?"

In June of 1870, the first section of the Atlantic City Boardwalk was opened to the public, and for nearly a hundred years it was America's crown jewel of classy escapism. In the '40s and '50s, as the song says, it was the place to strut and take in the fresh sea air while enjoying a relaxing vista of beach and sea. Decked out in their finest, from snap brim hats and double breasted suits to stockings and heels, this was the place to go if you wanted to put on airs a bit. The casual attire of burgeoning "theme parks" was considered déclassé because this was Atlantic City and it was all about style.

A stroll down the Boardwalk took you past the fabulous ocean front homes, the coffee shops and elegant restaurants that catered to the millions who would go "down the shore." You would pass the famous Atlantic City Convention Hall, home of the Miss America Pageant, and the world renowned Steel Pier where so many great Rock and Roll concerts of the '50s were held. Atlantic City was a magical place, a Mecca to see and be seen, to sun and socialize.

By the time I got there in the early '80s all that had changed. The charming little shops had been replaced by tattoo parlors and fast food restaurants. Sophisticates taking a leisurely walk along the Boardwalk had been supplanted by women in string bikinis, street punks with humongous boom boxes perched on their shoulders and the homeless. Bargain hunting vacationers cramming six in a motel room had replaced the bon vivants of another era.

Casting an eye on the growing popularity and success of Las Vegas, in 1976 the citizens of New Jersey passed the Casino Gambling Referendum in hopes it would revitalize Atlantic City. By that time, Atlantic City was in bad shape, having been nicknamed "South Bronx by the seashore." Buddy Hackett was far less kind in describing New Jersey's attempt to jump start the ailing city by introducing gambling casinos when he quipped, "They took a shithole and made it a shithole with carpets." Of course this has all changed in the intervening thirty years, especially since the Steve Wynns and Donald Trumps realized Atlantic City was within a tankful of gas to 25% of the U.S. population. But it's taken them nearly that long to clean the place up and elevate it to close to the standards of Las Vegas.

The problem with the initial version of the gambling referendum was that the politicians hamstrung it by making it inconvenient and, in some ways, downright dangerous. First they stipulated that any establishment offering gambling had to have at least 500 rooms. This caused the hasty remodeling of old hospitals and hotels located in the middle of slums. Then they agreed that 24-hour gambling was somehow indecent and set a cut off of 2 A.M. This caused a lot of ardent wagerers to be tossed out onto the streets while they waited for the casinos to reopen at six, making them sitting ducks for muggers.

The most bizarre ruling (which I believe stands to this day) was one that banned Keno and Bingo. This was done to protect churches in the community from losing their income stream. It also guaranteed that the legions of little old ladies bussed in each day would have nothing to do but wait for the bus once they blew their wad on the slots.

This was the world I saw when Resorts International made me an offer to come to town. Tibor Rudas was RI's first entertainment director and he had a flair like no other. He currently produces Pavarotti as well as the Three Tenors. Tibor approached me with an offer to produce three live audience participation shows a day. One of my first impressions of Resorts International's hotel (other than it was an old troop hospital) was the garbage trucks that made their pick-up fifty feet from the front door every morning. The surroundings were ugly and the neighborhood was in chaos. They tried blowing up an old building across the street to make way for a parking lot, and when the explosive charges went off smoke poured forth but the place stood firm. They had to bring in wrecking balls which were noisy and raised a lot of dust. I hadn't been there twenty-four hours before it was clear they would never outdo Vegas.

I was put in a small bar at the far end of the casino and given hosting duties for some of the oddest game shows you could imagine. One of our games was a compilation of every game show you've ever seen and concluded with a go-go contest capped off by a men's ballet contest featuring men in tutus. To prep them for the appearance, Charlene Trichon would take them to the back room, roll their pants up and put them in tutus. One day she got them all ready and came out to check where we were in the show. When she returned to cue them they were gone. A casino guard informed her that three men were spotted running through the casino in tutus, one of them shouting, "No way!"

One of my favorite games involved pitting an older lady against a younger man—to see who could put on a girdle faster. To make it harder to accomplish their task they were required to wear boxing gloves. Both contestants got the same prize regardless of who won, but I always made sure the lady was victorious. One young stud was on his way to winning, so while he was poised with one foot in the air I gently nudged him and, unfortunately, he fell right off the stage. Weeks later I got a call from RI's legal department informing me the guy was suing and they needed me to testify in a deposition.

I went to the courthouse which was filled with lawyers for both sides, a court administrator and a court reporter. The attorneys were glaring at each other from opposite sides of the table like roosters before a cockfight. When the Resorts attorney asked the plaintiff what happened you could feel the tension rise in the room. In his most serious and injured demeanor, the plaintiff began his tale of woe. Everyone was doing their best to look sympathetic, but when he said, "I was putting on a girdle wearing boxing gloves and Mr. Eubanks pushed me off the stage," the entire room exploded into laughter. Ultimately, the joke was on RI, which coughed up $100,000 to salve the man's ego and injured back.

In the late '70s I was contacted by Frank Gelb, a boxing promoter who had convinced the fledgling Turner network to do a live variety show from the Resorts hotel in Atlantic City. He asked me to host, so every week we resurrected the talent show format that had made Ed Sullivan so famous. The only difference was that instead of world class acts, we had magicians and local singing groups. We also tried to book whoever was playing at the hotel to enhance the quality of our talent line up.

One week we got sax man Sam Butera and the Witnesses. Sam made his mark after teaming up with Louis Prima and Keely Smith in the late '40s. He had developed a real Vegas style act—lots of energy and highly entertaining. I was excited to get an act of Sam's caliber and was thrilled when I took the stage to introduce him. He and the Witnesses struck up "That Old Black Magic" and immediately most of the heads in the audience were nodding to the beat. The stage Sam was performing on happened to be on the floor below the huge indoor swimming pool at Resorts. Right in the middle of the song—and a live national television broadcast—the ceiling caved in sending tens of thousands of gallons of warm water rushing onto the stage. As Sam floated by I can still remember his gurgled "last words," "What...the...hell?" Within seconds everything and everyone on the stage was carried away in the torrent. Nobody was hurt, but Sam's first choice of song might have been the

I'M ALWAYS ON A MOUNTAIN WHEN I FALL

WHEN THE TIME CAME to begin taping the 1979 season, the ratings of *The Newlywed Game* were rapidly declining. Since 1977, *The Newlywed Game* had found a new lease on life in the burgeoning field of television syndication. For years programs had been rebroadcast in what was commonly referred to as "reruns," but the new syndication was a different animal. Now, given the explosion of outlets through the growth of cable, program producers were finding an expanding and hungry market for their creations. Syndication was fairly new to all of us, but Chuck Barris saw a fresh audience in the heretofore untouched "prime time access" time slot, that is, the hour between 7 and 8 P.M. Previously left to reruns, news or local programming, that golden hour was now sought after by national syndicators. A sale to a TV station in a given city was called a "clearance," and the syndicator with clearances in all the major national markets was going to haul away truckloads of money.

Chuck Barris's approach to presenting *The Newlywed Game* to our new audience in the '70s was to juice-up the format by giving it an edge. Chuck felt the relaxed, casual atmosphere we had created and maintained since the inception of the show in 1966 was too staid for our new time slot, so he set forces in motion to change all that. In its new incarnation, the plan was to transform *The Newlywed Game* into a ratings smash by appealing to the audiences' most primitive appetites, a philosophy that later served producers of shows like Jerry Springer very well. Even the atmosphere back stage had changed. I saw a lot of new faces and there were even some celebrity fans of Barris's shows spending time on the sets. Once in a while I would see Andy Kaufman talking to staffers and acting bizarre. He even appeared in his Foreign Man character once as a contestant on *The Dating Game* and showed up at Sunset-Gower for a cast party.

Game show vet Mike Metzger was selected by Chuck to assume the duties of producer on *The Newlywed Game*, a function he was also fulfilling on *The Dating Game*. Metzger was quite a character, with long hair, a beard and a penchant for breaking with convention, both personally and professionally. Before I even met the man, I knew of Metzger's reputation. Though he was considered very hip and New Agey—years before that was a trendy label—Metzger could also be a hard-ass producer. In 1967, Chuck had a show called *The Family Game*. Metzger was the producer, with Bob Barker as host. One day in rehearsal, Metzger and Barker got into an extremely heated argument over a question Barker was supposed to ask a contestant. The question contained the word bellybutton, which Barker refused to say. Barker stormed away to his dressing room and Metzger summoned Barris.

"Barker's pissed," explained Metzger. "He won't say bellybutton."

"What are you talking about?"

"He won't say the word bellybutton. We almost got in a fight."

Barris's eyes narrowed. "We'll see about that," and he stalked off to Barker's dressing room to confront his host. A few minutes later Barris reappeared, looking sheepish. He passed Metzger without making eye contact and said quietly, "Bellybutton is out."

Barker won. He didn't have to utter the vile word, but when I heard the tale I was impressed that Metzger would nearly come to blows with Bob Barker over something as absurd as the word bellybutton. What Metzger probably did not know at that time was that Barker was a black belt in Karate. (I don't really blame Barker—I rejected about twenty percent of the questions the writers of *The Newlywed Game* put in front of me.)

I first perceived Metzger as a bit of a hippie, seemingly too laid back and bizarre to operate in the high pressure world of network television. Once I got to know him I learned that his style was one of his biggest assets, and that he had a solid reputation for getting results. Metzger was an extremely affable eccentric and I liked him. As a matter of fact, I once offered the fellow music lover a gift.

"I want you to have my gold Beatles album," I told him, holding out the rare collectible. Just before the 1965 press conference at Capitol Records, each of the Fab Four were presented with gold albums—which they promptly abandoned after the function. Not wanting to waste such a treasure, I got one of the homeless gold records. Capitol knew I had the album but had never said anything, so by then I assumed it was mine. Metzger and I had spent a lot of time talking about music so I decided I wanted him to have it. He was stunned and touched.

"I can't take this, Bob. It's too much."

"No, Metz, I want you to have it." I handed it to him.

His eyes glistened slightly as he admired the golden treasure nestled in its elegant glass and hardwood framed case. "I'll put it on my wall," he said reverently. A few days later I happened by his office and he excitedly waved me inside.

"Hey Bob! Listen to this!"

Next to his desk was a record player, and positioned on the turntable, to my horror, was the gold album. At first I was shocked he had dismantled the display case, but I was even more blown away when he dropped the tone arm on the valuable artifact and music actually issued forth. It was some obscure opera. Metzger looked up at me and shook his head. "Can you believe those cheap bastards? They didn't even use a Beatles album."

Some years later, Metzger ran into some financial trouble and tried to auction the album at Sotheby's. Apple Records, who has since taken over the catalog from Capitol, got wind of the attempted sale and called him. After tersely informing him it was not his to sell, they offered him three grand for it. He took the dough. When the story got back to me I was disappointed in Metzger, but also sorry he had been forced to sell his belongings.

To propel *The Newlywed Game* to where he felt it should be in the ratings, Chuck Barris issued an order to Mike Metzger to introduce whatever provocative elements he felt necessary to push the limits of allowable taste. Metzger had never been too fond of the steady stream of what he considered bland, clean-cut suburbanites that had been the staple of our contestant pool. His new interpretation of the ideal couples spawned a parade of red necks, misfits, oddballs and even the occasional midget spouses. Then, to complement the reduction in contestant standards, I was given the task of stirring up the freak show.

Armed with questions that had been written with a leer, my function was to seize on the contestant's every word, insecurity and, particularly, their response, and give them a spin in the sleaze cycle. The awful thing about this period—and the part for which I am least proud—was that I jumped into it with relish.

I had become very unhappy during this time, suffering the throes of a life crisis that seemed to come at me from all directions. There was this rising dread that at forty I had somehow missed the mark in achieving my goals. Between the years 1962 and 1973—despite my insecurities—everything I touched turned to gold. Now, it seemed, nothing that happened was any good.

One of the problems with celebrity is that, in my opinion, it elevates many of the wrong people. Not that some celebrities aren't worthy of admiration, but the members of society we should be asking for autographs are the doctors and teachers and soldiers and cops, not people who happen to be seen on TV. I think part of my crisis came from not feeling worthy of all of the attention. Why me? What had I done—really done—to deserve such adulation? For years I've joked that in the department store of life I live in the toy section. I guess I looked around, and fairly or not, summed up my career with a so what? I did not see entertaining people as being anywhere near the same level as those who save or help or change others' lives for the better.

As hard as I tried, I also couldn't decide if what I wanted now was just wildly different than ten or twenty years ago, or that things had really stagnated, or worse, slid down hill. Intellectually, I knew that I had a number of seemingly significant accomplishments, but I had a gnawing, unresolved feeling of emptiness.

I had actually exceeded many of the dreams I spun as a young man starting out in radio, but no matter how I looked at it I could not convince myself I had done anything of real merit. Yet I had created a concert promotion company that had brought the Beatles and others to L.A.; I had helped my radio station become number one on the market; I had one of the first concert promotion companies that promoted all kinds of music; I had helped form the *KRLA Beat*, the first newspaper for teens and a precursor to Rolling Stone; and I had founded the first PR firm for rock groups. All these things were in my mind as I wrestled with my dilemma, but they didn't seem to carry the weight they should in satisfying my conscience that I had made reasonable contributions to the world.

I had experienced periods, whole years even, when I felt I was on track, living up to my expectations; then it would all come crashing down. I thought I had beaten the doubts many times, only for them to come back, every time, with a vengeance. And what I was feeling this time seemed considerably magnified compared to the other times. To sum it up, this was a very tough time for me.

As much as I loved doing *The Newlywed Game*, I had fallen into a hole where I couldn't shake the feeling that my life's work could be capsulized as a guy who pushed young couples to answer suggestive questions about their personal lives for the price of a toaster. This growing insecurity began to follow me like Marley's ghost, making me more and more uncomfortable. I feared my inadequacies were becoming increasingly obvious to everyone.

What undoubtedly heightened all of my other anxieties was my situation at home. Irma and I had been growing apart for some time and that distance had since lapsed into a downward spiral. Before we started that season's production, I did whatever I could to avoid going home, whether it was going on the road with Merle or throwing myself into various projects. As we settled into production I felt I had a place to hide for a while. Yet, as taping began I realized the production schedule of thirty-five work days would pass quickly and I'd have to look elsewhere for solace.

With my marriage fraying around the edges, I found the podium on *The Newlywed Game*'s stage to be the perfect sniper's perch. When life becomes overwhelming some men abuse their spouses. I abused my guests. I arrived at work every day with good intentions, but as soon as I took the stage my hostility welled up, and with eight easy targets in my cross hairs, I was often harder on them than I should have been. It was a sad irony that with my own marriage turning to shit, I used those bright, shiny new marriages to vent my anger and frustrations.

Of course, this mischief was all done under the flag of "good fun," but the shots I took were often inappropriate, and when I laughed it was usually at my contestants, not with them. Sometimes I felt just plain mean and would toy with them.

During one taping, the energy on the set was high and the contestants were very lively. There was a lot of laughter and one of the guests in particular, a husband, was really getting into the off-color tone that I had set. As the host I couldn't get too smutty but the contestants were, to some extent, protected from that restriction.

"In what room of the house would your wife say is your favorite place to eat?" I asked.

One husband answered, "Uh, the dining room."

Number two's was just as boring. "She'd probably say the kitchen."

The third, an apparent couch potato, replied, "I'd have to say the rec room."

But the fourth hubby, a smart-ass I had identified early on as a potential grandstander, lit up with a smirky expression. "I do my best eating in the bedroom, Bob."

Then he winked.

The answer was innocuous enough, but with his wink I decided to make an example of him. My face clouded over and my eyes narrowed with scorn as I stared a hole through him. "Hey pal, this is my show and I'm not going to have anyone take it into the gutter."

When everyone realized I wasn't joking, the poor guy shrank to about five inches tall and it got really quiet on the set. Metzger didn't bother to stop tape because he thought it was hilarious that I had verbally slapped a guest. The rest of that show was very somber, with the contestants carefully weighing their answers, terrified they might piss me off again. After the taping I would usually feel guilty and seek out the offended guest and apologize. Sometimes I didn't.

Although many of those shows were very funny, I had a creeping suspicion the price was going to be high. Instinctively, I felt what I was doing was bad for the show, and probably my career, yet I continued with my self-destructive behavior, running from my personal problems by hiding in my work. I also excused myself by rationalizing that it was the direction Chuck and Metzger had chosen and I was only "following orders," but I knew it would catch up to me.

I now recall those few seasons with some shame because the poor contestants trusted me and I dumped on them. I had always been a people-person, priding myself on my compassion for others, yet it was almost as if some malevolent spirit had inhabited my body. And the weirder the questions became, and the more increasingly off-center the guests Metzger threw at me, the more my rage simmered. Though the show was my place to hide during those times I look back at those tapes and see a deeply troubled soul bitterly lashing out.

The results of our misguided labors eventually paid off when two key sponsors, Ford Motor Company and Proctor & Gamble, shut their checkbooks. Both Ford and P&G's ad agencies finally had enough of the show's descent into questionable taste and let us know they were dropping their sponsorships. Then almost immediately, there was another attack on the show straight out of left field, this time from the home of the owner of KTLA, the station where we not only produced the show, but was also its outlet in the L.A. market. Gene Autry's first wife was a bit of a religious zealot and took it upon herself to become the watchdog of our show. After determining we were blasphemers and needed to be expunged from television, she let out the word that she hated what the show had become. She also began pressuring her powerful husband to find a way to get us off the air. With arrows now flying, we knew *The Newlywed Game* might be in trouble, but like all of show business, if the ratings are big and the dollars are big, then money wins over morality every time.

Having amassed considerable game show savvy, and with plenty of time on my hands, I teamed with my friend Michael Hill and formed a company to help satisfy television's seemingly unquenchable thirst for game and reality shows. Michael has the most brilliant mind I've ever seen in that unpredictable business, and I've seen them all. To anyone on the outside it would seem a simple chore to just wing off great show ideas, but the truth is game shows must work on many, many levels, most of which are not evident to someone sitting at home in the comfort of their Barcalounger. The Hill Eubanks Group came into existence to market and produce such ideas. Our partnership seemed like a good match, teaming the creative brain with the glad-handing celebrity. Michael was an idea machine but had a ferocious temper, and one of my primary functions was to step in and smooth things over when the fireworks began. In addition to peacekeeper, I would also assume host duties on run-throughs when my schedule on *The Newlywed Game* permitted.

When we formed The Hill Eubanks Group, Michael already had two projects in the works, one of which was called *Ask A Silly Question*. In the course of developing it we interviewed a number of prospective hosts. We particularly liked one of them, a former weatherman from Indiana in his early thirties who had originally come west to take a stab at stand-up comedy. David Letterman had been knocking around Hollywood a few years at that point, both as a writer and performer on variety

David Letterman and Allen Ludden during the shooting of our NBC pilot, *Smart Alecks*. NBC didn't buy the pilot, but they sure bought Letterman.

shows. He had also become a darling of Johnny Carson, making quite a few appearances on *The Tonight Show*. David was very, very funny and though *Ask A Silly Question* never went anywhere, the brass from NBC encouraged us to use David in our next project.

The second concept Michael had in the chute was a format he called *Smart Alecks*. It was based upon the premise that every time you get a great idea, some smart aleck will tell you what's wrong with it. When we got ready for the pilot, it was brought to Michael's attention that David didn't even have a sports jacket. Though we quickly found one, it didn't fit his lanky frame so we had it heavily clothes-pinned to avoid resembling a poncho on camera. David certainly made me laugh, but sometimes I felt his acerbic style of humor squashed the little guy under his heel for the sake of a joke and, given my recent propensity for similar behavior on *The Newlywed Game*, I was particularly sensitive when others did it. But he was wickedly funny and I knew he was headed for stardom. David had experienced some success by then, but still seemed unaffected by his steady rise, choosing to continue to drive the old red pickup truck that had brought him out to California. *Smart Alecks* didn't make it past the NBC suits, but David did and was soon given the daytime show that would launch him into the stratosphere. The last time I saw David was the 70s when he stopped by my dressing room while I was shooting *The Newlywed Game*.

Our lack of success on those shows points out another pitfall of the game show business: for every one that makes it, hundreds are developed, pitched and piloted. Though you're mostly panning for gold in a dry creek bed, what every game show producer dreams of is that Holy Grail, a *Wheel Of Fortune* or *Jeopardy*.

With the demise of *Ask A Silly Question* and *Smart Alecks*, the first true joint project of The Hill Eubanks Group to make it to pilot was *Celebrity Secrets*. I hosted and it featured three contestants facing five celebrity guests. The contestants were read a secret that pertained to one of the guests and they would try and uncover whose secret it was by eliminating the other celebs. The winner would be the one who made the most correct guesses. For every correct answer the contestants received cash, and in the end all of the players received lovely parting gifts, courtesy of our sponsors.

ABC's Michael Brockman liked the idea and ordered a pilot, which we produced. The pilot was good, but fate intervened when ABC head honcho, Fred Silverman, decided to fire Brockman and the show was dead at that network. But Brockman quickly landed at NBC, where he immediately ordered the show. There was a lot of dialing-in of details right up to the last minute, not the least of which was changing the name to *All Star Secrets*, just in time to make the deadline for TV Guide and all the newspapers.

Once we were off and running we booked celebrity panelists such as McLean Stevenson from *M*A*S*H*, Pat Boone, Buddy Hackett and Phyllis Diller. The show lasted about eight months; then Silverman moved over to NBC, once again fired Brockman and immediately pulled the plug on our show. I think poor Brockman was beginning to feel like The Fugitive as "Inspector" Silverman pursued him from network to network.

One celeb panelist was Soupy Sales. Soupy's secret was that he was an artist. He had painted a rather large oil painting and brought it to show his skill. Unbeknownst to Soupy, our art director was pretty talented himself and quickly painted a darned good copy of Soupy's painting.

All Star Secrets with panelists Pat Boone, Phylis Diller, Greg Morris, Mary Ann Mobley and McLean Stevenson.

When it was revealed that Soupy was the artist, I "accidentally" destroyed the fake masterpiece by ripping it in two on the nail I was supposed to hang it from. It was worth money seeing Soupy's face twist in horror. Another time, Wolfman Jack claimed to be the owner of a pig farm. Once he was matched to the secret his smile quickly faded when a stage hand dropped a pig in his lap and he acted like he'd never seen one before in his life. He looked up at me, "Do he bite?"

Celebrity panelist Wayland Flowers was a puppeteer who became famous in the '70s with his alter ego, Madame. Many say Madame, a ribald and crotchety old puppet, was really a surrogate for his mother. Wayland Flowers and Madame got away with a lot more than a lone comedian could because his use of Madame as a mouthpiece took much of any curse off what he said. During a show something about exotic birds came up and Madame quipped, "I've seen a Cock-or-two." From anyone else it would have been bleeped, but Wayland managed to get it through the censors. We would often hear Wayland, alone in his dressing room, arguing with Madame. I guess he had some Norman Bates-like issues with his mother. Wayland was a very funny man and I was sad when I heard he had passed away in 1988.

On the set of *All Star Secrets*.

In retrospect, one of the most interesting moments during the run of *All Star Secrets* happened in one of the last shows. A young Austrian body builder, who had in recent years been laboring at a career shift to movies, was selected as the celeb with the secret. And his secret? I smiled to myself as he informed us in his thick accent that within ten years he would become "a huge stah." But Arnold Schwarzenegger had the last laugh as his bold prediction not only came true, but years sooner than he foretold. I'm not sure even he could have predicted he would end up governor of Cal-ee-fornia.

An amusing anecdote from behind the scenes centered around one of the show's crew members. He had just bought a VW and was bragging incessantly about what great mileage he was getting. He was very precise about his calculations and terribly proud he'd bought such an energy efficient car, especially since we were experiencing an energy crunch. Some of his fellow crew members finally had enough of his boasting and took the situation into their own hands. They secretly began adding gas to his car, a little at a time, until he was getting some staggering, world record mileage. The man was on cloud nine, telling everyone on the set about his "miracle" car. I shared with him that I had owned a Bug years before and he pooh-poohed my old car as hopelessly out of date technology. Once he had gotten really full of himself, the boys began reversing his big gains by siphoning gas out. Suddenly his mileage plummeted, now no better than a land whale like a Buick Electra 225. The crew allowed this to go on for a while then let him in on their mockery. The VW owner never said another word about his car.

Though the shows we put forth weren't burning up the game show market, our efforts did not go unnoticed. We were soon offered similar first-look, overall deals at both Universal and Twentieth Century Fox. The nature of the deals were that each studio offered offices and staff in return for the first chance at whatever brilliant ideas we generated.

When we first received the offers, I phoned Michael to discuss what we should do. We hashed them over for a while then reached an impasse.

"The deals are almost identical. What do you think?"

"I don't know," I replied. "You're right, it's a tossup."

Michael paused a moment. "Hey, doesn't Twentieth have a better commissary?"

I visualized both eateries. "Yeah, I think they do."

"Well, what do think?" he asked.

"Twentieth," I confirmed.

"Twentieth," he agreed, and we hung up. I called our entertainment attorney, John Mason, and told him to make the deal. John is a helluva good lawyer and today represents some very big stars, including music giants Reba McIntire, Vince Gill and Kenny Rogers.

When it came time to hammer out the fine points of the deal with Twentieth, John invited us along to the negotiation confab with the head of their business affairs, Marty Groothuis. John is a wonderful negotiator because he has the balls to ask a drowning man for his last gulp of air, yet makes his demands in such a calm, rational voice many of his foes simply fold.

Not so with Marty. The meeting began on a very cordial basis, but soon John's wild ultimatums—outrageous profit percentages, ridiculous credit demands and ludicrous staff and office requirements—caused the meeting to rapidly degenerate into a shit-slinging fest. John didn't expect Marty to give us any of them, but threw them in as a tactical ploy to soften him. John's persistence seemed to cause Marty increasing distress, to the point where the poor man's face became so red I was afraid he was either going to have a heart attack or spontaneously combust. Eventually, Marty became so enraged he slammed his fist down hard on the desk.

"I don't have to take this!" he screamed, then jumped out of the chair and fled his own office.

We all looked at each other in surprise, then burst into laughter. John stayed in his seat but Michael and I couldn't sit still. Michael grabbed the phone and pretended to be speaking to someone. "Mr. Groothuis? No, I'm sorry, I believe he's resigned. Uh, huh. Actually, I'm not sure." He put his hand over the phone. "They want to know where he is."

I sat down in Marty's chair, put my feet up. "I heard he joined a commune in Oregon."

Michael set the phone down. "Should we order in?"

I nodded. "Pizzas for the whole building. On Marty."

"On Marty," concurred Michael.

John, the pragmatic kill-joy, looked at his watch. "Too early for pizza."

"So, how long do we wait?" I asked John.

He shrugged coolly. "'Till the other shoe drops."

Michael asked, "This ever happen to you?"

John shook his head, then smiled, "But you've got to admit... this is interesting."

Fifteen minutes passed, then the phone rang and the secretary answered. A moment later she appeared at the door, obviously shaken.

"Uh, Mr. Groothuis is uh..." she stammered.

"What?" prompted John. "Still in the men's room?"

She exhaled deeply. "Uh no. He just called me from a pay phone across the street and said he's not coming back until you leave."

Our consummate attorney put on his game face. "Well you tell Mr. Groothuis that when he gets back from vacation we'll be in touch."

Despite those inauspicious beginnings, the deal was eventually made. Our first project was *The Guinness Game*. Based on *The Guinness Book of World Records*, contestants would try to create a record that would find a place in the famed book. One of the lowlights of that show never made it on the air. We booked an elephant named Dolly who, her trainer alleged, could throw a ball and hit a target. When the poor pachyderm came in for the run-throughs it became readily apparent she was no Sandy Koufax, in fact, had the target been a barn she would have missed. When we canceled the booking her trainer turned around and sued us. With the prospect that two of their producers might be facing a rogue elephant in court, Fox shelled out 10,000 bucks to make Dolly disappear.

On another occasion, we booked Cormack the Incredible, a mystic who possessed such phenomenal mental powers he could stroll on red hot coals without so much as flinching. Cormack planned on setting a new fire walking record, so we created a huge run of coals for his attempt right in the parking lot at KTLA. When taping time arrived the coals had been simmering for hours and were fiery enough to make s'mores. Our host, Don Galloway, who had been a regular on the TV series *Ironside*, stood nearby as Cormack psyched himself up for his walk of fire. Finally, Cormack marshaled his resources and was ready.

"I'll need absolute silence," he commanded, then closed his eyes and took one last deep breath. After a very pregnant pause, Cormack, now seemingly in a trance-like state, opened his eyes and raised his arms for balance.

Suddenly, the dead quiet of the parking lot was shattered by four words: "I think he's ready," said Don, softly mothering his microphone.

Don's attempt to heighten the drama must have rung like a gunshot to Cormack who was in mid-stride as it was uttered. His concentration blown, Cormack hit the coals and his eyes bulged wide as the soles of his bare feet hissed like two tenderloins hitting the hibachi.

"Oooo! Aaahhh! Owww! Shit! Ouch!" he squealed, staggering down the lengthy open barbecue. We all looked on in horror, fearing he might fall. As soon as he gave up, we had Cormack the Incredible rushed to the hospital. I imagined the nurse dressing his blistered extremities with hickory-flavored BBQ sauce. Cormack didn't even come close to a record.

LOVE WILL KEEP US TOGETHER

The Beatles • Mick Jagger • Cary Grant
Merle Haggard • Bob Dylan • David
Letterman • The Rolling Stones • The
Beach Boys • Tina Turner • Leeza
Gibbons • Jerry Lee Lewis • Gene Autry
Roy Rogers • Monty Hall • Roy Orbison
Buddy Hackett • Barbara Mandrell

THE GUINNESS GAME ran on NBC's owned and operated stations (O&O's) until the Peacock decided to shed us for *Family Feud* five nights a week. With *The Guinness Game* over, Michael and I began searching for a new home for The Hill Eubanks Group. The Universal deal was still open and Al Rush, the executive under whom we would be operating, wanted us to pitch them on developing two shows, a one-hour talk format starring Toni Tennille, of the Captain and Tennille, and a remake of *You Bet Your Life*.

Al informed us there was existing pilot for Toni's proposed show, but Toni and the producer of that pilot, Alan Thicke, had suffered some sort of falling-out, so the slate was clean on what the show might be. The only catch was, in order to get the deal Al told us our company had to more or less audition for two people: Toni's husband, the "Captain," Daryl Dragon, and her manager, Bruno Saccotti. Bruno's only previous management experience had been the baseball team at Cal State, Northridge, but Bruno and his wife had been devoted fans of The Captain and Tennille at the Smokehouse in Burbank years before the act was discovered. When it came time to find a manager, loyalty won over acumen and Toni and Daryl tapped Bruno to steer their career.

Regarding the presentation of our ideas to Daryl and Bruno, Al's advice was simply "put on a show" to impress them. We took it to heart and decided the way to get their attention was to really put on a show. In a town where impressions are often far more important than substance, Michael hit on a brilliant idea that was more Mission: Impossible than game show pitch, but it made crazy sense when he laid it on me.

Backstage at the *Tony Tenille Show* with the Captain and Tenille.

Our offices were grouped around a large common area. When Daryl and Bruno arrived for the meeting, that space looked more like the Situation Room at the White House than a television producer's office. Parties of earnest young TV mavens sat around tables holding meetings on the myriad shows we had in development. As Michael and I casually ushered Daryl and Bruno on the tour from office to office, they overheard even more discussions of projects with the biggest names in the business. In one room photos of Frank Sinatra adorned the walls while heated discussion ensued about Frank's demands for his accommodations. In another office, work was progressing on a prime time show for CBS. Everywhere they turned they saw charts, graphs, photos, file folders labeled with big star's names, energetic phone calls with agents and busy people everywhere—the general hubbub of an insanely busy (and by association, successful) production company.

As soon as the meeting concluded and a starry-eyed Daryl and Bruno walked out the door, I stepped into the common area, raised my hands and addressed our staff.

"Thanks everybody. Great job! You can all go home, now." The truth was that most of our "staff" had been assembled from a local casting agency and, as Daryl and Bruno were exiting our parking lot, our "development executives" were shuffling out the back door to rejoin the actors' breadlines. And our "big deals?" None were real. Later that day we got a call from Al Rush over at Universal.

"Hey Michael, I don't know what you guys did, but Daryl and Bruno think you're the biggest and best producers in town."

Michael feigned surprise. "No kidding? That's great. All we did was show 'em around, then gave them a pretty straightforward pitch. Nothing special, really," he said, attempting modesty while I crossed my fingers that our deception had succeeded.

"Well, whatever you said you've got their show. Congratulations."

The second he got off the phone I let out a cheer. At that moment, a quote from a good friend of mine, Bob Geddes, never seemed more true: Life is timing and lighting. It didn't hurt having a genius for a partner, either.

Toni's production was slated to replace Dinah Shore's *Dinah!* on NBC's O&O's. Ironically, though there were many production venues available, we were assigned the same sound stage at KTLA where Dinah's show had been produced. Toni threw herself into the production, working long hours and honing everything until it was perfect. I was impressed with her ability to conduct a brilliant interview one moment, then, after the briefest set-up, jump into a musical number. Toni was always prepared, never complained, and made life ridiculously easy for Michael and myself as her producers.

For reasons that were never made clear to me, Daryl, an accomplished musician, was not directly involved in the show. I had assumed early on they were a package and, at the very least, Daryl would be handling the music. When Michael and I were informed that wasn't the case, we brought in an up and coming young musician and former actor named Ira Newborn. Ira would go on to a very distinguished career, composing the music for such films as *Ferris Bueller's Day Off*, the *Naked Gun* films and *Ace Ventura, Pet Detective*.

Another asset we had going was our ability to draw great guests, which could probably be attributed, to a large extent, to Toni's heat in the business. She and the Captain had not only had some big musical hits recently, but had also hosted their own prime time show on ABC just two years prior. When the film *9 To 5* debuted as a sure box office

success, we contacted the female leads to book them on the show. It
made me look foolish when Dolly Parton declined us since everyone
knew we'd been close.

The worst guest we had during the tenure of the show was Chevy
Chase. Flush with his recent success in *Caddyshack*, Chase was hot and
Universal, our show's backer, wanted us to give Chase some face time.
We had been hearing a lot of inside (and reliable) buzz about Chase's
uncontainable ego. Consequently, Michael and Toni and I were reluctant
to book him. We finally contacted his manger and made the offer, not
only to appease Universal, but also because not to have such a hot star
would be seen as a fumbling oversight. Even worse, failure to book him
could create the perception within the industry that we were unable to
land a big name, which could become a self-fulfilling prophesy—Hey,
they can't get Chevy Chase ... why would I want to do that show?

Chase agreed to do the show, but then phoned Michael directly and
laid down the law. The moment Michael got off the phone he came
down the hall to my office.

"You're gonna love this," he said.

"What is it?"

"I just got off the phone with Chase. He has one stipulation."

"Okay ... " I said warily, sensing a punch line.

"He insists we have no audience during his interview."

"What?" I asked incredulously. "It's a damn talk show. There's gotta
be an audience."

"Not with Chase."

"That's complete bullshit ego. No audience? Who does he think he
is, the Pope?"

"No," said Michael with a slight smirk, "he's Chevy Chase. And
you're not."

I had to laugh. "What an asshole."

"I agree. But we need him."

We acquiesced to his dictate for no audience and hoped for the best.
It wasn't long after Chase breezed in for the taping that we began to
regret it. We all wondered what was wrong with him. Seemingly spaced-
out, he was not only rude, but pompous to the point of being a carica-
ture of himself. His attention constantly wandered, as if to say he didn't
give a shit and wanted everyone to know it. Despite Toni getting such
an off-putting vibe from him, she was a trouper and waded through the

interview, but Chase threw her questions back with flippant retorts and wisecracks that went nowhere. Finally, Toni's lovely face darkened, her eyes narrowed, and it was very apparent she had had quite enough of Mr. Chase. She abruptly stopped the interview, told him to leave her show, then got up and walked off the stage. I couldn't help but smile a dozen or so years later when I watched Chase squirming on his own very short-lived talk show on Fox.

Maybe Chase's failed interview portended bad things, for despite all the indications and elements that seemed to assure success, for some reason our numbers never really jelled on the West Coast. Back east our ratings were fine, but viewers on our side of the Mississippi stayed away in droves. And when your numbers flag in the TV business, panicked network execs start doing all manner of stupid things.

When we created the format for the show, we wanted to showcase our star's terrific voice, so we planned to have her singing as often as possible. Unfortunately, her management company, and our boss MCA, didn't want her to give away on television what they might be able to sell to the public, so they forbade us from letting her have more than one solo song. Stupid, yes, but we managed to get around it somewhat by getting them to agree, that in addition to her solo, she could do at least one duet per show. Toni was dying to sing as much as possible so the duet allowed her to sing one extra song. Toni's solo had always been one of the last elements of the show, sort of the show closer, and it was always a production number, done with appropriate fanfare. Yet when the latest Nielsens came in, some nervous brainiac in programming pointed out that we had no ratings for the last fourteen minutes of the show and cried, "Oh my, what to do?" It's not that Nielsen changed their whole system since the last ratings book, it's that the show was under a magnifying glass.

Michael got a call from Chuck Gerber, head of NBC's O&Os.

"There aren't any numbers for the last fourteen minutes of the show so we want to cut Toni's song."

Michael knew it was simply a cost cutting move on NBC's part because the cheapskates had to pay MCA a licensing fee every time Toni sang. My partner bristled.

"That's ridiculous. Cut her song? No."

"We can't justify it."

"You want to cut her song completely? She's a singer."

"She can still sing, just move it somewhere else."

"There's only the middle and she does a duet in the middle."

"So drop that and let her do her production number then."

Michael dug in. "No. I'm not changing anything. You're saying no one watches the show in the last fourteen minutes? Everyone just tunes out?"

"No, it just we don't have numbers, Nielsen..."

"I'm not changing a thing." And he hung up.

It wasn't long after that conversation that the NBC bean counters looked at the bottom line and gave us the thumbs down. We did well in every market but L.A. The network replaced us with *Mary Tyler Moore* reruns and did bigger numbers. I always felt that if they had given our show a chance to grow it would have been a success. Years later, NBC exec Wes Harris stated at his retirement party that canceling *The Toni Tennille Show* was the dumbest thing he ever did. Of all the shows I've been involved with, I'm proudest of that one.

Once in a while your ego takes a hit, yet when it comes from your own back yard it's a surprise. I was scheduled to act as Grand Marshal of the annual parade in Hidden Hills. Although we spent most of our weekends at the ranch in Santa Ynez, we still spent most of our time at the Hidden Hills home and considered ourselves members of the community. The parade was well known for attracting far more participants than spectators, but it was a tradition. Even my kids rode in the parade each year on their bikes. At the last minute something came up that required me to be out of town so I called Dan Walling, the parade organizer.

"Dan," I said, "I'm really sorry, but I'm going to have to cancel on you."

"Oh, okay, Bob. That's fine."

I was surprised he took it so well. "Really?" I asked. "You're okay with this?"

"Oh yeah," he continued, sounding almost relieved. "As a matter of fact, it's a real coincidence, because our first choice just became available."

I knew our lovely neighborhood likely offered a number of celebrity residents with more drawing power than I, but I was curious, hoping it was a real big name I was losing out to.

"I'm glad to hear that, Dan. So who did you get?"

Dan paused, then sounded almost apologetic. "Uh, Lassie."

I nodded numbly, picturing Dan on one end of the phone and the famous collie on the other, hind legs propped on his desk, a cigar in his left paw. Eubanks? Dan, Dan, Dan, he's the best you can do? Alright already, I'll do your damn parade! Woof, woof.

"Well," I said, mustering a smile, "I'm happy it worked out." Being sued by an elephant was bad enough, but to be on someone's list beneath a dog? Ouch.

Despite the failure of Toni's show Michael and I still had a deal with Universal, so we moved on to our next project. It was a remake of *You Bet Your Life*, the wildly popular show Groucho Marx hosted from 1950 through 1961. Our version was to be produced for syndication; in other words, it was not to be aired by a single network at a specific time, but rather sold to stations across the country to be aired at their convenience. To follow in the footsteps of the legendary Groucho, our host also needed to possess some degree of legendary status, so our choice came back to a guy who had been a recurring guest on *All Star Secrets*, the brilliant but difficult Buddy Hackett.

Throughout his career, Hackett had distinguished himself as a stand-up comic, movie star and variety performer. For a guy in his mid-fifties, he seemed to have been around forever, and to some extent he had, given his first network gig was with Dumont in 1949. Despite playing the professional goofball, to those who knew him Hackett engendered the highest respect for his intellect, if not his charm. He may have played dumb, yet he was anything but. He would complete both the *New York Times* and *Los Angeles Times* crossword puzzles religiously every morning. I also heard a story that after spending only six months in Hungary doing a movie he became fluent in the language.

During the production of *All Star Secrets* I hadn't really gotten to know any of the guests, including Hackett, but with the new show he and I would be spending quite a bit of time together. I immediately decided to take steps to insure we understood each other. For years I had been hearing tales about Hackett's famous temper, what a giant pain-in-the-ass he could be and how he loved to yell at everyone, so one day I tracked him down on the set.

"Buddy? You got a minute?" I asked, cordially, but not overly friendly.

Hackett shrugged. "Yeah, sure."

We stepped into a room off the set, and as I closed the door behind me I saw a subtly quizzical expression come over his face. "Whassup?" he asked.

I stepped close to him, my six feet towering over his squat little body. Then I leaned in so our faces nearly touched, as Dirty Harry might with some punk who was thinking of crossing him. My demeanor was suddenly so threatening I actually heard him gulp.

"I don't like anybody yelling at me," I said, my voice calm but forceful.

"Yeah..." Hackett acknowledged, his eyes widening.

"So if you yell at me one time, Hackett...one time...we're through. I'll walk away and you'll never see me again. Understand?"

Hackett's goofy mug blossomed in surprise and he reached out and softly patted my shoulder. When he spoke I realized at that moment that Buddy Hackett's trademark corner-of-the-mouth articulation sounded like a Long Island mobster on helium.

"Bobby," he said, "I would never yell at you! Believe me."

Our eyes met for a moment and I felt he was sincere. I relaxed my posture a bit and unclenched my jaw. I smiled slightly, then he smiled.

"Okay," I said and held out my hand. "I believe you."

He shook it, then exhaled deeply. "Geez, Bobby, I thought you was gonna punch me or somethin'."

Hackett never yelled at me. But he yelled at everyone else.

The show began airing on September 8, 1980, and, at least initially, the audience numbers were decent. Hackett turned out to be fairly well behaved, but he did have his moments. He made it known he had certain unbreakable rules, one being that nobody was to be seated while he was on stage. One of the pages, a hapless kid of about eighteen, hadn't gotten the word. He began ushering some audience members to their seats while Hackett was doing his warm-up monologue. The second Hackett saw the small procession he stopped in mid-sentence and his face clouded over in a scowl.

"Hey! You!" he screamed.

The stunned page and the audience members froze and turned toward the stage.

"Yeah, you!" raged Hackett. "You stupid son-of-a-bitch! You don't seat anybody while I'm on this goddamn stage!"

This excessive display really pissed me off. After the taping I found the whimpering page being comforted by several people. I calmed him, then took him by the arm and marched him to the door of Hackett's dressing room. I knocked and we entered. Hackett was in his undershirt and boxers. The compliant look on his face told me he knew he had crossed the line. It was the first and only time I ever yelled at him.

"Damn it, Hackett! You owe this young man an apology!"

Hackett hung his head as if he were a little boy who had been caught, his trademark lower lip more prominent than usual. There was a long pause, then he whispered, "I'm sorry."

"He didn't hear you," I said firmly.

Hackett made brief eye contact with the kid, cleared his throat and repeated, "I'm sorry," with a bit more authority.

"Okay," I gestured, "now shake hands."

They did so and I never mentioned the incident again.

Buddy Hackett always played the buffoon, but in fact was an authority on some fairly esoteric subjects. On occasion, Buddy had scholars from around the world phoning or writing for his opinions. As a game show host he had some great qualities, with his rapid fire delivery and acid tongue, but sometimes I felt he went too far, scalding his contestants with hilarious but brutal put-downs. Once, we had a woman who could hum and whistle either the same song in harmony or two different songs at the same time. She was very talented and in no time had the audience in hysterics. That was her fatal mistake because Hackett was quite jealous of his kingdom and woe be to anyone who tried to be funnier than he. The moment he felt she was taking control, he launched a merciless but viciously funny attack on her. In mere moments he had reduced her to tears and we had to stop taping.

Hackett had some other idiosyncrasies that caused problems. One was the studio temperature: He required it be just slightly above meat locker levels, a balmy sixty-four degrees. I went to him one day to plead for the audience.

"Buddy, can't we warm up the studio? I'm afraid some of the people will get frostbite."

He shook his head adamantly. "No Bobby, you don't get it. It's gotta be cold in there."

"Why?" I wondered. "If the audience gets hypothermia how is that good?"

"'Cause if it's too hot in there the laughs'll rise and nobody'll hear 'em," he said with a knowing nod then walked away. I was left standing there, pondering the inexplicable Mr. Hackett.

One thing about Buddy Hackett, he was short and had naturally clownish features, and though he rode that shtick for years, God help anyone else who mentioned it. Hackett had a very thin skin for such remarks except among his closest friends, and then only in private. Outside of that small group, only Hackett made fun of Hackett. But I can recall one exception. On *The Tonight Show*, Johnny Carson asked Hackett if he got a royalty on Cabbage Patch dolls. The audience exploded and Hackett laughed along, taking the joke well, but only Carson could have gotten away with that in such a public forum.

We made a deal with a clothing manufacturer for Hackett to wear their clothes on the show in return for a promotional fee. Hackett was very conscious of his weight and once at 3 A.M. during pre-production, Michael got a phone call.

"Hello?" Michael answered sleepily.

"Michael?" came a small voice. "It's Buddy."

"Buddy?" asked Michael, suddenly alarmed and fearing the worst. "What's wrong?"

"I gained two pounds," he said contritely.

"What?"

"I've gained two pounds. You think those suits will still fit?"

Relieved that Buddy had not been in a car wreck or arrested, Michael relaxed.

"Yes Buddy, they'll still fit. Don't worry. If they don't we'll let them out a little."

"Okay, goodnight." Then he hung up.

Hackett could also be very warm and generous. One day a deliveryman showed up at our office with a large, wrapped item on a hand truck. It turned out to be an ornate and extremely garish grandfather clock, compliments of Buddy. However ugly the thing was we knew Buddy had spent a lot of money on it so we proudly displayed it in our office. Several years later during a move it fell off the back of a truck and was demolished.

Despite his habits of killing guests when they were too funny, or his occasional rampages, Hackett was an absolute scream. The set was a riot and I would often head for home with my gut aching from laughing all day. But one night on the freeway, as I was laughing to myself about the fun that day, I had a sinking moment of clarity and suddenly understood why the show was probably not going to make it. What slapped me in the face was the realization that, despite my sore jaw, the shows were not funny because almost all of the laughs came during the commercials. Hackett sometimes needed to have his ass booted or his hand held, but generally, he and I and Michael got along great.

A month or two before we went into production, my wife and I drove to his home in Beverly Hills for dinner. Hackett said the dress was casual so this old cowboy took him at his word and slid into my favorite jeans and cowboy boots. You couldn't miss his house because right in front was this enormous concrete elephant. When Irma and I arrived at their door, Hackett's wife Cheri greeted us warmly. George Segal and his wife had just arrived and Segal was decked out in a crisp blue blazer, gray slacks and a fire-red tie. He looked like a timeshare salesman from Phoenix. I take that snipe only because he was not even remotely pleasant to me. As soon as the introductions were over, he worked hard at ignoring us. Cheri escorted us back to where the party was warming up. I kept one eye on Segal the dandy, slightly concerned this might be turning into one of those party blind-sides where they tell you casual and everyone is dressed like they're going to a reception for the Queen of England.

We arrived at a large recreation room with a pool table, and behind the expansive bar was our host, making drinks. When I saw Hackett's casual powder blue shirt I relaxed a bit, concluding I wasn't guilty of a fashion faux pas. The house was spacious and elegant, but an exotic glassed-in room adjacent to us caught my eye. Hackett noticed my questioning expression.

"It's where I keep my pea-shooters, Bobby."

I gave him a confused look. "Your what?"

He grinned, "C'mon."

Inside that room was an absolutely massive collection of firearms. He had everything from Gatling guns to antique hand-inlaid pistols to state-of-the-art assault rifles. I'm no gun aficionado, but I knew he had enough firepower to invade a small country.

"Planning a war, Buddy?" I asked, not completely joking.

"Nah," he shrugged, playing down his arsenal, "I'm just a gun nut."

And he was. Even in his own home Buddy was packing heat. In his pocket was a small revolver. And I thought he was just glad to see me.

Hackett and Carey Grant during a party at Hackett's house circa 1978.

BOB EUBANKS ARCHIVE

BOB EUBANKS ARCHIVE

Glen Ford and Buddy Hackett at Hackett's house.

Hackett was handing out a few more drinks as Glen Ford and his wife Cindy arrived. Cindy and Glen had met in the late '60s while Cindy was a Golddigger dancer on *The Dean Martin Show*. Ford's brown, western-style suit and shit-kicker boots made me feel right at home. I noticed that Segal even warmed a bit in the presence of a bigger fish. Not long after that, another even larger legend arrived, Cary Grant, with his fiancée, Barbara. I found it telling how the screen giant interpreted "casual attire": a crisp, double-breasted dark blue suit.

With Cary Grant's presence, the change in Segal was complete. Though he wouldn't give the game show guy the time of day, I watched with amusement as Segal transformed from swaggering to kowtowing as the big dogs appeared. Once the party got going, we settled on an array of sofas, indulging in drinks and light conversation. Soon Hackett announced, "Okay! Everybody ready? Let's go eat!"

As we strolled to the dining room, Cary Grant took me aside.

"Bob, I've got to sit next you at dinner," he whispered.

"Sure. Why?" I was taken aback that Cary Grant seemed interested in sitting next to me. Given that Segal wouldn't even talk to me, I was surprised Cary had even noticed I was there. His tanned face lit up and he laid an arm over my shoulder.

"You know," he said, continuing to whisper, "Barbara and I never miss *The Newlywed Game*. I wanted to talk to you about it."

I thought, "Cary Grant watches *The Newlywed Game*? How cool is that?"

Later, as the dinner table conversation hummed, Cary continued his unbounded praise of *The Newlywed Game* "We play along on your show. We do quite well," he said, catching Barbara's eye with a wink.

Housewives from Minneapolis gushed like that about the show, but not Cary Grant. It was almost surreal. "I'm really glad to hear you and Barbara watch the show," I answered, trying to sound gracious.

"Oh, we're much more than that," he said seriously. "We live it. We won't even have a car that has a division between the front seats."

Unsure how to respond, I just smiled.

He continued in his whisper.

"We're big fans. Barbara and I are a real couple."

"What do you mean you're 'real couple'?" I asked, now also whispering.

"Barbara and I only have one toothbrush."

I winced. "Oh God, Cary, that's really more than I wanted to know."

Later, as the dinner table conversation hummed, Cary continued his unbounded praise of *The Newlywed Game*.

"We play along on your show. We do quite well," he said, catching Barbara's eye with a wink. Housewives from Minneapolis gushed like that about the show, but not Cary Grant. It was almost surreal. "I'm really glad to hear you and Barbara watch the show," I answered, trying to sound gracious.

"Oh, we're much more than that," he said seriously. "We live it. We won't even have a car that has a division between the front seats. Like I told you, we're a real couple." Unsure how to respond, I just smiled. The Hackett's home was just down the street from a mansion once owned by the gangster Bugsy Siegel's girlfriend. The underworld impresario met his maker one night in a Mafia version of a drive-by shooting. Everyone at the dinner table not only claimed to know who bumped off Bugsy, but had many of their own mob stories. Cary had some wonderful tales of Cuba, from the pre-Castro, Meyer Lansky days. The table was abuzz with colorful anecdotes about the criminal element in Las Vegas in the '50s and '60s. As the energy in the room grew, Cary announced he had a joke. He started, and it went on and on.

The momentum of the previous half hour flagged a bit, but we were all waiting expectantly for his killer punch line. Just as he was coming into the home stretch, Ford did it again. Giving Cary a soulful look, he blurted out, "I love you, man, I really love you." Once again, the room went dead silent.

Cindy Ford patted her husband's arm. "Poopsie? You alright?"

Hackett stood. "Alright you guys, anybody wants to smoke, go outside on the terrace. I'm gonna stretch my leg."

Hackett had just endured arthroscopic surgery and was still in some pain. He also hated smoke, but his remarks were obviously timed to cover Ford's embarrassing moment. The party started to disperse at that point. Later, as the last guests stepped out the door, I paused to ask Hackett about Glen Ford.

"He didn't really drink anything," I observed, trying to understand his strange outbursts. Hackett nodded. "Yeah, it isn't that. See, Glen was with one of the first camera crews that got into Auschwitz. It's sort of like what the Vietnam guys are going through. It really affected him, and only now is he startin' to have flashbacks of the people and smells and all that. It's finally gettin' to him."

As we drove away from the party I couldn't help but feel for Glen Ford and wonder what horrors he'd seen that even thirty-five years couldn't dim.

The Beatles • Mick Jagger • Cary Grant
Merle Haggard • Dolly Parton • David
Letter SOMEDAY WE'LL • The
Beach Boys • Ike and Tina Turner • Leeza
Gibbons • LOOK BACK ene Autry
Roy Rogers • Monty Hall • Roy Orbison
Buddy Hackett • Barbara Mandrell

MY CONCERNS ABOUT THE FATE of *The Newlywed Game* came true when, in September of that year, after the completion of the 1980 run—almost simultaneous with the debut of *You Bet Your Life*—the show was once again canceled. Not only had the loss of those big sponsors hurt us, but I think everyone in the business could feel the face of daytime television changing. Cable was starting to offer greater variety, and producers were beginning to explore new avenues for attracting viewers. As the months after the show's cancellation ticked by, it began to hit me that this time it was really over. I had never heard of a show coming back after two cancellations. Michael and I were getting by with The Hill Eubanks Group, but I knew one disturbing and inexorable secret about Hollywood: Nothing lasts forever. For that matter, rarely more than a season, which was exactly how long *You Bet Your Life* survived.

Now my concern was what to do, given my identity had been so tied to *The Newlywed Game*. With the show called out after two strikes and the slide into my early forties, I had to ask the question: How do I reinvent Bob Eubanks? *The Newlywed Game* had always been a safe harbor for me but now it seemed gone for good. The show did come back, but it took five long years.

Meanwhile, I had the mall shows and my time on the road with Merle and his band. Off and on, I saw an entire decade pass with Merle Haggard. You spend that much time with someone you discover a lot about them, who they are, what makes them tick, why they are who they are. Hag and I rode the highways of America together, ate in truck stops and mom and pop joints, and saw the inside of countless motels and hotels across the Heartland. I saw him and his musicians perform at everything from high school auditoriums to sold out sports arenas and opera houses. And the White House. It was a helluva ride, but in 1982 I knew I had to get off. The last concert I ever produced for Merle was in March of that year.

I got off an airplane in Beaumont, Texas, rented a car and headed toward the venue. On the drive from the airport I got to thinking about my wife and children. My kids were all in their early to mid-twenties and I was heartsick I had not watched them grow up. I had been spending their time with the Hags and the Dollys of the world, but not the people who really counted, Irma and Trace and Theresa and Corey. I remembered Hag's sad words to me about his role as husband and father and knew I was no better. Something inside me snapped, and it was time to salvage what I had left of my most important relationships. As I pulled into the hotel I realized I was done with music promotion and life on the road. I had to get home.

I found Merle and the band in the coffee shop and asked Merle if we could speak in private.

"Hag, I can't do this any more. The road is killing me. I've got to get back and start being a husband and father again."

His eyes had sympathy for a pain he knew all too well. "I know exactly what you mean." He told me to go home and that he and the band would be just fine. As far as the road goes, the only difference between me and Hag is that I quit cold turkey and he's still addicted. Many was the day I would get back from a long road trip cursing life lived out of a suitcase, then three days later be climbing the walls, checking my schedule and wondering what was on the other side of the next hill. I soon got used to being back and never really wanted to be gone again for a protracted time. As for Merle, he and The Strangers are still out there, riding the highways from one gig to the next. I'll bet to this day, even on those rare occasions when he's home, that once in a while Hag'll go out and sleep on his bus.

You meet many people in Hollywood who are phonies. You also meet them in other industries, but they just don't seem quite as extreme. Then, once in a while you run into the real deal, a genuine person who actually does what he says he'll do. Michael Landon was such a guy.

In March of 1979, NBC sent a bunch of TV stars and suits to Minneapolis for the opening of a new network affiliate, channel 11, KARE. Tom

Brokaw and Jane Pauley broadcast *The Today Show* live, and there were many network celebs to mingle with. One of them was Michael Landon. After striking up a friendship, we were walking though the airport on the way out of town when a woman approached him. She had that combination smile and furrowed brow that nearly every celebrity has seen, and then asked him the one question every celebrity hates: "Who are you?"

For some reason I had always felt that if I answered, "Bob Eubanks," it would be construed as egotistical. And if I didn't answer they'd think I was a jerk. I will never forget Michael's response.

"Lady, who do you want me to be?"

He said it with such a gleaming smile and electric charm she was completely floored but certainly could not say he was egotistical or rude. I began using that response from then on. It's been a great way to avoid the inevitable corner you get painted into by anyone crass enough to ask such a dumb question. Most of the time they have no comeback and just stare blankly at you. Another problem with reality television is that people never remember your name. Over the years I've been asked by countless people if I was everyone from Bob Barker to Dick Clark, and even Clint Eastwood when I was younger. They've called me Wink numerous times and frequently messed up the name of the person they thought I was. At least in dramatic TV they'll only slightly insult you by calling you by your character's name. I swear, sometimes people are so thick headed you could hand them your ID and they'd argue with you.

I was back stage at a convention in Dallas waiting to be introduced when some idiot stage hand said, "Hey, you're that Ken Lange, from *The Dating Game* aren't you?" apparently mistaking me for Jim Lange. I smiled and politely said, "No, I'm not." He shook his head, "Oh yeah, you are," as if I were concealing some state secret. When the loudspeaker announced, "And now here's the star of *The Newlywed Game*, Bob Eubanks!" he gave me this sly little smile, "See, I told you so." People often mean well but can be exceptionally rude around people they have seen in television or movies over the years. Because they have the illusion that they personally know you, some of them tend to take liberties. My only pet peeve is that I will absolutely not answer anyone who yells at me. You yell at your dog. If someone approaches me during dinner in a restaurant I will politely sign an autograph. But if some loudmouth yells at me across a bar to impress his date I will look right through him.

I stayed in touch with Michael over the years and we developed a friendship. So many people you deal with in this town are merely acquaintances no matter how long you know them, but Michael Landon was a friend. When Corey wanted to get into the stunt business he asked for my help. I made a few calls and one of them was to Michael. Having been on *Bonanza* for so many years I figured he knew a lot of stunt guys who were still active. He was doing *Highway to Heaven* and explained there was no action on the show but if he ever needed a stuntman he would call me.

Meanwhile, Corey began to carve out a career that would eventually see him become one of the top stuntmen and precision drivers in the industry. About a year after my call to Michael he phoned to say they had decided to add a little action to *Highway to Heaven* and he needed a stuntman. He asked if Corey was available. With all the stuntmen he knew I was quite touched and impressed that he remembered.

Corey went to work for Michael until other commitments took him away. He suggested that Michael hire his older brother Trace, which he did. Trace not only became Michael's new stunt double, but eventually became the show's stunt coordinator. Just before Michael passed away from pancreatic cancer in 1991, Trace worked on a two-hour television pilot Michael was shooting called *Us*. Trace thought Michael was funny, fair and a man driven by his creativity and heart. To me, Michael Landon was a guy who was good for his word.

I may be the only American to host a live game show in the U.K. Michael Hill and I produced an American show called *Infatuation*. The folks at U.K. Living bought the reruns of the show and then decided to bring me over to host the original English version.

Talk about a fish out of water. I loved the English people but sometimes their culture baffled me. My dressing room looked out onto a cricket field and I watched that game for three weeks and in that time had less idea about how the game is played than when I started. And the English men were very proper and polite, but so reserved and apprehensive about showing their emotions it was very hard to get good reactions out of them. This from the land of *Monty Python*!

It also took me a while before I found food this old cowboy could palate. I finally found a pub around the corner from my hotel that served an edible burger with salad. Unfortunately the salad "dressing" was a glob of mayo. By my second trip I had learned my lesson and solved some of my problems with an "emergency food kit" which consisted of Cremora, Equal and ranch dressing. That saved the day.

By the time my tour of duty was coming to an end I'd become pretty savvy to the ways of jolly old England. I saw a man in the lobby of the hotel one day and walked up to him.

"You're American, aren't you?" I asked.

"Yeah," he said, "how did you know?"

I pointed to his shirt. "Blue shirt. Every guy in this country wears brown, gray, black or green. But never blue. It's like they're trying to hide."

Sometime in the early to mid-'80s, I was attending a bachelor party for my attorney John Mason. There were a lot of people there, and in the course of the evening I noticed Brian Wilson across the room. Accompanying Brian was his controversial therapist, Dr. Eugene Landy, who was later accused of seizing control of Brian, both financially and emotionally. I didn't know much about Landy at the time, other than he seemed to be just another of Brian's weird diversions, like filling his bedroom with sand or staying in his room for years at a time. I made eye contact with Brian several times and noticed he was staring at me with a sort of childlike curiosity. As I made my way around the room, speaking with several people, Brian finally came over to me. He held out his hand.

"Bob? Brian Wilson. Have we ever met?"

I didn't know whether to laugh or cry for him. I took his hand.

"Shit Brian, we used to spend almost every weekend together. You opened my club in North Hollywood in 1962."

It had been at least twenty years and I saw him strain to recall it. The confusion in his face felt like a man twisting in the wind so I let him off the hook.

"So how have you been?"

There was a sadness to him, a beaten resignation.

"I'm okay. How about you?"

We spoke for a few minutes and the highlight was when Brian told me about his brand new yellow Corvette and his eyes lit up. For a moment or two he was like a little kid with a new bike. Soon others joined our conversation and we both moved on, but I couldn't help but have the sense that he was a man in trouble. Brian eventually broke away from Landy, got his life reorganized, started a new family and in 1998 released "Imagination," his first album in many years. As wildly successful as Brian has been, I came to see him as a tragic figure, a musical prodigy who had it all but got lost in his own mind. I hope he's turned it around.

Over the years I have had some memorable encounters with some of the most influential people of our time. And, as time goes by, I realize how special those moments were. In the 60s, long before I ever did the Rose Parade, I was standing in the tunnel of the Rose Bowl waiting for the rain to stop so I could promote a rodeo with the Pasadena Jr. Chamber of Commerce. The Grand Marshal of the parade was Ronald Reagan and we passed the time talking about all sorts of things, but especially horses, from what a joy they were to their importance to mankind. This was a man who loved horses as much as I do. I'll never forget that conversation.

In the late 70s I was in Las Vegas promoting a concert at the Convention Center. There was a television crew out front and I went to investigate and ran into Muhammed Ali and Joe Louis. Muhammed remembered me from my participation in the Thrilla in Manila so I struck up a conversation with two of the greatest fighters to ever lace up gloves. It was strange and wonderful as they casually chatted with me as if I were one of them.

I spent some time backstage at a Variety Club Telethon in St. Louis with two other titans of a different field, Ray Charles and Chuck Berry. Although Chuck had worked for me years before, I have always been a huge fan, and I felt privileged to be among these legends. They spoke with such familiarity I figured they had been friends for years. They talked about everything from being on the road to artists being cheated out of royalties to gripes about the record business. It was fun to sit back and just listen.

I was invited to play in a golf tournament in San Antonio, Texas, and was told a private jet would pick me up. We made a short hop to the Van Nuys airport and to my surprise Bob Hope climbed aboard. We departed and not many minutes later we landed in Palm Springs where former president Gerald Ford joined us. As with the other men, I was in awe of my fellow passengers and honored to travel with them. At the golf tournament I was to host a stage presentation. Prior to being introduced I spent the better part of an hour chatting in the dressing room with former president George H.W. Bush. He's a brilliant, outspoken and fascinating man and we passed the time discussing everything from golf to world affairs to Democrats.

During the Reagan administration I went to a roping in Fort Worth,

Texas, and met president Reagan's Secretary of Commerce, Malcom Baldridge. Mac was a very serious roper and as we sat under a tree at the event and discussed the woes of the world we struck up a friendship. He invited me to come roping with him in Landover, Maryland, near Washington, D.C. He told me he had horses and cattle but no one to rope with. Mac was such a cowboy he was inducted into the National Cowboy Hall of Fame in 1984. Tragically, a few years later, in 1987, Mac died with his boots on when a horse flipped over backwards and killed him doing the very sport he loved the most, team roping. Mac, I'm sorry I never made it out to Maryland to rope with you.

One afternoon I was sitting in the American Airlines Admiral's Club in Chicago when a distinguished looking man sat down beside me. One of the reasons I noticed him was his silly red and white polka dotted carry-on case. As I glanced at him I thought I recognized him. It took me a moment and I suddenly realized this was a true American hero, the second human being to set foot on the moon, Buzz Aldrin. I introduced myself and he proceeded to captivate me with stories about his great adventure, what it was like to be on the moon and his relationship with Neil Armstrong. We sat together on the plane to Los Angeles and it was the shortest flight of my life. How often do you get to talk to a guy who has walked on the moon? Oh, and the polka dotted case? His wife's idea, so he wouldn't lose it.

Perhaps my biggest thrill at meeting anyone turned out to be a dream come true for the ten-year-old in me. I was at the Hollywood Christmas parade, walked into the green room and my jaw nearly hit the floor. Sitting there—all in costume—were Roy Rogers, Dale Evans, Gene Autry, Pat Buttram, Iron Eyes Cody and Clayton Moore, the Lone Ranger. I was in absolute heaven. I don't recall even saying a word; I just took it all in. It's the only time I really regret not getting a picture.

The worst interview I ever did was on national television. It was the *Conan O'Brien Show*. I was excited when they booked me because I admired Conan's work. When the interview started all seemed well. He asked several questions about *The Newlywed Game* and then wanted to know when I began using the term "make whoopee." I explained to him, as I have done many other times, that I came up with that word because it was innocuous, and saying "making love" or "having sex" might cause a child to ask their parents about the subject before they

Ask me a question about Roy Rogers. He was the best!

BOB EUBANKS ARCHIVE

were ready to explain it. And I certainly did not originate the phrase. I first heard it in a Frank Sinatra song, "Makin' Whoopee," and took it to mean any form of intimate contact, even kissing and hugging. The term felt pretty harmless. I told O'Brien *The Newlywed Game* that the term was intended to protect the children. What I didn't get into was the story behind why I came up with the euphemism in the first place.

When my daughter Theresa was around seven or eight I was taking her to her riding lesson. It was a cloudy day and we were listening to a deejay named Corky Mayberry who mentioned he got "horny when it rains." When she asked me what "horny" meant and I nearly drove off the road. I was so angry that I had to explain it to her before I had intended to I resolved never to put another parent in that situation. By the mid-'70s the world had changed, so I relaxed my policy about using "making whoopee" in lieu of more direct terms.

O'Brien seemed satisfied, but then the interview bogged down. After an uncomfortable silence he suddenly raised his hands and came toward me while letting out this insane shrieking cackle. It freaked me out so badly I nearly fell out of my chair. When I recovered I asked, "Why did you do that?" He gave me a blank look and shrugged, "I couldn't think of anything else to say." It was the worst interview of my life.

Before I close the chapter on Merle Haggard I have a few more things to say, including a parting anecdote that I think capsulizes his staggering talent. Not too long ago I was sitting on an airplane listening to my iPod. I'm blown away by this thing—it's an amazing little gadget not much bigger than a pack of cigarettes that holds 7,500 songs. As I've mentioned, anything technical messes with my head, so I thank God that my assistant, Joanie Perciballi, knows how to download all my CDs. I was listening to some of Hag's songs and had to marvel at his range. From his ruminations on love to his songs about prison, fighting, loneliness, heartache and just every day situations, Merle elevates everything he touches, opening a door that would give even the most unreflective person a true glimpse at the highs and lows of being a human being. I love Cash and I love Marty, but for my money, Hag is the real deal. He writes 90% of his hits and no two sound alike. His melodies are unforgettable and his lyrics can bring tears to your eyes.

· I think it was around 1978, and I was sitting in Merle's suite at the Holiday Inn in Hollywood. Merle and Bonnie and I were supposed to be having a meeting but Hag seemed distracted. I was trying to explain something about our next tour, but he wouldn't look me in the eye and kept mumbling to himself. I wasn't sure if he was being rude or just losing his mind, but I kept talking. After a few minutes, Merle shook his head and stood up.

"Aw, shit, Bob. I gotta go in the next room for a few minutes."

With that, he grabbed Bonnie's hand and disappeared into the adjoining bedroom. After about twenty minutes he reappeared. He looked relieved. "I had this damn melody in my head all morning and just hadda get it out."

That "damn melody" turned out to be "Everybody's Had the Blues," which became a huge hit for Merle. It was fascinating to watch that song come to life. Merle seemed almost tortured for a while, as if something inside was trying to be born, while he both fought and nurtured it. It spoke a lot about the process. Perhaps the creative mind doesn't always set out to make something. Maybe sometimes a breakthrough idea or song, or whatever it may be, forces its way into the mind and demands to be born. With my friend Merle Haggard, the Poet of the Common Man, it's a process he's been through many, many times.

About the time I quit promoting Merle, I was in Las Vegas on business and stopped in at the Hacienda Hotel to see my friend Paul Loudin, who was the owner and president. When his secretary showed me to his office he was chatting with a dark haired guy who wore large, tinted eyeglasses.

"Great to see you," exclaimed Paul as he came around the desk to shake my hand. "Bob, this is my good friend, Joey Cusumano."

Cusumano warmly greeted me. After some small talk, they returned to their discussion. "I'm telling Joey that my employees are robbing me blind, at least during the late shifts." This was just before high-tech surveillance like the Eye-in-the-Sky rendered cheating too difficult to attempt without detection.

"Joey has some experience on how to cure these problems."

Cusumano nodded. "Yeah, listen, there are definitely ways to cut down on the problems you're having. Let's go down to the floor and take a look."

I followed them down to the main floor of the casino and quickly got an education in gaming house management. As we walked between the tables and machines, and wound our way through the crowds, Cusumano pointed out what he thought was wrong. He suggested rearranging tables, moving the dealers around and changing the traffic flow. Pretty impressed, I assumed Joey Cusumano was some sort of consultant. Over the next couple years I would run into Joey in Vegas and always enjoyed his wit and sense of humor.

Years later I was watching a television show about the making of Martin Scorsese's film, *Casino*. To my dismay, I learned that writer Nicholas Pileggi had based at least some of Joe Pesci's character, Nicky Santoro, on Joey Cusumano. No wonder Joey knew so much about gambling.

I could have used Joey Cusumano's services several years later. In 1986, Irma got a phone call. On the other end came a husky male voice. "Tell Bob Eubanks he's a dead man. I'm going to kill him!"

We immediately contacted both the FBI and the police. They told us the same thing: that there wasn't anything they could do until we got some other calls. To me it sounded like *Call us as soon as he kills you.* It scared the hell out me knowing there was someone out there with murder in their heart, and whether it was serious or not, I couldn't take that chance. When I left the house I carefully watched everything around me. When I drove, I constantly scanned the vehicles around me for anything suspicious. I now understood Merle Haggard's state of mind the time we first met when he was packing a gun for protection. It surprised me when I decided to do the same.

I took my sons as escorts to a mall appearance in Orange County and the police gave me a bulletproof vest. During the crisis I got a call from a reporter with the tabloid *The Globe.* He didn't know about the death threats and began asking all sorts of stupid questions about where I went to high school and so on. Edgy from the situation I snapped, "What the hell are you looking for?"

Smarting a bit, he asked, "Why are you getting so defensive? Do you have something to hide?"

I explained that someone had threatened to kill me, I was taking it seriously, and because of the pressure I was particularly sensitive. Bad idea. The next week, a full page picture of me was on the cover of *The Globe* with the headline Death Threats to Host of Newlywed Game— Scared Bob Eubanks Packs a Gun.

I have always had a poor relationship with the press. I think it all started years ago when the famous documentarian David L. Wolper approached me when I owned the Cinnamon Cinder. He wanted to do a documentary on teenage nightclubs. I liked the idea and gave him full cooperation. When the documentary was released I was appalled. In it, he scathed non-alcoholic clubs like mine as "Modern Day War Camps."

Years later I was doing an interview over lunch with a reporter from the Philadelphia *Enquirer.* We had a good rapport and talked about our children, the business, and shared quite a few laughs. I left feeling we had connected, so I felt particularly deceived when I read the snarky article the next day that opened, "He strutted in with his Conway Twitty hairdo." Conway Twitty? Strutted? I don't think I've ever strutted anywhere and I damn sure didn't have as much hair as Conway Twitty.

Oh, and as for my gun toting days? Trace and Corey took me to a shooting range and I couldn't hit the target to save my life. I carried that gun for about three weeks. One morning I was getting ready to leave the house and looked at that gun and got mad.

"This is bullshit. I'm not going to run anymore, I'm not going to hide, and I'm not going to carry a gun. Whatever will be will be. I will not live in fear."

I left the gun, walked out of the house and quit looking over my shoulder.

The Beatles • Mick Jagger • Cary Grant
Merle Haggard • Dolly Parton • David
Letterman • The Rolling Stones • The
Beach B... ...Leeza
Gibbons • Jerry Lee Lewis • Gene Autry
Roy Rogers • Monty Hall • Roy Orbison
Buddy Hackett • Barbara Mandrell

MICHAEL & ME

AN INCIDENT THAT HAPPENED nearly two decades ago has continued to haunt me ever since. One of the reasons I wrote this book was to finally set the record straight about it. A few things said offhandedly during a brief interview have caused me more pain than I can describe. It created such an embarrassment that for a long time I truly believed my career was over. And when people I thought were friends deserted me I considered leaving the entertainment business for good. It was one of the darkest periods of my life. For years I prayed that God would hear my pleas and send a well placed bolt of lightning to take care of my tormentor.

In mid-August, 1987, Charlene Trichon booked me into Flint, Michigan, to present *The Newlywed Game* before a live audience. This was of particular interest to me because I was born in Flint. I had few memories, given I wasn't quite two when we moved and had only been back once when I was seventeen, so I was looking forward to the date. Though I would be there for just one day, I wanted to get a sense of the people of Flint and see what kind of place it was. Over the years I had read of the large scale factory lay-offs and wondered how it had impacted the community. General Motors, by far Flint's biggest employer, had been dismissing people in Flint since the late '70s and had laid off nearly 30,000 of the town's citizens over the intervening decade.

I arrived on a lovely sunny and breezy afternoon, and as I made my way to the Flint Fairgrounds, the place looked to me like a normal Midwest town. At the fairgrounds I said hello to some fans and was told the stage and sound system were set and ready to go. Just before I went on, the fair manager told me a local guy wanted to do an interview for a TV news story. A pudgy guy in jeans and short sleeves approached me. With eyeglasses that rendered him slightly bookish, he introduced himself as Mike Moore. He was polite, seemed reasonably witty and asked if he could interview me after the show. I readily agreed.

Moore's questions focused exclusively on what he characterized as the sorry condition of Flint. He was extremely insistent that Flint was in desperate trouble and seemed to want me to corroborate his opinion. I answered the first few questions by pleading ignorance. I repeated to him that I had left Flint when I was a toddler and had grown up in California. I told him I considered myself a Californian and that I knew little of Flint. He pushed me to say something negative about Flint but I wouldn't take the bait. Instead, I kept telling him it looked like a nice town and continued to plead that I knew nothing about it.

During the stage presentation of *The Newlywed Game*, I had asked the husbands how much their wives' "chests weighed." I've asked the question hundreds of times during the televised and live versions and felt it was harmless fun. In our interview, Moore asked about the question and used the word breast instead of chest. I took exception to his word, telling him the word breast made it a "dirty" question, whereas I felt chest kept it innocuous. Chastising him for his word over mine probably stemmed from my sensitivity over the years to people claiming the show was sleazy or suggestive. I jokingly called him a pervert. Big fluffy clouds flew by, occasionally obscuring the light and preventing the camera from getting a perfectly exposed image. At one point, the cameraman announced that the light was dropping. As the crew began chatting, he seemed to turn off his camera and then stepped away from it. While we waited for the sun to come out—and assuming the camera was off—I told a stupid joke. *Why is it that Jewish women never get AIDS? They only marry assholes, they don't screw 'em.* That it was told to me by a Jewish friend does not excuse it. The crew laughed and the cameraman asked if I had "any others." Attempting to bond with them, I told another one that was equally off color. *I mowed the lawn the other day with my shirt off and my back got stiff. So my wife asked me to mow the lawn with my pants off.*

Both jokes, at face value, seemed relatively silly to me, but they both cracked up the crew (including Moore) and, at that moment, that's all that mattered. The light levels returned to normal, the cameraman appeared to turn his camera back on and we finished the interview. I immediately forgot all about Moore and his crew and went on to my next job. About two years later, to my horror, I discovered that Michael Moore was a bit more than just some guy with a TV news crew. He was, in fact, a documentary filmmaker and his debut piece, *Roger & Me*, was hitting the film festivals. And, with the film's increasing exposure, word got out that I was in it—complete with my tasteless jokes.

With a seven-minute ovation at the Toronto Film Festival, and with everyone talking about it, the gravity of it all hit me. Suddenly I was hearing whispers that Bob Eubanks was anti-Semitic. That absolutely staggered me. In a state of shock, I called my lawyer Eric Weinstein and asked him if he could find out how I was portrayed in the film. Eric hired a stenographer and sent her to the New York Film Festival. She sat through the film and wrote down exactly what I had said. After the film Moore held a press conference during which someone asked if they had gotten a release from me. Moore stated they had one.

A few days later Eric phoned me. I'll never forget it: I was at the corner of Hayvenhurst and Ventura Boulevard in Encino. I pulled over as Eric read me the transcript. I literally felt dizzy and slightly nauseous when I heard the words. What probably heightened all the drama at the time was that the latest version of *The Newlywed Game* had just gone off the air and I was feeling a bit vulnerable.

By now, the visibility of Moore's film was increasing, and so too was my anguish. Through the fall of 1989 it seemed I heard some new bit of misery every day. I was also either being consoled by people I had not spoken to in years, or finding that many I had regarded as friends were distancing themselves. In late January 1990, I got a phone call from my friend Jeff Wald. He had just returned from a Superbowl party at Pierre Cossette's home. Cossette has been executive producer of the Grammy Awards since the early '70s, and the guests at his party constituted a virtual who's who of heavyweights in the TV biz. Jeff spent the afternoon mingling at the get-together and came away with an ominous piece of news for me.

"You have a major problem in this town."

His words sent a chill through me. Always proud of my image, I considered myself sort of a boy scout among many of my Hollywood associates. Jeff's perception was that people were now seeing me as a sleazy guy who told racist jokes—and many of them had not even seen the film. I was absolutely heartsick. Since beginning my career I had worked with lots of people, many of whom were Jewish. A great percentage of my friends were Jewish, as were quite a few of my partners. Many phoned to make sure I was all right. I asked them all the same rhetorical question.

"Do you think I'm anti-Semitic?"

I knew I wasn't the least bit anti-Semitic but I wanted to see how they perceived me. Most just laughed, but those who realized how serious and shaken I was gave me detailed explanations as to why I was not. Buddy Granoff, Chuck Barris's partner, went one further.

"Bobby, this is total bullshit. You're no anti-Semite. I'm buying some full page ads in the trades swearing that you're no anti-Semite. It's bullshit!"

"Thanks, Buddy, but don't waste your money. I'll be fine."

But I wasn't. My partner Michael Hill got another news flash from an agent at William Morris. "I've heard that Bob will never work at CBS again."

I was stunned. I phoned the exec at CBS who had supposedly made the statement and set a meeting to explain myself. I arrived at her office and told her the whole story. She had not even seen the film. She stared blankly at me the entire time. I might as well have been talking to the table. I have not worked at CBS since.

Prior to this disaster, my partner Dale Sheets and I had been pitching a story around town about the first days of the Israeli Air Force. It's an amazing tale and we were trying to get a film deal out of it. I went to one of the heroes of the story, a former fighter pilot named Lou Lenart, told him about my situation and he offered to take me to the Anti-Defamation League to get their opinion. Lou and I met with a very nice man, a member of their Board. After listening to a full description of what had happened, the man waved his hand.

"Bob, one joke does not an anti-Semite make."

With help from Lou's man from the ADL, we drafted a letter of apology from me to give to the press. I then contacted Entertainment Tonight and they generously offered me a spot the next evening and I went on and apologized to anyone I may have offended. Fortunately, I told the joke about a segment of the population that is pretty compassionate.

But none of these kind and gentle gestures and absolutions softened my humiliation. Frustrated, I turned to the source of my torture, Michael Moore, and tried to reason with him. I called his appropriately named Dog Eat Dog Films to plead with him to take me out of the film. The receptionist hung up on me as soon as I said my name. I contacted Warner Brothers, the distributor, and asked that they remove the footage of me, using the rationale that my segment could be taken out with no effect on the film. They said there was nothing they could do. I found it interesting that while everyone was going to town claiming I was this terrible anti-Semite, Warner Brothers would not remove the very footage that supposedly was so offensive, despite the fact their CEO was Jewish. I guess, in this case, money trumped ideology and ethics.

When Eric Weinstein had to drop out of the case because he also represented Warner, I got another attorney, John Weston, who had successfully argued before the Supreme Court. "We'll sue Moore," said John. "It'll cost you $150,000 and we'll win. Then he'll appeal it and he'll win. You can't win here."

Phil Donahue did a two-part program from Flint on the plight of the town and Moore was his guest of honor. When someone in the audience asked why he had "included the Bob Eubanks" segment, Moore self righteously answered, "To show that that kind of prejudice is out there." The big question is: who's really the anti-Semite? Few know this, but according to the *Washington Times*, when Moore left his job at *Mother Jones* he complained bitterly to the press about the "Jewish" and "Zionist" influences he claims he saw while working there. Hmmm. All I did was tell a stupid joke.

I phoned my next door neighbor in Santa Ynez, Bo Derek, and got the office number for famed trial lawyer, Gerry Spence, in Jackson Hole, Wyoming. We spoke for a few moments while I told my story. Then Gerry asked in his deep, Western Plains drawl, "Didja tell the joke?"

"Yeah," I sighed.

"Well Bob, ya shot yourself in the foot. You don't need a lawyer. You need a PR guy."

I've lost track of all the hate mail, death threats and terrible things people have said to me. Sometimes the brick on the head comes right out of left field. One evening I went to the stage play, "Tony and Tina's Wedding," a fascinating piece of performance art that makes the audience part of the show. I was really enjoying myself and thought I had put the horrors of Michael Moore behind me for one evening, when a wizened little old lady approached me. Pulling back her sleeve to reveal tattooed numbers—compliments of the SS—she remarked with withering scorn, "I vas in Auschwitz. How could you?"

Shaken by that encounter, I decided to get aggressive in my defense and the next day I called a reporter named Naomi at the *Jewish Journal* in L.A. and told her the story. In the course of our discussion, we touched on an interesting subject.

"So you're saying," I said, "that if I were Jewish, this whole thing wouldn't even be an issue?"

"Absolutely."

But that was no consolation. I proceeded to invest a small fortune to dispatch lawyers after Michael Moore to stop his film—or at least to take me out of it. When we asked for a copy of his alleged release from me, all we got was a ten-minute video tape and an audio tape. Thwarted at every turn, my lawyers finally concluded we were powerless to stop him. The film went on to critical praise and launched Moore's career as an activist and sociopolitical critic. After siccing my legal commandos on Moore, I searched for any way I could to exonerate myself. I contacted a lawyer in Flint who had actually sued Moore over how he was depicted in the film. Prior to appearing in *Roger & Me*, Larry Stecco had known Michael Moore for over a decade and had even loaned Moore money for one of his projects, while working to ease some zoning problems on another.

In the film, Moore showed a Flint garden party as a clueless and insensitive gathering of the town's rich snobs, wallowing in their excess. Heightening the gap between the haves and the have nots, African-Americans stood motionless in the background, painted white like marble and portraying living statues for the amusement of the ruling class. The truth was, a recent *Money* magazine article characterizing Flint as one of America's worst places to live had the locals motivated to show support for their city. The party's primary goal was to raise money for a local battered women's shelter. Larry told me that Moore knew all this yet led the party guests to believe that he was shooting a piece for the Junior League and the local educational channel. He also neglected to mention in the film that the "statues" were paid models, thus implying they were servants. Moore encouraged the party guests to ham up their portrayal of the Gatsby lifestyle. (It was set up scenes such as those along with other glaring discrepancies that scotched a campaign by some to have the film nominated for an Oscar for best documentary) The end result was devastating to those at the party. It would be like going to a *Sopranos* theme party and then having someone claim in a nationally released documentary that you were in the Mafia.

Roger & Me made the party guests out to be racist aristocrats, which stupefied Larry when he saw the finished product. Politically liberal, Larry Stecco had marched for many causes, including that of civil rights in the '60s—not to mention helping Mr. Moore with his own liberal projects. Now he looked like a callous plantation owner, the South ablaze in the background as he sipped his mint julep. So he sued. After a lot of legal wrangling, and great expense to himself, the jury awarded Larry a settlement. The jury also recommended that Moore apologize to Larry, but Moore refused. When Larry later ran for a local judgeship, he told me Moore contributed a thousand bucks to his opponent. Nevertheless, Larry prevailed and is now the Honorable Judge Larry Stecco.

Moore took quite a bit of license in the film, not only with his portrayal of various characters, but also with many of the facts he alleged. To Larry's credit, despite what Michael Moore put him through, he holds no grudge against the man he once helped and who stabbed him in the back. As Larry says, "The people who know me know I'm not that person. If they don't know me, it doesn't really matter."

I feel the same way. In 1992, PBS commissioned Moore to do a 30-minute follow up to *Roger & Me* entitled *Pets or Meat: The Return to Flint*, obviously borrowing from the element in the first film where the woman offered rabbits for either cuddly pets or dinner. In the new film Moore took yet another shot at me. "Oh, and Bob Eubanks apologized for his joke and, can you believe it, Bob Eubanks is still working?" I couldn't believe him. He was like this crazed Rottweiler with his teeth in my ass and wouldn't let go.

For more than fifteen years the mere mention of Michael Moore's name made my blood boil. I swore to friends that if I ever happened upon him in a men's room I would rearrange his dentition. When his book, *Stupid White Men*, shot up the bestseller charts, and then seemed to hang there forever, I was nauseous. When he won the Oscar for *Bowling for Columbine* I couldn't believe it. Now, with the tremendous box office of *Fahrenheit 9/11*, Moore has become a major Hollywood success. I said, "God, I thought what goes around comes around."

When Moore practically got booed off the stage during his acceptance speech for Columbine, I understood. I let God off the hook: "Okay, I guess you had a plan."

I have railed at Michael Moore for years, but with the writing of this book I realized it was time to put down the burden I've been lugging around all these years and to acknowledge who really got me into that pickle—me. While I do not agree with Mr. Moore's questionable style of ambush journalism, what he did was...well, I walked right into it.

It sounds nutty, but I've always been afraid of cameras. I tense up when I see them. Photographers have always put me on edge because I, and many celebrities I know, have been set up by them. Interviews have also been tough for me because I learned over the years that the friendly interviewer will stab you in the back if it suits his or her cause. Perhaps my tension came through that day with Moore's crew. When Moore tried to pin me down about Flint, a subject that was obviously dear to his heart, I got on my soapbox and lectured him about other cities that had—at least the way I saw it at the time—far bigger problems. Maybe that pissed him off. When he asked about the chest/breast question I gently scolded him for being a pervert, only to turn around moments later and tell my tasteless jokes. I'm sure when Moore looked over his footage in the editing room he realized he had a way to get back at me for selectively taking the moral high ground. Perhaps he would have done it anyway. A few years after the film came out I ran into one of his crew members at Caesars Palace in Las Vegas. He said to me, "Boy, did you get set up!"

Whether or not Moore and his cameraman conspired to make me think the camera was off doesn't really matter. I have to take full credit for what happened. I think most adults have done things they are not proud of. I've certainly been involved in more than my share of such situations. This incident became one of my worst. When Michael Moore held a mirror up to me, albeit slightly distorted, I didn't like what I saw. Because of what happened I have not told an ethnic joke since. Jokes like that seem harmless, but when they come at someone else's expense they're never harmless. One big fear I had was that people who didn't know what was really in my soul would judge me to be someone I wasn't. Worse, people might take it out on my children or grandchildren. And worst of all, someday my grandkids might see me differently because of it. That is something I don't think I could bear.

When I was unable to stop the message, I went after the messenger. I raged at Michael Moore for years, venting to anyone who would listen what a jackass I thought he was. I hated him and his films and his books, and the bile rose in me every time he chalked up another success.

Yet it has been said that life is too short to carry such hatred and anger and I feel no truer words have been spoken. And because I deeply believe that I must let go of it, it is essential I reach a peace in my heart toward the man who got it rolling. Mr. Moore, you succeeded, you wounded me. But I cannot imagine that the plague you visited upon me was truly what you intended. I don't think anyone could be that perverse. I think you were just doing what you do best. As for me, I plead mea culpa and am laying down this sack of rocks once and for all.

That is, Mike, unless if we happen to run into each other in that men's room somewhere . . . .

The Beatles • Mick Jagger • Cary Grant
Merle Haggard • Dolly Parton • David
Letterman • The Rolling Stones • The
Bea... ...eeza
Gibbons • Jerry Lee Lewis • Gene Autry
Roy Rogers • Monty Hall • Roy Orbison
Buddy Hackett • Barbara Mandrell

CECIL B. EUBANKS

*S*OMETIME IN EARLY 1989, my son Corey gave me a movie script he'd written. He called his story *Payback*. I read his script and thought it was very good. He told me he wanted to play the lead and proposed that we find the money and make the movie. I teamed up with my friends Don and Dennis McCoy, borrowed the money, and suddenly we were in the film production business. Another friend, Norman Levy, an icon in motion picture distribution, helped us line up a distribution deal. With that we were off to the races.

The first problem we encountered was about money. Originally slated to have a $350,000 budget, it became clear early on that the budget for *Payback* would run much higher. As we wrestled with the shortfall, we began casting. For such a low budget film we did get some terrific actors. Tough guy Michael Ironside played the hard-ass sheriff, and soap star Theresa Blake was the love interest. We also had Vince Van Patten, character actors Bert Remsen and Buck Taylor and Patrick Swayze's brother, Don.

One of the most interesting coincidences of my life occurred when we were casting. We wanted veteran actor and stuntman Richard Farnsworth to play the role of an elderly gentleman who owned a gas station. I tried a number of times to reach Richard at his home in New Mexico but never got him. A few days later I was coming out of a gas station in Santa Ynez and who do I see driving by but Richard Farnsworth! I flagged him down and we talked. Even though he was busy and couldn't do the film, he got a kick out of the coincidence.

Richard could be pretty crusty but he always had this twinkle in his eye that told you he knew a lot more than he let on. He and I had an ongoing joke and whenever we'd see each other one of us would say, "How do you get to Encino?" The joke came from a story Richard told me. Richard was walking out of Pickwick Bowl in Burbank when a guy in a Cadillac wearing a double breasted suit, pulled up. Richard was in his usual cowboy hat and boots. The guy sized him up and yelled, "Hey Tex! How do you get to Encino?"

Richard opened his mouth in fake surprise and in his quiet little voice said, "How did you know my name was Tex?"

The slicker in the Cad shrugged. "I just guessed."

Richard nodded matter-of-factly toward him. "Then why don't you just guess how to get to Encino?"

We shot most of the film in Santa Ynez and our little production had just about everything from zooming helicopters and explosions, to cars and a bus turning over. The music was composed by my friend "Captain" Darryl Dragon. I hated motion picture production. Compared to television it moved like molasses and on top of that it was cold during the shoot.

In the middle of the production of *Payback* a scary incident occurred that could easily have gotten Corey and me killed. We were coming back from the ranch late one night and saw a telephone pole hanging precariously by its wires. Then we saw the cause of the severed pole lying nearby in a pasture. It was the remains of a car and it was on fire. We raced to the wreck and found two young men in what we barely recognized as a horribly mangled Corvette convertible. The passenger was unconscious so I pulled him out. Meanwhile, Corey threw dirt on the fire then tried to rescue the driver, but his seatbelt was jammed. Now the flames were leaping higher and we feared the tank might blow, taking us all out in a big ball of fire. Although I thought the driver was probably dead, I dragged the passenger to a safe distance then ran back to help Corey save the other one. As Corey worked to get the belt off him, I tossed more dirt on the burning car. We got the driver out and as I turned around I was shocked to come face to face with the stunned but relatively unharmed passenger. The fire department arrived moments later and knocked down the fire, but had we not arrived those two young men would have been toast.

We later found that the driver had just gotten the car from his parents and to celebrate had gone out, gotten drunk and made his new car fly, at

With my friend Richard Farnsworth. "How do you get to Encino?"

least temporarily, until it sheared off the pole and rolled over and over, nearly killing himself and his buddy. When we later asked the two to take an AIDS test, because they had gotten blood all over us, the driver whined, "Oh man, I don't have AIDS. I'm a drunk not a druggie." Both men took the test. Oh, and neither of them ever bothered to thank us for our trouble. Then, to top it all off, Trace contacted writer Mitchell Fink at the *Daily News* in the San Fernando Valley and told him of our exploit. Unfortunately, this happened during the middle of the *Roger & Me* turmoil and Fink sneered, "Great, but if you think this makes up for *Roger & Me*, you're crazy!"

Corey did a good job acting, his buddy and fellow stunt man Russell Solberg showed he could direct, and all in all the finished product was pretty decent. The movie looked like it cost a lot more than $350,000— because it did. The completed film ran around a million and we lost a little money in the end. I did not enjoy making the film, mostly because I couldn't stand the self-importance exhibited by many people on the production. I think Scott Chester, our associate producer, said it best: "God made people to make movies, or to cater to those that do." I consider our biggest success to be the fact that the people of Santa Ynez still talk to us.

While I'm on the subject, allow me to vent a little. I believe the entertainment business offers some of the most wonderful careers in the world. Anyone who is really motivated can find their niche. Male, female, in front of, or behind the camera—even wearing a mouse costume and wandering around that theme park in Anaheim—there are many paths and even more exciting opportunities. My oldest, Trace, was a stunt coordinator before leaving the stunt world to become a full time L.A. County fireman. Daughter Theresa became a script supervisor and worked on many films and television shows, including ABC's *Life Goes On* and Fox's *Party of Five*.

As I've mentioned, Corey is one of the world's top stuntmen and stunt drivers. When directors need a particularly tough or risky stunt they know who to call. Not long ago, Corey was hired for a series of very dangerous BMW ads. He did the stunt driving in three five-minute movies for the Internet directed by people like Tony Scott and John Woo. He was paid the equivalent of a very large yearly salary—for just a few weeks of work—but nearly died in the process. Which brings me to the plight of the stuntman. Yes, they are often well paid, but in Hollywood they are, by and large, considered second class citizens.

Many of the people who contribute to the production of films have very specific rules as to how they are credited. Big stars and famous directors insist on their name above the film's title. Writers and producers have a little ballet at the beginning of movies and TV shows as to how and what order their names are presented. Even the schlub who gets the director his latte gets a mention. Worse, there's no formal recognition for stuntmen. Makeup people and costumers are lauded with Oscars, but what about stuntmen? I think they should be recognized by the Academy, given their own category and, of course, their own award. Perhaps most unconscionable, how could their own union, the Screen Actor's Guild, ignore their own by not offering an award category to the stunt performers on their nationally televised show? Shame on you, SAG.

Stuntmen are often treated like dirt. Even though they're members of the same union, while the actors are sitting in comfy little director's chairs, the stuntmen are relegated to the curb. Appallingly, in a town where credit is king, many times they receive no credit for their work. And worse, when actors have a chance to put in a good word for the people who made them look good, the actors often feel inclined to snatch the credit away.

Corey doubled Tom Cruise in Ron Howard's *Far and Away*, choreographed the fights, taught Tom how to fight and did the really dangerous elements of his horse stunt work. As a father I was very proud of Corey's work, so it was a shock when Cruise went on television and bragged to Jay Leno that he had done all his own horse stunts. Not to slam Tom Cruise—Corey says he's a great guy—but, c'mon, man, don't go taking credit from someone who's put his ass on the line for you. Eight years later, another Cruise movie, *Mission: Impossible II* got my blood boiling again when the nationally televised stunt awards wanted to nominate Corey for his exceptional driving and the powers that be wouldn't release the clip that would qualify him for the award. Could it be they didn't want anyone to think Tom didn't do his own driving? Another problem is stuntmen have to wait until 65 to retire at full pension according to the union. The difference between them and actors is that actors don't break their bodies pursuing their craft. Stuntmen, like professional dancers, suffer many debilitating injuries and can't make it to 65 to collect their due. Not all of them become stunt coordinators or second unit directors. Picture a 64-year-old guy falling off a railcar or out a three-story window onto some boxes or mattresses. Some stuntmen are pretty tough cookies and work until that age, but many are suffering from arthritis and old injuries by the time they're in their late thirties. They should be able to retire at a younger age than other actors.

Corey has doubled many, many actors, including De Niro, Stallone and George Clooney. Along with Kevin Costner, those actors respect, and perhaps more importantly, publicly acknowledge the efforts of these hard-working, and often under appreciated, pros. People have said De Niro can be a little standoffish, so when Corey was set to drive for him in *Midnight Run*, he was curious. When the two of them were sent to sit in a truck to be physically matched up for a shot, De Niro had not yet introduced himself to Corey. While the hair and makeup people labored to match Corey and De Niro's hairlines, the two sat patiently. As they had their hair adjusted, De Niro was silent but kept stealing glances at Corey. Yet when Corey would turn to make eye contact, De Niro would look away. Corey is very affable and finally, after about twenty minutes, he couldn't stand it. When De Niro turned to look at him, Corey turned quickly and their eyes met. Corey, who has never been intimidated by anyone, nodded casually.

My son Corey with Tyler Ann and Casey.

My oldest son, Trace, with wife Susie and kids Christopher, Cole and Kelly.

My beautiful daugher, Theresa.

"So," he asked, "what do you do?"

De Niro had to laugh. "I'm an actor."

A few years later, Corey saw De Niro on the set of *Backdraft*. As they passed each other, De Niro stopped and smiled, "Oh, the comedian."

Corey fired back, "Oh, the actor."

When Corey was the second unit director and stunt coordinator for *The Wedding Planner*, he was told, along with most of the rest of the crew, they were not to make eye contact with the star, Jennifer Lopez. If anyone wanted to talk to her they were to tell her bodyguard, who would inform her assistant, who would pass it on to J-Lo. Corey had heard all sorts of ego games from stars but this took the cake. Because he was responsible for Lopez's safety and it was critical they communicated clearly, he decided to level the playing field the first chance he got. When she arrived on the set and introductions were made, Corey smiled and feigned ignorance about the big star. "My daughter tells me you're a singer."

Once they got underway, Corey was supposed to follow orders and not speak directly to her. For most of the day it didn't interrupt his job, but as the time got closer to doing an important and dangerous stunt he knew he would have to talk to Lopez. The stunt involved Lopez getting the heel of her shoe stuck and a large dumpster sailing down a hill toward her. The dumpster was actually a rather elaborate device, remote controlled and quite expensive. As second unit director and stunt coordinator Corey was responsible for everyone's safety, including the star's. The light was also fading so they needed to get the shot quickly and he didn't have time for a lot of theatrics between himself and Lopez's interpreters. He decided to cut through the crap and waved Lopez over.

"Jen, Jen, c'mere."

Lopez looked a bit put out but walked over.

"Look Jen," continued Corey, "when the dumpster comes down the hill, you keep your eye on this mark. The second the dumpster passes that mark you get out of the way. Because if you don't, the dumpster will hit you, I'll have a big old dent in it, and the rental company will charge me a fortune. So, bottom line? Get out of its way."

Lopez had to laugh. With the ice broken filming went perfectly and J-Lo and Corey got along just fine.

Sly Stallone was shooting *Get Carter* in Vancouver, B.C. and wanted Corey to do a car chase for him. Stallone had become a fan after Corey impressed him with his driving in *Cobra*. When the Canadians refused to allow an American stuntman to come up there (they come down here all the time), Stallone moved the entire second unit to Seattle so Corey could do the driving. Way to go, Rambo!

When I was a boy there was only one thing more exciting to me than horses, and that was roping. Every year when the family would head out to southwest Missouri to visit my uncle, I would wear out his dairy calves chasing them around the pen with my rope. I seldom caught anything but I sure had a blast. When I was 20 I met Jess Todd, a calf roper and team roper who owned a ranch in Canoga Park. I bought a roping horse, went to roping schools and was soon living my childhood fantasy. Jess stirred my interest in team roping and I found it so much fun it was almost like an addiction.

Team roping was developed by cowboys on the open range when they needed to capture and doctor a sick cow or steer without the benefit of a fence. One man ropes the horns or head, while his partner ropes the hind legs. Eventually that activity was translated into a rodeo event. Today, professional team roping involves hundreds of thousands of cowboys and cowgirls and many of them make a decent living at it. Most people would think they only do team roping in places like Texas or Wyoming, but many would be surprised to find that within one hour of downtown Los Angeles you can go to a team roping event almost every night of the week.

I joined the Professional Rodeo Cowboy's Association (PRCA) in the late '60s and actually competed in a few rodeos. Had my kids depended upon dad to bring home the bacon from those events they would have starved. Nevertheless, I have my gold card from the PRCA and we have a roping arena on the ranch. I like nothing more than an afternoon roping with Corey or anyone else who'll join me. It was my team roping experience that lead me to one of the best jobs I've ever had.

Having been a cowboy all my life, my "day" jobs have often taken me far from my love of horses, the smell of fresh hay and dirt under my feet. So when I was asked to do live television commentary for the PRCA I was elated. I was set to comment not only on the regular rodeos, but the National Finals Rodeos as well. And if that weren't enough, when I found out who my broadcast teammates were I nearly flipped: Bob Tallman, the dean of rodeo announcers, Hadley Barrett, former rodeo ace, Larry Mahan, the six time All-Around World Champion Cowboy, and former Miss Rodeo America, Pam Earnhardt (now Pam Minnick). Pam and her husband Billy own famous Billy Bob's Texas, billed as the world's largest honky tonk. It's a vast club, so big, in fact, they don't have mechanical bulls like other clubs—they offer the real thing!

It was a helluva broadcast team and, after quickly bonding, we hung nicknames on each other. Tallman was the Count, Pam was Pete, Mahan was Bull and I became Bert. David Allen, our PR man, gave me that nickname because he loved Bert Parks. To get him back, we named him Brillo, in a dedication to his curly hair. PRCA president Bob Edison became Flash. It was a blast traveling around the country to the best rodeos, and I soaked up a lot of authentic rodeo culture hanging around that crew. Tallman, the Count, can describe a rodeo with the skill of a painter creating a masterpiece. Rodeo jargon just flows out of him. And Barrett and Mahan, with their decades of rodeo experience, offered terrific insights and analysis into what people were seeing.

I also picked up many expressions, one of my favorites being *I'm so tired, you could put a piece of chalk in my ass and follow me all over town.* Mahan also offered me many moments of amusement. He used to fly his own plane between rodeos and was considered an excellent pilot. He had one rule though, which was no farting in the plane. Offenders were fined five bucks. Unfortunately, he never applied that rule to himself.

One afternoon we arrived in North Platte, Nebraska, for a rodeo and checked in to our humble little motel. We hadn't been in our rooms two minutes when I heard Mahan let out a yell. I raced next door to find him lying on his bed, his head and shoulders covered by a huge painting. Apparently the moment he laid down the painting fell on him as if on cue. I miss the Count, Bull, Brillo, Hadley, Pete and Flash. I never made much money doing the shows but I gladly would have swapped that gig for just about any other job I've had.

I had heard a rumor that Mark Goodson and Bill Todman locked themselves in a room back in the '50s or '60s (depending upon who was telling it) and didn't come out until they had brainstormed up about fifteen different game show formats. Some of the ideas they put down on paper eventually became *What's My Line?*, *Price Is Right*, *Password*, *Concentration*, and *Card Sharks*.

Card Sharks debuted on April 24, 1978, and began a successful three-year run with host Jim Perry. A few years later Jim went on to host *Sale of the Century* for NBC, a job he had for around six years. Sometime probably in the early '80s, Michael Brockman left ABC and moved over to CBS. In 1986, Brockman decided to bring back *Card Sharks* and called to see if I was available to audition. Why he didn't call Jim Perry I don't know, but I agreed and auditioned, even though I had not auditioned for anything since *The Newlywed Game* in 1966. It came down to me and John Wayne's son Patrick, and I got it. And so began a run until 1989 on the most enjoyable show I have ever done.

The game was played with two contestants competing to guess which of five playing cards would be higher or lower than the last. You gained control of the board by guessing how many people out of a hundred would answer a question a certain way. If you made a guess and your opponent guessed higher or lower, and was closer, your opponent got control. *Card Sharks* was a host's dream.

I worked with two very pretty ladies on the show, Suzanna Williams and Lacey Pemberton. Suzanna was a gorgeous blond and Lacey was a drop dead beautiful brunette. The show was a lot of fun and allowed me a chance to use my skills in drawing out the most amusing answers from the players. Unfortunately, quite often when I would play with the guests to extract the most humor I was shut down by our producer, Jonathan Goodson. Jonathan was Mark's son, and I believe he was trying so hard to please his dad he frequently erred on the side of such conservatism that it hurt the results on the show. Nevertheless, the show was a big hit for CBS and we had a good run. I would bet if you talked to Michael Brockman today he would tell you canceling *Card Sharks* was one of his biggest mistakes.

While Jonathan could sometimes try my patience, we generally got along. His dad, on the other hand, was wonderful to work for but had some odd quirks as a person. Mark got the hots for Lacey Pemberton and began to shower her with all sorts of gifts and flowers. When Lacey got married Mark's heart was broken. Then Lacey got pregnant and continued to do the show until she was due. After she had taken what I thought was a maternity leave, Mark came to me and asked if I knew anyone who could replace Lacey because she would not be coming back. Apparently Lacey had other ideas because she soon engaged civil rights lawyer Gloria Allred and went to the press with the story that she'd been denied employment. Lacey finally made a financial settlement with Mark and returned to the show. The only thing good about Lacey's absence was that my daughter Theresa filled in as a model in her stead. If anyone asks I tell them that, hands down, *Card Sharks* was my favorite game show of all time. By the way, Lacey is now the casting director for *The Bachelor* and *The Bachelorette*.

Over the years I've been asked many times if I have any good stories about my fellow game show hosts. First of all, two things that I've learned over the years is that comedians make lousy hosts and that there are hosts for shows and shows for hosts. Some shows could be hosted by a number of people, and some shows require a very specific type of

PRCA PUBLICITY SHOT

A thorn between two roses. World's All-round Rodeo Champions, Casey Tibbs and Larry Mahan.

BOB EUBANKS ARCHIVE

One of my proudest rodeo moments—World's Champion Brad Smith and I won the buckle at the opening of the Professional Rodeo Cowboys Hall of Champions in Colorado Springs.

Calf roping on my
wonder horse, Floppy.

BOB EUBANKS ARCHIVE

My first roping horse, Roanie.

BOB EUBANKS ARCHIVE

On the set of
Card Sharks
(1980's) with
my co-hosts
Suzanna
Williams
and Lacey
Pemberton.

CBS PUBLICITY PHOTO

host. I've heard Barker described as a rascal, a label that's also been at-tributed to myself, and that's why I think he could have done *The New-lywed Game*, just as I probably could have handled *The Price is Right*.

Alex Trebek was great on *Concentration* and is the perfect host for *Jeopardy*. I couldn't have hosted *Jeopardy* to save my life. I believe Pat Sajak would much rather be hosting a talk show than *Wheel of Fortune*, but walking away from that much money would be very hard. Chuck Woolery is a terrific guy, a good friend, and he's just as genuine and sincere off camera as he is on. Chuck has a vulnerability that people love. He makes mistakes and laughs at himself. On the other hand, some hosts have quirks that might not be readily apparent when you watch them perform for the camera. I was doing *Card Sharks* at CBS and although it was a lot of fun. Sometimes shooting game shows can get a bit boring between tapings, so one of the people who probably did the most in keeping me from getting bored was Bob Barker. And he never knew it. *Card Sharks* and *Price Is Right* were shot on the same set, so sometimes I had a chance to have a little fun at Barker's expense and mess with his sizable ego.

The dressing rooms near the stage were at a premium, so Barker and I shared one. A week's worth of shows were usually taped in one day, and the two shows were not in production at the same time, so we didn't often see each other. We were never literally in the same dressing room together, but we tried to respect each other's belongings. I say, tried.

After sharing the room for a while I became curious about a large wooden sign that hung over the couch. In it were carved the initials "WGMC." I had no idea what it meant, but I did know that it was Barker's. So one day in a fit of boredom I took it down and hid it under the couch. I went on to tape my show, then headed back to the ranch in Santa Ynez and forgot all about it. A few days later I got a frantic call from producer Jonathan Goodson.

"Bob, where's Barker's sign?"

I knew exactly what he was talking about. "Barker's sign? What sign?"

"Jesus! His sign! The one over the sofa! In the dressing room."

"In the dressing room? Remind me what sign that is." I couldn't suppress a laugh.

"Goddamnit, Eubanks, where's the sign!

"Exactly what the hell does WGMC mean?"

"Bob, shit, just tell what you did with his sign. Barker's having a heart attack over it. He won't go on until he gets it back."

"It's just a sign for heaven's sake. It's under the couch."

I heard Jonathan sigh in relief.

"So what does WGMC mean?" I asked.

"World's Greatest MC."

I laughed out loud. "You gotta be kidding?"

"No, no I'm not. Now I have to go defuse a crisis. 'Bye."

Barker has a couple other quirks that aren't apparent to most. Number one, he does not like to be touched. Number two, he hates it when people come on stage and say "I can't believe I'm here" as if they'd just been beamed in like on *Star Trek*. Game show host Allen Ludden was another old schooler who took himself deadly seriously. In the early

'70s I had a dressing room near his and, ever the practical joker, pried the star off his dressing room door. As with Barker, I got the panicked phone call also saying the star refused to go on until that physical symbol of his status was returned to its rightful door. Ludden was also easy to fluster. In the late '70s he was hosting *Liars Club*, and I came on as one of the four celebrity panelists. During a run of banter between us panelists and Ludden (while we were actually taping) I asked Ludden how much he was making as the host. My question completely floored him. They almost had to stop taping because Ludden got tongue-tied for a long, uncomfortable moment and completely lost his train of thought. Someone else made a crack and got the show back on the tracks. Ludden was one of the all-time great game show hosts, and his work on *Password* will never be forgotten.

I DON'T WANT TO SPOIL THE PARTY

The Beatles • Mick Jagger • Cary Grant
Merle Haggard • Dolly Parton • David
Letterman • The Rolling Stones • The
Beach Boys • ... • Leeza
Gibbons • Jerry Lee Lewis • Gene Autry
Roy Rogers • Monty Hall • Roy Orbison
Buddy Hackett • Barbara Mandrell

IN EARLY 1984 the decision was made to bring back *The Newlywed Game*. I was busy trying to sell *Celebrity Secrets* and wasn't available, so they hired Jim Lange. ABC planned an experiment to do the show one week. At the end of the week the decision was made not to move forward with that version of the show. In 1985, Barris sold his company to Burt Sugarman. Sugarman, who is married to *Entertainment Tonight's* Mary Hart, was a very successful television and film producer. Sugarman's company brought back *The Newlywed Game* once again, and this time I was the host.

One of the first decisions they made was to paint the set blue and white and have me stand between couples two and three. The color made no difference, but I'm certain that moving me changed the dynamic of the show. The episodes shot during the run between 1985 and 1989 were the funniest we ever did. Putting me closer to the couples created a magic that worked wonders for the responses I got. I didn't think we could find anything new after nearly twenty years, but I feel those were probably the best days of *The Newlywed Game*.

But after four years the ratings began to drop, as they usually did after that period of time. Michael Hill and I had just sold *Celebrity Secrets*, so I decided to quit *The Newlywed Game* and host our new show. Unfortunately, the company assigned to distribute *Celebrity Secrets* folded about midway through the sales effort and I was left without a show. When I quit *The Newlywed Game*, Jeff Wald was managing comedian Paul Rodriguez and brought him in to replace me. I offered to help Paul make the transition, but after one session I could see Paul was going to do it his way, so I backed off.

301

The finished product didn't work. Watching it was like seeing somebody beat up my mother. It had no pacing and worse, Paul thrust himself center stage. The star of the show had always been the couples, and now here was Paul, stealing their thunder and trying to out vamp his guests. That's the problem I have with comedians being hosts—they make lousy ones. They're too busy being funny and not listening to their guests as they try to come up with their next line. I also think good hosts make lousy comedians. Meanwhile, Burt Sugarman sold his company to former Sony chief Peter Guber, who eventually sold it to Sony.

The Paul Rodriguez incarnation of *The Newlywed Game* went away pretty fast and the show lay dormant until 1996. In that year, new owner Sony decided to bring it back to the marketplace. As with all big companies, the suits at Sony decided to meddle with a formula that had worked for thirty years. They concluded they needed a new, younger host. Their choice was a guy named Gary Kroeger, an alum of *Saturday Night Live* in his late thirties. When I heard they were bringing the show back I was momentarily excited until I heard they had a new host. I couldn't bring myself to watch it so I have no idea how Kroeger did. The new version also changed the format, with three couples instead of four. That version lasted a year.

Not long after that I got a call from Russ Krasnow, the new head of programming at Sony.

"Bob? We fucked up. If you're interested, I would like to talk to you about coming back and hosting the show." I had mixed feelings. I was surprised and happy, but I was also irritated. They had taken my baby, assaulted it with a new host and format and it had crashed and burned. My response was, "Get out your checkbook." I was curious as to what Krasnow would offer. When I walked into his office, to say we hit it off on the wrong foot would be a gross understatement. For a guy trying to woo me back he had a very strange approach. We shook hands, and as I sat down he laid a book in front of me. The author was Michael Moore. I sensed an ugly turn of events.

"Before we get started, I want you to know this guy is a friend of mine."

Still stinging ten years after the incident, I lashed out. "Then before we started, let me tell you, you have a friend who I think is a liar and a cheat and not a very nice man."

That meeting set the chilly tone of our relationship for the next two years. Sony cried poor-mouth, so in lieu of a decent salary I was given a producer's credit. But it was in name only because whenever questions arose that related to the direction of the show, I was relegated to a corner while others made the decisions. You would think the people in charge would be interested in the opinions of a guy with three decades of experience with the show, versus their few months.

One of the few things they did right was going back to the original four couple format, but they made some blatant mistakes like the sets, which were poorly designed and executed. Another problem arose in miking the contestants. After they had spent some time warming up the contestants in their dressing room, a sound man would enter and put his hands up their clothing to install his mikes and wires. This tedious and invasive process took them out of the moment and ruined whatever magic we'd summoned in our preshow warm-up. I suggested we mike them before the warm-up, but was ignored. I believe it put a damper on the contestants' attitude and hurt the quality of their answers.

Sony assigned a new producer to the show. As with Russ Krasnow, Steven Brown and I got off to a rocky start. I had a wardrobe guy named Jim Hook who handled wardrobe on all the game shows I did. Jim has a sharp eye and always made me look good. Not long after Steven came on board, he waltzed into my dressing room and started going through my clothes rack.

"What are you doing?" I asked.

"I'm here to pick out your clothes."

"What are you talking about?"

"I pick out your clothes from here on."

"Sorry pal, but I'm the host and I'll pick out my own clothes."

"I'm the producer of the show and I'll be picking out your clothes."

"Like hell you will."

"I'm sorry Bob, but that's the way it is. I'm choosing them."

"Go ahead. I just won't wear them."

"That's the most passive-aggressive thing I've ever heard."

At that moment I felt like demonstrating that a punch in the nose was even more passive-aggressive, but I guess that just would have been aggressive-aggressive. I didn't wear his sartorial selections. Early on, Steven and I had a number of heated discussions and confrontations, but none reached the level of what happened during a taping one afternoon.

I was in the middle of a very funny bit with a contestant. We were slinging it back and forth and I was enjoying one of those rare moments on the new show when everything was working. Suddenly I heard, "Stop tape!" and the show ground to a halt. Annoyed, my annoyance quickly turned to rage when I discovered the show had been stopped because a word was misspelled on a cue card. I stormed into the booth and got into it with Steven and Sony exec Melanie Chilek. Something snapped inside me and the three of us got into a horrible screaming match. Suffice it to say I am not proud of that moment. Surprisingly, Steven and I eventually put our differences aside and have since become good friends. Despite our differences on the show, overall I feel he is an excellent producer. Oh, and the word was *not* misspelled.

As I mentioned earlier, in the mid-90s, Michael Hill and I produced a show called *Infatuation*. It was a reality show whose concept was ahead of its time. After seeing an episode of *Sally Jessy Raphael*, Michael and I thought the premise would work for a series. And the idea was this: Have you ever had a crush on someone but were afraid to tell them? We would put the person with the crush on camera and they would describe their infatuation with someone. Meanwhile, that someone would be backstage, in a soundproof area, waiting to find out who had the crush on them. Then we would unite the two and, as they say, see what happened.

The show hung on two magical moments, first, when the object of the crush came onstage and found out who had the thing for them, and second, when the person with the crush made their proposition. At that point the object of the crush had the option of accepting or rejecting the offer. That was what held the audience in suspense—anticipating the big moment, when the person with the crush either crashed and burned...or soared. While the concept later backfired with tragic results for Jenny Jones, about the worst thing that happened on our show was some ruffled egos.

One afternoon a little lady in her late fifties came on all starry eyed about a young man less than half her age she had met while they were extras on a film. While the film was shooting the two apparently hooked up, and during some downtime (as I mentioned earlier there's a LOT of downtime shooting a movie) the two ended up in his car and got jiggy with it. When they parted company he promptly forgot all about it. She did not. She contacted our show professing her love for him, so we began making arrangements to fulfill her dream. We contacted the young man and told him someone had a crush on him. He agreed to come on the show but had no idea who held him in such esteem.

With the camera catching every word, the older woman described in detail her fling with the young Latin Lothario. Then I said, "Okay, let's bring him out." The door opened and when he walked out on stage and saw who it was he almost died. I'm pretty sure he figured their quickie marked the last time they would ever see each other. Now everyone would see he had gotten it on with a woman probably older than his own mother. He was mortified.

Several days after the taping his lawyer contacted us, demanding that we not air the episode on the grounds his client's "Latin lover image" would be destroyed if the world visualized him rolling around in the back seat of his car with this older lady. We eventually settled it out of court, agreeing not to air the episode in Los Angeles to preserve his all important "Latin lover image."

One thing I have found very interesting in observing couples over the last thirty-five years was how much people—and our society—have changed. When I started doing the show in 1966, people tended to be more mean-spirited, almost as if they had bought into the notion of the war of the genders fostered by sitcoms and radio comedies of the '40s, '50s and '60s. It seemed almost a cliché for the men to try and "get away" with things behind their wife's back, or to hate their mothers-in-law or to generally be at odds with their wives. Though it made for good TV, I was often saddened by the lack of respect people showed each other—particularly when it was someone you supposedly loved above everyone else. Over the years I saw women start to take control of their roles and assume a power they never had—or possibly never embraced. By the '90s, couples seemed more like teams, with both of them working and sharing equally in the responsibilities of managing a home, careers and a family.

It's sad that all of the episodes from 1966 to 1974 were destroyed. Not that *The Newlywed Game* should necessarily go into the entertainment archives with *The Honeymooners* or *Citizen Kane*, but it was a slice of Americana. It represented, to some extent, the values of the average young newlywed living in the U.S. in the mid to late 20th century. Sure, it was a comedy show, but it used real people, and the questions not only sought laughs, but defined who they were and the nature of their relationships with their spouses. When you put anyone in front of a camera there will always be some manipulation, but there was also a lot of truth. Which brings to mind some of my favorite questions (and some of my favorite answers):

What's your favorite thing to put on your Pavarotti? In all deference to the great tenor I usually got "Spaghetti sauce."

Where does the electricity go when you turn it off? "From the vibrator to the wall plug."

How many digits does your husband have? "One, and it's a big one."

How many showers did your wife have before she got married? One stupid husband said, "She takes baths."

If you went to see *Henry the VIII* twice, would your wife say she went to see *Henry the XVI* or *Henry the IX* twice? Without apologizing to Mr. Shakespeare, two couples said "*Henry the XVI.*"

What's your husband's least favorite thing to put on his wiener? One wife said, "Ben Gay."

Sometimes during a show Metzger would come up to me and say, "We've got to replace this question." One time as we were trying to figure out a replacement question Metzger finally said, "Oh hell, just ask what their favorite rodent is." It got a laugh out of me so I asked it. Two of the women did not know what a rodent was. I urged them to answer anyway and one said, "saxophone," and the other said, "karate school." With those answers we knew we were on to something, so from then on we started asking questions with words that sounded a lot like something else. It spawned questions like "When's the last time your husband masticated?" which caused an embarrassed bride to declare, "Oh, he doesn't have to do that, we're married." When I asked another young lady "When's the last time your husband vacillated?" she shook her head: "We use baby oil."

And to show the art of manipulation, if I asked the ladies "In what direction does the sun come up?," intellectually, they would answer "East." But if I put them in a scenario in their kitchens on a warm summer morning with the coffee brewing and the sun on their back, then asked, "In your neighborhood, which direction does the sun come up?," I would get every point on the compass.

I watched America change over four decades on my stage and, in spite of all the fears that we're going down hill as a society, I feel confident that we're getting better.

In 1999, Sony pulled the plug on *The Newlywed Game*. Some of those

With the
legendary
Monty Hall.

ABC PUBLICITY PHOTO

original episodes did not air until the year 2000, making me and *Let's Make a Deal's* Monty Hall the only game show guys to host the same format in five different decades.

One particular episode on the show that was alleged to have occurred—or did occur—has spawned nothing short of an urban legend. It even inspired the title of this book. I am, of course, referring to the famous (or infamous) "In The Butt" incident. Did it happen? And if so, exactly what happened? I sincerely told people for many years that it never happened. Then someone showed me a clip and proved me wrong. It did happen, but not precisely the way mythology and collective memory have it happening.

Sometime in the '70s I asked a little lady in her early twenties named Olga, "Where's the strangest, most unusual place the two of you have ever made whoopee," fully expecting something relatively innocuous like "the garage" or "the dining room table." Olga took it another way and found herself on the spot, apparently feeling pressured to reveal on national television something that, up to that moment, had been intensely private. Her face very serious, she finally answered, "In the ass." I shook my head.

"No, no, no, give me a location."

She then gave me some innocuous answer. The "ass" line got bleeped but history, if you will, had been made. I don't know why I didn't remember it, or maybe like everyone else, I began to buy the myth and

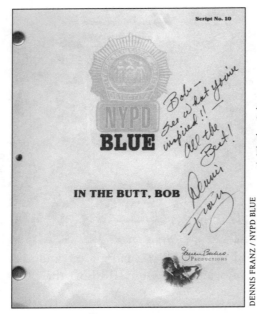

Script No. 10

NYPD
BLUE

Bob—
See what you've
inspired!!
All the
Best!

IN THE BUTT, BOB

PRODUCTIONS

DENNIS FRANZ / NYPD BLUE

Autographed copy of NYPD Blue "In the Butt, Bob" script. They were praying they didn't get an Emmy nomination.

not what actually happened. Perhaps the excuse, at least in my case, was living through nearly forty years of tapings—they tend to blur together. I heard the following story (I assume its true) and think it's a funny bookend to the "in the ass" story.

When the producers of *Confessions of a Dangerous Mind* (based on Barris's book alleging his spy escapades), were putting their film together they wanted to use the clip. They contacted Olga and asked for permission. She refused, claiming, "Oh no, I'm a grandmother, you can't use that." When the producers countered, "We'll give you $5,000," Olga quickly replied, "Okay."

Finally, I was hosting a Hollywood Christmas Parade some years back and was interviewing multiple Emmy winner, Dennis Franz.

During the interview he chuckled, "We've immortalized you."

"How is that?"

"We did an episode we called 'In the Butt, Bob.' After we aired it we started worrying we might get an Emmy nomination for it."

"And how is that a problem?"

"We'd have to announce the title of the episode."

They didn't get that nomination for "In the Butt, Bob," but they have certainly received plenty of others over the years, along with many well deserved golden statues.

COWBOYS AND INDIANS

The Beatles • Mick Jagger • Cary Grant
Merle Hag~~gard~~ ~~Dolly Parton~~ • David
Letterman • ~~The Rolling~~ Stones • The
Beach Boys • Ike ~~&~~ Turner • Leeza
Gibbons • ~~Jerry Lee Lewis~~ Gene Autry
Roy Rogers • ~~Monty Hall~~ Roy Orbison
Buddy Hackett • Barbara Mandrell

I N 1976, MY FIRST WIFE, IRMA, and I were up at the ranch in Santa Ynez. Early one morning I looked out the window and saw her sitting on the fence staring at the barn. A little while later I glanced out again and she was doing exactly the same thing. I went out to see if she was okay.

"I want to do something, be in some kind of business," she said as she heard me approach.

"Like what?"

We had taken a shot at horse racing and it proved to be a tough field. I figured out very early you didn't have to own them to watch them being saddled. We had talked about raising thoroughbreds. Irma had also investigated the brood mare business but concluded, after a great deal of research, that even if you're lucky enough to find a fantastic horse, it's still a total crap shoot. She kept eyeing that barn.

"What about art?"

"Huh?" her comment seemed like an absolute non-sequitur. "Art?"

"Yeah...," she said, as the idea gelled in her head. "I don't want to have to depend on anybody again. I want to be in business for myself. I have a background in art. I've got a good eye for it...."

"Yeah...you do."

Irma had taken some art and design in college and had shown a real talent for the art she'd selected for our homes.

"How about an art show?"

"Uh, sure. Where?"

"There," she said, as she jumped down from the fence and started moving toward the barn.

For a few moments I thought she'd taken leave of her senses until she started explaining her vision. Inside the barn she swept a hand across the scene as if visualizing a painting. "Great art, displayed in a great setting." I looked at the stalls and the dirt on the floor and just couldn't picture it. It was, after all, a barn. "We'll redo it. Walls, lighting, everything. Make it a setting to enjoy terrific Western art." Irma had a very strong will and was also very practical. Though I didn't yet see what she saw, I thought she just might be onto something. A few months later, after she assembled an art collection and transformed the barn with her crew, I stepped inside for the big unveiling. My jaw dropped open. Irma had taken what had been an old hay barn and turned it into a spectacular art gallery. Spot lights created warm pools of illumination, while potted and hanging plants gave the place a feeling of serenity. The collection of art she had assembled was exquisite, and it was beautifully displayed, with each piece complementing the one next to it. Soft music created a mood perfectly conducive to enjoying the art. I was absolutely amazed.

The first show lost $9,000. Yet Irma was undaunted, and over the next twenty-five years the Peppertree Art Show evolved into one of the longest running and successful art shows in the West. Many consider our art show one of the premier exhibits of its kind. Irma put together a collection of the works of some of the best artists in the country, featuring beautiful paintings, striking bronzes and intricate wood carvings. Her idea was not only to display great art in a special way, but also to offer both the experienced and beginning collectors a chance to add to their collections at accessible prices. She began doing the show twice a year, in May and November. It was quite an undertaking, with months of searching for the right artists and pieces, to the weeks of prep and assembly just prior to the show's opening. In the mid-'90s, Irma's health began to fail so she cut back the show to once a year. When cancer took Irma from us, Trace and I sat down and talked about the future of the show. He had been working with his mother on the show for years and we both agreed she would have wanted it to continue. Since retiring as a fireman, Trace now runs the show and has it back on its bi-yearly schedule. Like his mom, he does a great job of picking the artists and keeps the show running like clockwork. In May, 2004, we proudly presented our 50th show featuring over 100 artists who had been with us over the years. It was an incredible success. If you are ever up in Santa Ynez in May or November, stop in and join us for the Peppertree experience.

In the early '90s, I received a phone call from a very pleasant man who had been referred by my friend Jim Wagner. Larry Donizetti had heard of my affinity for art, as well as my interest in anything having to do with Western American culture. Larry was a marketing man and told me about an idea he had to sell items on the Home Shopping Network. HSN is a Florida-based company that was founded in 1977. It started by selling closed out items and stuff many retailers wouldn't touch. Something about the thrill of buying things from the comfort of your own living room eventually made the network a huge success. Larry's idea was to sell unframed Western art lithos. He thought that with my name attached we could do well. We approached HSN and they not only liked our idea, but encouraged us to expand our scope. They suggested we include framed items as well as Native American jewelry and artifacts. We thought that was a great idea and set about putting together a line. With that, the Bob Eubanks Southwest Gallery was born. Larry and I immediately headed to Gallup, New Mexico. Though small in population, Gallup is a hub for the Navajo Nation. It also features the largest collection of Navajo artists in the Southwest. We began setting up contacts with many of the Navajo jewelry craftsmen and traders in the area. The locals had never considered such a volume of business. We went to the hogan of one Navajo silversmith and inspected his work. We really liked his jewelry, and when we asked if he could provide 500 handcrafted rings that looked identical, he almost fell out of his chair. He was deliriously happy with our order but a bit panicked, not only by the sheers numbers, but by the prospect that his hand assembly suddenly had to have the look and consistency of a factory.

We made deals with a number of craftsmen that allowed us to reserve the items, but did not require their production until we had orders. Once the orders were taken we would have the artisan fill them. We hoped we would swamp them with orders but really had no idea whether of not we'd be successful. HSN was predicting a large volume but in the end they didn't know whether we'd sell twenty rings or 2,000.

Because of my connections in the art world, I found a place that would frame our lithos at such a low cost it allowed us to make a decent profit per unit. We got our product line ready and HSN gave us a time slot. On the air date, Larry and I arrived at the studio just before I was to go on. We were hopeful, but a little nervous. I was shown my mark in front of the cameras and away we went. As each item is introduced, you can see a computer screen off to the side of the camera that instantly tells you your status. In one glance you could see how many items you started with, how many you've sold, what your gross sales are, and how much money you're making per minute.

Before I went on I realized I had to have some kind of hook to sell our items. They were very high quality and beautifully crafted, but I knew that a story would sell them. I had watched other people pitching their products and the most compelling (and the most successful) presentations were the ones with a story. One of my first items was the painting of a little Indian boy. A darling two-year-old, he was dressed in his full costumed regalia and strutting his stuff at a traditional pow wow. What made it unique was that the artist, Mimi Jungbluth, had painted the smallest corner of his diaper sticking out from beneath his costume. She told me that the little boy danced for hours and, as the day grew longer, the diaper got heavier and heavier. It was a sweet, charming story and I told it as the item went up for sale. In four minutes we sold 300 pieces. Unlike today, when HSN's time blocks are much smaller, we had two four-hour periods in which to sell our wares. The first day was a smash hit and HSN had us back many times. We did ridiculously well. It was not uncommon for us to gross $700,000 to $800,000 in those eight hours.

All was well for a couple of years and then Barry Diller came along. Diller had been the head of Paramount Pictures for a while and went on to run HSN's rival QVC. By the mid-'90s, he left QVC and bought HSN. With the arrival of Diller things changed for the worse for vendors like us. Other than increasing competition for his network, along with Diller's reign came the institution of a system at HSN they called "guaranteed sales." That meant the vendor not only had to have a large number of the items ready to go, they also had no guarantee from HSN if they didn't sell. I tried to picture going back to the guy in the hogan and telling him I needed to return half of the thousand rings he'd just scrambled to make for us.

Larry and I moved on from HSN but had many other ventures, some profitable, some disastrous. We created, along with Michael Hill, a live game show in Branson we called "The $25,000 Game Show." What we failed to take into account was that people would be hard-pressed to pay for what they've come to expect for free on television. It was a good idea but just in the wrong place. Over the three years the show was presented we lost around $400,000.

We've also marketed videos of *The Newlywed Game* and a Christian workout tape called *Connection*. We got into book publishing, infomercial production, golf club manufacturing, and even helped start an airline called Tahoe Air, running daily jet service to Lake Tahoe. We marketed ladies' sandals that had interchangeable colored and textured tops so women who were traveling could take a whole closet full of shoes in one bag. We even sold an acne remedy and a multi-level marketed vitamin supplement.

When Larry and I were looking for new products to sell on HSN, I came across an item in Branson I thought was very cute. It was this goofy little Felix the Cat clock, but the hook was it talked to you. And in Japanese. When you set the clock and the alarm went off it would politely say "Ohio," which I believe is Japanese for hello. If you hit the snooze it would come back for a second time, this time a bit more insistently, "Ohio!" On the third try, Felix was downright pushy and yelled, "OHIO!!" When you finally turned it off it would thank you with a snappy little, "Domo."

The clock was perfect for HSN, and when I showed it to Larry he laughed. We thought we'd give it shot with HSN. We were getting ready to leave town so he stuck it in his bag and we went to the Springfield/ Branson airport. While waiting for our plane there came an announcement, "Would TWA passenger Mr. Larry Donizetti please come to the TWA ticket counter."

I looked at Larry. "What's that about?"

"No idea."

When we arrived at the counter there were two big cops looming.

"Mr. Donizetti?"

"Yes?"

"Come with us, please."

Larry and I nervously followed the cops into the back room. On a table was Larry's bag.

"Could you explain that?" asked one of the cops.

From inside Larry's bag came a muffled little, "Ohio, ohio, ohio...," from our now malfunctioning Felix. The clock never made it on HSN.

Larry and I have had many ideas, some good, some bad, but none crazier than getting into the wrestling business with the Navajo Indians. We had spent enough time in Gallup and the surrounding area to get to know the locals and in that time we learned two things: they loved bull riding and wrestling with equal passion. We teamed up with the mayor of Gallup and a local jewelry trader and businessman named Dominic Biava to hold "The Rumble at Red Rock." When this was all coming together I remembered a story Fuzzy Owen told me about a concert he had booked on the Navajo Reservation at Window Rock. At 8 P.M., when the concert was to start, there were literally five people in the audience. Having been assured the concert would be a sell-out, a slightly worried Fuzzy went to the building manager.

"What's goin' on? Where are all the people?"

The guy seemed unconcerned. "They'll be here pretty soon, don't worry." Then the man looked up and nodded. "Oh, here they come now."

Fuzzy turned and saw a great cloud of dust as around 400 concert goers arrived at the same time. When the dust settled the concert went on with a full house. With Fuzzy's experience in my mind I knew that regardless of what happened, at the very least it was bound to be interesting.

Red Rock State Park features a stunning natural amphitheater and rodeo arena just outside Gallup. With permanent bleachers affixed to the ancient red rock walls that surround the venue on three sides, it's a very dramatic place to hold any event. Working with the mayor and the reservation, we got a great deal on both the advertising and price of the facility. Then we shopped around for wrestlers. At that time, Ted Turner owned the WCW (World Championship Wrestling for those of you out of the wrestling loop) so we went to his organization to buy our wrestlers.

Turner charged us $20,000, and for that we got "Nature Boy" Ric Flair, "Macho Man" Randy Savage, Steve "Sting" Borden and Kamala, along with Jerry Saganovich and Brian Knobbs, better known as the Nasty Boys. In addition, the WCW supplied us with the ring, the referees, and the bus to bring the wrestlers from Albuquerque to Gallup. We were warned that in August it rained every afternoon and were urged to buy rain insurance, which we did. The policy stated that it had to rain 2 tenths of an inch before 8 P.M. before we could collect. At five minutes of 8 it started to drizzle. By 8:30 it had rained two inches (and we never collected a dime).

But the show must go on, and the wrestlers were absolute troupers.

None of them complained and they all did a great job despite being in the midst of a torrent. Of all the rock and country music acts I've ever handled, none were as courteous and professional as those wrestlers. While the wrestlers were milling around getting ready to go on, a huge blond-haired guy walked up and extended his hand.

"Hi Mr. Eubanks, I'm one of the Nasty Boys. It's a pleasure to meet you." It was one of those odd moments where you just have to step back from yourself and smile. Here was this massive man, preparing to go out and commit (staged) mayhem, and yet he was so low-keyed and polite. One of the stipulations in the contract was that we provide a place to shower and play gin after the match. It was quite a sight seeing muscle bound warriors like Randy Savage and The Nasty Boys sitting around in towels playing gin after they had just beat the shit out of each other in the ring. The match was a big hit, with the wrestlers putting on a full out show in the driving rain in front of 8,000 screaming fans. We didn't make any money but we didn't lose any either. It was so much fun I'd do it again in a minute.

Larry Donizetti and I have had a very good partnership. He is one of the kindest, most honest men I have known. We have made some great decisions and profited, and have also done some of the dumbest things you could imagine. How two reasonably bright guys have gotten into some of these situations we have I don't know. But I do know that no matter how bad it ever got Larry and I have never exchanged harsh words nor ever doubted each others' integrity.

In 2001, I got a call from a company called IGT (International Game Technology). They are manufacturers and distributors of gaming equipment, particularly slot machines. They wanted to use my name, likeness, and voice on a slot machine that featured *The Newlywed Game*. The amount of time I had to put into the project was minimal and the money was very good. As I considered their offer, something rather bizarre happened. Until IGT called I had never thought about appearing on a slot machine. Then, suddenly, I got another inquiry, this time from Bally Gaming, offering me yet another slot machine deal. So, in the course of a week, I now had two lucrative offers to lend my name and voice to a slot machine. Bally presented an interesting angle to their machine's concept. Their slot was to be called "Bob Eubanks Cash For Life" and literally provided the big winner with a sizable long term annuity.

Just as IGT was pressuring me to decide, and while I was also weighing Bally's offer, I went to Italy with my wife, Debbie. My first mistake
was not taking my cell phone. Then when I spent so much time on hotel
phones, AT&T thought someone had stolen my phone card and cancelled it. So now I was condemned to stand on the streets using public
phones to make collect calls as hundreds of little scooters buzzed by
like angry bees in the background. Pretty soon we seemed to be stopping every hour or two to resume negotiations between Bally and IGT
and something had to give. Finally, when Debbie turned to me with
huge tears in her eyes and yelled, "You're ruining my vacation!" I made
a decision. I went with Bally because they offered the most money and I
thought their concept might have a longer life.

Initially, I signed a two-year contract and Bally ended up spending
most of that time developing the machine and getting them placed.
They came back around when the contract was to expire and had me
re-sign—of course for the same amount as the first signing. Never in my
wildest dreams would I have ever thought someone would put my face
on a slot machine—and pay me so much for the privilege. If you ever
see a Cash for Life machine, drop a quarter in it. Pull my handle and,
who knows, maybe you'll win and get a check once a week for the rest
of your life.

I was asked to appear on Dick Clark's show, *The Other Half* (the male answer to *The View*) where I would host a version of *The Newlywed Game*.
There would be three couples, Dick and Kari Clark, Danny Bonaducci
and his wife and a couple off the street. I've always maintained that celebrities can be dull because they try to hard to perform, but this time
I was proved wrong. Much of the credit to the success of that segment
has to go to Dick and Danny's wives, who were hilarious. We learned
a lot more about the two celebrities than they probably had planned to
reveal.

I asked Kari where the strangest place was that she and Dick were
romantic and she told me that several months before, Dick had met
her at the airport with a sandwich that had a bracelet hidden inside
it. Then he "attacked" her in the car in the parking lot at LAX. Apparently sandwiches and airports really turn Dick on. She also told me that
Dick's most annoying habit was throwing things. He once threw his
eggs against the wall because he didn't like the way they were prepared.

Another time he tossed a computer out the window. Maybe we can all relate to that.

Danny Bonaducci's wife answered that the things that drive her craziest are Danny's habit of blowing his nose without Kleenex and that he bites his toenails. I got that same answer years ago when I did *The Newlywed Game* on *The Mike Douglas Show* in Philadelphia. The wife of then Phillies star (and now manager) Larry Boa admitted her husband nibbled his toenails. Now that's pretty flexible!

I also want to mention that when I was getting started in radio, Dick Clark was the guy we all looked up to. Dick showed deejays that we could use our position to go anywhere we wanted. He opened doors and created opportunities out of thin air and inspired us to move beyond radio. Among that group, we all owe Dick a huge debt of gratitude. He was and is a pioneer and I have always had the greatest respect for him.

When *The Newlywed Game* and *The Dating Game* went on the air in the mid-60s we literally saved ABC's daytime schedule. When they put both the shows on Saturday nights, we once again ignited the network during our time periods. We had good shows, were cheap to produce, and I believe we were a major influence in ABC becoming a strong and dominant network. Another show that came on the air during the '60s that revolutionized ABC's image was *Batman*, starring Adam West. Yet, a couple of years ago when ABC did its 50th Anniversary Special, they did not invite me, Jim Lange or Adam West to appear. I am angry because we had a hell of a lot bigger impact on the growth of the network than some of the stars who were invited.

To show you how strange this business is, in 2003, at the age of 65, I did five nighttime specials. The first one I did with Wink Martindale, Jim Lange, Ben Stein and Peter Marshall. We did so well against Fox's powerhouse, *American Idol*, that NBC ordered four more. The shows were called *America's Most Outrageous Gameshow Moments* and the powers that be at the peacock network asked if I would like to host the next two by myself. Those were very successful so they asked Chuck Woolery to join me for two more. In my wildest dreams, I would have never imagined that I would be hosting primetime specials.

While we were shooting the last one at Ontario Mills Mall in Ontario California, it was getting late and we were all pretty tired. Four or five

August 7, 1987

SISTERS OF
ST. BENEDICT

Convent of Immaculate Conception
R.R. 3, Box 201
Ferdinand, Indiana 47532
(812) 367-1411

Gentlemen,

I watch the TV show, "Newlywed Game" regularly & like it very much. Will you please send me the full name & address of the "star" of the show, known on the show as "Bob." I want to tell him I enjoy the show & he is a good actor. He seems to enjoy his role on the show. Thank you for your courtesy in sending me his name and address. My life work was with First Grade, 4000 in my lifetime. After 64 years teaching I am now retired and I do miss the little children.

Respectfully,

Sister Amata Alvey

Any show approved by Sister Alvey can't be all bad!

SISTER AMATA ALVEY

gang members walked up and every time I would open my mouth to say something they would shout some obscenity, snicker, and we would have to stop taping.

After several rounds of this I finally said, "Stop tape. I'll be right back."

I walked over to these guys, put my arms around them and formed a football huddle. "Fellows, I've been here all day. I want to go home. So do me a favor. Shut your fucking mouths."

They smiled sheepishly at me and said, "Okay, Bob," and that was the last we heard from them. That moment reminded me that to really communicate you just have to get down on people's level.

I have one final story that I wasn't sure where it fit in the book so I saved it for last. It's always good to go out with a laugh. Tex Earnhardt started a car dealership in 1951 in Chandler, Arizona, and from that single store turned it into a billion dollar empire. Like Cal Worthing-

My beautiful wife, Debbie, and our little angel, Noah.

TAD CRAIG PHOTOGRAPHY

ton, Tex still does his own commercials, which are quite colorful. He concludes each commercial standing next to a huge Brahma bull that has been sexually altered, so his famous tag line, "And that's no bull!" is quite accurate. Aside from being Arizona's biggest car dealer, Tex and his ex-wife Pam are friends of mine.

When I was doing the television commentary for a series of rodeos with Pam, she told me this story. Tex and Pam had a chimpanzee named JJ. As much a character as his master, every morning JJ would roll out of bed, use the toilet (sometimes going through an entire roll of toilet paper) and then proudly don a smart little cowboy suit. He would go to the kitchen, pour himself a cup of coffee, and after dumping in a judicious helping of sugar, he would stir it with his foot and start the day.

After their morning routine, Pam and JJ would head to the barn to feed the horses. One day, Pam got busy in the barn and lost track of JJ. Pretty soon the phone rang. It was Tex, sounding upset.

"Pam, where's JJ?"

She looked around but JJ was nowhere to be seen. Apparently JJ had gotten bored and decided to go on a short field trip. Across the street, a little Hispanic lady was breast feeding her baby. She looked up just as a chimp in a cowboy suit walked in the front door and flashed a smile at her. Hysterical, she damn near dropped the baby as she ran into the bedroom, locked the door and phoned 911. Unimpressed with her hospitality, JJ saw a bottle of codeine cough syrup on the coffee table and decided to have a party on his own. He chugged it. When the police arrived they found a drunk monkey dressed like Tex Ritter collapsed on the sofa.

EPILOGUE: WHAT AM I GONNA DO? (WITH THE REST OF MY LIFE)

NOT LONG AGO, I was walking in the hills at the ranch. I was trying to figure out what I wanted to do for the rest of my life. I have done so much and yet I was feeling unfulfilled in my business world. I have re-married to a beautiful and loving woman and we have a wonderful little boy named Noah. How about that? The old boy can still get it on! My 10-year-old granddaughter says she can't wait to baby-sit her uncle!

I thought about teaching, but there is no money in teaching. Yet, I wanted to do something where I could use my past experiences. What do I have to offer? Well, I am a people person. I know how to make people talk. And I have had some incredible experiences. So I decided to join the world of corporate speaking. I had no idea what to do or who to turn to.

I met my friend Mark Mayfield at a speakers showcase in New York City. After watching me, he said, "you're doing it all wrong." Mark is one of the best and most knowledgeable men in the speaking industry. So, after spending two or three days with him in Kansas City, we crafted a very funny one-hour keynote speck using my past experiences. It's called, "It's All About People." I then joined Mark and five other wonderful speakers and we formed a marketing group run by my friends Melinda Batchelor and Melody Alexander. Sometimes you are judged by the company you keep and I am proud to be part of First Class Speakers.

There is nothing in the Bible that talks about retirement and I don't intend to do so in the near future. My business is great. I go out and tell stories and make people laugh. They give me a check and I go home. They don't care how old I am or what my ratings are. So maybe I'll see you down the road. I'm the guy wearing the Tony Lama boots and Wrangler pants. If you see me wearing a necktie, you'll know I'm getting paid. I was born a cowboy. I am a cowboy and I'll die a cowboy. I don't want to go anywhere where I can't tie up my horse. God Bless.

A JOURNEY WORTH TAKING

It's when we're looking back
That we learn to laugh with life
Seeing all the opportunities
We had to seize the prize
We were running for the goal line
Always looking at the time
Never stopping long enough
To feel where the peace resides

We could choose to walk as God
Seeing life through loving eyes
With acceptance in our hearts
With commitment as our guide
Letting simplest of pleasures
Be what we now hold so dear
Knowing it's not the destination
But the journey that we revere

Which ever path we choose
There is happiness in life
Straight and narrow, twisting turning
Always knowing deep inside
That what we show the world
Is what we in turn receive
To reach the highest star
We need only to believe

—Susie Eubanks

323

INDEX

The Andrew R. Cecil Lectures on Moral Values in a Free Society

established by

The University of Texas at Dallas

Volume III

CONFLICT AND HARMONY

Conflict
and
Harmony

ANDREW R. CECIL
DONALD W. SHRIVER, JR.
ERIK SUY
ERNEST W. LEFEVER
WILLIAM P. MURPHY
STERLING M. McMURRIN

With an introduction by
ANDREW R. CECIL

The University of Texas at Dallas
1982

Library of Congress Catalog Card Number: 82-70278
International Standard Book Number 0-292-71081-X

Distributed by the University of Texas Press,
Box 7819, Austin, Texas 78712

FOREWORD

The Andrew R. Cecil Lectures on Moral Values in a Free Society, established by The University of Texas at Dallas in 1979, have come to fill an important part in the intellectual life of the community. This series has brought to the campus of the university prominent scholars, statesmen, businessmen, and religious leaders, who have shared their insight on some of the most vital, and sometimes controversial, moral and ethical questions of our time.

In their presentations on campus and in the community, the 1981 lecturers in the series offered challenging and inspiring ideas to the students and faculty of the university as well as to the general public. This program reaches beyond the horizons of mundane practical concerns and offers the opportunity to analyze the philosophical and moral basis of civilized society. An institution of higher learning has the responsibility to provide a forum in which public values are examined and debated, in which the heritage of our nation may be revitalized and passed on to new generations.

It was to this end that the Lectures on Moral Values in a Free Society were founded and named for Dr. Andrew R. Cecil. Dr. Cecil first participated in the life of our campus as President and Chancellor of The Southwestern Legal Foundation. His leadership of that institution earned him the highest respect in educational and legal circles throughout the United States. After he consented to serve as Distinguished Scholar in Residence at The University of Texas at Dallas, these Lectures were established and named for him.

In November 1981, Dr. Cecil was joined by Ernest W. Lefever, Sterling M. McMurrin, William P. Murphy, Donald W. Shriver, Jr., and Erik Suy for the memorable third series of Lectures on Moral Values in a Free Society. We are especially happy to be able once again to publish the proceedings of the Lectures, so that the thoughts of these men may not be lost to memory. Through the generosity of the contributors to the series, who make possible the appearance of the lecturers on campus and the publication of the proceedings, we are delighted to offer this volume to a wider audience.

I am confident that you will find that *Conflict and Harmony* will stimulate your consideration of many of the important issues facing our society and the world community of nations.

ALEXANDER L. CLARK, Acting President
The University of Texas at Dallas

January, 1982
Dallas, Texas

CONTENTS

INTRODUCTION

by

Andrew R. Cecil

Harmony in the most general sense connotes an accord, a congruence which gives proper direction to the actions of the individual and to the functions of society. Plato sees justice and harmony fused in one universal virtue of perfect coordination and compares justice in a society to the harmonious movement of the planets that holds them in an orderly relationship. The Psalmist also refers to this perfect coordination when he praises the Lord who by wisdom made the heavens, stretched out the earth above the waters, and made the great lights—the sun to rule by day and the moon and stars to rule by night. (Psalm 136:5-9.)

In the Old and New Testaments, harmony is identified with the essence of divinity and represents the fulfillment of the divine will. For Plato, the harmony of three faculties—wisdom, temperance, and courage—constitutes justice. When this harmonious condition is achieved, the just man "sets in order his own inner life, and is his own master and his own law, and at peace with himself." When strife arises among the three faculties, injustice and conflict occur.

Although justice is not identical with harmony, these two virtues are reflected in each other. Both demand from everyone a certain abnegation of individual sovereignty, of self-respect, in favor of the common order and the welfare of others. Neither should be confused

11

with mere legality. Harmony and justice have a transcendent validity that is loftier than any established legal order.

According to Herbert Spencer, the nineteenth-century British philosopher, the idea of justice can grow only as fast as the "external antagonisms of societies decrease and the internal harmonious cooperation of their members increase." This harmony, he believes, can be obtained through freedom, and the formula of freedom is: "Every man is free to do that what he wills, provided he infringes not the equal freedom of any other man." This principle reduces the purpose of justice to the prevention of breaches of mutual freedom. It provides equality of opportunity and permits each individual, in the course of his pursuit of happiness, to prosper according to his desires and abilities.

That formula of freedom does not meet the expectations of a society governed by the principles of the attainment of the greatest general happiness and of concern for the welfare of one's fellowman. For the flowering of such principles, the society needs the general direction of a moral code. In this country, religion has provided the essential elements of such a code. Religion is interwoven into the texture of our society. The separation of church and state, the "wall of separation" concept embodied in the Establishment Clause of the United States Constitution, does not imply that the government or state institutions should be contemptuous of religion or religious principles, such as those in the Christian concept of morality. No constitutional requirement makes it necessary for government to be hostile, suspicious, or even unfriendly to religion or to throw its weight against efforts to widen the scope of religious influence.

Church and state, despite their separation—which is

so fundamental a part of the American system—each have their own sphere and may profitably interact with one another. The 1981 lecture by Dr. Donald W. Shriver, "Collision and Community: Church and State in a Humane Society," addresses the question of the responsibility of religion and of religious people in a democratic society. After surveying the various attitudes possible to believers in a Judaeo-Christian tradition in our nation, Dr. Shriver concludes that Jewish and Christian citizens—indeed all citizens—have a responsibility to inject the beliefs of their consciences into the political process. He also warns that no single conscience is infallible and that one of the greatest virtues is the humility that allows its possessor to realize that he may be wrong.

Dr. Shriver sees the interaction of church and state as important for the vigor and progress of society and suggests that religious faith bears an important relationship to faith in the future of our nation and of mankind in general. The biblical virtues of faith, hope, and love, he suggests, are especially relevant in our society today, when so many citizens have a pessimistic outlook on the world and its future. Only through these virtues can we hope to build the harmonious world that should be our children's heritage.

There is also a need for the general direction of a moral code to attain harmony on the international scene. We must discharge our responsibilities not only toward our community and our country but also toward world society. Continuing apprehension and distrust in international relations create persistent conflicts in world affairs. Yet, in spite of turmoil and tension pressing from all parts of the globe, no effort should be spared to establish harmony and peace as the essential and decisive substitutes for conflict and force.

Some believe that international harmony can be achieved by a balance of power. History teaches us that a balance of power alone has never brought permanent peace and that countries outside the centers of power demand, and will continue to demand, a fair measure of participation in the handling of global problems. A parity of military capabilities between the superpowers will not secure peace and harmony with freedom and justice. In our desire for an easing of the international tensions and conflicts that have torn the globe for generations, we must seek other means than a "balance of power" to obtain harmony in a world of ever more closely interacting economic, environmental, and legal institutions.

The peoples of the world are partners in a great world partnership of nations in which every peace-loving nation wishes to determine its own life and institutions and to be assured of justice and fair dealing by the other partners. A faith in the essential worth and dignity of each individual, when applied to international relations, demands that we be prepared to put forth all our resources and energies to maintain a union of self-respecting free nations and to protect their freedom and dignity from oppression. To want to live in a free world means also to want freedom for others. The basis of any system of freedom is, therefore, the ethic of humane respect. Ethical and moral standards applicable to individuals should become generally accepted as applicable, also, to international conduct.

In his paper, "Harmonious Settlement of International Conflicts," Dr. Erik Suy argues that on the international scene the growing emphasis on points of dispute and conflict becomes more and more dangerous. In order for civilized culture to survive on this globe, all nations must change their outlooks from one of imposing their own viewpoint and self-interest to one of striving for peace. On all fronts—education, law, economic and military institutions—he suggests a new emphasis on harmony and cooperation.

Dr. Suy sees many channels of cooperation between nations already in existence but points out that many of them have not been used to the fullest extent possible. Among these channels, he lists education, disarmament negotiations, development aid, regional economic organizations, the recognition of human rights, and United Nations peacekeeping forces. Among the indispensable requirements for maintaining and strengthening international harmony, Dr. Suy sees a sense of justice and respect for others. These moral virtues must be shared by all if true international harmony is to prevail.

When we examine the essence of harmony, whether on the international or domestic scene, by stripping away its multiple layers, we will find that human rights are at the very core of its meaning. In the United States, our commitment to promote human rights and to enhance the dignity of the individual has a rich tradition that goes back as far as the Massachusetts Body of Liberties of 1641. That document provided that "No man's life shall be taken away, no man's honor or good name shall be stayned, no man's person shall be arrested . . . no man's goods or estate shall be taken away from him . . . unless it be by vertue or equitie of some express law of the country." In this century, Woodrow Wilson sought to place the power of the United States at the service of mankind and to make the doctrine of service to humanity a guiding principle of world politics.

Experience shows that in international relations, where power relationships always remain relevant, inconsistency in implementing a human rights policy may be inevitable, since in addition to human rights there are other foreign policy objectives and fundamental national interests to be considered, such as national security, arms control, and international trade. The rule of morality, as Alexander Hamilton wrote, "is not precisely the same between nations as between individuals" because the responsibilities of the state differ from those of individuals. An action of the state can influence many millions of lives, even those of generations to come, while, according to Hamilton, the consequences of a private action of an individual are ordinarily terminated with himself.

Our human rights policy becomes incoherent when it directs its fire at right-wing, anti-Soviet authoritarian regimes and takes less interest in using the human rights issue against left-wing totalitarian nations, such as the Soviet Union, China, Cuba, and North Korea. This incoherence creates the impression of a contradiction between the human rights policy and the national interest of the United States.

Another human rights policy calls for a distinction between authoritarian regimes—which are not in principle hostile to our conception of human rights—and totalitarian ones—which do not hesitate to commit the most brutal acts to repress any concept of individual freedom and natural rights. The advocates of this distinction believe that while quiet diplomacy might be effective in dealing with authoritarian governments the systematic violations of human rights by totalitarian governments demand strong international measures.

History gives ample evidence of the complexities involved in relating humanitarian concern with national interest and safety. Acknowledging these complexities,

Reinhold Niebuhr, only weeks after Hitler plunged the world into World War II, remarked:

> "It is important that Christianity should recognize that all historic struggles are between sinful men and not between the righteous and the sinners; but it is just as important to save what relative decency and justice the western world still has, against the most demonic tyranny of history."

In his address on "Freedom, Dignity, and Foreign Policy," Dr. Ernest W. Lefever classifies the injustices perpetrated by present-day Soviet Russia with Hitler's in its expansionist as well as totalitarian policies. He stresses the distinction between totalitarian and authoritarian regimes; he argues that authoritarian regimes not infrequently evolve into democratic rule while totalitarian regimes can never allow this to happen. The ruthless uses of force in East Germany in 1953, in Hungary in 1956, in Czechoslovakia in 1968, and in Poland in 1981 sadly bear out his distinction.

A principal concern of Dr. Lefever's address is the major weapon—terrorism—which he argues totalitarianism is using to further its ends around the world. Opposing himself to those who see shades of differences between various terrorist activities, Dr. Lefever condemns all international terrorism as one of the most serious threats to worldwide human rights. He doubts that it is possible to export our own domestic concern for human rights and respect for the rule of law through pressure on our allies, since our ability to influence other countries politically has diminished in the last two decades. In Dr. Lefever's view, there should be a moral constraint on efforts designed to change domestic practices, institutions, and policies of other states. The exam-

ple we set within our own country, according to Dr.
Lefever, remains the most effective method of influenc-
ing others.

Turning to domestic issues, the conflict too often experienced between labor and management brings into
prominence a vast number of social problems. Industrial
peace is essential for a harmonious society. The Marxian
anticipation of a cataclysmic split of our society into
two hostile camps—the bourgeois and the worker
classes—has never come. The communist hope that the
American economy would collapse in the common ruin
of the contending classes has proved to be ill-founded. In
order to prevent or remedy conflicts and avoid the predicted downfall of the capitalist system, the United
States has succeeded in large measure in integrating
harmoniously into the society all its members by means
of responsible livelihood and active participation in the
life of the society.

About a century ago, Pope Leo XIII in his famous en-
cylical *Rerum Novarum* (1891), defending private property as a natural right, emphasized that "labor is not a
commodity" and that "it is shameful to treat men like
chattels to make money by." The encyclical stressed the
dignity of labor and the right and duty of the state to
prevent the exploitation of labor. On the ninetieth anniversary of *Rerum Novarum*, May 15, 1981, Pope John
Paul II in the encyclical on Human Work *(Laborem
Exercens)* also stresses the importance of human work.
According to the encyclical, the right to private property
should be subordinated "to the right of the common use
of goods." It predicts that new technological developments and changing economic and political conditions
will influence the world of work and production no less
than the industrial revolution of the last century did.
The new conditions and demands will require a reorder-

ing and adjustment of the structure of the modern economy and of distribution of work.

The Pope reminds us of the principle of the primacy of the person over things. He sees the danger of treating work as a special kind of "merchandise" or as an impersonal "force" needed for production (the encyclical alludes to the expression "work-force"). Work is for the human being and not the human being for work. Work is a source of right on the part of the worker but is also a moral obligation. Man must work because the Creator has commanded it and because of man's responsibility toward his family, toward the society in which he lives, and toward his country and the whole human family. Man "is the heir to the work of generations and at the same time a sharer in building the future of those who will come after him in the succession of history."

The encyclical accepts labor and capital as indispensable components of the process of production. Acknowledging the universal right to strike, the Pope warns against the abuse of this right for "political" purposes since such an abuse can lead to the paralysis of the whole of socioeconomic life. In the final analysis, the encyclical reminds us that social and socioeconomic life is like a system of "connected vessels" and that every social activity directed "toward safeguarding the rights of particular groups should adapt itself to this system."

Professor William P. Murphy, in his lecture "Moral and Ethical Values in Labor-Management Relations," traces the history of the struggle of labor for the recognition of the right to be organized and to participate in collective bargaining in the United States and notes the importance of *Rerum Novarum* in this process of recognition. Professor Murphy demonstrates the importance of moral considerations to the flow of history, showing that moral considerations played a crucial role in the passage of the labor laws that all Americans now take for granted. Although he sees less evidence of conscious moral forces at work in the enforcement and litigation of labor issues than in the original enactment of the statutes in this field, he leaves no doubt that labor-management relations is an area in which the consciences of Americans have contributed to a growth in harmony and justice.

The harmony we are seeking can be effectively forwarded through a sound and morally aware system of education. Whether the miraculous inventions which play such an important part in our society enhance social harmony by being consecrated to man's life or increase conflict by being dedicated to destruction and disruption depends upon the goals we establish for our educational efforts. Education to promote harmony calls not only for the fostering of intellectual development but also for the training of spiritual perception in order to understand God's purpose in creating the universe and the divine law governing the world. Recognition of the eternal values is essential to the existence of harmony.

Dr. Sterling M. McMurrin, in his lecture "Education and Moral Values: The Moral Responsibility of the Schools," observes that an educational system has no choice but to impart moral values; it does so either consciously or unconsciously. In fact, Dr. McMurrin argues, all systems impart moral values more effectively by their underlying structures and by the unspoken values of the cultures which they are passing on then by their conscious attempts to implant moral attitudes. While emphasizing that the primary duty of an educational system is to foster intellectual growth, Dr. McMurrin warns of the importance of nurturing the maturity of the individual person. He accuses American education of too often having failed to provide for the consideration of such vital aspects of experience as meaning and purpose and counsels educators to strengthen their resolve to address the essential moral values.

We seek a system of education and a form of government which will provide leadership to prevent tension in a highly organized industrial society. People desire to live in a decent law-abiding society, and the crux of their aspirations is understanding human nature. Because of the importance of understanding the true meaning of life and of the need of a public philosophy of civility, our forefathers recognized that religion, morality, and knowledge are necessary to good government. True religion includes true morality, and the inculcation of religion takes place through diffusion of knowledge.

As I point out in my lecture on "Morality, Religion, and Knowledge—Essential Elements of Harmony in Government," knowledge, religion, and morality fused into one force—which is understanding—can guide individuals and nations into harmony and prevent conflicts. This is the essence of the interrelation between knowledge, religion, and morality.

The 1981 Lectures on Moral Values in a Free Society stress the point that harmony and not conflict is the natural state of the world. Conflict is a symptom of radical disorder in man's relationship with God and, consequently, with his fellowman. Whatever the causes and circumstances that have carried us into the present disorder, the fact remains that the world is faced with constantly deepening conflicts. The rising danger of war and of nuclear weapons creates a frustrating sentiment of constant peril. Harmony can be restored, if temporarily, through negotiations and settlements but not through appeasement.

Appeasement augments the danger of conflicts and encourages those responsible for creating the conflicts to seek new rewards through turmoils and tensions. This fact caused Churchill to speak of World War II as an "unnecessary war." It could have been prevented. If all the nations that united to defeat our common enemy in 1941 had been equally united when Japan first started aggression against Manchuria in 1931 and Italy against Ethiopia in 1935, the subsequent German aggression might have been prevented and the war of 1939–1945 would not have taken place.

Although the aggressive intentions of Germany were well known before the First World War, the intended victims of aggression, blinded by wishful thinking, learned the bitter lesson of complacency in a perilous world when Germany occupied their country. Before the Second World War, throughout Europe the claim was popular that peace can be obtained through disarmament since only the arms makers are the "war makers." Most Western nations apathetically watched the Nazi atrocities and acts of aggression in the hope that they would be spared. The awakening came with the global war.

After the Second World War, Soviet Russia expanded its imperialistic ring of tyranny to Eastern Europe, invaded and imposed a government of its own choice on the people of Afghanistan, and with tanks and guns shattered the dreams of freedom of nations suffering under the heels of communist regimes. After the Second World War, the United States did not gain one inch of new territory, although it was the only undamaged industrial power in the world and had a monopoly of nuclear weapons with the ability to deliver them anywhere. Instead of militaristic expansion, the United States offered the world the Marshall Plan, the Point IV program, and other foreign aid programs to rebuild the war-ravaged economies of the world, including Germany and Japan, who had been our enemies. These two diametrically different courses of activity demonstrate the difference between the policy of conflict by use of force and the policy of harmony by assisting nations plunged into the tragedy of war and economic disasters.

In this decade of the eighties, demonstrations are taking place to ban nuclear arms. Everyone with a sound mind looks with horror on the specter of a nuclear war. Yet no one expects that these voices of protest will change the aggressive ambitions of Soviet Russia. Peace cannot be obtained by banning the bomb unilaterally unless we make the choice to live as slaves under the heel of communist tyrants rather than to risk our lives. No, there is no need for appeasement or for surrendering the world to the dehumanizing barbarism offered by the totalitarian enemies of the free world.

There is also no need to give up hope or to cease our efforts for restoring harmony in this world of conflicts. Such efforts call for patience. At the Peace of Westphalia of 1648, which brought an end to the Thirty Years War, it took six months to decide in what order the delegates of the participating countries would enter and be seated at the conference table. Yet this peace signalized the end of the greatest religious war and the first wide attempt at tolerance. Efforts to restore harmony call for firmness, understanding, vision, and love of our fellowman, who has God's given right to be free. "Be alert: stand firm in faith, be valiant and strong. Let all you do be done in love." (I Corinthians 16:13.) There is no reason why people in any part of the world should live in the tension of conflict or in fear of war.

MORALITY, RELIGION, AND KNOWLEDGE: ESSENTIAL COMPONENTS OF HARMONY IN GOVERNMENT

by

Andrew R. Cecil

Andrew R. Cecil

Dr. Cecil is Chancellor Emeritus and Trustee of The South-western Legal Foundation and Distinguished Scholar in Residence at The University of Texas at Dallas.

Associated with the Foundation since 1958, Dr. Cecil has helped guide its development of five educational centers that offer nationally and internationally recognized programs in advanced continuing education.

In February 1979 the University established in his honor the Andrew R. Cecil Lectures on Moral Values in a Free Society, and invited Dr. Cecil to deliver the first series of lectures in November 1979. The first annual proceedings were published as Dr. Cecil's book The Third Way: Enlightened Capitalism and the Search for a New Social Order, *which received an enthusiastic response.*

Educated in Europe and well launched on a career as a professor and practitioner in the fields of law and economics, Dr. Cecil resumed his academic career after World War II in Lima, Peru, at the University of San Marcos. After 1949, he was associated with the Methodist church-affiliated colleges and universities in the United States until he joined the Foundation. He is author of twelve books on the subjects of law and economics and of more than seventy articles on these subjects and on the philosophy of religion published in periodicals and anthologies.

A member of the American Society of International Law, of the American Branch of the International Law Association, and of the American Judicature Society, Dr. Cecil has served on numerous commissions for the Methodist Church, and is a member of the Board of Trustees of the National Methodist Foundation for Christian Higher Education. Dr. Cecil also serves as a member of the Development Board of The University of Texas at Dallas. In 1981 he was named an Honorary Rotarian.

MORALITY, RELIGION, AND KNOWLEDGE: ESSENTIAL COMPONENTS OF HARMONY IN GOVERNMENT

by

Andrew R. Cecil

The Establishment Clause

Moral values are an indispensable part of human life, and morality has relevance to every decision made in the life of a man or a nation. These values may not always be clearly articulated, but they are there, determining which of the several alternatives facing us will lead toward evil or toward the common good. When moral guidance as a basis of action is overlooked in favor of other forces molding human events, the usefulness or even the possibility of defining the ultimate worth of human beings is denied. The result is an impoverishment of the spiritual heritage of a nation and a dangerous heedlessness in its public life.

In 1955, Walter Lippmann decried the growing disorder in the public life of Western civilization that grew out of the neglect and denial of the moral values that underlay the founding of this country. Convinced that there is a "body of positive principles and precepts which a good citizen cannot deny or ignore," he wrote, "I believe there is a public philosophy. Indeed there is such a thing as a public philosophy of civility. It does not have to be discovered or invented. It is known. But it does have to be revived and renewed." (*The Public Philosophy*, Little,

27

Brown and Company, 1955, p. 101.) Lippman located
this philosophy in the tradition of natural law, a position
I defended in the inaugural series of these lectures in
1979.

That there is indeed a public philosophy of civility that
provides a moral grounding for all our institutions was
assumed by our forefathers, even before the formal birth
of our nation. The Ordinance of 1787 for the government
of the Northwest Territory declared that "religion,
morality, and knowledge being necessary to good government and the happiness of mankind, schools and the
means of education shall forever be encouraged." In our
day, when all too often the practical ends of education
are stressed, it is inspiring to look back on this rationale
for the public fostering of education. In the interpretation of the Ordinance, the courts held that true religion
includes true morality and that all that is comprehended
in the words "religion and morality" and can be the subject of human instruction must be included under the
general term "knowledge." Since knowledge is the
"hand-maid of virtue," religion and morality are aided
and promoted by the increase and diffusion of knowledge.

The Ordinance was followed by the adoption of the
Constitution of the United States. It is the First Amendment to our Constitution which states that "Congress
shall make no law respecting an establishment of religion" and is thus known as the Establishment Clause.
Strengthened by the Fourteenth Amendment, which
made the Establishment Clause applicable to the states,
the First Amendment has been one of the great pillars
of American liberties. But it is important to distinguish
between the proper effects of that amendment and those
effects that were not intended by the drafters of the Bill

of Rights. The proper effects include legal separation of church and state as well as the religious liberty which is such a great part of the American heritage. Among the effects that were not intended is the attempt to bar the search for ultimate truth or preclude the application of religious and moral principles to public life.

The first and most immediate purpose of the adoption of the First Amendment was the belief that a union of government and religion tends to destroy government and degrade religion. "United with government, religion never rises above the merest superstition; united with religion, government never rises above the merest despotism; and all history shows us that the more widely and completely they are separated the better it is for both." (*Board of Education of Cincinnati v. Minor*, 23 Ohio St. 211, 13 Am. Rep. 233 [1872].) This separation of the domains of government and religion was designed to give each realm its proper place in the lives of the citizens of our country.

Our Founding Fathers strove to find the proper expression for their desire to protect both government and religion from mutual interference. In opposition to the bill establishing provision for teachers of the Christian religion introduced in 1784 in the House of Delegates of the State of Virginia, James Madison prepared the widely circulated "Memorial and Remonstrance," in which he demonstrated "that religion, or the duty we owe the Creator" was not within the cognizance of civil government. The proposed bill was defeated, and another drafted by Thomas Jefferson was passed.

Jefferson's bill "for establishing religious freedom" defines that freedom in its preamble. After stating that "to suffer the civil magistrate to intrude his powers into the field of opinion and to restrain the profession or propagation of principles on supposition of their ill tendency is a dangerous fallacy which at once destroys all religious liberty," the Act declared that "it is time enough, for the rightful purposes of civil government, for its officers to interfere when principles break out into overt acts against peace and good order." In these two sentences, stated the Supreme Court of the United States, "is found the true distinction between what properly belongs to church and what to the state." (*Reynolds v. United States*, 98 U.S. 145, 163, 25 L. Ed. 244 [1878].)

The First Amendment to the Constitution forbids legislation that will prohibit the free exercise of religion, thus guaranteeing religious freedom. Belief in religious freedom and in the separation of church and state does not, however, preclude the conviction that the three qualities discussed in the Northwest Territory Ordinance—morality, religion, and knowledge—are essential components of good government. The search for truth and for a basis of actions that will promote the common good calls for scholarly and critical examination of the basic concepts of religious faith, of moral value systems, and of facts and experiences offered by mankind's knowledge.

To pursue such examination we have to define morality and religion—terms which countless philosophers and scholars for many generations have sought to define. In search for definitions we shall endeavor to analyze the principal values that morality and religion have in satisfying human yearnings. The critical questions to be answered are: What is the common ground between morality and religion? Have all systems of morality religious roots? To what extent have attempts to repudiate the religious roots of a moral system succeeded in creating conflict and to what extent have faith and the values that are enshrined in religious traditions brought harmony to the world? To answer these questions it is imperative to define morality and religion.

Morality Defined

Jesus, when asked by Pilate whether He was a king, replied, "My task is to bear witness to the truth. For this was I born; for this I came into the world, and all who are not deaf to truth listen to my voice." To which Pilate retorted, "What is truth?" (John 18: 37–38 NEB.) Scholars have not yet agreed on the answer to Pilate's question. Morality, like truth, belongs to a group of terms that includes values such as religion, justice, beauty, and conscience, which have a great impact on human life.

In searching for the substance of these terms, however, we are confronted with a great variety of definitions often conflicting with one another, because some of them are too narrow and others too exhaustive. To demonstrate the difficulty of defining the nature of morality because of the diverse views of the theorists, we shall examine the contrasting concepts of morality embodied in the philosophies of two giants in the history of ethics, Plato and Aristotle. These two philosophers lived in the same period and represented the same Greek tradition. Indeed, Aristotle even began as a pupil of Plato. Although we might expect to find essential agreement, instead we find a great discrepancy in these two philosophers' ideas of morality.

In the Greek tradition, the inquiries of both Plato and Aristotle and the theories which developed from their teaching are directed toward discovering the nature of human happiness—toward search for the "good life." Both believe that reason is the highest part of man's nature and that the life which accords with reason is the happiest life. The ultimate knowledge upon which moral virtue is based is the knowledge of "good." According to Plato, "good" is the universal author of all things beautiful and right, independent of circumstances and human experience:

> "[I]n the world of knowledge the idea of good appears last of all, and is seen only with an effort; and when seen, is also inferred to be universal author of all things beautiful and right, parent of light and the lord of light in this visible world, and the immediate source of reason and truth in the intellectual. . . ."

Plato is absorbed in mental abstraction, in a subjective future. Aristotle, on the other hand, is a realist, resolved to concern himself with the objective present, with the external presence of reality. He agrees with Plato that the "good" for man is happiness, but insists that this basic moral principle is inherent in our activities and that it can be discovered through their study, although opinions about its nature may differ. The "good" we are seeking is different, for instance, in medicine, in military strategy, in architecture, or in any other realm of human endeavor. In medicine it is health, in military strategy victory, in architecture a building both useful and beautiful—"for it is for the sake of this that all men do whatever else they do." Some find happiness in pleasure, others in wealth or recognition, because men differ from one another and often even the same man identifies "good" with different things: with health when he is ill or with wealth when he is poor. Aristotle disagrees with Plato that apart from these many "goods" there is another "good" which is self-subsistent and above our comprehension and causes the "goodness" we are able to observe, study, and comprehend.

The name "man," for instance, has a universal application to all members of the human race, but the universal man exists only in our thoughts, he does not exist in reality. We are surrounded, maintains Aristotle, not with universal generic man but with specific individuals, present in reality. In his view, *nomina* (names) should be distinguished from *res* (things); hence comes the clash between the nominalists and the realists. This conflict between the nominalists—the followers of Plato—and the realists—the followers of Aristotle—runs so deep throughout the history of philosophy that the German philosopher Friedrich von Schlegel (1772–1829), the originator of the Romantic school of thought, remarked, "every man is born either a Platonist or an Aristotelian."

The contrasting views of Plato and Aristotle on the nature of the ultimate moral principle should perhaps discourage the attempt to define morality, yet we are driven on by Voltaire's warning, "If you wish to converse with me, define the terms." It may well be profitable to conduct our search on a more mundane plane than that of the Greek philosophers. According to common understanding, the term "morality" or "morals" refers to the common sense of the community, its sense of decency, propriety, and respect for established ideas and institutions, among other things. In a legal context, Benjamin Cardozo defined the moral standards of the community as the "norm or standard of behavior which struggles to make itself articulate in law." (*Paradoxes of Legal Sci-*

ence, New York, Columbia University Press, 1928, pp. 17, 41–42.) Morality has also been referred to as synonymous with character (*Warkentin v. Kleinwachter,* 166 Okla. 218, 27 P.2d 160 [1933]), or as a generic term, containing the sum total of moral traits, including honesty, fidelity, peacefulness, and so on. (*State v. Moorman,* 321 P.2d 236, 240, 133 Mont. 148 [1958].)

Because of the countless meanings which scholars have given to this term—some pointless to our discussion—and at the risk of some simplification, we define morality as the aggregate of rules and principles which relate to man's right or wrong conduct and prescribe the standards or norms by which man guides and controls his actions in his dealings with others.

Consideration of the conditions requisite to the fulfillment of man's moral duties leads into discussions of the terms "ethics" and "conscience." While jurisprudence deals with actions in their relation to law, for the most part independently of a consideration of motives, it is the province of ethics to examine the relationship between actions and the motives behind them. Ethics has thus been defined as "the science of the moral," as "moral philosophy," or as "the study of standards of conduct and of moral judgement."

The word "moral" derives from the Latin word *mores* and "ethics" from the Greek word *ethos;* both source-words refer to traditional human behavior. The word "ethics" is most often used in reference to professional conduct. A professional code of ethics is generally understood as the accepted standard of professional people in business relations peculiar to their professional employment. Such a code is the consensus of expert opinion as to necessary standards within a profession.

The courts have taken the position that in the general treatment of professional ethics sometimes so much stress has been put on the adjective "professional" that the substantive "ethics" has been lost sight of. It should rather be understood that "there is no difference between personal and professional ethics." (*In re Williams*, 50 P.2d 729, 732, 174 Okla. 386 [1935].)

Conscience

Because of the manifold and often contradictory connotations of the word "conscience," the theologian Richard Rothe suggests that we exclude this term from the scientific treatment of ethics. Conscience, however, plays such an important part in our discussion of the role of morality in public life that we cannot fail to consider what it is and what its function should be. Moral scientists explain conscience as the "moral sense" which gives us the power to distinguish between right and wrong. According to some moralists, conscience connotes a form of intuition. To the British philosopher Anthony Shaftesbury is attributed the term "moral sense"—man's natural sense of right and wrong in a universe which is essentially harmonious. Another British philosopher and theologian, Ralph Cudworth, representing the seventeenth-century group called the Cambridge Platonists, argued that moral ideas are innate in man.

In the eighteenth century, the British philosopher and clergyman Bishop Joseph Butler saw the springs of all human action in two of the principles which regulate man's behavior, benevolence and self-love. The natural principle of *benevolence*, he wrote, "is in some degree to *society*, what *self-love* is to the *individual* . . . though the former tends most directly to public good, and the latter to private: yet they are so perfectly coincident that the greatest satisfactions to ourselves depend upon our having benevolence in a due degree; and that self-love is one chief security of our right behaviour toward society."

There is no natural opposition between these two principles, according to Butler, because of another principle in man that reflects upon his own nature, that approves, disapproves, or remains indifferent to our actions. This principle in man, "by which he approves or disapproves his heart, temper, and actions, is conscience." In one form or another this principle of reflection, inner perception, or conscience is regarded as important by those moral philosophers known as intuitionists. Foremost among them is Immanuel Kant, who in his revolutionary metaphysical system accepted a universal moral law as pragmatically necessary. Kant called the supreme moral principle which man ought to follow the "categorical imperative," the unconditional command of the conscience: "Act as if the maxim from which you act were to become through your will a universal law of nature." The moral imperative is absolute and the moral sense innate, not derived from questionable self-experience; we act in obedience to this inner sense of duty, to these *a priori* principles of morals that command our behavior.

Opposed to this idea is the theory advocated by the empiricists, who hold that there is no moral faculty as such which distinguishes between right and wrong, but that all our knowledge comes from experience and through our senses. John Locke denied the existence of innate ideas of right and wrong, ideas inherited in the mind from birth, inborn in every human soul. He taught that a man enters the world not equipped with ideas but with a mind that is a clean sheet—a *tabula rasa*. Sense-experience begets ideas of right and wrong, and moral judgment comes from man's voluntary actions with regard to human or divine law.

According to Spinoza, conscience is the deposit of the moral traditions of the group and varies with geography; it is not innate but acquired. Thomas Hobbes makes a distinction between the public conscience, which is the law of the commonwealth, and private conscience. He rejects any thoughts that every private man is to be the judge of good or evil as "diseases of a commonwealth, that proceed from the poison of seditious doctrines." This doctrine, he states, is "directly against the essence of a commonwealth." Evaluations of good and evil are transient, vary from occasion to occasion, and are relative to the individual.

The study of human evolution has in some measure brought about a reconciliation of the two conflicting theories we have been discussing. Acceptance of the doctrine of organic evolution, according to the nineteenth-century British philosopher Herbert Spencer, determines certain ethical conceptions. Conscience, like everything else, has evolved and, through the process of adaptation to the ends of life, has become the product of age-long experience. By admitting also that certain moral conceptions may have become hereditary with the individual, Spencer reconciles the intuitionists and the empiricists. Harmony in a society can be obtained through the application of the formula of justice, which, Spencer believes, should be: "Every man is free to do that which he wills provided he infringes not the equal freedom of any other man." This formula is conformable to the belief that there is an inborn moral sense, as well as to the ideas of those representing the evolutionary view.

It frees the individual from aggression, protects his right to life, liberty, and the pursuit of happiness on equal terms with all and also permits each individual—through natural selection—to prosper according to his ability and willingness to work.

Whenever the belief in a moral sense is weakened by a loss of respect for the law, a rising volume of crime, an increasing threat of terror, acts of aggression, or atrocities of war, we should be reminded of the sentiments of honesty, generosity, sympathy, paternal love, and other impulses of altruism that strengthen and undergird this belief. Thomas Jefferson asserted that "morality, compassion, generosity are innate elements of the human condition." Without such forces at work in the heart of man, we may as well give up our hopes for a free and civilized community.

In answering the question "What is conscience?" our courts have taken the position that every man of ordinary intelligence understands, in whatever words he may express it, that conscience is that moral sense which dictates to him right or wrong. This sense may differ in degree in individual members of society, but no reasonable being, whether controlled by it or not in his conduct, is wholly destitute of it. "Greatly enlightened it is in some by reason of superior education, quickened in others because of settled religious belief in future accountability, dulled in others by vicious habits, but never altogether absent in any." (*Miller v. Miller*, 41 A. 277, 280, 187, Pa. 572 [1898].)

This moral sense led the Greek poet of the New Comedy, Menander (342–291? B.C.), to state, "Conscience is a God to all mortals," and almost twenty-two-hundred years later moved the English poet William Wordsworth to characterize "duty" as the "stern daughter of the Voice of God." This moral sense impelled Martin Luther to nail his theses on the door of the church at Wittenberg and, when he was summoned before the Emperor Charles and the Diet at Worms, gave him strength to hold his ground and to pronounce the historic words, so often quoted, "I neither can nor will recant anything, since it is neither right nor safe to act against conscience. Here I stand. I cannot do other. God help me. Amen."

The "moral sense" is a source of our moral obligations—obligations arising from the admonitions of conscience, out of a state of facts appealing to a universal sense of justice and fairness—which cannot be enforced by legal action but which are binding in conscience and according to natural justice. It is more than acknowledgement of gratitude or a desire to do charity. The court distinguishes gratitude and charity from a moral obligation as follows: "It is an obligation which, though lacking any foundation cognizable in law, springs from a sense of justice and equity, that an honorable person would entertain, but not from a mere sense of doing benevolence or charity." (*State ex rel. Holmes v. Krueger,* 271 Wis. 129, 137, 72 N.W.2d 734, 738 [1955].)

Legal actions are not always accepted as moral by certain segments of our society. Pope Pius IX in 1869 decreed that the soul enters the egg at conception. When the Supreme Court declared abortion legal, the National Conference of Catholic Bishops declared two days later on January 25, 1973, "Although as a result of the Court decision abortion may be legally permissible, it is still morally wrong, and no Court opinion can change the law of God prohibiting the taking of innocent human life. Therefore, as religious leaders, we cannot accept the

Court's judgement and we urge people not to follow its reasoning or conclusions."

There is also an important distinction between conscience and principle. Conscience, considered by some philosophers as an original faculty of our nature, springs from an internal source of self-knowledge that decides what is right and wrong, bows to no superior human authority, is governed by no man-made laws, is unaccountable to human tribunals, and rests alone with its possessor. Principle is the result of judgment, tested by reason, and yields to the decision of an intelligent mind in approving or condemning our actions.

There may be no connection between conscience and principle. A man may be opposed on principle to what he conscientiously believes to be right. One example may be capital punishment. To quote one decision of our courts: "Many men are opposed on principle to capital punishment, because as often remarked, they believe that the worst use that can be made of a man is to hang him; they believe that society would be benefited by the adoption of some other mode of punishment, and yet, as long as the law provides that certain crimes shall be punished with death, would feel no conscientious scruples in finding a verdict of guilty against one accused of such a crime." (*The People v. Stewart*, 7 Cal. 140, 141 [1857].) The situation, we believe, is different with the man who opposes the death penalty from considerations of conscience—he opposes the infliction of death as contrary to the laws of nature, of God, and of the rule of right.

We may be opposed in principle to negotiations with extortionists and kidnappers, yet feel no conscientious scruples when such negotiations to save the victims of criminal acts take place and ransom is paid, even when the act of terrorism is performed by a foreign government. We may be opposed in principle to interference in the domestic affairs of small nations, yet feel no conscientious scruples when the purpose of the interference—subordinated to prudent consideration—is to counter the intervention of another foreign power when the smaller nation offers an unfriendly foreign power military bases or when it pursues policies that endanger our vital strategic and economic interests.

Freedom of Conscience

The ancient Egyptians and Jews did not have an articulated concept of the individual conscience. They saw as inherent in God's order a system of collective virtues, rewards, and punishments. In the Old Testament, although we find a sense of sin among the Hebrews ("For I know my transgressions, and my sin is ever before me. Against thee, thee only, have I sinned and done that which is evil in thy sight." Psalm 51:3-4), there are no direct references to the notion of conscience as such. Yet we do find many examples of the workings of conscience. In the first chapters of the book of Genesis, both Adam and Cain are confronted with the reality of their sins by the voice of God Himself. David is brought to repentance by the accusations of the prophet Nathan. The entire book of Job is devoted to the story of an attempt to reconcile Job's conscience—which is clear of any sense of wrongdoing—with the apparent punishments that have been visited upon him. In the end, Job's assertions of his own innocence are silenced by the vision of the power of God.

The New Testament refers on several occasions to conscience as an element of human nature, as a witness to the law written on human hearts and to man's knowledge of natural law and its moral principles. "When Gentiles who do not possess the law carry out its precepts by the light of nature, then, although they have no law, they are their own law, for they display the effect of the law inscribed on their hearts. Their conscience is called as witness, as their own thoughts argue the case on either side, against them or even for them." (Romans 2:14–15.) Moral conscience as a witness of faith is stressed in Hebrews 9:9 ("According to this arrangement, gifts and sacrifices are offered which cannot perfect the conscience of the worshipper.") and in I Timothy 1:19–20 ("So fight gallantly, armed with faith and a good conscience. It was through spurning conscience that certain persons made shipwreck of their faith."). Thus the New Testament amplified the idea of conscience that it inherited from the Jews and the Greek philosophers by asserting the unique personality of each individual and the immortality of his soul.

An individual's judgment may not always be correct, yet he has to follow his conscience, even if objectively it is an erring one. Freedom of conscience is paramount to all human activities. It is more important than subjection of the moral personality to an objective truth. In the fourteenth chapter of his Epistle to the Romans, Paul spells out the obligations of a man to his conscience, since the primary principle is that no one should act with an uneasy conscience. This emphasis on the freedom of conscience gave birth to the ideas of inalienable rights, of the rule of a law that can be invoked against the state, and of the maxim that governmental authority must always be kept in check. This maxim proclaims that a person is more than a political pawn enjoying only the privileges bestowed on him by the state. This maxim also proclaims that in matters of conscience there is a moral power higher than the state.

Salus Populi

The freedom that conscience demands is not, however, absolute. This liberty does not altogether supersede the operation of the principle "salus populi suprema est lex"—the welfare of the people is the highest law. This principle is expressly recognized in the constitutions of many states. Article 38 of the New York Constitution of 1777, for instance, provides: "[T]he liberty of conscience hereby granted shall not be so construed as to excuse acts of licentiousness or justify practices inconsistent with the peace or safety of this State." The same limitation is repeated in the constitution of 1812 and in that of 1846, and parallels may readily be found in the constitutions of other states.

Our courts consider that the peace and good order of the community must prevail over conscience wherever the community's mental or physical health is affected. This category is a broad one and defers the dictates of individual scruples to the physical examination of school children and of prospective brides and bridegrooms, to the exclusion of obscenity, to vaccination to prevent epidemics, to elimination of drug addiction, and to suppression of mail frauds and other schemes.

The peace and good order of the community must prevail over conscience whenever the violation of generally accepted moral standards of the community makes a breach of the peace reasonably foreseeable. Because of the violation of the community's sense of reverence in

a monogamous civilization, legislation punishing polygamy was upheld, even though the Mormons conscientiously believed that their religion sanctioned and com-
mended that practice. Polygamy could, in the courts'
opinions, arouse passions leading to breaches of the
peace. As mentioned earlier, one of the rightful purposes
of civil government, according to Jefferson, is "to interfere when principles break out into overt acts against
peace and good order."

Peace and good order must also prevail over conscience when the defense of the country is imperiled. The
principle of *salus* is not limited to maintaining the well-
being of citizens within their own community but extends to protecting the community from exterior aggression. In seeking to balance *salus populi* and individual
conscience, one of the most widely discussed conflicts is
that between scruples concerning the bearing of arms
and the safety of the nation. From the inception of the
republic, religious objectors have been expressly or implicitly exempt from bearing arms. Claims based solely
on disbelief in war as an instrument of human policy
have been disallowed by our courts, and only those who
objected to service in war because of religious scruples
have been exempted. Conscientious scruples concerning
economic support of governmental activities have received no encouragement whatsoever by the courts.
Since the state's existence has material foundations
other than the martial one, conscience cannot be used
as a reason for tax avoidance.

Even though the freedom of conscience is not, therefore, absolute, the fact remains that this freedom is
the crowning glory of American liberties. It gives to
each person the untrammeled and unquestionable right

to worship God according to the dictates of his own conscience, without interference from any person or from any source. In the cause of religion, man is prepared to act and to suffer beyond all other causes. History instructs us that many men have died or suffered worse than death for the right to worship according to their consciences. Daniel Webster pointed out that the freedom which conscience demands and the love of religious liberty form a compound sentiment—made up of the dearest sense of right and the highest conviction of duty—which "is able to look the sternest despotism in the face." ("Speech in Commemoration of the First Settlement of New England," Plymouth, 1820.)

Lord Mansfield, one of the most illustrious luminaries of the common law, declared in a famous speech in the case of *Evans v. Chamberlain of London:* "Conscience is not controllable by human laws, nor amenable to human tribunals; persecution or attempts to force conscience will never produce conviction, and were only calculated to make hypocrites or martyrs." Whenever laws have been enacted to force conscience, bloodshed and confusion have resulted because, "There is certainly nothing more unreasonable, nor inconsistent with the rights of human nature, more contrary to the spirit and precepts of the Christian religion, more iniquitous or unjust, more impolitic than persecution against natural religion, revealed religion, and sound polity."

The first legislators to establish religious freedom, Lord Baltimore and William Penn—one a Roman Catholic and the other a Friend—by passing their memorable laws in favor of liberty of conscience and religious freedom secured two of the highest privileges of the human race. These liberties do not diminish the claims of morality and religion or the individual conscience. The tie between morality and religion was stressed by George Washington when he remarked in his Farewell Address:

> "Religion and morality are indispensable supports
> ... great Pillars of human happiness ... the firmest
> props of the duties of men and citizens ... And let us
> with caution indulge the supposition, that morality
> can be maintained without religion. Whatever may
> be conceded to the influence of refined education on
> minds of peculiar structure, reason and experience
> both forbid us to expect that national morality can
> prevail in exclusion of religious principle."

This leads to the question: Is morality always rooted in religious faith? To answer this question, we have to define religion and to classify the moral traditions by the values which they consider most important.

Religion Defined

Benjamin Franklin, though often cited as an unbeliever, thought of Christianity as the best religion for the mere purposes of civil government. In his letter to Ezra Stiles, the President of Yale University, in 1790, Franklin called Christianity the "best system of religion and morals the world ever saw or is like to see." On a similar note, our courts have expressed the view that Christianity "is the purest system of morality, the firmest auxiliary, and only support of all human laws." (*Updegraph v. Commonwealth* 11 Serg. 394, 406 [Pa., 1824].)

Yet the founders of this country and the courts have repeatedly stressed that in any action a magistrate takes in regard to the belief or disbelief of religious principles there is always the danger of trampling on the rights of conscience and of destroying religious liberty. God is the only arbiter and sovereign Lord of conscience and to Him alone man is accountable. The courts of law are not the *forum conscientiae* or *custodes morum* (conservators of morals) and, therefore, have no jurisdiction over "crimes against God" unless they are by necessary consequence crimes against civil society, either consisting of an actual breach of the peace or liable to provoke or excite such a breach. Even in this case, our courts have explained that "we have no right to interfere one inch further than is necessary to prevent outrage and infractions of the peace."

Those who wrote our Constitution never sought to make proselytes by coercion. Whenever the Christian religion is offended without licentiousness endangering the public peace, the courts should leave Christianity to fight her own battles because, "Christianity requires no aid from force or persecution; she asks not to be guarded by fines and forfeitures. She stands secure in her armour of truth and reason. She seeks not to establish her principles by political aid and legal enactments. She seeks mildly and peaceably to establish them in the hearts of the people." (*The State v. Chandler*, 2 Harr. Del. 533 [1829].)

Religion does not need an alliance with the State to encourage its growth nor laws to enforce it. Christianity, as the Supreme Court of Illinois reminded us, "had its beginning and grew under oppression. Where it has depended upon the sword of civil authority for its enforcement it has been the weakest. Its weapons are moral and spiritual and its power is not dependent upon the force of majority. It asks from the civil government only impartial protection and concedes to every other sect and religion the same impartial civil right." (*People ex rel. Ring et al. v. Board of Education of Dist. 24*, 245 Ill. 334 [1924].)

What religion is right is not a question to be determined by a court in a country which enjoys religious freedom, but since the Constitution of the United States does not contain a definition of religion, our courts of necessity have defined religion. Without such a definition, the courts could not assure the enforcement of the first amendment, which demands that Congress shall make no law respecting the establishment of religion or forbidding the free exercise thereof. Without such a definition, religion could not be distinguished from cults or particular sects, which—as the recent events in Guyana demonstrated—may have as their tenet human sacrifices on special occasions or advocate promiscuous intercourse of the sexes as prompted by the passions of their members and leaders.

A definition by our highest court is found in the case of *Davis v. Beason* (133 U.S. 333, 342, 10 S.Ct. 299, 300, 33 L.Ed. 637 [1890].): "The term 'religion' has reference to one's views of his relations to his Creator, and to the obligations they inspire of reverence for his being and character, and of obedience to his will. It is often confounded with the *cultus* or form of worship of a particular sect, but it is distinguishable from the latter." Our courts have promulgated what has been referred to as a "minimum definition." We may also find quoted in court opinions some definitions offered by religious philosophers, such as: "Religion is squaring human life with superhuman life . . . What is common to all religions is belief in a superhuman power and an adjustment of human activities to the requirements of that power, such adjustment as may enable the individual believer to exist more happily." (E. Washburn Hopkins, *The History of Religions*, New York, The Macmillan Company, 1918, p. 2.) Or, religion is "a propitiation or conciliation of powers superior to man which are believed to direct and control the course of nature and of human life." (J.G. Frazer, *The Golden Bough*, One Volume Edition, New York, The Macmillan Company, 1951, pp. 57–58.)

Laws are made to maintain peace and order, and while they cannot interfere with mere religious belief and opinions, they may interfere with religious practices. Can man excuse his practices which violate existing laws because of his religious belief? To permit this, stated the Supreme Court in the case of *Reynolds v. United States*, "would be to make the professed doctrine of religious belief superior to the law of the land, and in effect to permit every citizen to become a law unto himself. Government could exist only in name under such circumstances." (98 U.S. 145, 25 L.Ed. 244 [1878].) As Mr. Justice Cardozo pointed out: "One who is a martyr to principle—which may turn out in the end to be a delusion or an error—does not prove by his martyrdom that he has kept within the law." (*Hamilton v. Regents of University of California*, 293 U.S. 245, 55 S.Ct. 197, 206, 79 L.Ed. 343 [1934].) Crimes are not less odious because sanctioned or asserted to be a part of the religious doctrine advocated by a particular sect that denigrates them as a part of religious nature.

The courts have defined religion only of necessity, because no attempt to define religion in a satisfactory way can be crowned with success. The content of the term "religion" is incapable of compression into a few words or sentences. It is found throughout the history of the human race, common to man in the most primitive and in the most highly developed modern societies. Because it has to do with the entirely personal nature of the experience, belief, and performance of every human being, it is subject to the widest diversity of interpretation. Religious matters are so intimately related to the individual that even in one lifetime his interpretation and conception of what religion is may change, from one period of his life to another, depending upon his changing understanding of the value of life itself. Each religion, from the primitive form of fetishism to the modern form of monotheism, may present special features unlike that of any other, but all religions at every time and place have helped to determine man's thoughts, emotions, and behavior.

The way in which all religions resemble one another is that they include the interrelation between the human and the superhuman or the supernatural. The theologian Paul Tillich summarizes the fundamental concept of religion as "the state of being grasped by an ultimate concern, by an infinite interest, by something one takes unconditionally seriously." (*Morality and Beyond*, Harper and Row, 1963, p. 30.) The history of religion, as an activity involving an interplay between the human and the supernatural, leads us through various states of development from naturism (the worship of the objects of nature), through spiritism (the worship of ancestors), polytheism, brahmanism, neoplatonism, and other steps to the end point in historical analysis—monotheism. In modern times, and for the purpose of our discussion, we may safely say that religion has reference to man's relation to divinity and to his obligations to his Creator.

The bond uniting man to God entails a moral obligation to render God the reverence and obedience due to Him as the sustainer of all life and the source of all being.

Recognition of God as an object of love and adoration implies an obligation to act in accordance to the present principles of morality discovered by our reason and our feelings. Webster defines the distinction between religion and morality as follows: "As distinguished from *morality, religion* denotes the influences and motives of human duty which are found in the character and will of God, while morality describes the duties of man, which true religion always influences."

Morality Rooted in Religion

The influence of religion on the moral duties of man find its expression in our consciences, and we may find the terms "conscience," "morality," and "religion" used interchangeably. Asks the court: "For what is religion but morality, with a sanction drawn from a future state of rewards and punishments?" (*McAllister v. Marshall*, Pa., 6 Bin. 338, 6 Am. Dec. 458 [1814].) The identity of meaning given to such terms as "religious impulse," "religious belief," "the voice of conscience," and "moral obligation" points to the close interrelationship between morality and religion. Reason and logic without the aid of religious belief are not adequate to relate the individual to his fellowman and to his universe.

We have remarked earlier that Kant accepted a moral universal law as pragmatically necessary. He expressed his sentiments as follows: "There are two things which, the more I contemplate them, the more they fill my mind with admiration—the starry heavens above me and the moral law within me." In commenting on this sentiment of Kant, the prominent American jurist John Forrest Dillon wrote in his commentaries *The Laws and Jurisprudence of England and America:*

> "Not less wondrous than the revelations of the starry heavens and much more important . . . is the moral law which Kant found within himself, and which is likewise found within, and is consciously recognized by every man. This moral law holds its dominion by divine ordination over us all, from which escape or evasion is impossible. This moral law is the eternal and indestructible sense of justice and of right written by God on the living tablets of the human heart and revealed in his Holy Word."

The importance of revelation within the moral law was stressed by Sir William Blackstone. The illustrious English jurist expressed in his famous *Commentaries on the Laws of England* the opinion that because of our first ancestor's transgression our reason is "corrupt" and our understanding "full of ignorance and error." This, he argues, made it necessary for Providence to reveal its laws. These precepts are revealed to us in the Holy Scriptures, which are to be a part of the original law of nature as "they tend in all their consequences to man's felicity."

What is the impact of the Judaeo-Christian tradition on the morality of our laws? The Supreme Court of Appeals of West Virginia, reviewing a case of the removal from office of a prosecuting attorney found guilty of gross immorality, analyzed the governing standards of morality and reached the conclusion that our morality is more in harmony with the Mosaic interpretation of the moral law than with the "truly divine" interpretation given to man by Christ. According to Christ's teaching, man holds his body, mind, soul, and property by divine grant in trust for the benefit of his fellowman. This teaching calls for complete devotion to the welfare of humanity and for the establishment of a kingdom of perfect righteousness. "It makes," states the court, "the laws of morality concur fully with the laws of religion. According to it, he who serves man best worships God best, and he who worships God best serves man best."

While this divine interpretation of the Commandments is intended to secure perfection, the Mosaic interpretation, states the court, is "founded on absolute justice between man and man." Every man belongs to himself, has the right to do as he pleases, so long as he does nothing to interfere with his environment and accords the same right to others. The morality of our laws, concludes the court, "is the morality of the Mosaic interpretation of the Ten Commandments, modified only as to degree or kind of punishment inflicted." (*Moore et al. v. Strickling*, 46 W. Va. 515, 33 S.E. 174 [1899].)

Some may not accept this distinction between the two interpretations of the Commandments. Spinoza, for instance, looked upon the Jewish and the Christian religions as one and made no separation between the Old and New Testaments. The eternal wisdom of God, he wrote, "has shown itself forth in all things, but chiefly in the mind of man, and most of all in Jesus Christ." There is no doubt that the New Testament reaffirms and emphasizes the moral standards and obligations laid down in the Ten Commandments. Furthermore, the morality of our laws is not in fact limited to the Mosaic interpretations of the Ten Commandments. In analyzing these laws, we shall also discover the great impact of Christ's teaching, to mention only the special consideration that repentance has received in our courts and the qualities of forgiveness and compassion that are bound up in our judicial system.

The concept that morality is rooted in religion goes back as far as Plato and Aristotle. Plato believed that a nation cannot be strong unless it has faith in God. According to Aristotle, God is the first cause and the final cause—the purpose—of the world. The question that remains to be answered is: Are all systems of morality rooted in religion? In reviewing the various ethical traditions, we will, of course, find that some of them are consistently atheistic or agnostic. It remains to be seen whether these ethical traditions are fully consistent with the body of laws on which our nation is based.

We find two central groups of values glorified by ethical tradition. One is distinctly religious or remains in some sort of religious context; the other is divorced from religion. To the first group belong the traditional cardinal virtues listed by our courts: justice, prudence, temperance, and fortitude. (*Lyon v. Mitchell* 36 N.Y. 235, 238 [1867].) We may add wisdom, duty, truth, love, liberty, fidelity, honesty, and other similar virtues that develop the whole man. These in their origin are related to some kind of belief in God and consequently have special meaning within the context of religious faith. "Sound morals as taught by the wise men of antiquity, as confirmed by the precepts of the gospel . . . are unchangeable. They are the same yesterday and today." (*Zorach v. Clauson*, 343, U.S. 306, 313, 72. S. Ct. 679, 684, 96 L.Ed. 954 [1952].)

In our discussion of the various concepts of conscience, we pointed out that the moralists who are known as intuitionists believe that moral ideas are innate in man, that they are the inner law of our true being, the "silent voice" of our nature as man. Among them, Immanuel Kant believed that the supreme principle which man must follow is the categorical, unconditional moral imperative. Paul Tillich considers this unconditional character as the imperative's religious quality: "[T]he religious dimension of the moral imperative is its unconditional character." (*Morality and Beyond*, p. 33.) The divinely revealed natural moral law is in full harmony with the divinely created human nature. The ultimate moral principle is love, which should not be identified with charity or pity. Love is the highest work of the divine spirit, as described in the book of I Corinthians: "[I]f I have no love, I am nothing. I may dole out all I possess, or even give my body to be burnt, but if I have no love, I am none the better. . . . There is nothing love cannot face; there is no limit to its faith, its hope, and its endurance." (13:2–3, 7.) Love, therefore, includes and even transcends all the other virtues. In social institutions, spiritual freedom and human brotherhood are expressions of love.

Morality Not Rooted in Religion

Among the chief "virtues" of the second group of values—without roots in religion—we might list the desire of pleasure and the desire of power. The intrinsic aim of man—which according to Plato is "to become as much as possible similar to God" or as defined by Aristotle is participation in the eternal divine self-institution—is what gives the moral imperative its unconditional character. Such an unconditional character is lacking when man's aim is the greatest possible amount of pleasure to be derived from life. Contrast this view with the biblical one: "Set your affection on things above, not on things on the earth" (Colossians 3:2) and "It is the spirit that gives life, the flesh has nothing to offer." (John 6:63.) The hedonistic tradition, which extols pleasure, did not come from the Hebrew prophets and lawgivers and is not a part of the Judaeo-Christian morality which is the heritage of Western nations.

The doctrine that pleasure is the highest good, known as hedonism, has its own ancient roots. The principle that pleasure is the supreme good and indeed the only intrinsic good with moral significance for the individual was advocated by the Cyrenaic doctrine formulated by Aristippus, the Greek philosopher of Cyrene (5th-4th Century B.C.). In the dialogue *Gorgias*, Plato presents Socrates rejecting the contention that pleasure is the supreme good and showing the logical inadequacy of identifying pleasure with good.

Hedonism—which is egotistic and atheistic—is often unjustly confused with epicureanism and utilitarianism, which have different conceptions of the pleasant life than Cyrenaicism. The Roman poet and philosopher Lucretius Cavus in his *De Rerum Natura* (On the Nature of Things) follows Epicurus in granting that there is a god immortal and blessed but remote, who never intrudes in the affairs of men and who, therefore, is above dealing with rewards and punishments. This god lives, as a good epicurean should, in a garden of Epicurus in the clouds. Epicurus and his followers sought a pleasure that could lead to true happiness. Mere sensual enjoyment, he argued, brings unhappiness, "for it is not continuous drinkings and revellings, nor the satisfaction of lusts . . . which produce a pleasant life, but sober reasoning." The most important virtue, the beginning and the greatest good, is prudence, which is "a more precious thing even than philosophy," for it is not possible "to live pleasantly without living prudently and justly." In community life, the epicurean way consists of a pledge to assure mutual help among men, to restrain men from harming one another, and to save them from being harmed.

The British utilitarians Jeremy Bentham and John Stuart Mill replace the idea of pleasure with "happiness." Bentham taught that the individual's happiness depends upon the happiness of the greatest number. Such happiness represents the ethics of enlightened self-interest, calling for the individual's self-restraint in his search for happiness. Mill advocated the "Greatest Happiness Principle": "as rich as possible in enjoyments, both in point of quantity and quality." The individual's standard of conduct should be the best interests of society, "the greatest happiness of the greatest number." This transition from a sole interest in one's selfish happiness to a more general interest in that of others implies the natural moral law with its principle of love for our fellowman. Mill admits this principle by pointing out: "In the golden rule of Jesus of Nazareth, we read the complete spirit of the ethics of utility. To do as one would be done by, and to love one's neighbor as oneself, constitute the ideal perfection of utilitarian morality."

Far removed from philosophies allied closely to systems based on the moral imperatives rooted in religion are those so-called moral systems based solely on the prerogatives of power. When man's aim is merely a restless desire for power, he has divorced himself from the Judaeo-Christian tradition. The condemnation of such a position is richly illustrated in the Holy Scripture, to mention only Jezebel and Haman. Those who seeking power disobey God may expect the punishment described in Leviticus 26:19-20: "I will break the pride of your power . . . and your strength shall be spent in vain." The writers of the Old Testament realized that such retribution did not always occur in this life—Job expressed his dismay in his cry, "Why do the wicked live, reach old age, and grow mighty in power?" They concluded that a just God would somehow right things in the end, and goodness would prevail over naked power.

Thus the ethical position that extols power for its own sake—like the hedonistic tradition—is alien to the Hebrew prophets and lawgivers, as well as to Christ's teachings. It begins with the Sophists as portrayed in the first book of Plato's *Republic* by Glaucon and Thrasymachus, who argue that "all men believe in their hearts that injustice is far more profitable to the individual than justice" and that "the just is always a loser in comparison with the unjust." They believe that injustice applied on a large scale is particularly rewarding, since "injustice, when on a sufficient scale, has more strength and freedom and mastery than justice." From them a straight line leads to the power politics represented by Hobbes, Machiavelli, Nietzsche, and Marx.

In his uncompromising atheism and materialism, Hobbes exalts absolute monarchy. Machiavelli divorces the prince from ethical principles, recommending that he use hypocrisy, force, and fraud to gain power. The validity of law is also derived from force: "Nothing causes a prince to be so much esteemed as giving proof of prowess."

For Nietzsche, life is will to power and, therefore, it is essentially "injury, conquest of the strange and weak, suppression, severity . . . and at least, putting it mildest, exploitation." Exploitation, he believes, is a primary organic function of living, "it is a consequence of the intrinsic Will to Power, which is precisely the Will of Life." According to Machiavelli, "it is much safer to be feared than loved . . . For it may be said of men in general that they are ungrateful, voluble, dissemblers, anxious to avoid danger, and covetous of gain." Karl Marx, in order for the proletarians to seize power, calls for a merciless revolution which will bring the collapse of capitalism.

The power politics advocated by Machiavelli and Nietzsche influenced the minds of Mussolini and Hitler. The totalitarian communist countries are carrying out the gospel of Marx. The fruits of such abuses of power are only too well known. Today we continue to witness the atrocities taking place in countries under the yoke of communist dictatorships. We find tyranny instead of democracy, injustice and slavery instead of justice, equality in general poverty instead of prosperity, nationalism and imperialism instead of peace, and hypocritical slogans to conceal the darkness of oppression.

This darkness is the effect of a desire for power combined with a dismissal of conscience; it is expressed most effectively by the title character in Shakespeare's *Richard III:*

> "Our strong arms to be our conscience, swords our
>   law.
> March on, join bravely, let to't pell-mell;
> If not to heaven, then hand in hand to hell."

Shakespeare's villains, in fact, often speak doctrines derived from the teaching of Machiavelli, who was regarded as an infamous atheistic writer in Elizabethan England.

There is, indeed, something that the teachings of those who extol power as the supreme virtue have in common—they hated religion as an opiate, as an invention of the weak to limit and to deter the strong. As Nietzsche revels in the strength of the Superman, he pours contempt on the Judaeo-Christian ethic. The "spiritual men" of Christianity, he argues, have given comfort to the sufferers, courage to the oppressed and despairing; by preserving the sick and the suffering, they have caused the European race to deteriorate. "I regard Christianity," he write, "as the most fatal and seductive lie that has ever yet existed—as the greatest and most injurious lie. ... I urge people to declare open war with it." Hitler and Stalin did declare war against religion and revived cruelty in a form never known before.

In our generation, we have witnessed the fall of fascism in Italy and the fall of Nazi Germany. These events give us hope in the principle that nothing established by violence and maintained by force in opposition to what is right can endure. Nor can anything which is based on a contempt for human personality and which degrades humanity endure. Power not undergirded by spiritual force must destroy itself. Only the constructive power of spiritually creative resources can isolate the destructive forces of tyranny, divert us toward positive goals of human welfare, and help to build bridges of understanding and fellowship among peoples by mastering the moral and material resources latent in this world.

The only supreme power is God. Those who have rejected His commandment of love and who have attempted to seize that power which is His alone have brought into the world as a corollary of their power unparalleled destruction of human beings, terror, slavery, and concentration camps; they have plunged the world into wars of unprecedented ferociousness. We are reminded of the warning Aristotle issued in his *Politics:* "For man, when perfected, is the best of the animals, but when separated from law and justice, he is the worst of all; . . . wherefore, if he have no virtue, he is the most unholy and the most savage of animals." What distinguishes man from animal is the freedom of choice between the moral values whose roots are in religion and the values separated from religion. This fundamental choice can be made only by means of the profound understanding which comes from knowledge of the purpose of life.

Conflict or Harmony

According to Spinoza, the endeavor to understand "is the first and only basis of virtue," because "the greatest good is the knowledge of the union, which mind has with the whole nature . . . The more the mind knows, the better it understands its forces and the order of nature; the more it understands its forces or strength, the better it will be able to divest itself and lay down the rules for itself." Throughout the great philosophical tradition which we have tried to trace, there is the deeply rooted idea that understanding leads to right action. For Socrates, knowledge is virtue. For Plato, only knowledge produces a harmonious man capable of governing his desires and passions. Our forefathers declared in the Northwest Ordinance, to which I have referred previously, that knowledge is necessary for good government along with religion and morality, because the inculcation of religion and morality can take place only through the diffusion of knowledge. The kind of knowledge to which all of these referred is not mere abstract reasoning or the accumulation of facts. Knowledge, in order to explain the purposeful creation of the universe and guide our actions, must be grounded in the true values of life provided by religion and morality.

Knowledge in this deeper sense can flourish only when it is related to some kind of belief in God and immortality; by itself it cannot accomplish the aim of human life, which searches for something beyond mere survival. Without the direction of a moral code, knowledge becomes aimless and meaningless; but when supplemented by moral principles, it creates a climate in which commitment to service may emerge. Supplemented by moral principles, it shatters the illusions of those who refuse to acknowledge the dependent character of man's life and put their trust in wealth, security, pleasure, and power.

As John Wesley insisted, only the blended light of knowledge and vital piety, by controlling our violent, unsocial impulses and uncoordinated passions, can guide individuals and nations into harmony and prevent conflicts. This is the essence of the interrelation between knowledge, religion, and morality. When knowledge and religion are fused into one force—which is understanding—it is capable of grasping the highest truths: "The Lord by wisdom hath founded the earth, by understanding hath he established the heavens." (Proverbs 3:19.) It is the only force which can lift up humbled humanity and help it to fulfill God's call for a holiness of life which Wesley called "social holiness," love and service to all mankind.

COLLISION AND COMMUNITY: CHURCH AND STATE IN A HUMANE SOCIETY

by

Donald W. Shriver, Jr.

Donald W. Shriver, Jr.

Dr. Shriver has been President of Union Theological Seminary in New York since 1975. Before that he was professor of ethics at Emory University and professor of religion at North Carolina State University. He is an ordained Presbyterian minister and has spent most of his career in university and church settings in the south.

A native of Norfolk, Virginia, he holds degrees from Davidson College and Yale and Harvard universities.

As a teacher, writer, and administrator, he spent many years organizing dialogue and study around ethical issues in the professions of science, engineering, business, politics, and medicine. A number of his books have been co-authored with persons from these professions. His books include: The Unsilent South, Rich Man/Poor Man, Is There Hope for the City?, Medicine and Religion, *and* Spindles and Spires: A Restudy of Religion and Social Change in Gastonia.

He currently teaches courses at Union Seminary in business ethics and the urban ministry of the churches. His travels have taken him to thirty-five countries, and with his wife Peggy—who is Assistant General Secretary of the National Council of Churches—he recently spent two months in six Asian countries, including India, South Korea, and the People's Republic of China. He has been an elected leader of all levels of the Democratic Party, and was a delegate from North Carolina to the 1968 Democratic Convention. In Raleigh, N.C., from 1966 to 1971, he served on the Mayor's committee on human relations, and was active in various aspects of the Civil Rights Movement. In Atlanta, he participated in the city planning movement called "Atlanta 2000."

COLLISION AND COMMUNITY:
CHURCH AND STATE IN A HUMANE SOCIETY

by

Donald W. Shriver, Jr.

"My kingdom is not of this world." (John 18: 36.)

"Render unto Caesar the things that are Caesar's, and unto God the things that are God's." (Luke 20: 25.)

"Be subject to the governing authorities."

(Romans 13: 1–4.)

"Obey God rather than men." (Acts 5: 29.)

In his recent comment on these four passages from the New Testament, Max L. Stackhouse says:

"This cluster of teachings represents one of the most revolutionary social doctrines ever conceived. It is not a natural thing for people to draw a sharp separation between religion and politics as distinct realms, to demand responsible participation in both and simultaneously to say that the object of one (God) is the criterion for the object of the other (the exercise of power). The natural tendencies are, on the one hand, towards a world-denying spirituality that views religion and politics as absolutely irrelevant to each other, or, on the other hand, toward an accommodationist stance that uses one to 'legitimize' the other."

Then he adds: "We are always tempted by these 'natural' pagan tendencies." (Stackhouse, "The Church and Polit-

65

ical Life: A Loss of Confidence," *The Christian Century*, Vol. XCVIII, No. 24. July 29–August 5, 1981, p. 767.)

So long as Christians pray the prayer their Teacher taught them—"Lead us not into temptation"—they.will have reason to fear their vulnerability to "natural pagan tendencies" in the relation they prescribe and enact for the relation of faith and politics, churches and governments. The purpose of this lecture is to review summarily the major historic forms of this relationship in the theories and the institutional life of the Christian movement; and then to inquire what contributions, if any, the churches of the United States may have to make to the political culture of this land, given the historical circumstances of the 1980s and this particular historical tradition. In particular, I shall be interested in the two sides of this relation which Stackhouse calls "the most decisive indicators of social righteousness in society . . . the structural freedom of religion and the ethical dependence on an ecumenically shaped 'public theology.'" (Ibid.)

The Ancient Dialogue of Christ and Caesar

Almost every debate in contemporary America and the world about the role of religion *vis à vis* politics roots in some assumptions of long tenure in human history. The late H. Richard Niebuhr of Yale, who taught a whole generation of theological ethicists to think twice before they promoted any idea as something new under the sun, was one of those students of history who teach us to grasp history by reducing its themes to a typology. Niebuhr's five-fold typology of the historic Christian ways of relating "Christ" and "culture" may not summarize these varieties of Christian social ethics exhaustively, but he comes close to doing so. His book *Christ and Culture*

(New York, Harper and Brothers, 1951) remains just about what Paul Ramsey called it: "the one outstanding book in the field of basic Christian social ethics." The subject of the book is far broader than "church and state"; but one can break open any contemporary theological discussion of this relation by availing oneself of Niebuhr's honest historic memory and his exemplary sense, communicated in all his writing, that Christians have been wrestling with these matters for a long time.

The Collision of Church and State: "Christ Against Culture"

Stackhouse is right. It is *not* "a natural thing for people to draw a sharp separation between religion and politics." To detect the "natural thing" in the world of the Bible one must make reference to such ancient polities as Egypt and Babylonia, from which ancient Israel distinguished itself in the Exodus, in the struggle against the worship of the Canaanitish gods of fertility, and in its odd tolerance for the institution of prophet. That uniquely religious politician, the prophet, was always calling kings to account for their deeds before the bar of Yahweh, the true King of Israel. The makings of a sharp distinction between a religious authority and a governmental authority emerged in this Israelitish history. It lies like a foundation and platform under the religious experience, the political attitudes, and the social institutional life of the early Christians. Systematic thinkers have always had difficulty harmonizing the various epigrammatic sayings of Jesus on the subject of religious faith, the political order, and political crisis. Was he a mystic quietist, a secret revolutionary, or something else *vis à vis* the great Roman empire of his day? As recent New

Testament study might suggest, this is an abstract, ultimately impossible inquiry. Prior to the words attributed to Jesus as a teacher is the memory of those words in the collective mind of the early church; and prior to the memory, or contemporary with it, was the collectivity itself, the worshipping church.

Too little do most modern Christians appreciate the truly revolutionary "social doctrine" contained in the *fact* of the early Christian church. Sociologists will tell you that there were only two powerful social institutions in the Roman world, the state and the family. When the Christian church emerged in the first several centuries A.D., it was inserting itself, so to speak, as a third mode of human identity, related to but independent of the other two. What internal explanation did Christians give for this relative independence of the church from the family and the state? The answer is in the context of Acts 5: 29:

> "We ought to obey God rather than men [because] the God of our fathers raised up Jesus whom you had done to death. He it is whom God has exalted with his own right hand as leader and saviour, to grant Israel repentance and forgiveness of sins. And we are witnesses to all this, and so is the Holy Spirit given by God to those who are obedient to him." (Acts 5: 29–32.)

We read that the religious authorities of the time, in good standing with the Romans, heard these words and "wanted to put them to death." That is the natural reaction of an establishment informed of a fundamental, principled revolt against its authority. But an "unnatural establishment" was already at hand in the prophetic tradition of Israel; there, close to the birthday of the Christian church, that prophetic tradition found a spokesman in the great Pharisee Gamaliel.

> "Keep clear of these men, I tell you; leave them alone. For if this idea of theirs or its execution is of human origin, it will collapse; but if it is from God, you will never be able to put it down, and you risk finding yourselves at war with God." (Acts 5:38-39.)

Gamaliel in this instance shows himself a true *Jewish* conservative; the God of Israel has trustworthy connection with no government whatsoever. The Spirit of the Lord goes and comes from kings; history and the consensus of a certain religious community finally indicate where the Spirit was truly present. In this, Gamaliel was both conservative *and* liberal, if "liberal" is to be defined as Judge Learned Hand once defined it: "the spirit that is not too sure it is right." By what Spirit, Christians ask, shall our spirits be humbled and tutored? By the One who raised Jesus from the dead, the Jesus in whose name we worship the God of Israel and in whose name, if necessary, we resist the *dominium* of Rome. They resisted it, Acts 5 shows vividly, by the internal act of worship and the external act of evangelism. They undertook both activities in the belief that the teacher of Galilee had a reversed judgment passed upon him when, after execution at the hands of a religious and a political establishment, "the God of our fathers raised (him) up . . ."

No wonder, in this context, that the oldest Christian "theory" of the relation of church and state propounds a radical separation between the two, an antagonism centered upon the crucifixion of Jesus and a restructuring of worldly authority in the declaration of the Lordship of Jesus over the lordship of Caesar. For almost three hundred years this theory held controversial sway over the Christian churches as they multiplied like amoebae in every nook and cranny of the Roman empire. When they arrived, twelve generations away from the crucifixion, at new treaty-relations with Rome in the person of the Emperor Constantine, they had a long memory of church–state relations that added up to the radical caution: "Beware!" This caution Christians, in their historically conscious moments, have never forgotten.

There are places in the modern world where the Christian movement lives very much in a pre-Constantinian era. One such place is South Korea, where a Confucian culture, as near to "natural" religion as any religion in the world, strives to refute the strange propensity of the Christians to make their religion a method for keeping their distance from government and sometimes launching a protest against government.

That is the earliest Christian disposition for the relating of worshipping churches to reigning governments. The next earliest, strangely or naturally enough, was nearly the mirror image of the first.

The Merger of Church and State: "The Church of Culture"

Even before Constantine's Edict of Toleration in 312 A.D., some Christian theologians—like Clement of Alexander—were looking for ways to attach the message of the church to the message of Graeco–Roman culture. Clement and his intellectual relatives were uncomfortable with the thought that the worlds of the university, business, and government were foreign affairs in the Kingdom of God. Had not Jesus said to render to Caesar his due? The intellectual side of this "Christ of Culture" school makes a long story. Its political form under Constantine and his successors must interest us most. Two symbolic events—such events as to sweep pious celebrators of the early Christian church off their confident feet—shaped church-state relations in the Roman empire between the years 312 and 395. In the several centuries prior, Christians had struggled to acquire legitimacy at least to worship; in no small sense, the only sure revolutionary act of the early church, in the eyes of Rome, was the act of worshipping Jesus as Lord rather than Caesar as lord. The essential battle between churches and their host governments, in the jargon of later social science, was *symbolic:* Was there to be room in the human social world for (what the medievalists would call) "two swords"? (The sword of political authority and the churchly sword of the Spirit.) With the Edict of Toleration in 312, the official government finally answered "yes." After 83 years, another Edict—that of Emperor Theodosius—declared that the *only* religion henceforth to be granted political rights of legitimate worship was Christianity. In the 380s, Jews had been denied the right to become soldiers in the Roman armies; that was a vocation, now so quickly, reserved for Christians. By 395 it was illegal to be anything else but a Christian throughout the Empire.

So hard does natural religion die! For such natural reasons does a government spring supportively to a religion that "works," for the period of Theodosius in the East was the period of Augustine in the West, and there the very existence of government was in doubt under

mounting pressures of the "barbarians." There the
church assumed quasi-governmental responsibilities for
keeping the body and soul of crumbling society together,
thus building the foundations of a new European age
that we call medieval. In that new responsibility for the
care and nurture of human culture—the economy, the
polity, the society—the church was learning a sort of
emergency-ethic. Little in the New Testament suggested
that the church had a vocation for learning agriculture
(as did the new monasteries), or for policing the city of
Rome (as did Pope Leo facing Attila the Hun), or for
legitimating a new social order of landowners and serfs
(as did the great medieval social thinkers); but there it
was—human need crying out for church power in the
Western half of the empire, and human power offering
benefits to the church in the Eastern half. Thus, for the
next thousand years in both halves, the idea of the "separation of church and state" was hardly conceivable. The
history was far more complicated than this, of course;
but the startling truth for later ages of politically minded
Christians was the rapidity with which a "Church against
culture" can become a "Christ of culture." Make it an
ironic, skeptical rule: Persecute Christians for twelve
generations, begin to tolerate them, and in three generations they will gladly become the persecutors of other
religions! They will even put the governmental foot upon
the root from which their own faith sprang; they will
start a millennium of political disqualification of Jews.
So swift and so apparently contradictory is the coming
of the Christ of culture in mirror-opposition to the Christ
against culture.

  We may wonder if there was anything in the Christian
religion itself to bring it to this strange pass. Explana-

tions will differ with the critics and their respective centuries; St. Francis, John Calvin, and John Dewey would eventually have their very diverse explanations of what is wrong with the authority of the Christian religion when it mates itself closely with political authority, legitimates political power, and loses its vocation for political prophecy. Suffice it to say, for historical honesty's sake, this and other religions are vulnerable to the seduction of the godly by the government. Whatever else Paul had in mind when he said, "Be subject to the governing authorities," he did not have this in mind. Otherwise he would never have ended his life on a Roman chopping block.

The Hierarchy of State and Church: "Church Above Culture"

A thousand years after those who claimed to be witnesses to the resurrection, a combination of experience, reflection, and social circumstance brought the theologians of Western Europe to make subtle, careful, even beautiful distinction and connection between the realm of "nature"—ordinary human life—and the realm of "grace"—the extraordinary world of the divine Kingdom. When Ernst Troeltsch makes his famous distinction between a "sect" and a "church," he has this medieval model in mind for the church. Unlike those who merge the Christian truth too closely with other truths and the power of the Spirit too intimately with the power of government, the medieval mind saw everything in the image of the "great chain of being," an upsweeping hierarchy that began in the dirt of Tuscany but ended at the feet of Christ the King in Paradise. Dante tells it all: how a culture-transcending vision fortifies the culture-superintending church that legitimates without simply baptizing all the lower human orders of economics, politics, and the family.

Through later Protestant lenses, church-state relations of the Middle Ages were likely to be characterized as a formula for tyranny, exploitation, and the utter politicization of religion for trivial secular ends. To read the history of the Crusades, the papacy, and the wealthy mendicant orders in this era gives excuse to this view; but it is not a very accurate view, failing as it does to understand how nicely ordered, comprehensive, unified, and variously human the medieval system could be. In a century far removed from that time and in a country with no firsthand institutions rooted in that time, few American Christians think of the medieval hierarchy as a way to organize a society or one's thinking about society. But our nineteenth-century American Protestant relatives talked a lot about their dream of a "Christian America"; in so dreaming, they imagined a version of what Thomas Aquinas, Innocent III, and Henry VIII imagined. The Christian faith concerns everything in the human world, has a potential positive relation to every good and negative relation to every evil, and must exert through the church a great effect upon the world.

Government too has a role in producing that effect, as do other organized human agencies. The church is not in charge of the whole world, though it may be peculiarly able to recognize the rule of God in the whole world. Certain kinds of truth and power belong to the secular part of the world, and other kinds to the church, which must be at home on earth as the cathedral is at home in the marketplace, while pointing the village to Heaven.

It is a neatly ordered, seductive version of the articulation between the sacred and the secular. It was, for the Protestant mind that owes much to it, more seductive than the Caesaro-papism of the Eastern emperors or the straightforward clerical rule of Islamic fundamentalism. The medieval vision of church-state relations remains as the fond memory of many a modern Roman Catholic. What many still mean by the phrase "Catholic country" has overtones of this memory, and in an era when the parts of the human community seem so perpetually vulnerable to dissolving their social unity, who can blame us if we occasionally think that medieval Europe was the one and only great attempt of the Christians to influence a whole culture?

One remarkable feature of the Jews and the Christians, however, is their capacity to draw from their faith new reasons to protest against things that a previous generation saw as high achievement. True to its origin, the community of Christians seems always capable of pulling apart some current relation of Christ and Caesar to put them together again in more compelling fashion. This is one way to talk of the capacity for *change* latent in some versions of biblical religion. The medieval vision called for the great change of the human from the earthly sojourn to the heavenly home, but on earth humans had little time or reason for changing their society. Mostly medievalists believed that change is suspect, the orders of nature and grace are in their places, and the power of church and government must be exerted to keep things in those places. Order was the great social virtue; freedom had a very small place indeed. Perhaps the most free of places was the monastery, ostensibly a retreat from the world on the way of the soul to heaven.

But it was one of the ironies of the medieval synthesis that the politics of both church and state sometimes suffered disturbance in powerful forms from thinkers and leaders trained in the monasteries. Never underestimate the political implications of a religious lifestyle that ostensibly scorns politics!

The Conflict and Complementarity of Church and State: "Christ and Culture in Paradox"

Such a monastic disturber of the medieval peace was Martin Luther. Not a great questioner of church-state relations, he was hardly a precursor of politically guaranteed religious freedom. But he exercised his monastic freedom to study the Bible in Hebrew and Greek, to preach the conclusions of his study, and, above all, to share his personal religious experience with other interested Christians in the church. The result was a strange combination of revolution in religion and conservatism in politics, a new ordering of spiritual and secular truth that more or less compartmentalized them inside the same social structure. American Protestant Christians, reared so pervasively upon a Calvinist version of the Reformation, find it hard to appreciate Lutheran political ethics; for like Aquinas, Luther thought that order and the justice of order were the purpose of government, and like most medievalists, he anticipated little benign change in what governments do to curb the aggressive, evil impulses of human beings. He demanded a new specialization in the function of the church — to preach the loving grace of God without political intent or direct political expectations. He saw no smooth harmony between the justice of God and the grace of God, and none between the justice of government and the grace of Gospel-preaching. The two exist, in concept and in institution, in a paradoxical relation. They contradict each other, in a way that reflects the relation of a holy God to an unholy humanity. Thus, the church preaches salvation by divine grace to all people, while government holds all people accountable for doing the works of the human law. One speaks the word of divine love, the other the word of divine judgment. While the one testifies to the forgiveness of sins, the other imprisons and executes sinners.

It was a harsh theory of politics, fortified by the grim political realities of the sixteenth century. Few American theologians or politicians have been enthusiastic about Luther's grim vision of government, but many have agreed with him about the essentially quietistic role of the church regarding secular politics. The "two-kingdoms" of the Lutheran social order mingle in contradiction and hold together by the providence of God, not by simple principles of human reason. "Religion and politics don't mix" is a good Lutheran slogan, based on a profound sense of the distance between the righteousness of God and every human righteousness. Said Luther:

> "He would confuse these two kingdoms . . . who would put wrath into God's kingdom and mercy into the world's kingdom, and that is the same as putting the devil in heaven and God in hell." (Niebuhr, pp. 171–172, quoting Luther, *Works* Vol. IV, pp. 265–266.)

In the twentieth century, some critics have blamed Martin Luther for laying the groundwork for the weak resistance of German Christians to the tyranny and terror of Adolf Hitler. This, again, as in all the history of church-state relations in western history, is very complicated. But there is enough truth in the statement to have compelled "confessing Christians" like Bonhoeffer to revise their theories of the relation between a faithful church and a corrupt government. Sitting quietly by, preaching the Gospel, while the devil works away in government, seems contradictory to a biblical faith in the world-rule of God. Yet another vision of church-state relation seems plausible. The architects of this relation in the United States were influenced principally by that other vision.

Loyal Opposition: "Christ the Transformer of Culture"

Any survey of historical collisions between the Christian movement and political institutions will have to conclude that the two seem unable to leave each other alone. The reasons are both theological and pragmatic: From Exodus on, the biblical faith in God testifies to an unceasing negotiation between the ruler of the universe and the mundane history of humans. The terms describing this negotiation are frequently political, and ever and again, representatives of human government appear in the story. One theological reason for this recurrence is the universalism, the comprehensiveness of the Divine-human relation. One pragmatic reason is that governments in history are more or less "monarchs of all they survey." Everything and everybody in a territory come in some way under their jurisdiction. If religion and its institutions exist in that territory, the two are bound to meet up with each other.

We know what a fractious meeting that can be. No wonder that Martin Luther, somewhat against the odds, tried to pack the two into two contradictory, insulated cells. "Two kingdoms" are inherently unstable; one is always trying to "one up" the other. This seems to be an inherent tension in both the logic and the practice of church-government dialogue. "Sovereignty" at some level is indivisible. The locus, the nature, and the limits of supremacy are key concepts in both theology and political theory. What is the authority that settles all disputed questions, resolves all conflicts, and authorizes all right continuity and change? It is a question perennial in theology and practical politics, and no group of Christians in history has asked the question more persistently than the *Calvinists*.

They are not H. Richard Niebuhr's only example of the theory of "Christ transforming culture," but they are a very strong example, especially in their own American revised version. Ernst Troeltsch said that the spiritual descendents of John Calvin in Scotland, England, and America all shared the most distinctive idea of their founder: the idea of a "holy community," a civil society organized under laws derived from the Bible and laws derived more or less from popular political participation. How the will of God could become a positive basis for government "of the people, by the people, and for the people" may be a mystery of theologic and history. It is surely true that the spirit of Calvinism seems to offend against the spirit of liberty, for Calvinists in history have often been only "too sure that they are right." But Oliver Cromwell's famous remark to the two Scot regiments about to argue themselves into a fight still expresses a fundamental bit of political wisdom that took many centuries for the Christian churches of the West to perceive: "I beseech you, by the mercies of Christ, *think* that you may be wrong!" It was a thought not far from that of Gamaliel and every other true believer in a supreme, often hidden, will of God, distinct from all human wills and institutions. What Calvinists did for the Protestant notion of the supremacy of God was to take it out of the static structure of medieval society and out of the equally static boxes of Luther and to understand that divine will as restlessly at work in the whole human and nonhuman world. Calvinists, said A.S.P. Woodhouse, "lived in a world of particular providences." (Woodhouse, *Puritanism and Liberty*, Chicago, The University of Chicago Press, 1951, p. 42.) To them the whole world was "the theater of God's glory," which could never be tamed or institutionalized. Human beings are obliged, by this vision, to be constantly at the work of seeing, obeying, institutionalizing, and reinstitutionalizing the ever-transcending intentions of their divine ruler. That rule aims at unceasing *transformation* of all things human in the direction toward which God impels the world.

The implications for political philosophy in this Calvinistic version of Christianity were abundant enough in the period of the Puritan revolution in England, but that revolution had its largest continuation in the next 150 years of European settlement of America. Lord Acton called John Calvin "the virtual founder of the United States of America." That may be a strange opinion to Americans of the 1980s, but it would not have been as strange to anyone who listened to James Madison plead the case for no legislative financing of religious teaching in the schools of Virginia in 1785. Madison, a prominent "father" of the federal Constitution, had been a student of Presbyterian President John Witherspoon at Princeton. He was among the few members of the Constitutional Convention who exhibited the signs of some profound personal understanding of the Christian faith and loyalty to it. As a young man he had stood outside the jail in Orange, Virginia, "and heard an imprisoned Baptist minister preach from the window—the only pulpit legally available to him." Later he became an advocate, not of mere religious toleration but of "the right of every man to liberty" of religion. (Anson Phelps Stokes and Leo Pfeffer, *Church and State in the United States*, Revised One-Volume Edition, New York, Harper and Row, 1964, p. 55.) Baptists may have had a different church government from that of Presbyterians, but along with the Congregationalists they were heirs to the same Calvinism. Madison was one with Gamaliel in believing that if Baptists are "from God, you will never be able to put them down." We know from his eloquent "Memorial and Remonstrance" to the Virginia Legislature in 1785 the key theological ideas at issue in his call for a true separation of church and state. The major idea was thoroughly Calvinistic:

> "Before any man can be considered as a member of civil society, he must be considered as a subject of the governor of the universe; and if a member of civil society, who enters into any subordinate association, must always do it with a reservation of his duty to the general authority, much more must every man who becomes a member of any particular civil society do it *with the saving his allegiance to the universal sovereign*." (Stokes and Pfeffer, p. 56.)

Madison was both a Protestant and an enlightened eighteenth-century educated person in his belief that every human had potential access to some knowledge of God, that any attempt to bind the religious liberty of a human being was an affront to God, not simply to the human. *The God of the biblical faith does not need institutional human protection,* says Madison. The bill before the Legislature must be defeated,

> "Because the bill implies, either that the civil magistrate is a competent judge of truth, or that he may employ religion as an engine of civil policy. The first is an arrogant pretension, falsified by the contradictory opinions of rulers of all ages, and throughout the world: the second is an unhallowed perversion of the means of salvation. . . . The establishment proposed by the bill is not requisite for the support of the Christian religion. To say that it is, is a contradiction to the Christian religion itself; for every page of it disavows a dependence upon the powers of this world." (Stokes and Pfeffer, p. 57.)

Madison asks rhetorically, "What influences, in fact, have ecclesiastical establishments had on civil authority?" He answers with the mind of one who knows church history from Constantine to George III:

> "In some instances they have been seen to erect a spiritual tyranny on the ruins of civil authority; in many instances they have been seen upholding the thrones of political tyranny; in no instance have they been seen the guardians of the liberties of the people." (Stokes and Pfeffer, p. 58.)

The impressive thing about this eloquent plea for popular religious liberty is that it is based, not merely upon enlightenment rationalism and individualism, but upon a classic Calvinist appreciation of the authority and liberty of the Sovereign Lord of the Universe. Government has its place, along with all other human things, subordinant to that divine authority and liberty. The freedom of God precedes and authorizes freedom among his human subjects.

When he visited the United States in the 1830s, Alexis de Tocqueville, a practicing French Catholic, was impressed with a combination of religious freedom and the diminished powers of government in the young country.

> "For the Americans the ideas of Christianity and liberty are so completely mingled that it is almost impossible to get them to conceive of the one without the other; it is not a question with them of sterile beliefs bequeathed by the past and vegetating rather than living in the depths of the soul." (De Tocqueville, *Democracy in America*, A New Translation by George Lawrence, ed. by J.P. Mayer, Anchor Books, Garden City, N.Y., Doubleday and Co., 1964, pp. 293-294.)

American democracy, he claimed, requires the undergirding of a strong religiously defined morality to make its liberties no invitation to license; the authority of God, rather than being the support of tyranny is, in America, its arch enemy. "Despotism may be able to do without faith, but freedom cannot." (De Tocqueville, p. 297.) The vigor of such a religion, adds de Tocqueville, requires its separation from the state; for, along with Madison, he observes that every liaison of a universalistic faith with a particular state undermines universalism.

"By allying itself with any political power, religion
increases its strength over some but forfeits the hope
of reigning over all. . . . Like our years upon earth,
the powers of society are all more or less transitory;
they follow one another quickly, like the various
cares of life; and there has never been a government
supported by some invariable dispostion of the
human heart or one founded upon some interest that
is immortal." (Ibid.)

De Tocqueville toured America in the years of the
Second Great Awakening. In that period, large numbers
of newly converted or newly revived Christians were
seeing visions, not only of heaven but of a purified, re-
formed America. In these years, abolitionism was born,
as well as new movements for the rights of women and
children. Utopian communities spread across the land.
Where government had scarcely set up its bureaus,
evangelists were setting up their congregations. As in
so many "developing countries" of the twentieth-century
world, in developing America the churches provided
social networks of continuity for a society with very fluid
boundaries, human and geographical. No wonder that
the idea of "Christ transforming culture" should appeal
so much to American Christians in the nineteenth century. Theirs was a culture changing faster than any
European ancestor could have imagined, and it seemed
only fitting to the faith and the circumstances of Christians that they should take part in defining and explor-
ing the meaning of the "New World." For the first two-
thirds of the century, no one expressed these things
better than Abraham Lincoln, whose second Inaugural
Address embodies echoes of biblical faith in the Sov-
reign God of politics as do few other documents from

American political history. There has never been a
better statement of how a great, tragic political event
like a Civil War can be interpreted as an event with deep
human and theological meaning. Perhaps only in a country whose "virtual founder was John Calvin" could a
chief executive talk as Lincoln did in this address. Reviewing devastation of the four-year war, about to end,
he said that neither the North nor the South

> "expected for the war the magnitude or the duration
> which it has already attained. Neither anticipated
> that the *cause* of the conflict [conflicting regional
> interests surrounding the institution of slavery]
> might cease with or even before the conflict itself
> should cease. Both read the same Bible and pray to
> the same God, and each invokes His aid against the
> other. It may seem strange that any men should dare
> to ask a just God's assistance in wringing their bread
> from the sweat of other men's faces, but let us judge
> not, that we be not judged. The prayers of both could
> not be answered. That of neither has been answered
> fully. The Almighty has His own purposes. 'Woe
> unto the world because of offenses; for it must needs
> be that offenses come, but woe to that man by whom
> the offense cometh.' If we shall suppose that Ameri-
> can slavery is one of those offenses which, in the
> providence of God, must needs come, but which,
> having continued through His appointed time, He
> now wills to remove, and that He gives to both North
> and South this terrible war as the woe due to those
> by whom the offense came, shall we discern therein
> any departure from those divine attributes which

the believers in a living God always ascribe to Him?"
("Second Inaugural Address" in Henry Steele
Commager, Ed., *Documents of American History*,
New York, Appleton-Century-Crofts, 1962, pp. 442–
443.)

And at the end, having discerned the grim justice of God
in American history, Lincoln discerns a healing mercy:

"With malice toward none, with charity for all, with
firmness in the right as God gives us to see the right,
let us strive on to finish the work we are in, to bind up
the nation's wounds, to care for him who shall have
borne the battle and for his widow and his orphan, to
do all which may achieve and cherish a just and last-
ing peace among ourselves and with all nations."
(Ibid.)

Although the biblical Jesus is quoted without being
named in this classic of American presidential theology,
one could aptly designate it as a classic statement of
"Christ Transforming Culture" in American history.
Lincoln's deity is actively, ceaselessly at work ruling the
nation of which he, Lincoln, is President. How far from
a Roman emperor this president is! This deity measures
and never simply legitimates human purposes, delivering judgment upon the very standards of judgment basic
to the historic constitution of the nation. Along with
William Lloyd Garrison, Lincoln believed that the original great document of 1789 was deeply flawed in its
inclusion of slavery as a legal institution in a new nation
established on principles of "liberty and justice for all."
Not for Lincoln or any of the abolitionists the notion that
they lived under a perfect documentary constitution,

subject to no criticism from the more ancient Bible or from the new wisdom of a later generation. Lincoln is a *liberal* on these points; he has been willing to fight a war because he both interprets the Constitution in a certain way and criticizes the Constitution in an equally certain way. Above all he believes that God is at work in the world of human politics, rendering terrible judgments and amazing benedictions thereupon.

In the hundred years that followed the American Civil War, few American Presidents were able to draw so confidently and so profoundly from Hebrew-Christian biblical sources for the shaping of their political rhetoric. In Lincoln we catch sight of a religious faith sometimes being "used" in the service of a particular political cause but somehow always slipping away toward transcendence. Government remains subject to the purposes of God; it is never identical with them. Politics involves evil and tragedy as well as the victory of the good; God must judge the sins of the righteous and heal the wounds inflicted by the well-intentioned. Presidents cannot escape subjection to the "living God"—nor can whole peoples.

One reason why such rhetoric appeared so seldom in the next century of American political speechmaking was the decline of belief in the "living God" among some politicians and their constituents. Another reason was the increase in the varieties of religious experience in the American people as a whole. We call that increase "religious pluralism," and in our own time we are beginning to face its reality in ways little known to nineteenth-century America. Yet another reason was the retreat from the rigors of true Calvinism among American Protestants to the marshy depths of subjectivistic, apolitical personalism in religion. Companion to this development was the rise of single-issue political thinking among the Protestant churches, not so well grounded in the study of the Bible as was their thinking about slavery and not so appreciative of the ambiguous rightness of all political action, whether it be for the prohibition of alcoholic beverages, the refutation of Marx and Darwin, or the prohibition of abortion. For lack of a Lincolnesque respect for that ambiguity, Protestants in the early and middle twentieth century acquired a reputation for identifying the will of God with certain reforms of law. A living religious faith relates to politics partly by transcending politics, partly by calling into question some of the oldest assumptions of political culture, and partly by legitimating some of those assumptions.

At least a convert to the "Christ Transforming Culture" school of thought must say something like this. The rest of this lecture is an attempt to say, from the standpoint of this school of thought, what might be some "transformations" needed in current American political culture.

Religion in American Politics: Some Questions for Churches and Governments to Reconsider in 1981 and Beyond

What are the moral-political restraints appropriate to the personal-institutional freedom of religion in our society?

To summarize an important stream of biblical theology: The God of the prophets, the Father to whom Jesus prayed, rules the public world. Faithful disciples of this World-Ruler draw apart from the political collectivity to call attention to the Lord of lords, stopping the mouths of kings with their totalitarian rhetoric and subjecting all citizens, even Presidents, to the living God. The churches are as concerned with the public world as with the private. The public world, allegedly owned by government, is in fact disputable turf. Both church and government carry out their responsibility "under God" in that public world; by their impacts upon it, measured by standards inherent in the content of the faith, their works good and bad are to be judged. Jesus called his disciples to be the "light of the world" and "the salt of the earth." A public test of "good works" seems implied in this teaching.

We hear much about "freedom of religion" and little about "the public responsibility of religon" in the churches of America. When we do, as in the church folk who help compose the "Moral Majority," we are not sure what "public" this minority-majority is being responsible to.

The problem of the public accountability of religion extends all the way from identifying the tax-liabilities of religious organizations to identifying the line between civil and uncivil disobedience. Of all countries on earth, the United States may be the most difficult for the drawing of such lines, for ours is a political culture where the very word "freedom" is an argument-ending word, the last word in a hierarchy of widely shared values. Someone has said that "explanation is where the mind is at rest." Most Americans find it easy to rest in the word "freedom." It has direct religious connotations for many of us, especially in the matter of religious freedom. Above all things, American courts and government bureaus want to avoid seeming to violate the religious con-

science of the individual and the rights of religious
organizations to promulgate their messages. Some may
assess our current culture as endangering these rights;
but, after travelling to many a foreign country, one can
only testify that America is still an amazingly free country for religion. Public law, public police power, and
public tradition support this freedom. *Freedom* is a
strong element in our public *order;* and the society at
large *supports* religion in the sense that, with powers of
law, taxation, and violence at its disposal, it leaves religion unmolested.

But it cannot with utter consistency do so, and that is
the theoretical and practical problem of church–state
relations that will haunt our logicians and our legislatures for a long time to come. People with religious con-
victions can have impact on society for good or ill, just
as the cry "fire!" may have impact for good or ill in a
crowded public place. Institutions for the promulgation
of religion also have social economic political *power.*
They own property, spend money, educate children, and
talk politics. In the name of the biblical tradition, they
"obey God rather than Caesar," but in doing so they may
help or hurt Caesar. They exercise public responsibility
according to their own interests and definitions. *To
what extent should they be responsible to the public according to the interests and definitions of government?* Or
to put the question theologically: On some points, is
government a better loudspeaker for the voice of God
than the churches?

To raise this question is to raise the specter of political
spirits that both believers and atheists think they have
exorcised from American political culture. Madison
explicitly rejected the idea that government could speak

for God; that was the hopeful business of the churches. That God can use government rightly to oppose the "free religious conscience" of church people seems so profoundly antithetical to the American political tradition that it would be a brave Supreme Court Justice who put into his brief the statement, "On this point my reading of the Bible is more accurate than yours." Yet again the Lincoln precedent is full of suggestion for the possibility that the all-judging Lord of history can use government to cut down the pretensions of the righteous just as they, on occasion, must stand in protest against the righteousness of the governor. To reduce the question to an illustration, one might claim that on matters like civil rights for minorities, abortion rights for the poor, and radical toleration for religion itself, a Congress or a Supreme Court may on occasion speak a word for the public *interest* that no separated church is likely to speak.

To speak personally, the principles of my own theology and ethics compel me to ask a question like, "What is good for all the people of our society?"; but the insularity of my personal and churchly experience may also compel me, in all due realism, to confess that I have less reason to *know* the public good than does many a person and agency in government. Who defines the public good? That is the root question. And for churches and synagogues there is a parallel question, "What is our part in defining the public good?" My next two political-religious questions are specific expressions of these two general ones. Here I want simply to point out that neither of these two general questions has a sure, common answer in our national society; and openness to *new* answers to both questions may be a fundamental contribution to American democratic culture by religious-minded citizens.

On this point, the theology of Reinhold Niebuhr and even the combined testimony of Adam Smith and Karl Marx have some wisdom to share: All versions of the "public interest," whether touted by religious or governmental organizations, are tainted with provincial interests. Somebody's neglected interest is at risk in every proposal for serving the public interest. A humane society does well, therefore, not to trust the self-definition of its total interest to any one of its components. "Separation of powers"? Yes, in the name of larger interests than any one power is ever likely to represent in any society. *If they have not wrestled with the fundamental taints of self-interest in all their proposals for "the public good," no human being, organization, or institution is ready to take its part in the defining and enacting of that public good.* It is not really a paradox. It is a recipe for political humility, grounded, for the religiously minded, in the faith that God alone knows and does good for the whole.

Should the churches inject their political opinions directly into the political process?

My answer is first an unambiguous "yes," followed by a touch of ambiguity, both sides of the answer flowing out of the history of the church's dialogue with political power over the centuries. As a review of the early Christian church will confirm, the church has been injecting some opinions into the political process from its very beginning. Most powerfully, as we have seen, it did so by organizing itself for the worship of Jesus the Risen Lòrd, injecting into the world of the Roman Empire the "opinion" that Caesar was *not* Lord. That opinion rankled the Romans exceedingly; they hauled many a Christian to the lions on the strength of that single

opinion, which was ultimately to transform the relations
of religion and government in all ages of modern history,
right up to the history of Nazi Germany, authoritarian
Argentina, and Confucian Korea. In the same sense, the
early Black churches of America were visible protests
and opinion-makers on the subject of the conflict between the freedom of the children of God and their en-
slavement by a supposedly freedom-loving government.
Especially in the case of the Black churches of the pre-
Civil War period, we see the politically transforming
mission of a Christian community, gathered in anticipation of a different sort of political order, gathered in
preliminary experience of that order inside the church.
As Professor Lawrence W. Levine describes that early
Black American church, it was a "sacred space" for
maintaining "spiritual freedom."

> "Slave music, slave religion, slave folk beliefs—the
> entire sacred world of the black slaves—created the
> necessary space between the slaves and their owners
> and were the means of preventing legal slavery from
> becoming spiritual slavery . . . They created and
> maintained a world apart which they shared with
> each other and which remained their own domain,
> free of control of those who ruled the earth." *(Black
> Culture and Consciousness*, New York, Oxford
> University Press, 1977, p. 80.)

The political concepts in that description are unmistak-
able. A political assertion was embodied in the very existence of that illegal, secret, stealing-away-to-Jesus Black
church: *Slavery is contrary to the Gospel of the Lord!*
It was the hottest political issue in nineteenth-century
America, and the consensus of reflective Christians now

is that on that issue the Black church was on God's side of the political struggle.

Against the background of such history, no secularist should be surprised that reflective Christians and Jews cannot go along with the old adage, "Religion and politics don't mix." So far as such precedents in church history take us, the recent discovery of politics by a large number of evangelical Christians is long overdue. Black evangelical Christians discovered politics a long time ago. The very birth of their church was a political event. The coming together of ten Baptists to form a new congregation in Dallas, Texas, can be a political event, too. If they form that congregation as a part of a struggle over church property, or in opposition to the liberal politics of their former minister, or in protest over the control of their previous congregation by people of wealth, they will have among themselves all the makings of things political, for they will be concerned about how people shall relate to each other in terms of *power:* Who shall lead them, what powers leaders shall have, and how they shall distribute the resources of the community.

As church people do all this, they are acquiring political experience. It is a fact of church history—the history of the Wesleyan movement in Wales and England, for example—that many new Christians have their first political experience in the church. There they learn that they count for something in the eyes of God and that they can speak up in public because their voices are important to their neighbors. A primitive beginning of democracy is here, but here also is the beginning of the moral ambiguity of politics. It has often puzzled me that some secularists and some proponents of the "wall of separation" doctrine are sure that the opinions of religious people are dangerous in politics. Religious people are people. They have as much right, individually and organizationally, to voice their opinions in a democracy as anyone else. They have the right to lobby, to buy ads in the newspaper, and to corral votes. What they do not have, on grounds of their own religion, is the right to pretend to speak authoritatively for God. Government has no such right—we settled that with Constantine. Churches have no such right—we settled that with Luther and Calvin. Majorities have no such right—from Amos to Martin Luther King we know that majorities are frequently resisters of the will of God. No human being has the right to confuse his or her opinion with that will of God. "All have sinned, and come short of the glory of God." "There is none righteous, no not one." *There* is the beginning of democracy in the Kingdom of God, where God respects his own wisdom more than the wisdom of human beings!

A prosaic way of putting all this is "Do not think too highly of yourself." (Romans 12:3.) Why not? Because, as a believer in God, you are committed to something higher than yourself, your opinions, your point of view on the world.

To put it this *religious* way is already to suggest an answer to the third question I am about to pose, concerning positive contributions that a vigorous Christian church might make to the political culture of this country. This one is a negative contribution: humility regarding the opinions of religious citizens, a humility that might extend—Gamaliel-like—to listening to the outrageous opinions of citizens whose religion is different from their own. The collision between religion and government sometimes consists of a collision between equally and oppositely inclined religious people. The quarrels of the body politic are often quarrels inside the churches. That is hugely evident these days when Congress is treated to a great variety of religiously-grounded testimony on issues like abortion, patriotism, and crime. By their conflicts over the right specification of their faith to political policy, religious folk pose problems for the policy-making politician. No problem is so great as the clash of equal certainties on a legislative floor where "public interest" may sometimes mean compromise between the several interests to the public.

Should religious persons and organizations make their views known on specific public issues? Yes, especially if they can do so in resistance to the temptation to turn their particular opinions into an idolatry, a substitute for the wisdom of God, which is likely to elude the combined powers of church and state. If they could avoid this temptation more consistently, religious people would not stir up such a flurry of anxiety when they flood a legislative hall. Too often the religious have impressed politicians as Calvinists impressed the one who said, "I had rather face an army of men armed with pikes than one Calvinist convinced he is doing the will of God." Human beings are capable of doing the will of God, and at times in our public life a religious citizen or a religious body may inject singular political wisdom into legislation or policy. Everett Dirksen said of the 1964 Civil Rights Bill, "It was the fault of those damn preachers." That included many a Black preacher, who remembered that his ancestors were right to read the Bible as a book of freedom rather than a book of slavery. We can believe that those Black ancestors read the book more correctly on this point than did many white ancestors of Mr. Dirksen himself.

Yet that brilliant conservative Senator had some wisdom on his side if he believed that it would take more than law to bring justice to Black people in America, more than a Supreme Court decision to bring them good education, and more than a friendly federal government to bring them friendship in a local community. Give Mr. Dirksen his day in court. Acknowledge the possibility that every citizen has *some* access to the knowledge of good and evil, justice and injustice. This is the provocation of democratic institutions such as the vote, jury trials, and legislative hearings. It is possible that churches and corporations, labor unions and college professors have some clues to the public's interest. If we do not believe that, we will not long be defenders of democracy. We shall fall victim to despair and cynicism toward "the popular will." One takes courage at the new involvement in politics among those who call themselves a "Moral Majority." One can take no comfort or courage from their blithe assurance that they are so clearly moral or in the majority; pride and "being too sure that you are right" lie in that direction. But let no liberal Christian or intellectual elite tell us that "ordinary people" have nothing to tell president, legislators, and judges on the bench. If religion requires us not to make an idol of "the popular will," it requires us also to love our neighbors enough to *listen* to them, even when, embroiled in single-issue politics, our neighbors seem to play only one note on the scale of political virtues.

The religious and ethical tests of our humanity are many, and the search for a combination of virtues in our personal and social action is often very long. Often it is given to individual groups in a society to see only one virtue in a controversy, and it is their contribution to inject that virtue into the debate. As the historian G.M. Trevelyan said, "The world is moved in the first instance by those who see one side of a question only, although the services of those who see both are indispensable for effecting a settlement." *(England in the Age of Wycliffe,* London, Longmans, Green and Co., 1925, p. 181.) In a democracy we are likely to call that second sort of person a politician, and the contribution of the multiple-side-seeing politician is frequently underrated. In the long stretch of history we have to confess that some single-minded prophets of justice have made larger contributions to the humane society than have those politicians who are always cautioning the prophets, "Easy does it." Only a few, like Wilberforce, Lincoln, and Adlai Stevenson have combined a sense of righteousness with the irony and humility of political experience. Neither slavery nor the Vietnam War may have been good candidates for moral uncertainty; and I am inclined to think that the case against preparation for nuclear war is equally subject to some central, unmoving moral-religious principles. But even when the principles are clear, the strategies may not be so. The tactics may be various indeed, and the policy that can command the assent of the total public may be far from a perfect match with principle. It is hard to imagine a major political issue of our time which would not benefit, on some level of its discussion, from humility among the discussants. Religion is one source of such humility, an ingredient of light and salt in the public arena which may be sadly lacking if religious people do not put it there. So, along with the right to inject their opinions into the political discourse of the community, religious people have an obligation, on grounds of their own faith, to do so with the restraint of the finite.

What might the Christian churches contribute to the development of new language and new modes of public discourse in an increasingly secular, pluralistic American culture?

In a recent lecture, Professor Robin Lovin of the University of Chicago Divinity School suggests that in western history religion has been preoccupied with two contrasting relations to politics and government: either the legitimation of social *order* or the protection of religious *freedom*. As Stackhouse pointed out, concern for social order is "natural" in human societies, and the Romans saw the freedom of the early Christians as a threat to their social order. Finding, over three centuries, that they could not destroy their will to resist the government, the Romans in turn adopted Christians as allies in the fight against social disorder, especially on the frontiers of the empire. For the next fifteen hundred years, the Christian movement was chiefly such an ally. Even today, the idea that churches might take the lead in order-threatening public marches, demonstrations on behalf of peace and civil rights, and the like, sends a shiver through the hearts of many "good" Christians. "Religion is supposed to be a force for peace and harmony, is it not?" No person acquainted with *American* church history can consistently believe that! As Professor Lovin says, most of America's churches left the Massachusetts Bay Colony with Roger Williams. They have been leaving social order in the name of religious freedom. Down to today, most American Christians see "freedom of religion" as a more obvious priority for the church in society than "upholding law and order."

But mere preference for one or the other does not seem to be the major need of our national society today. It is time, says Lovin, for the churches to work harder on the task of reshaping, reforming, and inventing a political language, a political mode of dialogue that fits the requirements of a society that is more pluralistic, less uniformly religious, and more subject to major disagreements than has been any America in history. What will the churches be able to contribute to the political fabric of this country when it celebrates its three-hundredth birthday in 2076? None of us will be alive to find out. But we might begin now to shape that culture in certain directions by the particular tilt of our work in the church, in politics, in private conversation, and in public dialogue.

I have suggested that a Christian people, one people among many in a pluralistic democracy, can contribute the salt and light of principled *humility* to their political negotiations with their neighbors. There is a twin to this suggestion: We can on occasion make a point of *public repentance* for our political mistakes.

Soon after the conclusion to World War II, a Synod of the Evangelical Church in West Germany awoke to its record of lukewarm opposition to Hitler's near-destruction of the Jews. In an act of public confession, the Synod repented of its failure to raise a loud voice of protest when it might have done some political good, in the early Hitler era. It repented also of longtime Christian fueling of the dark fires of antisemitism. To this outbreaking of belated repentance, German public response was furiously negative. Religious and nonreligious people alike blamed the church for blaming itself. "What did any of us have to do with the policies of the Nazi madman?" they said, in effect.

Political repentance is a hard nettle to grasp. It hurts

the hand that signals the little cry, "We're sorry!" Such a cry requires a perception of wrongdoing (an intellectual achievement), a willingness to seek a different future (an act of repentance), and the humility to confess publicly to one's neighbors (an act of honesty and courage). Most of one's neighbors will shrink from imitating such an action. Repentance is never popular because it pushes us all towards questioning our own collaborations with evil. The repentance of a neighbor is harder to defend against than the moral judgments of a neighbor. One can always point the accusing finger back; it is hard to join in the suspicion that nobody, including oneself, is wholly innocent.

In their personal political witness and in the corporate political witness of the churches, Christians need to be publicly honest about their collaborations with public evil. From the prayer of confession we utter in public worship to the resolutions we pass in our assemblies, we need to assume the ordinary mantle of our humanity and to say to the world: "We were wrong on that one." My own denomination, the southern Presbyterian Church, for example, took a long time to acknowledge, even quietly in its own deliberations, that it was wrong to read a justification for slavery out of the pages of the Bible in the mid-nineteenth century. Many southerners have come to repent so slowly of their one-time approval of the institutions of racial segregation that their passage into acceptance of desegregation was too gradual for them or others to notice. I hardly know a southerner, white or Black, who would be willing publicly to recommend that we go back to a segregated society. But many have not yet known the personal liberation of saying out loud, "On this point our grandfathers and grandmothers

were wrong." I have often thought that the great political mistake of Lyndon Johnson was his refusal to let
Hubert Humphrey take a new point of view publicly on
the Vietnam War in 1968. There are times in political
affairs when the only escape from disaster lies in a
change of direction, a change of a previous mind, a
metanoia, a repentance in public policy. Public resistance to repentance is ordinary among politicians and
their constituents. Yet how is a democratic system to
work if it does not, on occasion, lead people to change
their minds? What can be moral about our political
opinions if on occasion we do not change them in the
name of new moral clarity? The church, the religious
citizen, should exert leadership in making repentance
a public virtue, one healthier for society than any
amount of stubborn self-righteousness or silence about
past sins now to come to light.

One of the directions in which religion should move
our repentance is the direction of a more *inclusive* political community. De Tocqueville was right: One good
reason for the separation of churches and their host
states is the preservation of the universalistic vision of
biblical religion. The Jewish people have been uneasily
at home among the nations of earth because their vision
of God's purposes for themselves could never be limited
to the politics of one nation, not even the state of Israel,
ancient or modern. Christians spread across the boundaries of the Roman Empire because the Gospel of Jesus
was good news for human beings as such, not just for
people who spoke Latin. The nineteenth-century mis-
sionary movement and the twentieth-century ecumeni-
cal movement among Christians embodied the global
loyalties of the Christian churches; it is no exaggeration

to say that at their best the churches of each nation are constantly qualifying their national loyalties with that global loyalty. It is too small a thing for an American Jew or an American Christian to be Americans only. They have worldwide communal obligations, and if those obligations seem sometimes to dampen their patriotism, that is only consistency between their religious profession and their political behavior. Some of the saddest chapters in church history were written by Christian churches who loved Mother Russia, the Fatherland, or America the Beautiful more than God the Father Almighty, Creator of Heaven and Earth.

To enunciate this theological-ethical principle of universality is not to be sure how to translate it in public policy in one's own nation. But no Gospel-respecting church will stand for a public law that favors white people over black and brown people in immigration policy, a foreign economic aid policy that ignores the hungry people of a country that happens to be of little military worth to the United States, or a national defense policy that treats a thousand American lives as worth more than a million Russian lives. How discomforting it is to put it that concretely. But what is politics about if not the specifics of law and policy? And how can the conscience of any universalistic religion be comfortable at the natural national tendency to remember the needs of one's own people and to forget the needs of the foreign? We live in a moment in American history when the "foreigner" is present in our lives in discomforting numbers and frequency. Whether by the inflow of Asian immigrants in unprecedented numbers (a fact made possible by the Immigration Act of 1965, one of Lyndon Johnson's great services to international justice by the

revision of the racist quotas of the 1920s), or by the formation of Korean and Mexican churches, or by the instant presence of the nations to each other via television
and airborne weapons, we know that we are in a new
pluralistic time in American history. The great time of
internationalization of our nationalism is still ahead
of us. Again on the basis of much traveling, I am convinced that the United States is one of a handful of
nations whose own national history equips it to take some
leadership in the answering of a perplexing political
question: How in one nation can the peoples of many
nations be at home with each other? I was struck, for
example, during a recent trip to Rumania, at the great
cultural resentments which still persist between the
German Rumanians and the "old" Rumanians. The
Germans arrived in Rumania as immigrants "only"
five hundred years ago. In the eyes of older Rumanians,
Germans are newcomers. One has to think of the chasms
between white and Black and Hispanic immigrants in
our own country to make a historical comparison. Along
with Brazil, Canada, and perhaps India, the United
States has a chance to pioneer in the art of building a
public culture whose contributors come literally from
all the earth. Can we build such a culture? With the help
of a religious conviction that God really *is* "no respecter
of persons," we might do so. If we let our naturally inherited prejudices, our age-old human propensity for
favoring our own kind, take charge of our political
language and action, we will not make it as a unified
nation far into the twenty-first century. The time is upon
us when we shall prove or disprove *the possibility that
world strangers can become national neighbors.* Nothing
but a religious definition of our humanity, in my opinion,

will enable us to make the transition to that larger functioning political community.

The real test of our ability to make such a transition will come in the fusing of our moral and political capacity to do what the Bible and Lincoln saw as the tests of a truly humane society: "to bind up the nation's wounds" and to care for *widows* and *orphans* and all others who must be numbered among the weak and powerless people of the earth. On this issue there may be reason for much mutual humility and much public searching for just law and policy among citizens who differ in their religion, ethics, and political attitudes. But the Christians and Jews among us need soon to clarify a certain basic theme that runs like a thundering underground river, straight through the Old and New Testaments: *A society is judged by the God of mercy according to its treatment of its weakest and neediest citizens, who are most in need of mercy.* On this point Jews and Christians must undertake to challenge and change some popular public rhetoric in the United States of America. It is time to say out loud, with conviction and compassion and humility, that we may not believe in "welfare chiseling" but we do believe in welfare. We may not believe in multigenerational dependence upon government giveaway, but we are ready as a people of abundance to give away food to the hungry if that is the only way to keep them from starving. We believe too much that we are our brother's keeper to believe that we are our brother's moral superior because we have a job and he does not. We believe too much in the social dependence of us all to expect any person to become self-supporting before he or she has experienced a lot of support from somebody else. We believe too much in the mercy of God upon us to refuse mercy for our neighbor in the ditch.

To be sure, all this moves against the grain of traditional American individualism. We are a people who tell each other that we are self-made. That is a theological and a social-psychological absurdity. We will never be a humane society nor will we be political realists unless we discover in our national life some political form of the great biblical definition of the church: "One body with many members. . . . If one suffers, they all suffer together. If one flourishes, they all rejoice together." (I Corinthians 12:26.)

The humane society is the compassionate society. Whatever your political party or ideology, if you mean to be a biblically religious citizen, you cannot sidestep this principle. You can stop being a Christian or a Jew and go on to other religions or to no religion, but the integrity of this religion requires this political implementation. We are far from such consistent implementation in American society. We remain a society in which it is very embarrassing to be poor or disabled or disadvantaged. Biblical churches and biblically-oriented people may never be so numerous in the United States as to tilt its political ethos toward an analogy with the church, whose members "have the same care for each other." But the analogy is an appropriate one for anyone who believes in the possibility of transforming a culture in directions revealed to the world in the face of Jesus.

Is it possible so to transform culture, even to make progress towards such a transformation in America in the year 2076? We cannot be sure that there will be a United States of America in that year, and many of my younger friends these days have a nagging certainty that there will hardly be a human race around in that far-off year. They think that we may not make it past a nuclear war into the twenty-first century, and they are making only short-range plans for their own futures. As a result they are not much committed to politics, for to them the world of politics seems either too complicated or too disaster-prone to worry about. How shall we entertain realistic, long-term hope for the societies in which we now live? It is a question that has often come to people in world crisis, such crisis as the early Christians confronted in themselves and in their Roman neighbors who could not imagine a worthwhile life apart from the integrity of the Roman Empire. Augustine wrote his book, *The City of God,* in response to the anxieties of his time, when the barbarians were literally at the gates. He took his text from the Book of Hebrews: "Here we have no continuing city . . . we look forward to a city with foundations, whose builder and maker is God." Traces of that godly city meet us on our historical way, he said. We live by faith in our Creator, architect of our destiny; this "faith gives substance to our hopes," even our hopes for some changes in this earthly scene.

Some years ago the Harvard psychiatrist Robert Coles came back from interviews with a sample of mountain folk in Appalachia. He had found that they were, for the most part, very religious. A reporter asked him, "Do they use religion, as Marx said, as a way to make themselves content with their poverty?" Coles answered, "Oh no, they are likely to tell you that, 'if it were not for our belief in God, we would not have the courage to believe in a better earthly future for ourselves.' Faith in God is what keeps them going."

Many Americans in the 1980s are pessimistic about the future, and this is a worrisome *political* fact. A few years ago in North Carolina some of us carried on research around the question, "Who are the people in our society who have strong persistent commitments to public political activity?" (Cf. Donald W. Shriver, Jr., and Karl A. Ostrom, *Is There Hope for the City?*, Philadelphia, Westminster Press, 1977, especially Chapter 5.) In brief our answer was "People who have a philosophy or a religion that sustains them, who have at least a few friends whom they can lean on, and who have already begun to put their philosophy into practice politically." Some of the most frustrated people among our interviewees were those with high moral standards for a just society who had a low number of personal friends and a record of only episodic involvement in politics. You have more chance of suffering from stomach ulcers and insomnia, we found, if you have high ideals, no friends, and no political track record! You cannot sustain political action without friends and personal conviction, nor can you sustain personal conviction without friends and political action. Faith without works is dead; works without faith are equally dead. And you cannot love your neighbor unless someone loves you. These are simple, basic truths that link religion and politics. In America of the 1980s, politics will need a religion that supports the political process by helping people to put their confidence in a cause, a kingdom, a purpose beyond their own. Religion will need a politics that invites people to experience incremental advances in the achievement of a just, compassionate, and peaceful society. "The best use of a life," they say, "is to give it to a cause that will outlast it"; it is one office of religion to convince people that there is such a cause. It is one office of politics to offer us an arena for the pursuit of that cause.

Not many among us can believe, on biblical grounds, that the mere survival of our country is such a cause. The moralist in us is convinced that only through its service to larger causes does a nation deserve to survive. The realist in us knows that in today's globally interdependent world no nation is an island. We sink or swim together with our global neighbors. Can we fit that vision to the practical politics of our cities, states, and nation? Religious faith will incline us to the positive answer to the question. Some positive political hopes abound in certain of the churches and religious movements of our time: the insistence of the National Council of Churches, against our composure, that justice for the poor in Latin America may not be as achievable under conventional economic development; the willingness of the United Presbyterian Church to launch a peace*making* program; and the conversion of Billy Graham to the view that Christians must oppose the nuclear arming of the nations. Billy Graham's conversion, by the way, suggests that conversion—especially in political terms—is a process extended in time as well as an instantaneous event. Putting religious faith, hope, and love together with the facts of political life takes time. You have to think about it, consult your neighbors, try it out in political practice, and then think, consult, and try it all over again. Out of such a "cycling" come hopes for the twenty-first century based on something more substantial than wish fulfillment. Neither Billy Graham nor the signers of the New Abolitionist Covenant hail the twenty-first century through rose-colored glasses. The signers of the Covenant are examples of what Paul Tillich once called "beliefful realism." This is how they write about the challenge of the nuclear peril to both the theology and the politics of Americans:

"As the foundation of national security, nuclear
weapons are idolatrous. As a method of defense,
they are suicidal. At stake is whether we trust God
or the bomb. . . . [Therefore] in light of our faith,
we are prepared to live without nuclear weapons.
We will publicly advocate a nuclear weapons freeze
as the first steps towards abolishing nuclear weapons altogether." (Available from Fellowship of
Reconciliation, Box 271, Nyack, N.J., 10960.)

Political foolishness? Not so foolish as those 70 percent
of Americans who, according to *Newsweek*, expect a
nuclear war within the next ten years and who do not
expect to survive it. That 70 percent, I fear, have little
effective, invigorating link between their faith and
their politics. Perhaps they have no faith to link to their
politics. Without faith and its link to politics, humanity
may have no long-range future, for both faith and
politics are the preparation of the present generation for
the coming of a future one. Faithless politics leads us
to a short and stingy future. Unpolitical faith hopes only
for some other world, despising this one. The God of our
fathers and mothers, the God of Abraham, Jesus, and
the Circuit Riders, long ago loved *this* world. It is our
happy heritage also to love it, for our neighbor's sake
and for that of all our children.

HARMONIOUS SETTLEMENT OF INTERNATIONAL CONFLICTS

by

Erik Suy

Erik Suy

Dr. Suy has served as the Under-Secretary-General and the Legal Counsel of the United Nations since 1974. A Belgian national, he studied law and political science in Ghent, Geneva, and Vienna. He received his Doctor Juris degree in Ghent in 1956, and graduated from the Geneva Institute of International Studies the following year. His doctorate in political science was earned in Geneva in 1962.

Subsequently Dr. Suy served as a lecturer and then professor of international law at the University of Leuven, Belgium. He has had appointments as visiting professor at universities in many countries.

In 1967–1968, Dr. Suy acted as adviser to the Belgian Minister of European Affairs, and in 1968–1973 to the Minister of Foreign Affairs. He was a member of the Belgian delegation to the Vienna Conferences on Diplomatic Relations in 1961 and on the Law of Treaties in 1968–1969. He served as a member of the Belgian delegation to the United Nations General Assembly sessions from 1969 to 1972, and was Chairman of the Sixth Committee (Legal) during the 27th Session of the General Assembly (1972).

A founding member and member of the board of the International Institute of Humanitarian Law (San Remo), Dr. Suy is a member of the American, Belgian, French, and German Societies of International Law. He is an Associate of the Institut de droit international *and a member of the Permanent Court of Arbitration. During the course of his career, he has written five books and over fifty studies in the field of European and international law.*

HARMONIOUS SETTLEMENT OF INTERNATIONAL CONFLICTS

by

Erik Suy

The study of international relations over the ages reveals that nations, under whatever names they were organized—tribes, cities, feudal dukedoms, principalities or kingdoms, confederations, and even episcopal sees or other spiritually ruled entities—have always lived in a state of war and conflict. Conquest of and hegemony over others are the themes of the history lessons and textbooks with which we grew up. The periods of prolonged peace, even though only in a particular region, could probably be counted on the fingers of one hand if we could only remember them at all, whereas the seven-year, the thirty-year, and the hundred-year wars among so many others are the unforgettable landmarks of which most of us know the dates and the places where important battles took place. If our memories should fail us, there are enough monuments to glorify those heroes who slaughtered other men for the lofty ideals of freedom and justice.

A dispassionate and objective observer might come to quite a different conclusion, namely, that the only creation of God gifted with reason has behaved totally irrationally, unable to organize peace in a durable way. Let us not be confused by the innumerable peace treaties. They prove only that war has been the constant preoccupation of man and that episodes of peace were only momentary pauses between and preludes to new, ever greater and more devastating wars. The history of international relations is basically the history of wars—and only occasionally of peace—between nations.

History, moving from war to war, has another lesson to teach us. As a consequence of wars, nations have grown through the destruction and absorption of those who were defeated. Through conquests, tribes and cities became nations and states, growing ever more powerful by gaining manpower and goods. Wars were no longer decided by a single battle. They became continuous and far-reaching struggles in which the fiercer or the technically more advanced party normally became the victor, leaving behind not only a defeated army but a ruined country. War was no longer a mere clash of armies but became a total and deadly affair affecting entire nations. Wars became matters between bigger and bigger nations. Consider that at one time, Athens and Sparta, Rome and Carthage, duchies and counties in the Middle Ages, and the various states in Germany and Italy were important entities. The formation of larger nations has no doubt been a consequence of past wars, leading to conflicts between huge entities which it is correspondingly difficult to unify.

However, the more devastating and widespread wars became, the more responsible leaders have sought to find a road to permanent peace. The first truly global conflict gave rise to an international—and under the then prevailing standards—universal organization for peace: the League of Nations. However, the League soon disappointed humanity. After the Second World War, which it was unable to prevent, it was replaced by the United Nations, for which there will never be a substitute.

Although the achievement of near-universality by the

international community, linked with an awareness of the interdependence of the problems facing all nations, should reasonably have led to a decreasing emphasis on national sovereignty, the contrary seems to be true—at least in respect of relations that do not affect international trade and economics. The driving force in this resurgence of nationalism seems to be the newly independent or, indeed, newly created states. Though perhaps grateful to the international community that helped them achieve freedom and often greatly dependent thereafter on that community for economic and technical assistance and for protection, they also are still suffused by the satisfaction and the pride of having achieved independence and the feeling that exercising anything short of full national sovereignty would be a sign of weakness, a betrayal of hard-fought ideals.

Still, the concept of sovereignty may not be the unshaken pillar of international relations it is supposed by many to be. At least in its absolute expression, sovereignty has come under attack since World War II and has been increasingly challenged by philosophers, social scientists, jurists, and students of international relations. Already in the 1920s, it was pointed out that the use of the term "sovereignty" had ceased to facilitate contemporary discussion of political problems and had become a mere source of confusion because it is a notion taken out of its historical setting. It was suggested that the term "authority" is entirely adequate and carries none of the distressing historical connotations attached to "sovereignty." In the words of James Brierly, "The history of the doctrine is one of the most fantastic in the whole history of ideas. For us today it stands for international disorder." As Hersch Lauterpacht put it,

Brierly's denial of the dualistic view of the law led him "as it has led others, to an emphatic rejection of the validity, in the international sphere, of the notion of sovereignty as the supreme will not subordinated to any overriding legal obligation. Any such notion he conceived to be inconsistent with the very concept of international law." Other outstanding jurists, such as Duguit, Kelsen, Politis, and Scelle, have also repudiated the traditional and absolutist concept of sovereignty.

Recently Lord Wilberforce placed on lawyers the blame for the whole unhappy situation resulting from emphasis on national sovereignty. "Let us remember," he said, "that the present structure of the world society is lawyer-made—its concepts are lawyer-devised." As an example he cited sovereignty, a concept which he claimed "was unknown in the Greek and Roman world. It is a concept devised by lawyers in the 19th century with the rise and increase of nation states. Then someone devised the powerful slogan 'The power of a sovereign is incapable of legal limitation.' This was fine when there were only a few recognized Christian States—to which the lawyers all belonged—all speaking the same language. It comes under strain when you have 150 with far from the same cultures and ideas."

Nineteenth century jurists never anticipated the misuses to which the concept of sovereignty has lent itself or the degree to which it has become an obstacle to world integration. For example, in respect to human rights, it has been persuasively argued that since the promulgation of the Universal Declaration, these rights have achieved international status and recognition; but those to whom such recognition is inopportune, argue that how a state treats its own nationals is an exercise of its sovereignty and as such is not liable to interference by the international community. This dilemma, and others like it, seem insoluble. In the long run, the degree to which national sovereignty gives way to the needs of an integrated and more humane world order will be the measure of what Dag Hammarskjold aptly called "our will to find a synthesis between the nation and the world."

In any event, in its current state the international community is burdened by actual and potential conflicts. At the worst, those conflicts give rise to the use of force by one state against another. That this is still a frequent reality is a measure of the wide gap between the "ought" and the "is" in the international legal order. What is worse, the international community, having failed time and again to prevent the start of an armed conflict, is frequently unable to exert itself to bring such conflicts to a speedy halt. Since the Charter of the United Nations outlawed the threat or use of force, Member States have legally renounced this instrument of advancing national policy. That this norm is often observed in the breach is a sad feature of the present condition of our world. The use of force—outside the very limited exceptions provided for in the Charter—is not only unlawful but is also fraught with unthinkable dangers in this nuclear age. The consequences for mankind of an armed confrontation involving the use of the weapons of mass destruction that man has managed to devise are literally too awful to contemplate.

I should like to quote here what one of the most learned observers of human behaviour had to say about this state of affairs. "The fateful question for the human species seems to me to be whether and to what extent their cultural development will succeed in mastering the dis-

turbance of their communal life by the human instinct
of aggression and self-destruction. It may be that in this
respect precisely the present time deserves a special
interest. Men have gained control over the forces of
nature of such an extent that with their help they would
have no difficulty in exterminating one another to the
last man. They know this, and hence comes a large part
of their current unrest, their unhappiness and their
mood of anxiety." This was written in 1928 by Sigmund
Freud in his book *Civilization and its Discontents.*

As there can be little doubt that the foregoing analysis
of the contemporary state of international relations is
correct, namely, that the use of force is not only illegal
but highly dangerous in that it can lead to the complete
destruction of human civilization, then the only solution
is to settle disputes peacefully or, better still, to avoid
disputes entirely.

Although dispute-settlement has traditionally received a predominant share of attention from students
of international relations, dispute-avoidance is perhaps
equally, if not more, important. Success in this area
would prevent disputes from developing and would do
away with the need to devise methods of settling them
peacefully. It is rather amazing that a world order that
claims to be civilized and progressive has not yet succeeded in avoiding disputes. Not that the means for
achieving that goal are missing. We have the principles
of the Charter and additional ones proclaimed by the
United Nations in the field of friendly relations and cooperation among states. If these were faithfully followed, it is likely that few disputes would arise. What
seems to be lacking in order to achieve such harmony is
the political will necessary to subject the individual

interests of states to the general interest of the international community in maintaining and furthering peaceful and harmonious relations among its members.

It is, by far, not sufficient to proclaim a willingness to avoid conflicts or to have, as an only recourse, methods for the peaceful settlement of disputes. There must be a real ongoing battle for peace—requiring in the first instance, a programme of education and training towards peace. As peaceful behaviour does not seem to come naturally to man, one cannot hope to achieve success without a purposeful effort to engage in such education and training. This may sound highly idealistic and entirely impractical, but there are other fields in which human beings are trained to acquire nonnatural behaviour. There are several areas where a good start could be made:

First, schoolbooks should eliminate passages that highlight past and present controversies between nations or that glorify military victories. Rather, history texts should focus on the mistakes made and the chances lost to achieve peace.

During the last two decades, an attempt has been made, especially in Europe, to introduce new courses and to initiate research on problems of peace and war. In the United States, steps are now being undertaken to establish a National Peace Academy. In the United Nations, upon the initiative of the President of Costa Rica, an International Agreement for the Establishment of the University for Peace was reached in December 1980. The Charter of this University, headquartered in Costa Rica, which will formally open its doors before the end of this year, proclaims the following aims and purposes: "The University is established with a clear determination to provide humanity with an international institution of higher education for peace and with the aim of promoting among all human beings the spirit of understanding, tolerance and peaceful coexistence, to stimulate co-operation among peoples and help lessen obstacles and threats to world peace and progress, in keeping with the noble aspirations proclaimed in the Charter of the United Nations. To this end, the University shall contribute to the great universal task of educating for peace by engaging in teaching, research, postgraduate training and dissemination of knowledge fundamental to the full development of the human person and societies through the interdisciplinary study of all matters relating to peace."

Recently, a proposal has been made in the United Nations to proclaim a year of peace, a month of peace, and a day of peace. Personally, I tend to be skeptical about this proposal because it is my belief that each day, year in and year out, should be dedicated to the immense task of learning how peace is maintained and secured.

Another, and perhaps an even more important, educational effort would be for all states to abstain from war propaganda and other expressions of hatred directed against other countries, their leaders, and their people. This would comply with a principle solemnly proclaimed by the General Assembly of the United Nations in 1970: "In accordance with the purposes and principles of the United Nations, States have the duty to refrain from propaganda for war of aggression." (Declaration on Principles of International Law Concerning Friendly Relations and Cooperation Among States in Accordance With the Charter of the United Nations.)

This strictly circumscribed interdiction of propaganda is of course insufficient. In more recent attempts to refine the principle of the nonuse of of force, greater emphasis has been given to the much broader concept of "hostile propaganda"—however ill-defined—because it was felt that the peaceful settlement of international disputes implies, as a first step, the duty to abstain from all acts or measures that might aggravate those disputes. Experience teaches that wherever and whenever the slightest conflict of interest develops between nations, hostile propaganda erupts, with the purpose of mobilizing the masses and bringing about a climate favorable for confrontation. Thus it is not surprising that such propaganda aggravates rather than heals such conflicts. The modern mass media help—indeed prefer—to dramatize such conflicts. However, this same media technology could be used as a powerful tool to bring people and nations closer together and to defuse tensions. Alas, such restraint and responsible action seems to be the exception rather than the rule. In a society that believes in the free flow of information and where the mass media are in private hands, the responsibility of the journalist, as a potential vehicle of peaceful ideas, is immense, but so are the temptations, because it seems to be more rewarding to report confrontations rather than quiet gatherings of leaders searching for peaceful solutions.

In a recently published report, the International Commission for the Study of Communications Problems stated the following:

> "Communication's role in international relations is . . . indeed vital, because it governs the ability of international opinion to come fully to grips with the problems which threaten mankind's survival—prob-

lems which cannot be solved without consultations and cooperation between countries: the arms race, famine, poverty, illiteracy, racialism, unemployment, economic injustice, population growth, destruction of the environment, discrimination against women. These are but the principal problems, and it is essential to highlight how very serious, deeprooted and far-reaching they are, and even more, how the same challenges and the same dangers affect all nations. The mass media have a vital role to play in alerting international public opinion to these—and other—problems, in making them better understood, in generating the will to solve them, and equipping ordinary people, if necessary, to put pressure on authorities to implement appropriate solutions. Only if the media put more stress on what joins people together rather than on what divides them will the peoples of the world be able to aid one another through peaceful exchange and mutual understanding." (*Many Voices, One World*, London, Paris, 1980, pp. 34–35.)

Another means of dispute-avoidance is to foster the establishment of international norms, for disputes are less likely to arise and fester where the relevant legal principles according to which they should be resolved are clearly expressed and generally accepted. It is therefore necessary to strengthen the processes whereby international law is made—that is, the international legislative process. This process, though not generally known and insufficiently understood, nevertheless functions relatively actively, especially within the present structure of international organizations, to produce, *inter alia*, twenty to forty significant global or regional multilateral treaties each year, as well as resolutions, declarations, and other provisions of more binding later instruments. For some years now, the most important aspect of this process, that by which multilateral treaties are made, has been studied both by the United Nations Secretariat and by the General Assembly, as well as by the highly respected *Institut de droit international*. Though these studies may not result in any immediate improvements in or rationalization of this process, the very fact that critical attention is now focused in this direction cannot but have a positive impact on this important mechanism for building a cooperative and, thus, more peaceful world.

At a time when the world economic situation is deeply troubled, the industrialized "North" is afraid that the development of the "South" will cause even greater difficulties in that it will increase competitive exports and, thus, the jobless rate in high-wage countries. On this, employers and employees for once seem to hold the same view. But just because we are uncertain of the effect that the industrialization and development of the South might have, we cannot abstain from trying to resolve a problem which—if left unsolved—will surely seriously disturb international peace and security throughout the foreseeable future. The North-South negotiations and generally the search for and the establishment of a New International Economic Order are prerequisites for world progress and, perhaps, even for world peace. Diplomats, politicians, bankers, and other experts agree that the questions of population, food, energy, and trade have attained global dimensions and that the problems of the North affect the South—and vice versa. Addressing these problems recently before the U.N. General

Assembly, the French Minister for External Affairs, Cheysson, said, that "never before in history have the principal factors of economic life been so unpredictable . . . We are living in a world without order, a chaotic world, an insane world." He therefore urged that a system of law be gradually introduced into world economic relations. The efforts to do so have started—it would take too long to enumerate the drafts of global and regional codes of conduct, agreements, uniform statutes and contracts, and other instruments designed to pave the way towards more harmonious international economic cooperation. Harmony in international economic relations has become the key to harmony in the overall relations between states.

At the dawn of the next millenium, in less than one score years, the earth will have to provide food, shelter, and employment for an additional two billion inhabitants. Meanwhile, however, approximately the same number will have died in another holocaust, not in gas chambers or through executions but through starvation and disease, mostly in the southern part of this globe. It is not only likely but virtually certain that this scandalous situation carries the seeds of explosions which will affect international relations, peace, and security. This is not a prophesy nor does it relate to the distant future: This is the major preoccupation of our generation. We, in the industrialized West, have, perhaps for too long, been obsessed with the idea that peace is exclusively a matter of balance of power between East and West. We are now beginning to understand that development too is a prerequisite for peace and that in this respect we cannot merely close our eyes and sit idly by, waiting for some miracle to happen. Decisions need to be

made quickly in order to come to grips with unprecedented problems. Those decisions must be global, not
national. They must be negotiated, not imposed. They
must be expressed in mutually advantageous long-term
agreements, not merely in nonbinding declarations of
intent or programs of action. Dr. Andrew Cecil, in his
1979 lecture on "World Peace Through Law and Unity,"
said: "Answers to the world's problems can be found
when common objectives are identified and pursued. No
nation, acting alone, can assure its people peace, or
achieve prosperity at the expense of others by limiting
its cooperation to simple reaction to events in the world
economy." (*The Third Way*, 1980, p. 172.)

If harmony in international relations were indeed the
sincere desire of all nations, it would become evident that
there is no need for them to maintain enormous armies
and huge arsenals of weapons of mass destruction. The
security of our world is not improved through the ex-
penditure, year after year, of $500 billion for soldiers
and for military hardware.

While the two military alliances of "East" and "West"
still are responsible for two-thirds of this figure, the
developing countries account for 70 percent of world
arms imports. The annual half-trillion dollars spent
worldwide on preparations for and sometimes the execution of wars—compared with some $30 billion spent
on official development assistance—underscores the link
between arms control and development. It is easy to play
with figures and to dramatize statistics. But one thing
remains certain: International harmony and stability
would be better served by diverting the money spent on
military hardware to the much more rewarding task of
fighting hunger and poverty.

From the end of the Second World War until about twenty years ago, international relations were viewed exclusively in an East-West context. The decolonization process added a new dimension to world politics: Roughly one hundred new states have been created, almost all of which are still classified as developing countries. Consequently, attention has shifted from great power confrontation to the problems of development. But today, we are witnessing a growing number of conflicts between these new countries—mainly territorial conflicts but some exacerbated by East-West tensions—that absorb tremendous quantities of resources that could be better used for development.

The decolonization process and the consequent increase in the membership of the international community have also multiplied the potential for conflict between the young nations, whose boundaries were drawn by the colonial regimes, which took scant account of such important factors as the ethnic origins of populations and the rational distribution of natural resources. Many of the conflicts that originated during the period of colonization still persist and are the cause and source of constant conflicts among the states of Africa and of Latin America. Moreover, these conflicts often provide a pretext for intervention by outside powers.

Each region has established its own international organization (the Organization of American States and the Organization of African Unity) with conflict-solving mechanisms best adapted to their own needs. Although recourse to good offices, mediation, and conciliation has resolved some tense situations, it is frightening and discouraging to see how these states still resort to saber rattling and military buildup.

While it is true that in the respective immediate post-colonial eras the principle *uti possidetis iuris* was accepted both in Latin America and in Africa in order to avoid territorial disputes, in the long run this principle may not always be strong enough to provide a guarantee of permanent territorial stability. This seems to be an area where judicial settlement might prove useful, and one could further explore means of improving methods of settling territorial disputes through judicial or arbitral proceedings. But it may also be worthwhile to examine the possibility of establishing, within each regional organization, a permanent expert body charged with monitoring and studying territorial and boundary situations in all their aspects, historical, geographical, economic, and legal, as well as taking into account the views of the governments concerned. Such studies or surveys could be most useful as background material in settling future conflicts.

One of the major achievements towards peace in our times has undoubtedly been the creation of the European Economic Community. The persistent conflict between France and Germany has permeated the history of the last centuries and has been the cause of two world wars. It was the genius of Jean Monnet which successfully pursued the idea that, by bringing together first the coal and steel resources and then extending this experiment to the whole range of the economy, a major cause of conflict between the major European powers could be eliminated. In less than thirty years, this economic community has grown into a powerful entity in the political field as well, and its example is being followed, albeit slowly and cautiously, in some other areas. It would seem that the creation of genuine integrated economies in Africa,

Asia, the Carribean, and Latin America is indeed a major prerequisite for a successful *entente* among the countries in these regions, which because of economic weakness and/or geographical position are individually often at most marginally viable.

In searching for harmony in international relations, one should not overlook another important development in the basic structures of which those relations are constructed. Until some two decades ago, the prime—indeed, almost the exclusive—movers and actors on the international scene were nation-states. Gradually intergovernmental organizations have started to play more and more important roles in international politics, and other actors have also appeared on the scene, such as nongovernmental organizations, individuals, and transnational corporations. This is not the place to elaborate on the significance and impact of the latter, except to mention that the international community has become fully aware of the role—whether constructive or disruptive—these corporations have played and can play. Efforts are consequently being made in various international fora, in particular the United Nations, in order to maximize the contribution of these corporations towards development and peace, while at the same time curbing any potential abuse of power.

The role and position of the individual under international law have become significant in recent times. First, it has been acknowledged that the ultimate purpose of all politics, including at the international level, is the well-being of the individual. In the long run, no state can afford to conduct domestic or foreign policies that do not ultimately benefit its nationals, while grave and persistent violations of human rights may affect the international standing of a government and lead to its isolation. Furthermore, history teaches that continuous oppression leads to turmoil and uprisings, which may have international repercussions. Thus, internal stability, order, and harmony, which can only be achieved through respect for human rights, are seen as prerequisites for international stability and harmony, because conflicts arise when economic and political conditions generate the basis therefor.

Finally, it cannot be ignored that potential threats to international peace and security are often of a non-state origin. Due to the ever-greater interdependence of all societies, including the international community as a whole, hostile activities of individuals and groups tend more and more to affect and destabilize the fabric of orderly relations among states. Thus, *inter alia*, the problem of international terrorism needs to be dealt with in all its many complex aspects.

Significant progress has been made in the United Nations toward the elimination of aerial hijacking, the protection of diplomats, and the curbing of hostage-taking through the elaboration of international instruments dealing with these topics. But states will have to continue the search for solutions of this most disruptive evil of our times.

Although I have dealt with some conflict-preventing measures, such as education, disarmament, development, the strengthening of the rule of law, regional integration, and human rights, it would not be fair if I were to omit at least one promising way of maintaining peace even when a conflict has already arisen or even when a breach of the peace has actually occurred or is about to occur. Article 33 of the United Nations Charter provides that the parties to a dispute should settle these through peaceful means, and it specifically mentions negotiations, inquiry, third party mediation, conciliation, arbitration, and judicial settlement, as well as resorting to regional agencies and arrangements. These techniques are well-known and some are used extensively, even though they may not be equal to situations where the conflict is so profound that the parties are on the verge of using or have actually resorted to armed force.

In this type of situation, the United Nations has developed "peace-keeping operations," which have been defined as "[T]he use by the United Nations of military personnel and formations not in a fighting or enforcement role but interposed as a mechanism to bring an end to hostilities and as a buffer between hostile forces. In effect, [they serve] as an internationally constituted pretext for the parties to a conflict to stop fighting and as a mechanism to maintain a cease fire." (Brian Urquhart, "International Peace and Security: Thoughts on the Twentieth Anniversary of Dag Hammarskjold's Death," *Foreign Affairs*, Fall 1981, p. 6, footnote 2.)

During the past decades, United Nations peace-keeping forces have been interposed in a buffer zone to separate the conflicting parties, as well as truce supervisors. In recent years, there has been an increasing tendency to call for similar international forces with a peace-keeping mandate to function within the framework of the Camp David Agreements, or in Chad and in Namibia.

This novel institution needs to be further encouraged and developed. In the United Nations, the major problems are the consent of the country in whose territory the force is to be established, as well as its financing.

Possibly, forces established by regional organizations or even by a more limited group of states will have less difficulty with the former requirement. Though the need to secure financing can be a serious obstacle, it should be recognized that this is a lesser and more acceptable burden than the overall costs of a military adventure.

Ultimately, peace-keeping operations can only be viewed as interim devices for defusing and cooling off, giving the parties a new opportunity to assess the elements that could lead to a permanent settlement of their dispute. I therefore earnestly believe that the time has come to look into the potential of using international forces of a nonstrategic character, both within and outside the framework of the United Nations. First, the willingness of states to accept a peace-keeping operation and also to participate in such forces must be ascertained. Detailed mechanisms must be designed and developed. The difficulties are, however, not insurmountable, and the effort may prove to be rewarding.

State relations, like all human relations, involve two types of interactions: conflict and integration. By inhibiting conflicts and promoting integration, conflict resolution should become more effective and harmony should begin to replace conflict. When states realize the preponderance of their shared regional or global interests as compared to their individual and, mostly ephemeral, immediate interests, conflicts should arise less frequently and, if they do arise, they should be more amenable to resolution. The international community would thus succeed in removing tensions between its members or maintaining them at nondestructive levels consistent with the continued pursuit of states of both their individual and their collective goals. If this does not ensure perfect harmony, it should at least bring about Horace's *concordia discors* (harmony in discord), which would be a not insignificant achievement in human affairs, judging by man's conflict-ridden history.

Ideally, the settlement of international conflicts should be based not on expediency nor on a precarious balance between antagonistic interests but on the twin pillars of justice and respect for others. To be effective, these pillars will have to constitute the support for the moral canopy of each nation. In a Greek legend related by Protagoras, Zeus, fearing the total destruction of our race, sends down Hermes to impart to men the qualities of respect for others and a sense of justice, so as to bring harmony into our cities and create a bond of friendship and union. Hermes asks Zeus in what manner he is to bestow these gifts on men. "To all equally," replies Zeus, "for if only a few shared in these virtues, there could never be cities." Similarly, unless all nations share equally in the sense of justice and in the respect for others, on which international harmony must be based, there could never be a world which we could truly call the City of Man.

FREEDOM, DIGNITY, AND FOREIGN POLICY

by

Ernest W. Lefever

Ernest W. Lefever

Dr. Lefever is President of the Ethics and Public Policy Center, an independent, nonprofit, research organization in Washington, D.C. The Center publishes studies on a wide range of domestic and foreign policy issues. From 1964 to 1976, Dr. Lefever was on the senior foreign policy studies staff of the Brookings Institution. His most recent Brookings book, Nuclear Arms in the Third World, *was published in 1979. Currently he is a member of the Values Education Commission of the State of Maryland.*

He has an A.B. from Elizabethtown College and a B.D. and Ph.D. in Christian Ethics from Yale University. Dr. Lefever is a member of the International Institute for Strategic Studies (London), the Washington Institute of Foreign Affairs, and the Johns Hopkins University Society of Scholars. He serves on the editorial board of Policy Review.

Dr. Lefever has written, edited, or co-authored fourteen books, including Ethics and U.S. Foreign Policy *(1957);* Profile of American Politics *(co-author, 1960);* Arms and Arms Control *(1966);* Crisis in the Congo *(1965);* Uncertain Mandate: Politics of the U.N. Congo Operation *(1967);* Spear and Scepter: Army, Police, and Politics in Tropical Africa *(1970);* Ethics and World Politics *(1972);* TV and National Defense *(1974);* Amsterdam to Nairobi: The World Council of Churches and the Third World *(1979);* Will Capitalism Survive? *(1979); and* The CIA and the American Ethic *(1980). He has written for many American journals and newspapers, including the* New York Times, Wall Street Journal, Washington Post, Washington Star, Boston Globe, *and* TV Guide.

He has done research at the Johns Hopkins School of Advanced International Studies, taught political science at the University of Maryland, American University, and Georgetown University, headed the Foreign Affairs Division of the Library of Congress, and was associated with the Washington Center of Foreign Policy Research. He has lectured at the National War College, the Army, Navy, and Air Force War Colleges, the Japan Defense College, the Foreign Service Institute, and many universities.

FREEDOM, DIGNITY, AND FOREIGN POLICY

by

Ernest W. Lefever

We live in a dangerous and troubled world where people everywhere reach out for peace, freedom, and bread. I remind you of two menacing realities: the continuing threat from the Soviet Union and a relatively new specter that haunts the world—international terrorism.

At the same time, we need to be reminded that there is hope. Freedom, dignity, and human rights are realities—aspirations, to be sure, but sometimes and in some places they are given life and breath. The forces of good and evil are in a constant struggle. Freedom has ever been under siege, but no tyranny has quenched man's persistent thirst for liberty, no dictatorship his demand for dignity.

Human Rights Are Central to Politics

Human rights and security are what politics is all about. Fifteen centuries ago Saint Augustine said that if it were not for government, men would devour one another as fishes. But governments often become corrupt, cruel, or tyrannical. When this happens, they are the most monstrous fish of all. Depending on its character, government can be the most effective protector of human rights or the most vicious violator of them. Hence, the struggle for viable and humane government is the heart of politics and ethics.

But there are no human rights without security. Order

is the necessary but not sufficient precondition for justice and respect for human dignity. Chaos is the enemy
of justice and freedom because it invites the law of the
jungle, the survival of the fittest in the most brutal sense
of the term.

My hypothesis is that there is no fundamental contradiction between human rights and security, if both these
concerns are properly understood. And neither can be
advanced or fulfilled without freedom.

Three Concepts of Human Rights

We should distinguish between three frequently confused concepts of human rights. The *first* has more
immediate and universal application because it is rooted
in the religion and ethics of virtually all cultures and
calls for sanctions against political authorities and
others guilty of genocide, brutalizing innocent people,
and similar atrocities.

The *second* and more precise concept of human rights
is the fruit of the recent Western democratic experience
and embraces a wide range of substantive and pro-
cedural rights and safeguards. Rights so defined are
fully respected in perhaps fewer than a score of states.
They include freedom of movement, speech, assembly,
press, and religion; equality before the law; periodic
elections; the concept of being innocent until proved
guilty; a judicial system independent from executive
authority; and a variety of safeguards for accused persons. Many of these Western democratic rights are unknown and unattainable in large parts of the world
where both history and culture preclude the development of Western-type democratic institutions, and they

are often violated in the West itself. There are, however, significant differences in the extent to which human rights, more generally defined, are honored in non-democratic states.

The *third* area encompasses so-called "economic and social rights," such as the right to a job and health care. These are really objectives and aspirations, not rights, because they cannot be guaranteed by any government unless it is totalitarian. The price of gaining these "rights" is the sacrifice of freedom.

The Difference Between Domestic and Foreign Policy

In our system of sovereign states, there is a profound difference between the domestic and foreign policies of any government. Each government is sovereign only within its territory. In domestic terms, the first task of government is to *govern*, to wield effective control over the territory and to exercise a monopoly over the legitimate use of force within the state. The second task of government is to *govern legitimately*, to exercise power in accordance with the constitution and other laws, including those in effect under a state of emergency. The third task of government is to *govern justly*. Justice, said Aristotle, is giving every man his due, adding that to treat all people equally is to treat some of them unjustly. In moral terms, the highest object of government is justice. There are different stages and qualities of justice which define the range of human rights that can be guaranteed by a government.

Foreign policy is also an essential task of government, but in sharp contrast to domestic policy, the government is severely constrained by the power and legitimate interests of other states. The external policy of all governments must be occupied primarily with external threats. Its chief object is to defend the territorial and political integrity of the state.

The foreign policy of smaller states seeks to mitigate threats from immediate neighbors by transforming enemies into neutrals and neutrals into allies. To this end, the government uses military, economic, diplomatic, intelligence, and informational instruments.

The foreign policy of large states, particularly a superpower like the United States or the Soviet Union, is also concerned with national defense, but it has a larger role commensurate with the state's power and influence. It seeks to create an international "order" conducive to its larger purposes. If its purpose is to adjust and change the status quo by peaceful means, it will pursue peace and stability.

If it is a revolutionary state, whether Hitler's Germany or Brezhnev's Russia, it will attempt to destabilize "unfriendly regimes" and thus prepare the way for expansion and the imposition of its will on alien peoples.

Hence, foreign policy is concerned about the external environment and its impact on the interests of the state, and domestic policy is concerned about the distribution of authority and freedom, control and consent within the state.

For the United States and all other democratic states, the principal objective of foreign policy, therefore, is peace, and the principal objective of domestic policy is justice.

The Soviet Union: A Conspiracy Masquerading As a State

Every day we see evidence of Soviet expansion and subversion. What was a Soviet submarine with nuclear arms doing in the territorial waters of Sweden? Why has Moscow invaded Afghanistan and subjected some of its hill people to chemical warfare? Why does the Soviet Union maintain 15,000 Cuban mercenaries to uphold a minority regime in Angola? Why do the Soviets send arms to the guerrillas seeking to overthrow the centrist government in El Salvador?

The Soviet Union is probably the greatest tyranny of all time. Its leaders are a conspiracy masquerading as a government. Moscow is motivated by utopian and messianic dreams, and is attempting to build a world order in its own image. It employs raw military power, threat, propaganda, disinformation, economic measures, subversion, and terrorism. In its view, the dream of a socialist paradise justifies any means. Hence, the Soviet Union and its clients are the major threat to peace, security, and freedom in the world today.

The Soviet Union is also the greatest violator of fundamental human rights at home and the greatest exporter of human rights abuses abroad. Moscow not only oppresses its own citizens, but imposes its brutal system on other peoples, as in Eastern Europe.

Totalitarian and Authoritarian States

The foreign policy debate has been confused by a persistent failure to recognize the profound differences between a totalitarian state and an authoritarian state. In terms of political rights, moral freedom, and cultural vitality, there is a great difference between the two types of regimes. Most Asian, African, and Latin American countries are ruled by small elites supported by varying degrees of popular consent. Authoritarian regimes permit a significantly greater degree of freedom and diversity than totalitarian ones in all spheres—political, cultural, economic, and religious. Authoritarian rulers often allow opposition parties to operate and a restrained press to publish. Foreign correspondents usually can move about freely and send out uncensored dispatches. These regimes often permit relatively free economic activity and freedom of movement for their citizens.

There is far more freedom of choice, diversity of opinion and activity, and respect for human rights in authoritarian South Korea than in totalitarian North Korea. There is also far more freedom and cultural vitality in Chile than in Cuba.

Authoritarian regimes can evolve into democratic rule. This has happened recently in Spain, Portugal, Greece, and India. In sharp contrast, a Communist dictatorship has never made a peaceful transition to more representative and responsive rule.

To put it in its starkest and yet most precise terms, the prison walls in a totalitarian state coincide with the borders of the state. Every subject is a prisoner. We need only note the denial of emigration from the Soviet Union and the "wall of shame" in Berlin to dramatize this point.

A New Specter That Stalks the Earth: International Terrorism

International terrorism—a new specter that stalks the earth—has become an all-too-common instrument of world politics. The recent assassination of President

Sadat and the assassination attempts against President Reagan and Pope John Paul II underscore the danger of this growing menace. All indicators suggest that this brutal scourge will be with us for the next two decades.

Terrorism is the use of violence or the threat of violence against a person or group to achieve political objectives. Terrorism seeks to shock or intimidate a far wider group than its immediate victims. Terrorists rob, murder, kidnap, torture, hijack, and bomb.

International terrorism refers to acts of violence across state borders. President Sadat may have been murdered by Egyptian soldiers, but President Qaddafi of Libya was calling for his assassination openly for months. We do not yet know whether the men who committed the act were trained or supplied by Libya, but certainly there was a psychological, ideological, and political connection. At the very least, Qaddafi created the climate which made the act more likely and which underscored its international significance.

Many knowledgeable people believe the nearly successful attempt on the Pope's life could not have been accomplished without the support of an international terrorist network with its string of safe houses, false documents centers, and logistical structure.

The Growth of Terrorism

From 1968 through 1980, more than 3,600 people were killed and 7,500 were wounded in international terrorist incidents. The principal target was the United States; over one-third of the attacks were directed against Americans or American facilities. In 1974, terrorism reached a greater scale than any previous time in modern history—it was called the year of the terrorist. But since then terrorism has increased and so the 1970s can be called the terrorist decade. Early indications suggest that the 1980s will be no better. In 1981 there has been a dramatic rise in kidnappings, especially of U.S. businessmen in Latin America, usually with large ransom demands.

In earlier years, the terrorists said: "Kill one person, frighten 10,000." But with modern instant and vivid communication we can say: "Kill one person and frighten ten million." Television often portrays terrorists in a dramatic and even heroic light. Consider the impact of these images on the young and confused who are looking for meaning and challenge in their drab lives. The brutal deeds of the terrorist cry out for imitation.

The New Warfare

Terrorism is the new warfare, the efficient way to achieve political objectives that bypasses the discipline of the ballot box and the cost of conventional war. Terrorism is the weapon of the minority who seek to impose their will on the majority. Terrorism is often the weapon of the weak and alienated, who wittingly or unwittingly may be serving the objectives of powerful and aggressive states.

The terrorist does not depend on popular support, an army, or a large arsenal to reach his human targets or material symbols of "bourgeois decadence," such as a bank, refinery, or power station. His trade requires only a few dedicated, trained, and disciplined fanatics who are willing to take high risks to achieve their twisted ends.

The Psychopathology of Terrorism

What makes a terrorist a terrorist? Many psychologists have concluded that most terrorists, or at least most of their leaders, are psychopathic criminals. They have criminal minds. Some of them like to kill and court death. In ordinary times and places they would be ordinary criminals rebelling against their parents and society.

But we live in extraordinary times when the talent for criminal violence can be tied to a movement or harnessed to highflown rhetoric about "exploitation" and "liberation" or to low-level hatred, like "murder the Satan Sadat."

Not all terrorists have enlisted in a larger cause. Some of them are nihilists—they believe in nothing, they kidnap and kill for their sadistic pleasure. Many come from the upper-middle class and are drenched in feelings of guilt about their privileged position. Many are alienated loners seeking to become a footnote in history, like the Arthur Bremers and Sirhan Sirhans whose tortured psyches told them that one final act of violence would enshrine them in immortality.

The International Terrorist Network

The international terrorist groups—the Baader-Meinhof Gang in Germany, the Red Brigades in Italy, or the IRA Provisionals in Ulster—do not work in isolation from one another. Quite the contrary, there is a worldwide terror network, which is fully documented in Claire Sterling's *The Terror Network*, published in 1981. Her conclusions, supported by U.S. Government research, demonstrate that the terrorist leaders operating in Northern Ireland, West Germany, Spain, Italy, Turkey, the Middle East, and Latin America all have close ties with one another. Many have been trained at the same camps in Algeria, Libya, South Yemen, Syria, Cuba, Eastern Europe, or the Soviet Union. They communicate with one another by frequent visits and a secret network. They have common sources of financing; many operations are bankrolled by Libya. Many of them draw upon the same sources for weapons and logistical support.

International terrorism today is largely a leftist or even Marxist movement with the Soviet Union and Libya being the chief sponsors. Their objective is to destroy the old order and their chief targets are America and other Western democracies. They seek to destroy freedom and democracy in the name of "liberation."

The terrorists pretend to support local causes like Catholic rights in Northern Ireland or Basque autonomy in Spain, but this is a cynical tactic designed to spread their influence and demoralize democratic institutions. Terrorist leaders, for example, have repudiated the democratic government of the Republic of Ireland, which they characterize as an illegitimate Quisling regime.

Another basic tactic is to discredit the existing regime, however just it may be, by forcing it to take harsh police or military measures against the terrorists. When this happens, the terrorist disinformation apparatus accuses the regime of "fascist repression" and thus attempts to gain wider sympathy for their cause. Unfortunately, articulate segments of liberal academic, journalistic, and religious communities are often soft targets for this propaganda.

Terrorist leaders may be psychopathic criminals and political fanatics, but this is not necessarily true of the storm troopers at the lower level of their rigid hierarchy of authority and command. These foot soldiers are often recruited by brutal means. The Provisional IRA, for example, recruits youngsters by threatening to kneecap them, that is, to drill holes in their kneecaps. This threat is made creditable by the fact that the IRA has kneecapped 800 of their own number "for backsliding or informing." (Sterling, p. 151.)

Are Terrorists Freedom Fighters?

It is sometimes said that one man's terrorist is another man's "freedom fighter"—that it all depends on one's perspective. I reject the contention that any terrorist is a genuine "freedom fighter." Of course, there is injustice and "un-freedom" in the world. There are wrongs to be righted. But terrorism is not the answer. It is part of the problem.

The international terrorists have shown no genuine interest in human rights. They talk about rights abuses in free and partly free countries, but they have ignored the massive violation of rights in the Communist world. They destroy human rights in the name of human rights. The inhumane means they use betray the ends they proclaim.

How Terrorists Use the Media

Logic would suggest that a brutal minority movement dedicated to the destruction of the rule of law would be universally condemned in the democratic West and among civilized people everywhere. Sadly, this is not the case. Articulate leaders of Western liberal opinion directly and indirectly, consciously or unconsciously give aid and comfort to international terrorists. That is due partly to ignorance and partly to a romantic notion that terrorists are fighting for high-minded causes.

The terrorists receive a considerable boost from the Western media of communication which provide the visibility they seek, need, and thrive on. Television is a godsend for them. Some terrorist acts, such as blowing up a plane in a Middle Eastern desert, are timed to get maximum world coverage via satellite. If the media gave the terrorists the attention their small numbers and narrow support deserved, their activity would certainly diminish. But the media cater to drama, violence, and brutality.

Some governments and corporations aid terrorists by yielding to their demands. The terrorists kidnap an ambassador or business executive and demand for his release the freedom of imprisoned terrorists or ransom money, or both. When a government or corporation capitulates, terrorist kidnapping serves the triple purpose of identifying "the enemy," raising funds, and springing comrades so they can return to active duty.

Some Religious Groups Support Terrorists

One strange source of support comes from some church leaders, notably the World Council of Churches through its Program to Combat Racism, which has repeatedly given large sums to Marxist guerrilla groups, especially in southern Africa. In August 1978, the World Council made an $85,000 grant to the so-called "Patriotic Front" guerrillas who by terror were seeking to overthrow the interracial regime in Rhodesia, now Zimbabwe. Here was a Christian group giving what it called "humanitarian" aid to terrorists who had recently murdered thirty-five Christian missionaries and their children and who bragged about shooting down two unarmed, civilian passenger planes.

As recently as September 1981, the World Council made a second $125,000 grant to SWAPO guerrillas based in Angola. Like the Front, SWAPO is Soviet armed, Cuban trained, and Marxist oriented. It is attempting to fight its way into power in South West Africa and to prevent a peaceful and orderly transition to an independent Namibia.

Some Roman Catholic missionaries have become closely identified with guerrilla movements in Latin America under the rubric of "liberation theology." Large numbers of Irish-American Catholics, most with the best of motives, have supported terrorists in Northern Ireland, but I am happy to report that many have stopped backing the Provisional IRA. There was a time, according to Claire Sterling, when nine-tenths of the IRA's "weapons and most of their funds came from the United States." Today, however, most of the fund raising is done "through protection rackets, brothels and massage parlors, drug running, and bank stickups." (Sterling, pp. 151–152.)

Limits of U.S. Influence

As the leader of the Free World, the United States should pursue a vigorous and humane foreign policy designed to maintain its own security and that of its allies and to help create a world community that respects diversity and is safe for peaceful development and change. Human rights are an inescapable concern in all our foreign policy decisions because we Americans believe in freedom, justice, and dignity for all peoples.

Torture, exile under brutal conditions, harsh emigration restrictions, disappearances, and other abuses are reprehensible whether committed by *friend, foe,* or *netural.* There must be only *one* moral yardstick.

Saying this, we must recognize the limitations of American power and influence and the moral dangers of attempting to reform other people or to reshape their institutions. We should not indulge in what Denis Brogan once called "the illusion of American omnipotence," the tendency to overestimate the capacity of our government to mold the external world, particularly domestic developments in other countries. America is powerful, but it is not all-powerful. Our considerable leverage of the 1950s, which was diminished during the 1960s, has been further eroded by OPEC, a weakened economy, the great leap forward in Soviet military might, and our abandonment of Vietnam.

Quite apart from our limited capacity to influence intractable realities abroad, there is and should be a profound moral constraint on efforts designed to alter domestic practices, institutions, and policies within other states. Neo-Wilsonian attempts to make the world safe for human rights seem to be rooted in the naive view that the rest of the world is malleable, responsive to our wishes, and vulnerable to our threats.

The sometimes crusading and paternalistic rhetoric of a Jimmy Carter or a Woodrow Wilson drew upon an idealistic stream in the American character. But there is another and quieter stream, equally honorable but less pushy and more persuasive—symbolized by the biblical parallel of a candle upon a stand or a city set upon a hill.

A former Secretary of State, John Quincy Adams, expressed this more modest understanding of American responsibility in 1821, appropriately on the Fourth of July:

> "Wherever the standard of freedom and independence has been or shall be unfurled, there will be America's heart, her benedictions, and her prayers. But she goes not abroad in search of monsters to destroy. She is the well-wisher to the freedom and independence of all. She is the champion and vindicator only of her own." (Quoted by George Kennan before the Senate Foreign Relations Committee, February 10, 1966.)

The impulse to impose our standards or practices on other societies, supported by policies of reward and punishment, leads inevitably to a kind of reform intervention. We Americans have no moral mandate to transform other societies, and we rightly resent such efforts on the part of the totalitarians. There is more than a touch of arrogance in any efforts to alter the domestic behavior of allies, or even of adversaries.

Other states may request assistance from friendly governments on mutually agreed terms. But external forces, however nobly motivated, cannot impose justice, human rights, or freedom on other states without resorting to direct or indirect conquest. It may be possible to "export revolution," as the phrase goes—but we cannot export human rights or respect for the rule of the law. Freedom and justice are the fruit of long organic growth nurtured by religious values, personal courage, social restraint, and respect for law. The majesty of law is little understood in traditional societies where ethnic identity tends to supersede all other claims on loyalty and obedience.

The United States should also avoid the peril of selective concern for human rights abroad. There are human rights zealots who are more upset about relatively small specific abuses against prisoners in a friendly authoritarian state than they are about massive abuses against the entire population of a hostile totalitarian state. Favorite targets of their moral outrage are countries like Argentina, South Korea, Taiwan, Chile, and El Salvador, each a faithful ally of the United States, each pursuing a constructive foreign policy that serves the cause of stability, and each under siege by a totalitarian adversary, either by direct threat or subversion.

Many human rights activists tend to underestimate the totalitarian threat to the West and the totalitarian temptation in the Third World. Hence, they neglect or trivialize the fundamental political and moral struggle of our time—the protracted conflict between forces of total government based on coercion and the proponents of limited government based on popular consent and humane law.

U.S. Responsibility for Freedom and Dignity

We start with the premise that the United States has a responsibility equal to its capacity to act and to influence external events and consistent with the principle of sovereign equality among states. Recognizing our limitations and working in the spirit of John Quincy Adams, there are five appropriate ways the U.S. government and the American people can serve the larger cause of freedom and dignity in the world:

(1) We can be worthy custodians of the freedom bequeathed us by the Founding Fathers and thus continue to give heart to the aspirations of people everywhere. We can give hope to those in bondage by demonstrating what the late Reinhold Niebuhr called "the relevance of the impossible ideal." We can never fully realize our own ideals, but we can strive toward them. In most other cultural settings, full respect for human rights cannot be expected in the foreseeable future. A quick change of regime will not enshrine liberty or justice. The message of our example may be clouded, but it is not without hope—the struggle for a bit more freedom of choice or a better chance for justice is a never-ending one, and after small gains have been made, eternal vigilance is vital to avoid sliding back into bondage. Serving as an example of decency may be our most effective way to nudge forward the cause of human dignity.

(2) Our government can advance human rights abroad by strengthening our resolve and our resources to defend our allies who are threatened by totalitarian aggression or subversion. This may require security guarantees, military assistance, and in some cases the presence of U.S. troops on foreign soil. Our combined effort to maintain a favorable balance of power has succeeded thus far in preserving the independence of Western Europe, Japan, and South Korea.

Misguided U.S. policies have helped deliver the peoples of Iran and Nicaragua into the hands of regimes that show far less respect for basic human rights than their less-than-perfect predecessors. Human experience demonstrates that the best is often the enemy of the good. Our fastidious opposition to an authoritarian regime may hasten the advent of a totalitarian one. To withhold economic or military aid to a besieged ally whose human rights record is not blameless may help assure a far more repressive successor. This would be tragic.

(3) By the discreet use of quiet (not silent) diplomacy, we can encourage friendly regimes to observe the rule of law. We should never condone the violation of basic rights anywhere, but we should recognize the severe limitations of public preaching and punitive measures directed against our friends and allies. An attitude of mutual respect supported by material assistance provides a much more favorable atmosphere for encouraging them to correct abuses, such as arbitrary arrest, prolonged detention without charges, and torture, and to observe international covenants to which they have agreed.

(4) Because human rights and national security are interdependent, it is clear that the United States cannot fulfil its responsibilities to peace and freedom if it is militarily weak or if it lacks the will to use its power and influence. We need military strength great enough to deter a nuclear or conventional attack, to resist nuclear blackmail, to support our Free World allies, and to undergird a worldwide coalition to counter conquest, subversion, and terrorism.

We are being severely tested in South Korea, Taiwan, Southeast Asia, Central America, and southern Africa. The stakes are high—the freedom, independence, and security of the scores of countries involved and a world in which freedom will have a chance to flourish.

(5) In confronting the growing menace of international terrorism, the U.S. government has launched a quiet but vigorous effort to deter, contain, and fight it. The effort is coordinated by the State Department's Office for Combatting Terrorism and includes more than a dozen U.S. agencies. Its five major functions are intelligence, protection of overseas missions, contingency planning, crisis management, and efforts to formulate international agreements designed to curb hijacking and to repatriate terrorists. A high degree of cooperation has been achieved in antihijacking efforts.

Underlying the U.S. approach is a dogged determination to make no concessions to terrorist blackmail. Our government will not pay ransom money to free a kidnapped ambassador. Nor will it yield to other demands, such as freeing so-called "political prisoners" in return for the freedom of a kidnapped ambassador. Washington has urged other governments and American corporations to adopt this sound policy, which is certainly a deterrent to kidnapping.

Can Freedom Survive?

In the mighty world struggle where freedom and free institutions are challenged at every turn, can the United States and the other democracies survive and prevail? The doomsday sayers insist that we are too rich, flabby, and permissive to sense the danger, much less to do battle against it. Democratic niceties, they say, are no match for disciplined totalitarians. The West is doomed.

I am not that pessimistic. The democracies have hidden strengths and the totalitarians have hidden weaknesses. But we must face the harsh realities of tyranny, repression, terrorism, and aggression if we are to give substance to the realities of peace with honor and freedom without fear.

Recognizing both the limitations and responsibilities of American power and influence, we must rededicate ourselves to the cause of ordered liberty both at home and abroad. We cannot fulfill these responsibilities if we are economically stagnant or militarily weak or if we lack the will to use our power to defend ourselves and our allies.

Abraham Lincoln said, "No man is good enough to be President, but someone has to be." We can say no country is good enough nor wise enough to lead the Free World, but that is our destiny.

MORAL AND ETHICAL VALUES IN LABOR–MANAGEMENT RELATIONS

by

William P. Murphy

William P. Murphy

Professor Murphy holds the Paul B. Eaton Chair at the School of Law at the University of North Carolina at Chapel Hill. He has also taught at the law schools at the University of Mississippi and the University of Missouri. He received his LL.B. degree from the University of Virginia and his J.S.D. from Yale University.

His teaching areas are Constitutional Law, Labor Law, Labor Arbitration, and Employment Discrimination. Included in his scholarly publications are law school casebooks in Labor Law and Employment Discrimination, contributions to several treatises and books, and numerous articles in legal periodicals and other professional publications.

In addition to his academic credentials, Professor Murphy has considerable practical experience in the field of Labor Law. In 1950–1953, he was an attorney for the U.S. Department of Labor. In 1966–1977, he served as a special legal assistant to a member of the National Labor Relations Board. In 1976–1978, he was a member and committee chairman on the NLRB National Task Force on NLRB Procedures. Between 1965–1969, he was a member of the Missouri Commission on Human Rights. Since 1965, he has been an active labor arbitrator. He is a member of the National Academy of Arbitrators, and has served on its Board of Governors and as a Vice-President.

For many years Professor Murphy has been a regular lecturer on programs sponsored by The Southwestern Legal Foundation. He is the Chairman of the Foundation's Short Course on Labor Law and Labor Arbitration and the Short Course on Employment Discrimination, both presented annually. Since 1977 he has been the Distinguished Scholar in Residence of the Foundation.

MORAL AND ETHICAL VALUES IN LABOR-MANAGEMENT RELATIONS

by

William P. Murphy

Introduction

Labor-management relations is a large field which includes, but is not confined to, labor law. Since I am a lawyer whose experience is almost entirely legal, I will confine my discussion to the law of labor-management relations. The paper will discuss the relevance of moral/ethical values in three contexts: (1) the making of labor law; (2) the enforcement of labor law; and (3) advocacy in labor law.

The Making of Labor Law

If we step back in time and survey the scene in the United States a hundred years ago, we see the Industrial Revolution and the growth of capitalist enterprise at full tide. It was an era characterized by the growth of trusts in major economic areas; the emergence of corporate, as contrasted with individual, employers; the development of the factory system and a numerous wage-earning class; and the advent of impersonality and ruthlessness in employment relations.

So far as labor was concerned, the new economic system produced, as it had in England, low wages, long hours, unsafe working conditions, child labor, poverty, squalid home environments, poor health, high death rates, little medical, educational, or wholesale recreational opportunity—in short, blunted and blighted lives. These conditions, under which millions of workers eked out their existence, were justified by employers and economists as the inexorable and inevitable by-product of free economic enterprise. There was no feeling that the state should intervene to protect the workers against exploitation, since the economic thinking of the day was strictly laissez-faire, a philosophy transplanted from England, where the Industrial Revolution and the teaching of Adam Smith had bloomed a century earlier.

More to the point of this paper, the social thought of the Gilded Age also supported the system by denying that there was any connection between economic behavior and moral conduct or values. Indeed, the victims were blamed for their own predicament. Thus, Henry Ward Beecher asserted in all seriousness that "No man in this land suffers from poverty unless it be more than his fault—unless it be his sin." The minister who ardently opposed human slavery could find no moral fault in the gross economic disadvantages to which workers were subject.

Beecher's statement epitomized the attitude of the church, which in those days was more the recognized custodian of moral values than it is today. The religious leaders of that time generally either actively supported the employers or manifested a silent indifference to the plight of workers. In the 1890s, an alliance of ministers strongly condemned Eugene V. Debs and the railroad strikers. A few years later, in connection with a strike of streetcar workers in Terre Haute, Debs in his paper *The Toiler* made the scathing and bitter rejoinder:

"Let the workers also remember that from no single pulpit has there come in this sore hour a note of cheer. No, not one. The church is true to its historical mission. It has ever been on the side of the oppressor. There it stands today. When a rich and soulless corporation assaults its weary, worn, half-homed, half-fed workingmen, the pulpit is as dumb as death and no echo of the voice of Christ is heard in the temple that profanes his name."

Some few dissident religious voices related the church's indifference to employment conditions to the fact that churches were dominated by the wealthy and propertied classes whose real God, it was alleged, was "the almighty dollar." These few critics noted that working class people were unwelcome in most churches, with the result that the instrument of Christ was cutting itself off from the very kinds of people to whom his ministry was dedicated.

Against this triad of economic exploitation, laissez-faire justification, and the indifference of religious/moral authority, there was raised dramatically in 1891 a powerful voice of opposition and a clarion call for reform. In that year, Pope Leo XIII issued his far-reaching and influential Encyclical on the Condition of Labor *(Rerum Novarum)*. Addressed primarily to European countries where a majority of the working class was·Catholic, the encyclical also had special relevance to the United States where, because of large-scale immigration from Europe, a substantial percentage, if not an actual majority, of workers were Catholic. In the face of the entrenched solidity and respectability of the economic system and thinking of the day, the Pope's language can only be described as revolutionary. The following quotations are illustrative of the tone of the encyclical:

"[T]here can be no question whatever that some remedy must be found, and found quickly, for the

misery and wretchedness pressing so heavily and
unjustly at this moment on the vast majority of the
working classes. . . . [B]y degree it has come to pass
that workingmen have been surrendered, all isolated and helpless, to the hard-heartedness of employers and the greed of unchecked competition."

The Pope referred to

"the custom of working by contract and the concentration of so many branches of trade in the hands of
a few individuals, so that a small number of very
rich men have been able to lay upon the teeming
masses of the laboring poor a yoke little better than
that of slavery itself. . . . [W]hen there is a question
of protecting the rights of individuals, the poor and
helpless have a claim to special consideration. The
richer population have many ways of protecting
themselves, and stand less in need of help from the
State; those who are badly off have no resources of
their own to fall back upon, and must chiefly rely
upon the assistance of the State. And it is for this
reason that wage-earners, who are undoubtedly
among the weak and necessitous, should be specially
cared for and protected by the commonwealth."

The Pope squarely rejected the idea that, at least in the
area of employer-employee relations, economic behavior
and religious/moral values were distinct and separable
from each other. The Pope's suggested remedies were
twofold. The first, as already indicated, was protective
legislation. Thus, the Pope challenged head-on the premise and practice of laissez-faire philosophy. He especially
noted the relation of fair wages to the stability of family
life, and the particular need to protect women and chil-

dren from oppressive employment. The other remedy advanced by the Pope was self-help and correction through private associations of employees, of employers, and of both groups together. These associations, through consultation and negotiation, would seek to ameliorate the many economic injustices which were prevalent. The encyclical is not very specific on exactly how these groups and processes would work, and the terms "labor unions" and "collective bargaining" are not expressly used. But later Catholic writers and interpreters have uniformly agreed that the Pope was endorsing unionism and some form of bargaining or negotiations with employers over the terms and conditions of employment.

Along with his indictment of economic injustice and his recommendation of the proper ways to correct it, the Pope specifically repudiated another remedy which was being widely advocated by others—the adoption of socialism. The papal encyclical affirms strongly the institution of private property and ownership of the means of production, and condemns socialism and political radicalism as fervently as it does the abuses of capitalism.

At this point, let me digress for a moment. The American labor movement has always been essentially conservative compared to labor movements the world over, a fact not recognized or admitted by American employers. The approach has been what has been called "business unionism"—acceptance of the private enterprise system and an effort to obtain within that system, through legislation and collective bargaining, a fairer share for workers. The radicalism of the short-lived Wobbly movement of the early 1900s had no large-scale or permanent appeal for American labor. And in the late 1940s the CIO took decisive action to expel those few unions which were found to have come under some degree of Communist control. I have long been puzzled by the historical fact that the American labor movement has always accepted capitalist enterprise and eschewed socialism or radicalism rather than going the route followed by labor movements in other countries. Preparation of this paper has given me at least part of the answer. As exemplified by Pope Leo's encyclical, Catholic social doctrine was reformist within a private enterprise economy, but conservative in its rejection of socialism or any kind of political radicalism. Studies have shown that the leadership, as well as the membership, of the trade union movement in this country in the early decades of this century was heavily Catholic. A book published in 1981, *Catholics and Radicals* by Douglas P. Seaton, fully investigates the influence of Catholic social ideology and Catholic labor activists on the conservatism of American labor unions.

Pope Leo's encyclical had great influence in the United States in encouraging the development of labor activism in the church. The names of Father (later Monsignor) John Ryan and Father Peter Dietz are preeminent. Institutionally, the National Catholic Welfare Council, Catholic Workers Societies, and the Association of Catholic Trade Unionists supported the cause of labor. In 1931 Pope Pius XI issued his Encyclical on Reconstructing the Social Order, usually referred to as *Quadragesimo Anno* since it was in commemoration of the Fortieth Anniversary of Pope Leo's 1891 encyclical. Pope Pius reaffirmed the principles enunciated by Leo, noted the progress which had been made, and discussed the problems which remained. Pius's encyclical is more muted in its criticism of socialism which may be compatible with democracy and which was distinguished from communism, the real enemy. It is also more specific in its recognition of unionism and collective bargaining as appropriate private mechanisms to move toward greater economic justice.

The Protestant counterpart in the United States to the Catholic influence was the Social Gospel Movement of the early 1900s. In 1903, the Presbyterians created a Department of Church and Labor, which advocated reform measures. In 1908, the Methodists adopted the Social Creed, which was ratified by the Federal Council of the Churches of Christ (later the National Council of Churches). The Social Creed advocated protection against dangerous machinery and occupational disease and injury, the abolition of child labor, special regulations for the protection of workingwomen, the suppression of sweatshops, a six-day week, and provisions for retired workers. In 1912, the Methodist Conference of the North condemned the use of blacklists by employers and advocated collective bargaining. The latter recommendation finally found its way into the Social Creed in 1932. Church leaders in the early decades of the century were also active in investigating and reporting on labor disputes, in proposing solutions, and in pressing for mediation and arbitration between the contending parties. In the steel strike of 1919, Catholic, Protestant, and Jewish leaders combined in public support of the strike and urged reforms in the steel industry, which was then working employees a twelve-hour day seven days a week.

The foregoing summary makes clear the judgment of the major religious faiths in America that moral values, derived from religious precepts, were intimately involved in employment relations, that the existing conditions under which employees in America worked were incompatible with those moral values, that reform was necessary, and that the two principal avenues of reform should be protective legislation by the state and collective bargaining between employers and labor unions. Pressures for reform did not emanate solely from religious sources. Political, legal, educational, literary, and journalistic voices were also raised. Moral values, of course, may be derived from humanistic sources as well as religious ones, and the indictments of economic injustice from the secular areas of American thought and opinion formulation were therefore frequently moralistic in tone. The main point is that both religious and secular leaders considered economic justice to be a moral ideal.

The effect of the rising tide of protest on management was nil. Confident of their premise, secure in their positions of entrenched power, and with the law as their powerful ally, employers were indifferent to the demands for change. Their attitude was given classical expression by George Baer, head of the bituminous coal operators during a 1902 strike by the United Mine Workers. About 350,000 employees were involved. Violence broke out, martial law was declared in several states, and thirty people, including eighteen strikers, were killed. When urged by a group of churchmen to seek a solution for ending the strike "as his Christian duty," Baer replied: "The rights and interests of the laboring man will be protected and cared for, not by the labor agitators, but by the Christian men to whom God in his infinite wisdom has given the control of the property interests of this country."

Similarly, the law was indifferent to the problem of

economic injustice in employment relations and in all important respects supported the position of employers. The attitude of the judges was critical, since in those early days there were no statutes dealing with unions and collective bargaining, and the legal standards were developed by the courts. As declared by judges drawn from the same social and economic strata as were the employer class, the unlawful purpose/unlawful means doctrine was used to invalidate the collective action of workers which labor and its supporters thought should be legitimate. The enforcement remedy of the injunction, developed in the 1870s, was given the judicial imprimatur of the Supreme Court in 1895 in connection with a railroad strike *(In re Debs)*, and was used frequently until the 1930s as a potent divide to stifle union efforts to organize workers and establish bargaining status. During this period, the courts enjoined strikes and picket lines, which are clearly lawful today.

In 1908, the Supreme Court turned the Sherman Antitrust Act, which had been enacted by Congress in 1890 to rectify the concentration of corporate economic power, into a vehicle to restrain and paralyze union activity. In the infamous Danbury Hatters case *(Loewe v. Lawlor)*, the Court found that a strike by employees of a hat manufacturer and a national boycott by the union of the employer's hats constituted unlawful restraints of interstate trade. The employer obtained a judgment of $250,000 for which not only the union but also the individual members were liable and which was collected by the employer by attaching the homes and the bank accounts of the employees whose actions were declared unlawful only after they had engaged in them. If one wanted an example of a judicial decision which is not only bad law but bad morality, Danbury Hatters would be a choice candidate.

In 1914, in the atmosphere of the New Freedom of the Wilson administration, Congress enacted the Clayton Act for the twofold purpose of eliminating federal court injunctions in labor disputes and immunizing labor activity from lawsuits under the Sherman Act, thus repudiating the Court's decision in Danbury Hatters. Samuel Gompers, President of the American Federation of Labor, called the Clayton Act labor's Magna Carta. In 1921, however, the Supreme Court *(Duplex Mf'g Co. v. Deering)* gave the Clayton Act an interpretation which emasculated it and left the legal situation largely as it had been before the Clayton Act was enacted.

One of the favorite devices of employers to prevent unionism was the so-called "yellow dog" contract under which an employee or job applicant had to agree in writing not to join a union. Obviously, any effort to unionize employees who had signed such contracts was an inducement to violate them. In *Hitchman Coal and Coke Co. v. Mitchell* (1916), a federal court had issued an injunction against United Mine Workers organizers for what the district court called "foul and injurious prostitution" of employees. This use of the injunction was approved by the Supreme Court. At one time, an estimated 1.25 million employees were covered by such contracts, and at least sixty injunctions were issued against union organizing campaigns on the authority of the Supreme Court's decision.

Both Congress and state legislatures passed laws to protect the right of unions to organize by outlawing yellow dog contracts, but the Supreme Court again protected the interest of employers. In 1898 in the Erdman

Act, Congress prohibited yellow dog contracts in the railroad industry, but in 1908 the Court in *Adair v. United States* held that the statute exceeded Congress' power to regulate interstate commerce and that it unreasonably interfered with the freedom of contract of employer and employee contrary to the due process clause of the Fifth Amendment. Many persons, including, as noted, Pope Leo XIII, maintained that when the employer had all the economic power, there could be no real freedom of contract. In 1915 in *Coppage v. Kansas*, the Supreme Court invalidated a state law prohibiting yellow dog contracts and in the process addressed itself to the question of the inequality of bargaining power between employers and employees. Compare the language of the Pope with the following language of the Supreme Court:

> "No doubt, wherever the right of private property exists, there must and will be inequalities of fortune; and thus it naturally happens that parties negotiating about a contract are not equally unhampered by circumstances. This applies to all contracts, and not merely to that between employer and employee. It is from the nature of things impossible to uphold freedom of contract and the right of private property without at the same time recognizing as legitimate those inequalities of fortune that are the necessary result of the exercise of those rights."

In other cases, the Supreme Court invalidated the kinds of labor-protective legislation advocated by the Pope, the Social Gospel Movement, and the secular reformist leaders. The prototype case was *Lochner v. New York* (1905), a 5-to-4 decision in which the Court struck

down, again for unreasonable interference with freedom
of contract, a state law prohibiting bakers from working
more than sixty hours a week. An abundance of evidence
demonstrated the relationship between long hours of
work and the health of bakers under the conditions of
the industry as it existed at that time. The so-called
"police power" of a state is defined as the power to protect
the health, safety, welfare, and morals of the people. The
Court majority simply disregarded all the empirical
evidence and denied that the law was in fact a health protection measure. The real purpose, the Court said, was
to regulate the hours of work, and thus viewed as a
"purely labor law" it was beyond the state's legislative
power. The Court stated that "we do not believe in the
soundness of the views which uphold this law," described
such laws as "meddlesome interferences with the rights
of the individual," and lamented that such interference
"seems to be on the increase." Justice Holmes in dissent
accused the Court majority of deciding the case "upon an
economic theory which a large part of the country does
not entertain," i.e., laissez-faire, and asserted that "a
constitution is not intended to embody a particular economic theory."

Even with respect to laws for the protection of women
and children, whom the Pope had said were entitled to
special protection from the state, the Supreme Court
nullified reformist legislation. As to state legislation
protective of women, the Court's position was inconsistent. Contrary to its position in *Lochner*, the Court in two
decisions, *Muller v. Oregon* (1908) and *Bunting v. Oregon*
(1917), upheld ten-hour maximum hour laws for women
working in laundries and factories. But a District of
Columbia minimum wage law for women was held in-

valid in *Adkins v. Childrens Hospital* (1923) as being unreasonable interference with the freedom of contract. In *Hammer v. Dagenhart* (1918), another 5-to-4 Court majority struck down an act of Congress prohibiting the shipment in interstate commerce of goods produced by oppressive child labor. The Act regulated production, the Court said, and not the commerce in goods. Again Justice Holmes dissented, and the following language from his dissent has some relevance to the subject of this paper:

> "But if there is any matter upon which civilized countries have agreed . . . it is the evil of premature and excessive child labor. I should have thought that if we were to introduce our own moral conceptions where in my opinion they do not belong, this was pre-eminently a case for upholding the exercise of all its powers by the United States. But I had thought that the propriety of the exercise of a power admitted to exist in some cases was for the consideration of Congress alone and that this Court always had disavowed the right to intrude its judgment upon questions of policy or morals. It is not for this Court to pronounce when prohibition is necessary to regulation if it ever may be necessary—to say that it is permissible as against strong drink but not as against the product of ruined lives."

In summary, the Supreme Court, the ultimate judicial authority of our nation, in this period of our history by its broad scale approval of the use of the injunction, its gratuitous extension of the Sherman Act to labor unions, and its invalidation of federal and state protective legislation, aligned itself squarely with employers and refused to respond legally to the reformist sentiments of the time which, as we have seen, were based on the perception that the status of employees was an economic injustice not compatible with religious or secular moral values.

But the pressures for reform continued and increased and eventually prevailed. In 1926, Congress enacted the Railway Labor Act, recognizing the right of employees in that industry to form unions without employer interference and requiring employers to bargain collectively with those unions. In 1930 *(Texas & N.O. Ry. Co. v. Railway Clerks)*, the Supreme Court upheld the RLA as a valid exercise of Congress' power to regulate interstate commerce. In 1932, Congress passed the Norris–La Guardia Act, which deprived the federal courts of their wide-ranging authority to issue injunctions against the full panoply of union activities which were specified in the statute. State laws put similar restraints on state courts. The validity of such anti-injunction laws was upheld 5-to-4 by the Supreme Court in 1937 *(Senn v. Tile Layers Protective Ass'n)*. In 1935, Congress enacted the National Labor Relations Act, which recognized the right of employees of all employers whose operations affected interstate commerce to form unions free of employer interference and required employers to bargain collectively with such unions. In 1937, the Supreme Court, again 5-to-4 *(NLRB v. Jones & Laughlin Steel Corp.)*, upheld the NLRA under a broader view of Congress' commerce power than it had earlier espoused. In 1937, the Court upheld 5-to-4 a state law minimum wage *(West Coast Hotel Co. v. Parrish)* overruling its earlier decision in *Adkins.* In 1935, Congress enacted the Social Security Act, providing unemployment compensation for out-of-work employees and pensions for retiring workers. In 1937 the Court (5-to-4) sustained the Social Security Act *(Helvering v. Davis; Steward Machine Co. v. Davis).* In 1938, Congress enacted the Fair Labor Standards Act providing for a minimum hourly wage (25 cents) and overtime pay for hours worked in excess of forty a week and once again prohibiting oppressive child labor. In 1941, the Court upheld the FLSA *(United States v. Darby Lumber Co.)* and expressly overruled its earlier decision in *Dagenhart.* In 1940, the Supreme Court concluded that the Norris–La Guardia Act had the effect of immunizing labor union activity from the Sherman Act, specifically repudiating its Duplex decision *(United States v. Hutcheson).*

Thus, by the early 1940s, every grievance which labor had against the law had been corrected. Congress and state legislatures had responded to the reformist pressures, and the Supreme Court, under changed constitutional interpretations, upheld the validity of the new laws and gave them broad and generous application. It would be too much to say that the invocation of moral values in the efforts to improve the status of workers was directly responsible for the revolution in labor-management law and relations. Perceptions of injustice and reform efforts were based largely on political, economic, and legal grounds divorced from moral considerations. But in a democratic society, changes in law and behavior can occur and succeed only when they enjoy the support of dominant public opinion. It seems beyond dispute that the sustained argument by religious and secular groups that moral values demanded reform was a powerful force in the creation of a national climate of opinion which made possible the enactment of laws encouraging unionism and otherwise protecting the status of workers.

Under the aegis of the new legal regime, the labor movement grew in numerical strength and economic power. With the rise of the CIO, most of the mass production industries in the nation were organized. From a membership of only about 2 million in the early 1930s, organized labor mushroomed to about 15 million in the mid 1940s. This was roughly a third of the work force of the time, a peak of strength percentage-wise which has been gradually declining ever since as unionism has failed to keep up with the growth of the work force.

With the large victories won, the issues in labor-management relations became more narrow and refined. One controversial question was union security provisions in collective bargaining contracts requiring union membership as a condition of employment. The National Council of Churches supported labor in its opposition to legislation restricting such agreements. Congress decided in the Taft-Hartley Act in 1947 not to prohibit all such agreements by federal law but to authorize the states to do so. Some twenty states, mainly in the Southeast, enacted so-called "right-to-work" laws which labor alleges are a serious obstacle to its growth in those states. Another important issue, which continues to this day, is the status of agricultural workers who, because of the strength of the farm lobby, have been excluded from the legal protections accorded to other American workers. Organized labor and the church have continued in alliance in the effort to improve the status of farm workers, through legislative lobbying and support of Cesar Chavez in his organizational activity and boycotts of farm products. In both of these issues, the church discerned significant moral values at stake.

By and large, however, as labor grew strong it looked less to the church for support. In turn, the church and other groups which had supported labor for moral reasons became critical of some union practices. It is an interesting phenomenon that advocates of reform tend to attribute to disadvantaged and mistreated groups and individuals an innate nobility and virtue which transcends the immediate context. Once the injustice has been alleviated and the former victims have achieved power, it comes as a severe shock and disillusionment to learn that they too are capable of adopting goals and methods which offend social and moral values and may even be unlawful.

So it came about that in the 1950s the issues of financial corruption and undemocratic practices in some unions became prominent, and the phrase "labor reform" took on a different meaning. No doubt antiunion forces used the occasion to restrict unions in other ways, but the effort to regulate intraunion affairs was led largely by those who had long supported the cause of labor. Although only a few unions were found guilty, the image of the entire labor movement was tarnished. (It was an interesting happenstance that the Chairman and Chief Counsel of the special Senate investigating committee which probed into the malpractices of unions were both Catholic—Senator McClellan of Arkansas and Robert F. Kennedy.)

The infusion of moral values into employment relations is nowhere more obviously and vividly manifested than in the problem area of discrimination. Employment discrimination is but one aspect of the civil rights revolution of modern times. The civil rights revolution differed in an important respect from the labor revolution we have been discussing. In the labor revolution, the law responded to a social movement. In the civil rights revolution, one vitally important Supreme Court decision, *Brown v. Board of Education* (1954), outlawing racial segregation in the public schools, generated the social movement, which quickly extended to other areas of discrimination—notably voting, housing, public accommodations, and employment—and also to other bases of discrimination—religion, national origin, sex, age, and handicapped status. Organized religion, particularly the black ministry, was in the vanguard of the civil rights revolution, declaiming that discrimination was not only unlawful but also immoral.

In the larger struggle against discrimination, employment discrimination has been a major battleground. Employers are not the only guilty parties. Labor unions, particularly in the railroad and construction industries, historically have been some of the worst perpetrators of racial discrimination. The principal statutes are the Equal Pay Act of 1963, requiring equal pay for women who perform work substantially similar to that performed by men; Title VII of the Civil Rights Act of 1964, amended in 1972, prohibiting discrimination by employers and unions with respect to every kind of action relating to employment opportunity and advancement; the Age Discrimination Act of 1967, amended in 1978, prohibiting discrimination against employees between 40 and 70 years of age; and the Vocational Rehabilitation Act of 1973, amended in 1978, prohibiting discrimination against the handicapped by contractors with the federal government and employers receiving federal financial assistance.

All these laws are based upon a common premise—that

employment opportunity and advancement should be based upon ability and work performance and that it is wrong and unfair to restrict opportunity because of such factors as race, sex, national origin, etc., which are generally unrelated to work performance. Strong arguments against employment discrimination can be made on purely economic grounds, but it seems clear that the basic premise is a moral one. It is interesting to note that both proponents and opponents of the Civil Rights Act of 1964 recognized the preeminence of the moral issue. Proponents urged that the Fourteenth Amendment Equal Protection clause be utilized to the extent constitutionally permissible because it was more appropriate to deal with a moral evil such as discrimination and that the use of the commerce power downgraded discrimination to an economic problem and obscured its primarily moral dimensions. Opponents argued that Congress was abusing its commerce power for the very reason that it was being used to deal with a moral issue. In its decisions upholding the provisions prohibiting discrimination in places of public accommodation, the Supreme Court held that such use of the commerce power was not invalid because it was directed against a social and moral evil.

The moral ideal of economic justice for employees continues to find new frontiers. The last five years have seen an interesting development in the area of employee discharges. As noted, federal law prohibits discharge because of race, color, sex, national origin, religion, and age. About 25 million employees receive additional protection under collective bargaining contracts. These contracts require that discharges be for just cause. Under the grievance and arbitration provisions of the collective bargaining contracts, any employee who believes that he or she has been unjustly discharged, say for violation of a company rule or for poor work performance, can file a grievance. That grievance may be taken ultimately to an arbitrator before whom the company must justify the discharge. If the company cannot do so, the arbitrator has the authority under the contract to order the employer to reinstate the employee to his job and to reimburse him for his loss of earnings.

There are in the United States between 50 and 60 million employees who are not represented by labor unions and who do not enjoy the protection of a collective bargaining contract. As to these employees, the law for generations has been that their employment is at the employer's will and that the employer may discharge them for whatever reason he pleases without any legal recourse (unless, of course, one of the federal statutes is applicable). This is a legal doctrine which originated at a time when the law, acting to protect economic individualism, was heavily weighted on the side of the employers. One academic student has estimated that a million private industry employees are dismissed annually without any right to a hearing and a decision by an impartial tribunal as to the justness of their termination. Analogizing from data in the area of discharges under collective bargaining contracts, he estimated further that 150,000 to 200,000 of these employees would have been entitled to reinstatement under a just cause standard. This situation is virtually unique in the United States, which is the only major industrialized nation in the world that does not provide general protection to employees against unjust dismissal.

In the past several years, there has been a substantial

amount of writing by legal authorities urging reform in this area of nonprotection. Of more significance is the fact that over a dozen state courts, which are the custodians of the common law of their states, have under various legal theories repudiated to varying degrees the at-will doctrine and are extending judicial protection to employees against unjust dismissals. So far no state legislature has enacted a general protective statute, nor is there any likelihood that Congress, in the foreseeable future, will enter this arena. But at least the reform movement is under way. How far it will go, what directions it will take, the scope of the protection afforded, and the procedures and remedies which may be developed are only some of the important aspects of this significant and exciting legal development. It is particularly interesting that it is the state courts, not generally known as agencies of reform, who are taking the lead in responding to this newly identified problem of economic injustice.

The Enforcement of Labor Law

Up to this point, the inquiry has been focussed on the influence of moral values in the making of law which, in a short space of time, radically and permanently altered employer-employee relations in the United States. Once laws are enacted, those who are subject to them must govern their conduct to conform to the law's requirements. No matter how well a law may be drafted (and I certainly do not mean to suggest that all laws are well drafted because they are not), honest differences of opinion arise as to its scope, interpretation, and application to various factual situations. These disputes must be resolved through whatever processes the law provides, usually proceedings of an adversary nature before administrative or judicial tribunals. In these legal proceedings, whatever moral values were considered in the enactment of the law usually become muted, and the dispute is resolved through legal procedures and standard modes of legal analysis and argumentation. These sometimes become so refined and technical that the original considerations which led to the enactment of the law seem to have been completely lost. The advocate does not plead the case in terms of right or wrong in a moral sense but in terms of the textual meaning of words; the legislative history, if any, as to what the words were intended to mean; and judicial precedents which aid in the proper interpretation of the words.

Even when the jargon of the law seems most dominant, however, the moral values are frequently there without our awareness. Legal argumentation is replete with the use of such terms, to use familiar examples, as "fair and reasonable" as contrasted with "arbitrary and capricious," conclusory terms which I submit do reflect accepted underlying moral values. What advocate would admit that his position is arbitrary and capricious? All advocates favor fair and reasonable interpretations and results. Having said this, however, I think it must be recognized that in the enforcement of laws, through the adversary proceedings in which the laws are interpreted and applied to particular factual contexts, the language of legal analysis and argument takes over and obscures whatever moral or social values were originally articulated in the enactment of the law. On occasions, these legal techniques are used by advocates and decision-makers who are unsympathetic with the purpose of the

law to emasculate the law and defeat the accomplishment of its purpose through interpretation. The characteristics of the law just discussed are the very reasons
why so many people become disenchanted with our legal
system.

What I propose to do in the next portion of this paper
is to identify several controversial problems in the area
of the enforcement of labor laws and to suggest that, although these problems are commonly approached and
dealt with in legal terms, they do in fact present significant moral questions.

Intentional Violations

Perhaps the single most effective way for an employer
to keep a union out of his plant is simply to discharge
those employees who join or show support for a union.
This gets rid of the troublemakers and serves as a potent
object lesson to the other employees. Such discharges
were very common in the early decades of this century.
In 1935, the NLRA made such discharges an unfair
labor practice. The sad fact is that many employers, then
and ever since, have disregarded this legal prohibition
and continued as before. Today, more than forty-five
years after the law was passed making such discharges
unlawful, this is the most frequent kind of case which
arises under the NLRA. Indeed, Labor Board statistics
show that about two-thirds of all the unfair labor charges
filed against employers and about 40 percent of all
charges filed under the statute allege violation of this
particular provision.

The typical case is one in which the General Counsel
of the Board, the enforcement officer, alleges that the

employer discharged certain employees for their union membership or activity and the employer denies this and instead maintains that the discharges were for a valid reason such as insubordination, poor work performance, or the like. These cases seldom involve any question of statutory interpretation. Typically they turn on the resolution of a factual question—what was the employer's real reason for the discharge? I do not mean to suggest that the employer is guilty in all cases. Indeed, many of the charges filed by unions and employees are dismissed as having no merit. In many other cases, after a hearing is held, the employer wins the case. But this is the employer unfair labor practice which employers are most frequently found, after a hearing, to have violated. In many of these cases, the defense of the employer is so clearly specious and pretextual that the conclusion is justified that the employer's violation of the law was intentional.

I do not believe you could find one labor lawyer in this country, including those who represent management, who, if he answered honestly, would deny that many employers in this country today deliberately and intentionally violate this provision of the law in order to prevent their employees from exercising their legal right to have a union if they so desire. And what of the large-scale employer with many plants in different states who repeatedly over the years is found to violate this provision of the law, and even as the violations at one plant are being adjudicated, is busily engaged in committing the identical violation at another plant? Is it only the law which is being violated in separate instances? Can the entire course of conduct be properly deemed immoral? Obviously, the question transcends labor law. What kind of society would we have if all persons and groups deliberately and repeatedly violated those laws which did not suit them?

It is not only employers who intentionally violate the law. One form of union conduct which has been prohibited by the NLRA since 1947 is what is known as the secondary boycott. This occurs when a union which has a dispute with employer *A* brings economic pressure on him by exerting pressure on employers *B*, *C*, or *D* on whose activities *A* is dependent. All business enterprises depend upon other business enterprises, for example, for the purchase of supplies or raw materials, the rendition of special services, and the sale, transportation, and advertising of products. A union which has a dispute with one employer (called the primary employer) may legally strike and picket that employer. If this is not successful in winning the union goal, however, the union may seek to bring additional economic pressure on him by cutting him off economically from the other enterprises (called the secondary employers) on whom he is dependent. This may be accomplished by the union's instigating a strike of the secondary employees or by picketing the secondary employer in order to compel him to stop doing business with the primary employer. Such secondary activity is capable of inflicting great economic harm on the secondary as well as the primary employer. In order to confine the dispute to its primary context and to protect neutral secondary employers from being used involuntarily to resolve a dispute between two other parties, the law makes such union conduct an unfair labor practice.

In unusual situations, especially where both the primary and the secondary employer are doing business at

the same time at the same location, it becomes very difficult to determine whether the union's conduct is primary
and lawful or secondary and unlawful. In the original
and classical situation, however, the union activity is
frequently so clearly secondary and therefore unlawful
that it is impossible to conclude that the union did not
violate the law deliberately and intentionally. Usually
successful secondary activity requires advance planning. This is the unfair labor practice which, since 1947,
unions have been found most frequently to have violated.
I doubt if you could find one labor lawyer in the United
States, including those who represent unions, who, if he
answered honestly, would deny that many unions deliberately and intentionally violate the secondary boycott provision of the law in order to win some immediate
victory they were unable to win through lawful methods.
Is this merely a legal problem, or can the union's conduct
be judged also by moral standards?

To complicate matters a bit, consider the remedies
provided by the law for the two violations we have noted.
In the unlawful discharge case, the legal proceeding
may take several years, during which time the employee
is out of the plant and the object lesson on the other employees continues. If the discharge is finally found to
have been unlawful, the employer will be ordered to
offer reinstatement to the employee and pay him the
back wages he would have earned if he had not been unlawfully discharged. The back pay award, however, is
reduced by the amount the employee earned in other
employment which typically he was forced by economic
necessity to seek. The amount of back wages may be well
worth it to a large employer if the violations are successful in keeping the union out of the plant. Indeed, unions

commonly refer to back wage orders as "license fees for union busting." As to reinstatement, the union employee who returns to his former job frequently becomes a "marked man" from then on. In short, the remedy is an inadequate deterrent to unlawful discharges.

By contrast, the remedy provided by the law for union violation of the secondary boycott provision is swifter and more drastic. The matter does not drag on for years in litigation. If the General Counsel after investigation concludes that the union has acted unlawfully, he is required by the statute to seek immediately an injunction from the federal district court to stop the union activity from continuing. One of the major accomplishments of the Taft-Hartley Act was to revive the labor injunction against certain kinds of union activity. Furthermore, both the primary and the secondary employer may obtain money damages from the union. Obviously, the deterrent to unlawful secondary action is much more potent than that to unlawful discharges.

Unions and neutral observers have long noted the inadequacy of remedy for unlawful discharges and branded the disparate remedies for employer and union misconduct as unfair. Additional remedies such as double or treble back wage awards, elimination of earnings in other employment from the amount of back wages, and even the denial of government contracts to recidivist employers have been proposed for unlawful discharges. Bills have been introduced in Congress to provide these additional remedies, but employers have always had sufficient political clout to defeat them. What kind of judgment will you pass on a law which provides such unfair remedial structure—is it just bad law or is it also bad public morality? Is fairness a moral value or not?

Public Sector Strikes

Under a series of Executive Orders initiated by President Kennedy, about 1.5 million federal employees are represented by unions in bargaining with federal departments and agencies. Under more than thirty-six state laws, about 3.5 million state and local employees engage in collective bargaining through their unions with various state and local public bodies. Unlike the private sector, where the right to strike is protected with numerous objections, the strike is almost always prohibited in the public sector. The federal ban is comprehensive (Title 5, United States Code, Section 7311), providing for discharge from employment, fines and imprisonment for individuals, and loss of recognition status of violating unions. State prohibitions vary in their penalties. No-strike bans in the public sector have been challenged repeatedly in the courts, but no court has ever held that such a law is invalid or that there is a constitutional right to strike. (See *United Fed'n of Postal Workers v. Blount*, 325 F. Supp. 879 [D.D.C.], *aff'd* 404 U.S. 802 [1971].)

Despite the clarity of the law, strikes by public sector employees have persisted. Such strikes are rare at the federal level. I can think of only two—a localized one by postal workers in 1971 and the recent air traffic controllers strike. At state and local levels, however, strikes are frequent and recurrent. Each fall brings schoolteacher strikes across the nation, and strikes by transit workers, sanitation workers, hospital workers, and even police and firemen are no longer rarities. In all cases, a public sector strike prevents the performance of some government service to the people, but some strikes clearly affect the public interest more adversely than others. A delay

in the beginning of school will interrupt but not permanently impair educational opportunity, and most citizens can cope temporarily with loss of public transportation. Most citizens cannot, however, respond adequately
on their own to crime and fire. Some years ago the police
in a Canadian city went on strike; widespread looting,
mugging, and property damage occurred. Citizens in
several communities in this country have watched their
property burn because firemen were on strike. I have
already raised the question whether intentional unfair
labor practices by employers and unions were morally
as well as legally reprehensible. Is not the question even
more pointed when illegal strikes result in damage to the
safety and property of citizens who are dependent upon
the public service?

The moral imperatives are not, however, one-sided.
Illegal public sector strikes normally occur when an impasse is reached in the bargaining process. In the private
sector, we recognize the strike as the natural concomitant of collective bargaining. The anticipated monetary
damage to both sides in case of a strike is a potent pressure to bring the parties into agreement. In the public
sector, the law recognizes the right to bargain but not the
right to strike. If the interests of the employees are not
satisfactorily met through negotiation, or if the employer does not bargain with the union in good faith, the
temptation to strike is frequently irresistible, even
though it is known to be illegal. If bargaining is lawful
but strikes are not, then does the government not have a
moral obligation to provide other techniques or procedures for resolving the bargaining dispute? Many
state and local governments have done so—arbitration
is one such process. At the federal level, arbitration is

provided only for grievance disputes over the interpretation and application of the terms of the agreement, but there is generally no arbitration of bargaining disputes if the parties cannot agree.

An exception is the Postal Service, where a special statute provides for arbitration of bargaining disputes. In spite of that provision, the postal unions threatened a strike in 1981 which, under the circumstances, would have been unlawful. The Postal Service went a long way toward meeting the unions demands; a contract was signed and the strike averted. The air traffic controllers, on the other hand, had no recourse to arbitration or any other procedure in lieu of a strike. Failing to achieve their goals, they resorted to an unlawful strike, and we know the result. My question is: Does the federal government have a moral obligation to provide substitutes for the strike for the air traffic controllers and other federal sector unions as it has done for the postal workers? Another interesting question may be posed. The air traffic controllers were relatively few in number, about 12,000, and despite their discharges airline schedules were substantially maintained. What if 600,000 postal workers had struck? Would the President have discharged them with the same self-righteous strict law enforcement posture that he manifested toward the air traffic controllers?

Plant Closings and Relocations

Let me describe an event which has been increasing dramatically in recent years. A plant owned by a national corporation has been operating in a community for many years, employing hundreds, perhaps thousands, of employees and contributing substantially to the economic life of the area. If the plant is in a mainly rural area, as many are, it may be the economic mainstay of several counties. Then one day the announcement is made. The corporate board in a distant city has decided to close the plant. The decision has been made for economic reasons deemed to be compelling. Perhaps a product line is being discontinued, perhaps the plant is to be relocated where it can show a better profit margin, in short, a legitimate economic decision. But here are employees who have given years of their lives in service to the company, and here is an entire community faced with a blow, perhaps a disastrous one, to its prosperity. Should the situation be viewed only in economic terms? Is it merely a normal incident of an enterprise economy based on the quest for profits? Or are there corporate moral and social obligations which are involved?

In contrast to some other countries, American law does not deal with this problem. Until very recently, there was some authority under the National Labor Relations Act, if the employees of the plant to be closed were represented by a labor union, for requiring the company to discuss the matter with the union before making a final decision to close the plant. The thought was that such discussion might produce ways of reducing labor costs so that the plant could continue to operate at a higher profit level. But a decision of the Supreme Court this past June *(First National Maintenance Corp. v. NLRB)* has virtually eliminated any duty under the labor law for an employer to bargain with a union over plant closings.

There is one industry in the country in which employees enjoy a special protection not shared by employees in American industry generally. Under the Railway

Labor Act, rail carriers may not close down operations, merge, or consolidate without the approval of the Interstate Commerce Commission. As a condition of such approval, the Commission has the power, which has been used on many occasions, to require labor protective conditions on behalf of the employees whose work will be discontinued by the economic action being taken.

For several years, bills have been introduced to deal wtih this problem in other areas of American industry. Notice requirements, severance pay, and retraining allowances for employees, as well as funding for local interests which may wish to purchase the plant and continue its operation, are only a few of the many possible approaches. Whether government should attempt to deal with this problem can be argued pro and con on the basis of legal, economic, social, and, I submit, moral considerations. But in the new "laissez-faire" climate of the 1980s, it is very doubtful if such bills have any chance of being enacted in the foreseeable future.

How to handle and cope with plant closings will therefore probably be left to private decisionmaking. Some corporations have accepted the proposition they do have a moral/social responsibility which should affect their actions in plant closings. Others have not, but the matter is receiving increasing attention. Management and other groups are sponsoring programs and seminars to discuss all the aspects of plant closings, not merely the economic problems which are internal to the corporation but also those areas in which moral and human values are starkly at stake—the effect on employees and on the community. It remains to be seen whether there is sufficient corporate conscience in America to respond adequately to the need.

Preferential Treatment for Minorities

Employment discrimination on the basis of race and sex is prohibited by two major federal programs. One is the Equal Employment Opportunity Act of 1972, an expansion of Title VII of the Civil Rights Act of 1964, which applies to employers generally. The other is the Executive Order program which applies to companies that perform contracts for the federal government.

The statute is enforced in the federal courts. For many years, these courts, when an employer has been found after trial to have engaged in discriminatory hiring practices, have required the employer to take various kinds of affirmative action to remedy the past discrimination. In one leading case *(Franks v. Bowman Transportation Co.)*, the employer refused to hire qualified black applicants for truck driver vacancies, and thereafter hired whites for the jobs. The employer was ordered to offer jobs to blacks on a preferential basis as the jobs became open and to reimburse them for the wages they lost between the date they were unlawfully refused employment and the date they were eventually placed on the job. This remedy for blacks did not disadvantage any white drivers who had been hired during the period. As an additional remedy, however, the court ordered the employer to award the blacks job seniority from the date they were refused employment. This meant that when they finally went on the job, they started with greater seniority than the white drivers who were hired after the discrimination and had actually earned their seniority by working on the job. Thus, if layoffs were necessary in the future, the white drivers with less seniority would be laid off before the blacks. The question whether such "fictional" seniority was a

proper remedy went all the way to the Supreme Court.
The legal question includes a moral one. From the point
of view of the blacks, the seniority award simply put
them in their "rightful place" where they would have
been if they had not been unlawfully denied the job in
the first place. But from the point of view of the white
drivers, they earned their seniority the hard way, they
were innocent of any wrongdoing, and yet they were
being penalized by a relative loss of seniority status. Will
you agree that this poses a nice moral question? The
Supreme Court majority reasoned that to deny the blacks
the seniority they would have earned if they has been
hired originally would forever put them behind the
whites who, but for the employer's discrimination, would
have been forever behind the blacks. Although the whites
were themselves innocent of wrongdoing, they were the
beneficiaries of the employer's wrongful conduct. Therefore, balancing the equities, which is a legal way of saying the rights and wrongs of the situation, the balance
was in favor of the blacks.

Another form of affirmative action by the federal
courts is to require the employer, as a remedy for his past
discrimination, to hire blacks and women in certain percentages or ratios until such time as the work force has
achieved the same proportions of blacks and women as
would normally have been expected in that job-market
area if the employer had not discriminated. The critical
difference between this remedy and the one in the truck
driver case is that there it was individuals who had personally been discriminated against who received the
preferential hiring and the seniority. In the quota hiring
situation, however, blacks and women are given preferential hiring status over whites and males even though

they might not have previously been discriminated against. All the federal Courts of Appeals have upheld quota hiring as a proper remedy for past discrimination against the argument that it is "reverse discrimination" against whites and males. Although the Supreme Court has not directly addressed the question, what the Justices have said in other cases indicates that they consider this a lawful remedy if the employer has been found guilty of past discrimination.

Suppose now that blacks are given preferential treatment by a voluntary act, as contrasted with the compulsion of a court order, and suppose there is no finding of past discrimination. Do the whites now have a stronger moral claim that they are being treated unfairly, strong enough that the courts will hold that they are the victims of unlawful discrimination? Depending upon the context, the question may be a constitutional one of equal protection of the law, or it may be decided on the basis of some applicable statute. The Supreme Court is much divided on this question and has given no definitive answer. In one case *(Bakke v. Board of Regents)*, a state medical school in California set aside sixteen spots in its entering class of 100 for minority applicants. This means no white applicant could be considered for those sixteen slots, even though his admission qualifications may have been superior to those of the minority applicants. Four Justices voted to uphold the quota as a valid means of correcting the imbalance of blacks and whites in the medical profession, four Justices voted against it on the ground that it was discrimination prohibited by a federal statute, and one Justice said that, while a fixed quota was unlawful, the medical school could use race as one of many factors in its admission policy. In another

case *(Weber v. Kaiser Aluminum)*, the Supreme Court
upheld a craft training program for higher paid skilled
jobs under a plan adopted jointly by the employer and
the union which represented the employees. The training program gave preference to black employees over
whites with greater seniority.

The Executive Order program has also required preferential hiring patterns by government contractors as
a condition of getting the contract, even in the absence
of any finding of past discrimination by the contractor.
Once again, innocent whites and males are disadvantaged in whatever percentage of jobs is reserved for
blacks and females. This program has been upheld by
the lower federal courts but has not been passed on directly by the Supreme Court.

The entire area of affirmative action programs poses
what to me is basically a moral and ethical question. In
the face of a legacy of unfair and unjust treatment of
blacks, other minority groups, and women, which to
some extent continues today, how can we rectify and eliminate the wrong without treating whites and males unjustly and unfairly? In this situation, what is fair and
what is just? To me it seems clear that this is essentially
a moral and an ethical question, the answer to which will
determine the legal response.

In the 1970s the tide generally ran in favor of affirmative action programs against strong cross-currents of
opposition. In the 1980s the situation may well be reversed. In the fall of 1981, the Justice Department, which
enforces the 1972 EEO statute against state and local
government employers, announced that it would no
longer seek preferential hiring remedies. It would not
be too surprising if a similar policy is adopted in the

future by the Equal Employment Opportunity Commission, which enforces the act against other employers, or by the U.S. Department of Labor, which enforces the Executive Order program.

Sexual Harassment

No current problem in labor law reveals more vividly the recognition of moral values than the problem of sexual harassment. This is a brand new enforcement area under the 1972 EEO statute. The first federal court case was in 1975. In that case (*Corne v. Bausch & Lomb, Inc.*), female employees alleged that they had been repeatedly subjected to verbal and physical sexual advances by their supervisor and had ultimately been forced to resign because of his unwelcome activities. The court dismissed the case, holding that the company was not responsible for the act of the supervisor, that he was not carrying out any company policy, but rather that his conduct was merely "a personal proclivity . . . satisfying a personal urge."

Subsequent cases have uniformly repudiated this early view. Several Courts of Appeal have now held that such supervisory conduct is a violation of the statute for which the employer is liable. Perhaps the leading case is *Tomkins v. Public Service & Gas Co* (1977). In this case, plaintiff, secretary to a company supervisor, alleged that he told her she should lunch with him to discuss his upcoming evaluation of her work; that at lunch he stated his desire to have sexual relations with her and that this would be necessary to a satisfactory working relationship; that when she attempted to leave, he threatened her with recrimination and told her that no one in the company would help her if she complained; that subsequently she was transferred to an inferior position in another department; and that she was subjected to false and adverse performance evaluations, disciplinary layoffs, and threats of demotion. The federal appeals court upheld the cause of action, stating the law in this way:

> "[W]e conclude that Title VII is violated when a supervisor, with the actual or constructive knowledge of the employer, makes sexual advances toward a subordinate employee and conditions that employee's job-status evaluation, continued employment, promotion, or other aspects of career development on a favorable response to those advances or demands, and the employer does not take prompt and appropriate remedial action after acquiring such knowledge."

Last year the Equal Employment Opportunity Commission issued guidelines on the subject of sexual harassment. They reiterate the court holdings but in several respects go beyond them. First, they impose liability on the employer "regardless of whether the specific acts were authorized or even forbidden by the employer and regardless of whether the employer knew or should have known of their occurrence." Second, they go beyond the supervisor/employee context and prohibit unwelcome sexual advances which have "the purpose or effect of substantially interferring with an individual's work performance or creating an intimidating, hostile, or offensive working environment." This means that the employer is liable for sexual harassment by fellow employees and by employees of other employers who are on his premises. It remains to be seen whether the courts will uphold these extensions of liability.

The EEOC Guidelines emphasize prevention as the best tool for the elimination of sexual harassment. Steps which should be taken by an employer are affirmatively raising the subject, expressing strong disapproval, developing appropriate sanctions, informing employees of their right to raise and how to raise the issue of harassment, and development of methods to sensitize all concerned. As a result of the new law and enforcement activity, much attention is being given to the problem. Hearings have been held in Congress, many federal agencies have issued directives, unions have published handbooks, and many employers are developing internal procedures for dealing with the situation. Sexual exploitation in the work place is an old problem. I take it I do not have to persuade you that it is basically a moral problem. At long last our law is responding.

Cost-Benefit Analysis

In 1971, Congress enacted the Occupational Safety and Health Act. Its stated purpose was "to assure so far as possible every working man and woman in the nation safe and healthful working conditions and to preserve our human resources." Such protective legislation had been urged on both economic and moral grounds throughout the century. Congress acted because neither voluntary employer action nor state laws were adequately preventing industrial deaths and accidents which were attributable to unsafe working conditions. The statute is enforced by the U.S. Department of Labor. One of the powers of the Secretary of Labor is to issue safety standards which employers in particular industries are required to observe. Compliance with the standard will cost the employer whatever amount of money is necessary to make the technological and production changes in his operation needed to comply with the standard. These costs may be quite substantial.

One question which surfaced quickly was whether the Department, in its determination of standards, should have to justify a standard under a cost-benefit analysis. This means to compare the cost to the industry in complying with the standard with the benefit the standard would give the employees. This would include at least consideration of the number of employees involved and the degree of additional risk prevention the standard is supposed to achieve. The statute itself is silent on whether the Secretary of Labor should consider cost-benefit.

The question was presented in the Supreme Court's first decision reviewing a standard. The case *(Industrial Union Department, AFL-CIO v. American Petroleum Institute)* involved a standard regulating exposure to benzene, a chemical substance which can cause cancer. The Department standard, which applies principally to the chemical and rubber industries, placed the most stringent limitation on exposure to benzene that is technologically and economically feasible. The Department denied that it was legally required to justify the standard on a cost-benefit basis. In July 1980, the Supreme Court set aside the standard for other reasons without deciding the cost-benefit issue. One Justice in the majority stated that he thought cost-benefit analysis should be required. The four dissenting Justices indicated they thought otherwise.

The Supreme Court ruled on the question in a case decided in June 1981 *(American Textile Manufacturers v. Donovan).* In this case the standard limited exposure to cotton dust, which induces byssinosis, a serious and potentially disabling disease commonly known as "brown lung." As in the benzene case, the standard imposed was the most stringent that was technologically and economically feasible. The Department did not seek to justify its standard on cost-benefit grounds, arguing again that it was not required to do so. The Supreme Court upheld the standard by a 5-to-3 vote, one Justice not participating. The five-man majority held that Congress, in enacting the statute, had chosen deliberately not to require a cost-benefit analysis. The three dissenters did not meet the issue but disagreed for other reasons.

The Supreme Court decision does not, however, end the controversy. The decision holds that the statute does not require the Department to consider cost-benefit. It does not hold that the statute actually prohibits the Department from doing so. Thus, the Secretary of Labor is arguably free to adopt a cost-benefit approach in setting standards if he wishes to do so. At this point, let me inject a little human interest into the matter. Both the benzene and the cotton dust standards were issued by former Secretary Ray Marshall, who before his appointment by President Carter was a Professor of Labor Economics at The University of Texas at Austin and who has now returned to that position. Both the benzene and cotton dust cases were commenced in the courts when Marshall was Secretary. The cotton dust case was argued before the Supreme Court on January 21, 1981, the day after President Reagan was inaugurated. In early February, the new Secretary of Labor, Ray Donovan, a building contractor from New Jersey, took office. On February

17, President Reagan issued an Executive Order requiring that cost-benefit be considered in future rulemaking by executive departments and agencies. On March 27, the Labor Department announced that it was reopening the rulemaking process for the cotton dust standard. The same day the Justice Department took the highly unusual action of asking the Supreme Court not to decide the case which had been argued. The Court disregarded this request and did decide the case. Now the interesting question is whether the cotton dust standard will be reduced after cost-benefit analysis and how that analysis will affect future safety standards which may be issued.

We are not talking about paltry amounts of money. In the cotton dust case, the Department estimated that the steps necessary to comply would cost the textile industry about $650 million. One industry estimate of the cost was $2.7 billion. When the bill was before Congress in 1970, supporters argued that if the statute were enacted, the cost to industry should be considered in light of the enormous economic impact of industrial deaths, accidents, and illnesses in the absence of preventive standards. This might be called a cost-cost analysis. Senator Eagleton stated: "Whether we, as individuals, are motivated by simple humanity or by simple economics, we can no longer permit profits to be dependent upon an unsafe or unhealthy work site." In its decision, the Supreme Court stated that "Congress viewed the costs of health and safety as a cost of doing business. . . . Indeed Congress thought that the *financial costs* of health and safety problems in the workplace were as large or larger than the *financial costs* of eliminating these problems." Thus, it is possible to state the problem in strictly economic terms. Former Senator Yarborough put it another way: "We are talking about people's lives, not the indifference of some cost accountants." If cost to industry must be justified in terms of benefit to employees, then a difficult judgment must be made. That judgment must balance financial cost and human safety, and it seems to me that to a large extent that judgment necessarily involves moral and ethical values.

The cost-benefit analysis will also become important when, perhaps I should say if, the government becomes more active in prohibiting employment discrimination against the handicapped. A largely accepted view up to now has been that the employer's duty not to discriminate includes the affirmative duty to reasonably accommodate to the individual's handicap if the individual is otherwise capable of performing the job. Such accommodation may involve cost to the employer, and the question becomes how much cost may reasonably be required. The answer to this question also seems to me to rest to a large extent on moral and ethical judgments.

Advocacy in Labor Law

In the final portion of the paper I will discuss briefly whether moral values affect the role of advocates—legal and nonlegal, management and labor—the day-to-day work of representing their respective parties. Let me say that labor law advocacy is highly adversarial, reflecting the basic nature of labor-management relations themselves. While cooperative and amicable relationships between employers and unions are not uncommon, they are grounded upon a basic adversarial concept in which each side ultimately acts, and is known to act, in its own economic self-interest to the extent that the law and the economic power of the other side will tolerate. When critical issues and interests are at stake, even the best and longest-established harmonious relationships can turn sour. Some relationships never get past the stage of mutual hostility, distrust, and contentious discourse. So far as I am able to determine, moral values play no role in determining the position that the parties take in the negotiation and administration of their collective bargaining agreements.

Advocates of management and labor, either by initial choice or as an acquired characteristic, tend to share the attitudes and patterns of behavior of their respective clients. Just as many employers refuse to accept the legitimacy of labor unions, so many management law firms and individual lawyers are known as "union busters." Some management advocates seem less interested in establishing healthy relations with a union and in settling or winning disputes than in the long-range objective of getting rid of the union. In my experience, this rabid antiunion attitude has no comparable antimanagement counterpart on the union side or among the union bar.

I have sounded out several management and union representatives, and a few law professors, on my topic. The reactions of my respondents included honest puzzlement as to the nature of the inquiry and frank admission that they had never thought about any connection between moral values and labor-management relations. Only one of my respondents showed any real interest or indication that the topic was even worth pursuing. To be sure, this was not a scientific sampling process, but I do believe that the reactions I received were representative and typical.

So far as attorney advocates are concerned, it is not surprising that no connection is made between law and moral values. Legal process is not conducive to such connection. Law schools pride themselves on teaching students to "think like a lawyer" in order to become successful advocates. Basically, this means being able to master the techniques of legal analysis and argumentation and to become skillful in the use of legal doctrines, precedents, analogies, and other standard forms of persuasion, all in order to support whatever result the advocate is seeking to achieve. The emphasis is on manipulation of the tools of the trade, and these tools can be used to justify any number of different results. The fact becomes obscured that some results are better than other results, and that the choice frequently must be determined by values from outside the law—economic, political, social, and sometimes even moral values. Some judges become aware of this reality, although they may not voice it in their opinions, but many apparently never overcome the obtuseness engendered by law-school training and advocacy. In any event, in accordance with the myth that courts simply apply and enforce neutral principles of law, the decisions are written and the results justified in the language of the law. This, in turn, means that the advocates must argue their cases that way, and the process thus reinforces and perpetuates itself.

In contrast to the virtual absence of moral values in advocacy, there is some awareness among lawyers of the ethical standards imposed by the code of professional responsibility. In the years since the events known as Watergate, law schools have given increased attention and more classroom hours to professional responsibility. The labor law practice, like all areas of the law, has its own particular situations which pose sharp issues of ethical conduct for the advocate. I sometimes wonder, for example, what role counsel on regular retainer has played in advising the client who repeatedly or apparently deliberately commits unfair labor practices or engages in unlawful economic action or in intentional discrimination. What about the management lawyer who makes clearly specious objections to a Board election and uses the law's delay to postpone his client's having to bargain with a union? And what about the union lawyer, to take an example which recently occurred in connection with my arbitration practice, who seeks to frustrate an award in favor of the company by judicially asserting an interpretation of the award which is patently absurd?

The law reviews published at the various law schools reveal that, in the period after Watergate, there were papers and symposia in many specialized areas of the law on the particular ethical problem in that area of practice. I have not been able to find any published self-examination by the labor bar or any labor lawyer of the ethical problems posed in the labor practice.

Conclusion

In the making of labor law, moral and ethical values play a very large part and are forthrightly and passionately articulated. Economic justice—which includes fair compensation, decent and safe working conditions, a recognition of the worth and dignity of every individual, and some degree of industrial democracy affording the worker a voice in the setting of the terms and conditions of employment—is demanded as a moral ideal. In the enforcement of labor law, the values are still there, but they are no longer recognized as such and will almost never be articulated. Legal analysis and argumentation take over. In partisan advocacy, there is virtually no recognition of any moral values, and too little recognition of even the particular ethical problems in this highly adversarial area.

EDUCATION AND MORAL VALUES: THE MORAL RESPONSIBILITY OF THE SCHOOLS

by

Sterling M. McMurrin

Sterling M. McMurrin

Dr. McMurrin is the E.E. Ericksen Distinguished Professor, Professor of History, Professor of the Philosophy of Education, and Adjunct Professor of Philosophy at the University of Utah. He earned his Ph.D. from the University of Southern California and has been Visiting Scholar at Columbia University, Ford Fellow in Philosophy at Princeton University, and Visiting Scholar at Union Theological Seminary.

Dr. McMurrin served as the United States Commissioner of Education. Among his other government appointments were the National Commission for UNESCO and the Chairmanship of the Federal Commission on Instructional Technology. In addition, Dr. McMurrin has served as a Trustee of the Carnegie Foundation, Chairman of the Mountain–Plains Philosophical Conference, Vice President of the American Philosophical Association, and President of the Utah Conference on Higher Education. He is Chairman of The Tanner Foundation and Director of The Tanner Lectures on Human Values.

Dr. McMurrin is co-author of A History of Philosophy *and editor of many books including* The Schools and the Challenge of Innovation, The Conditions for Educational Equality, *and* The Meaning of the University. *Now in the press are* The Tanner Lectures on Human Values, *Volume I, of which he is the editor, and* Religion, Reason and Truth: Essays in the Philosophy of Religion. *He has also written over 250 published monographs, articles, and reviews.*

In his travels to forty-nine countries, Dr. McMurrin has lectured at seventy-four colleges and universities. He is a member of the American Philosophical Association and six honorary academic societies, and has been awarded six honorary doctorates.

EDUCATION AND MORAL VALUES:
THE MORAL RESPONSIBILITY OF THE SCHOOLS

by

Sterling M. McMurrin

The question of the responsibility of the schools in matters pertaining to moral values entails some consideration of the meaning and purposes of education and the basic functions proper to educational institutions. The first part of this paper will treat the larger problem of meaning and purpose; the second part will be concerned with the more specific issue of the schools and morality.

Meaning and Purpose

Education is basically a function of the culture. Educational philosophy, the policies which govern educational systems and individual institutions, the curricula of those institutions, and to some degree the methods of instruction and even the structure of institutional administration and finance are determined by the character and substance of the culture of the society in which the schools are established. The major determinants of education are such factors as philosophical ideas, religious beliefs, moral practice, art, science and technology, historical consciousness, government, law, the economy, and politics, and whatever else is built into the structure of the culture and affects profoundly the conditions under which the people live and think. These factors give the culture its vitality and strength,

and its values are both generated and exhibited by
them. That actual educational thought and practice are
functions of the culture should be entirely obvious. But
this fact seems to be lost on those students of the philosophy of education who seek the foundations for education in metaphysical systems or in such strange places
as the theory of knowledge in the vain hope that here
they may find absolutes from which they can deduce
educational policies that will have the enduring value
of certainties, free from the contingencies of cultural
and social diversity and change. This effort to derive
educational philosophy and policy from highly intel-
lectualized philosophical theories or systems, a practice
that even today is not uncommon, is an exercise in fu-
tility that has contributed little more than confusion to
the discussion of the foundations of education.

The central task of the philosophy of education is the
definition of the purposes of education in terms of which
we fashion educational policies and set goals for institutions and prescribe the objectives of instruction. To
pursue this task primarily by reference to the several
types of philosophy—realism, pragmatism, existential-
ism, positivism, or some other "ism"—as some have
attempted to do, is to seek the meaning of education in
partial abstraction from the real world of which it is a
most vital part and in principle to commit it to a theory
of reality or other philosophic position which, whatever
its value, is in contention with other theories in age-old
arguments for which there may be no conclusive resolution. The task of the philosopher of education is not to
commit educational policy and practice to any particular type or system of philosophy. It is to examine the
substantive and structural values of the culture and the

social institutions which sustain those values in the interest of clarifying the ends that are proper to the schools, for those ends, the aims and purposes of education, must be defined by the forms of thought, attitude, and action that are of supreme worth to us. The values that are highest in our hierarchy of worth, that are most enduring and persistent, are most essential to the foundations of education.

Here it is important to respect a principle that was forcefully enunciated by John Dewey, one of the foremost moral philosophers and one who refused to separate education from the philosophical analysis of values, even while insisting that the psychological and social sciences should be brought fully to the service of education. Dewey's major contribution to moral philosophy was his insistence that end or intrinsic values should never be divorced from the means of their achievement; for to define end values in abstraction is to risk an absolutism that is indifferent to the facts of real experience and threatens to generate moral sterility, if not regression.

Since its central concern is with values, the definition of the purposes of education is essentially a philosophical rather than scientific task, as it is not possible to construct a science of values. It is possible to have in principle a descriptive science of values, as is common in the social sciences; or it is conceivable that there is in principle an instrumental science of values that relates means to ends, a science which might provide the basis for a kind of human technology. But the search for the broad and basic purposes of education is more a normative than descriptive matter that must be concerned at crucial points with intrinsic end values rather than simply instrumental values. There is a sense in which education may be regarded as a moral enterprise, that is, one concerned with what ought to be—not simply with what is or has been. It is in its broad moral dimension that in principle education reaches beyond the boundaries of scientific analysis and explanation and must, therefore, be treated philosophically.

However, to say that the determination of the aims and purposes of education is a philosophical task does not mean that it is or should be indifferent to science and scientific knowledge. On the contrary, any philosophical endeavor that fails to solicit and exploit fully the relevant work and findings of the sciences is gravely deficient and not deserving of serious consideration as a guide to conduct. Decisions on the purposes of education that are indifferent to the great fund of pertinent knowledge that is available or can be made available from scientific and historical sources cannot provide a firm foundation for educational policy—not only knowledge of the world of things and events, of human behavior and association, but also knowledge of values, of the nature of valuation and of what is valued. There is a related matter in the case of teaching and learning, functions that lie at the heart of education. Teaching and learning are not sciences; they are closely related arts, fine and applied arts. But a wealth of knowledge relevant to these arts is available, and any responsible treatment of educational philosophy must respect it.

In any society, education by its very nature must be defined initially as induction into the value system of the culture, and authentic educational institutions, schools that are not simply involved in the training of skills, are properly engaged in securing and perpetuating the culture. Every society, whether primitive or cultured, almost instinctively devotes a large measure of its resources and energies to the process of inducting each generation into the social and cultural values. This is its guarantee that its culture will survive. In a closed, totalitarian society, that process is carefully prescribed and guarded with the result that education is subject to overriding political forces and its critical capacities are severely limited if not totally destroyed. But a society that seriously attempts to be open and free places upon its educational institutions the moral obligation of both critical analysis and understanding and constructive and creative reform. The culture that is transmitted to future generations is to be a culture that has been critically examined and strengthened. Indeed, this commitment to education of critical, constructive responsibility is a component of any satisfactory and full definition of democracy. It is this that makes academic freedom in our educational institutions not a privilege afforded to educators, as many have regarded it, but rather a civic duty that is imposed upon them by the very nature of their vocation. Those who cannot properly bear such a responsibility should convert to some other line of work.

If education is a function of the culture, a multiplicity of cultures entails a multiplicity of educational philosophies, and fundamental variations in the culture may result in concomitant changes in the aims and purposes of education. Therefore, there can be no single true or correct or even ultimately best philosophy of education. Here there are no fully objective absolutes, as the grounds for judgment on the philosophy are within the culture itself.

This does not mean, however, that education cannot pass judgment on the culture. It is not possible to achieve a complete objectivity that would fully escape the cultural introversion that ties us closely, both emotionally and intellectually, to the very values that we must criticize and judge as worthy of conserving or in need of revision, reform, or even repudiation. But this predicament does not inevitably prevent a society from the self-criticism necessary to achieving reforms. In this matter, it is important to recognize that nonabsolutistic norms that are generated within the contingencies of individual, social, and cultural experience are entirely sufficient as grounds upon which to evaluate and critize social institutions and cultural values. Competent evaluation does not depend on absolutes. It depends on analytical talent, knowledge, imaginativeness, rational judgment, and predisposition to criticism and reform. Although the understanding and judgment of the culture and social institutions are bound to the conditions and criteria of the culture, within the culture, which embraces the totality of its own intellectual, artistic, and moral tradition, there may be those very factors that provoke and stimulate responsible criticism. The capacity and incentive for authentic value discernment rather than commitment to absolutes is the mark of a free society.

Advanced cultures and many which are regarded as comparatively primitive have complex anatomies whose fabric of values is marked by variance, incongruity, and even discord, as well as by consonance and compatibility. The values of a culture, those things, conditions, or states of mind that are of primary interest, that are prized, that are objects of commitment for their instrumental or intrinsic worth, commonly conform to rough though identifiable hierarchical structures whose summits in a sense are expressions of the maturity and the peculiar character of the culture. The genius of our culture, the factor that in general informs its values more effectively than anything else, that both articulates and exhibits its distinctive character, is the individual, the individual person. This individualism, or personalism, is the product of a long and complex historical process whose main outlines can be traced especially from Hellenic and Hebraic sources, but which has now something of an original quality that issued from the past but cannot be found in the past. Our religion for the most part is theistic and personalistic; our metaphysics commonly has the flavor of pluralism and nominalism; our typical methodology is empirical; our government is democratic; and our moral philosophy is grounded primarily in the intrinsic worth of the person. All this and more adds up to a culture of the individual. Despite our obvious social failures and notwithstanding the fact that the individual person cannot be abstracted from the social order and from the culture that produces, nourishes, and sustains him, and even though the person in our society is now severely threatened by the depersonalizing processes of an automated and cybernated technology, a rank bureaucratization of both civic and private affairs, and increasing collectivization that mechanizes the individual, the person is still the symbol of the culture, of its best efforts and aspirations.

This means that in our kind of society conserving, strengthening, and transmitting the culture requires directing educational efforts to the individual, to the satisfaction of his essential interests and needs and the cultivation of his natural endowments. To the question why in a democratic society in which the worth of the individual is at the summit of the value hierarchy, the individual person is not seen as virtually the sole task of education, it must be replied that because in every society there is an elementary drive to preserve the culture and communicate it to future generations, a kind of biocultural survival mechanism, and because every individual is a product of the culture to a far greater degree than is the culture a product of the individual, the culture has a kind of priority over the individual. Nevertheless, in our society there is not a real priority over the individual of either the social or the cultural as it is the faith of a democracy that if we do what should be done for the individual—perfecting his skills, cultivating his talents, and above all liberating his mind and providing him with the instruments of knowledge—we will at the same time and by the same actions rectify and strengthen the social fabric and build high quality and endurance into the culture.

To fail to see the individual person always in relation to the society and the culture, to assess him entirely in terms of particularity and individuality, is the opposite error of the absolutism and totalitarianism that has no genuine respect for the fundamental reality and worth of the individual. It is to treat him atomistically and mechanically as if there were no value structure in which his life is or should be rooted, no human and humane world of which he is a part and expression and which is the ground of his intellectual, moral, and spiritual values. If our educational policies and processes were effectively oriented to such an atomistic individualism, it would be destructive to both individual personality and the personal qualities of social and cultural life. Such an education might well perfect the skills of the individual, but his sense of value would be destroyed, for the values of the individual person, including a sense of the worth of individuality, are generated, cultivated, cherished, and preserved only within a solid social and cultural structure. Schooling in techniques and skills is both useful and necessary, but only an education that liberates the mind and spirit while inducting the individual into the vast world of knowledge of things and events, of ideas and values, of what has happened before and elsewhere, and of what may yet happen, and why—only such an education, however it may be achieved, can minister properly to the life of the individual person.

In the task of preserving, criticizing, and perpetuating the culture, strengthening the society, and cultivating the life and endowments of the individual, the schools are not alone. Education is a responsibility of the total society, of numerous and diverse institutions from the family to civic organizations, the churches, and the government. The schools have a specialized function in education, and to recognize and clearly define that function is a basic problem in establishing effective educational policy. Unless the limits on the proper role of the schools are identified and respected, the consequences can be disastrous, not only to education but as well to general social policy. Especially because of failures in other sectors of society, our schools today are seriously encumbered with social burdens that have little or no relevance to their basic purpose. The proper function of the schools in our society is the generation and dissemination of knowledge, the cultivation of the intellect, and the refinement of the arts of reason.

But to say that the primary function of the schools is

a matter of reason and knowledge is not to foreclose them
to other and important purposes. Clearly the schools
should cultivate the affections and discipline the practical will of its students, as well as instruct them in knowledge and induct them into the correct uses of reason.
From the earliest years, the schools should initiate them
in the culture and bring them to an appreciation and
understanding of the values of the culture that will afford the possibility of genuinely productive and rewarding participation in the life of their community, their
nation, and the world. This entails far more than a
simple training and discipline of the intellect and acquisition of knowledge. It requires as well the nurture of
whatever contributes to the maturity of the person—
sharpening the senses, quickening the imagination,
refining the artistic and spiritual sensibilities, and
strengthening moral commitment and the moral will.
The schools perform first a cognitive function, but their
task is affective and conative as well. That the foundation of schooling should be the discipline of the intellect
should never be forgotten; but the affection, feelings,
emotions, and passions are also central in the structure
of human personality, and they make a valid and persistent claim on the goals and objectives of education.
But it is not enough to define those goals simply in terms
of the cognitive and affective. For there remains those
facets of human nature and experience associated even
more directly with the practical life, with judgment,
moral decision, and action. Here are the conative factors
that involve the dispositions, inclinations, temperament,
impulse, and volition. Like the affections, these lie close
to the center of human character, and in the cultivation
of a genuine morality, which requires intelligent deci-

sion and action free from passion, zealotry, and fanaticism, they must have the instruction and discipline that come from reliable knowledge and the capability and habit of rationality.

Morality and the Schools

In the matter of the moral responsibility of the schools and their obligation in moral education, there is one thing that should be taken without argument, that the schools should provide in the highest degree possible a social and educational environment that is genuinely conducive to respect for the principle of morality and for the basic moral values of the community. This is a large order, as it entails such things as artistry in the physical environment; wisdom and skill in directing the social side of school life and in nurturing and discplining social aptitudes and behavior; and, most important especially through the secondary schools, personnel who are morally competent to induce in pupils and students high respect for those personal qualities that are valued by the society and who are qualified to provide association that is conducive to strengthening rather than depressing moral character. This last requirement is becoming more difficult to satisfy because even though it does not necessarily mean conformity to established social habit and mores, the judicialization of the teaching profession that now infects the schools, together with the extreme liberality that has progressively encroached upon traditional attitudes and practice, has produced a confusion in matters of morals that permeates the entire social structure and will doubtless continue to generate perplexing problems for education. The schools cannot be expected to successfully treat practical moral problems when the society which creates and supports them has not, and possibly cannot, make up its collective mind in matters involving competing values.

Ordinary instruction in moral values is not possible. That is, there cannot be instruction in morality that in principle is similar to instruction in such areas as mathematics, the natural or social sciences, or history and philosophy. Morals is not a cognitive discipline. Moral judgments of right and wrong, good and bad, are in principle different from cognitive propositions that describe particular objects in space or events in time or that express general laws in universal form. Moral judgments are neither true nor false and they have no probability value, for they have no genuine cognitive meaning. Rather, in principle they are allied to aesthetic judgments of beauty and ugliness or sublimity and disharmony. There is probably no firm justification for describing them simply as expressions of emotion, but at least they are not a basis for a science of morality which could provide the means for making correct or true moral judgments. The method of verifying hypotheses in the natural or social sciences cannot be employed to validate moral generalizations in some way. They are sentences of an entirely different stripe.

But although there is no science of normative ethics, ethical theories, conceptions of the nature of the good and proposals on how it may be attained, can be objects of instruction. There can be a descriptive science of moral ideas, attitudes, and behavior, a form of sociology or a history of moral thought and practice. In principle, as indicated previously, there can also be a science of instrumental ethics, a discipline that may be grounded in the psychological or social sciences that describes the relations of means to ends, that treats the means by which moral purposes and goals can be achieved. These can be and are important subjects of instruction.

There is a great wealth of biological, social, and psychological knowledge that pertains to values and valuation. It is here in the pursuit of knowledge that the schools must make their contribution to moral values, to the moral life of the individual person and the moral strength of society—here, and in the cultivation of reason, the reason that can grasp the universal in the particular, assess the quality of arguments, analyze the worth of competing values, expose prejudice, temper the emotions, and provide the ground for intelligent decision and action. Whatever else the schools may do pertaining to moral values, their primary responsibility lies with knowledge and reason because this is essentially what the schools are for. It is here that they are qualified, or at least should be qualified. It is here that they should concentrate their best efforts, since no other institution bears this responsibility and, for the generality of our people, nowhere else will it be satisfied.

The substance of education, the curriculum of the schools, should respect the elemental drives, interests, and values of the individual: physical, economic, intellectual, moral, artistic, and spiritual. These are in varying degrees interrelated; they cannot be entirely divorced from one another. The economic factor in religion is entirely obvious, as are the economic and biological components of moral values. In some interpretations of the relation of religion to art or religion to morality, there are points of virtual identity. In a phenomenological analysis, for instance, it is difficult to discrimi-

nate fully religious from aesthetic experience, and the
relation between morality and art is so intimate that the
main grounds for regarding some acts as morally bad
are that they are aesthetically offensive.

That moral values obviously are not found in an isolated status but rather are present only in a larger context of experience involving a seemingly limitless variety of human interests and encounters should confirm
the fact that education in morality cannot be an object
of study in abstraction from other educational efforts.
To suppose that success in pursuing a course or courses
in morality would make the student, and perhaps the
teacher, more moral is to be deceived by a frustrating
fantasy. Morality is a quality of attitude or motive and
of the practical will; the study of moral values and moral
behavior, as important and necessary as this is in moral
education, offers no assurance that the result in actual
practice will be a strengthening of moral character. But
wherever there is increased understanding of something
that is valued by society, there may be greater appreciation of it. Greater knowledge of the overt and subtle
causes and effects of human behavior may well affect
both the thinking and attitudes of the student with reference to matters of morality, as well as influence his behavior. At least, if the study of moral values, especially
in the context of real moral dilemmas and decisions, does
not strengthen moral character, it is not likely to weaken
it.

There are grounds for defending the autonomy of
science, religion, art, and morality and for holding that
they are fundamentally distinct. These cannot be reduced to one another, and no one of them should domi-
nate and subordinate another, for each is an expression

of basic human experience and interest. In the processes of education, each should be treated as an end in itself and never simply as a means to something else. But to say this is not to say that they are totally exclusive of one another as personal or social experiences or as cultural expressions and products. The complete abstraction of any one of them from all the others, if indeed such an abstraction were conceptually possible, would leave it somewhat barren and lifeless and would deprive it of important overtones of meaning.

It is not difficult to define science. It is a cognitive matter; it involves both inductive and deductive procedures, and is essentially a specialized structuring of propositions formulating explanatory theory. But the definition of art, like that of religion and morals, is a quite different problem. Here is something made up of experience rather than ideas. Whereas for science the properties of truth, falsity, or probability apply, the quality of art is expressed in such ambiguous categories as sublimity, beauty, or comedy.

Far too little attention has been given to the relation of morality to art. Certainly there is some reason for supposing that with the cultivation of artistic talent and especially of artistic appreciation, where the aesthetic sensibilities are encouraged and disciplined and an acquaintance and association with art forms developed, there is a concomitant deepening and strengthening of the moral consciousness. This is not to say that art and morals are the same thing, but rather that they are so intimately related in experience that they cannot be totally divorced from one another and in the educational process there is some interdependence.

The matter of the relation of morals to religion has

always received much attention. At best they are areas of experience which are both theoretically and practically ambiguous. Their differentiating characteristics are elusive and their boundaries are quite impossible to establish. But their meaning for this discussion depends in part on their distinction and theoretic separation, however unclear.

Morals is distinguished by the category of "goodness." Religion is distinguished by "holiness." Goodness and holiness cannot be defined by other terms, as they are elemental qualities of experience. But goodness has obvious associations with such concepts as "right" and "duty," and holiness has relevance to the sacred, the numinous, awe, and mystery.

It is obvious that religion in our culture, whether theistic or humanistic, supernaturalistic or naturalistic, is heavily laden with moral values. Indeed, it has been the chief error of recent religious liberalism to move so far in the direction of identifying religion and morality that it has often lost sight of the distinguishing character of religion. But quite certainly none will object to the theist's common insistence that the God of religion, the supreme person of communion and worship, should be in some way identified with the highest good or to the typical believer's confidence that God wills that he be morally good.

It is understandable that morality is commonly grounded in religion and that the religious sanction of morality is widely assumed. This is largely the consequence of the moral religion of the early Judaic antecedents of the culture and of subsequent centuries of moralizing theology. But that morality should stand on its own foundations should be entirely obvious to those who have seriously examined the theoretic facets of this matter. To hold that a religious believer should be moral does not mean that the nonbeliever would be justified in being immoral or, more important, that he would have no ground for morality. Whatever the truth of religion, there is no morality more theoretically defensible than one which is humanistically or naturalistically grounded.

But the practical side of this problem is somewhat less simple. Moral practice and moral education inevitably encounter difficulties pertaining to motivation and the causes of behavior. That morality should be freed of religious sanction as its theoretic foundation or justification does not mean that religious believers should not draw moral strength from their religious faith. Though in its essential nature religion is autonomous and should not be confused with morals, in fact most established religion as it is found expressed in institutions as a factor and force to be dealt with in the life of society is moral in character and to attempt to disengage it from morality would be both foolish and futile. To hold that a human being should be good because he is a human being, placing moral education squarely on a humanistic basis, does not mean that it violates logic or moral principle to support the effort to achieve moral action by bringing God into the picture.

In the relation of morals to religion, fear of punishment and desire for rewards have been grossly overstated as motivating factors in moral behavior. It is important that a mature morality be positively rather than negatively based, because a positive morality is stronger and has a more acceptable quality. But the main practical problem that morals has with religion does not lie here at the point of religious sanction but is found, rather, in the strong tendency of institutionalized religion to absolutize whatever comes within its grasp. It is not the function of education to place the stamp of eternity on established moral thought and practice. Morality should be kept living and viable. Granted that there may be some moral absolutes, the moral principles and rules by which we live must be kept relevant to the actual world of our experience, and this is a changing world where contingencies are real. To say the least, this relevance is endangered by the association of morals with typical established religion, even though the problem of relevance is now of major concern to both theologians and religious leaders.

American education has failed to provide a center of meaning and purpose for the life of the individual in which the segments of his experience can be grounded and integrated. The churches, and sometimes the homes, at times succeed in this, but it is a proper task also of the schools. The chief sickness of our time, from which issue many of the ills that plague our culture and take a heavy toll in social confusion and failure and in personal anguish and suffering, in the deterioration of human souls, is the meaninglessness and purposelessness which infect the lives of so many of us and for which we seem to have no evident cure. This is not simply a problem of morals, though the whole matter of morality is tied closely to it and is a part of it and cannot be effectively considered in abstraction from it. It is rather the large problem of the spirit, of the spiritual life of the individual and the spiritual ground of the culture, which contains and nourishes him and his society. It would be better to say "of religion," because the ambiguous word "spiritual" suggests many things which should not be countenanced in the public schools. But "religion" is in some ways even worse—a good word badly used and misused, it suggests creeds and churches, sacred books, dogmatisms, and ecclesiastical authority.

The concern here is not with these but with the integration and grounding of life in a foundation of meaningfulness and purpose which gives it value and direction and provides for social and cultural roots which may preserve it from total segmentation and deterioration. It is not that the churches with their creeds and sacraments cannot or do not sometimes effectively produce this foundation. Rather, it is the question of how it can be produced in a society whose culture is increasingly secular and humanistic and where there are large failures in the homes and the churches, those institutions which have traditionally communicated the religious culture from one generation to another.

It is the question of how the ingredients of a genuine spiritual life can be effectively generated, cultivated, and communicated without their perversion through association with attitudes, ideas, and practices which are tainted with superstition and myth and are inimical to the progress of thought and morals. It is the question of the enactment of symbols which can bear the profound meanings of the mystery of existence and the worth and sacredness of the person—symbols by which the individual can be inducted into these meanings and can incorporate them into his life.

Public education in the United States is afraid to accept this responsibility. Because of its distorted conception of the ideal of the separation of church and state and its pathological fear of invasion by sectarian religion, it fails to bring the individual face-to-face with those universal depths of value and meaning which lie at the center of his being. It justifies this failure by a pious misreading of the intention of the law and hides its incompetence by claiming that it has no function in matters that in any way pertain to religion. The result is generations of persons who are religious illiterates, who know little or nothing of much of the most important literature of the world, who are ignorant of much of the most fascinating and important history, and who are robbed of insights, appreciation, and wisdom that might have been gained from an education of greater breadth and depth.

It is entirely obvious that instruction in numerous areas pertaining to religion—the history, sociology, psychology, or philosophy of religion—is not illegal in the public schools. But the American schools, below the universities, have quite carefully refrained from such instruction, as have many colleges, with the result that we have invested great resources in much instruction that is trivial by comparison in both interest and value. This is not to countenance prayer or other religious services in public schools. Schools are for instruction; they should not invade religious privacy or become surrogate churches. But the churches, which quite properly author the creeds and administer the sacraments, are not the sole proprietors of the human spirit nor the sole agents of genuine spirituality.

The future of moral education depends on a complete new look at the curriculum, not new ways of doing old things but new ways of conceiving and organizing the total instructional pattern. The so-called curriculum studies rarely raise the most basic serious questions about the fundamental structure of the curriculum in terms of human needs and interests. Too often today they are concerned simply with such matters as the job market and activities which more than anything else may be catalogued as entertainment. Education must bring science, religion, art, and morality into a just relationship. Unless this is done, neither the individual nor the culture will be properly nourished by it.

This difficult task will be accomplished only if the schools keep their sights on their reason for being, generating and strengthening those moral values of which they are the special guardians: commitment to the life of reason, respect for fact and evidence, love of knowledge, and passion for truth.

The Future and the Schools

Our future is precarious. There are no grounds for genuine optimism on what lies ahead for the nation or the world. The apocalyptic destruction that now threatens our survival is so appalling that it is unthinkable and unspeakable. But even aside from this dreadful prospect, we cannot deny that our society is suffering a severe moral deterioration, a condition evident not simply in the increase in violence and crime, in the weakening of the familial foundations of the social structure, in conflict and confusion in sexual ideals and practice, or in the apparent decline in civic virtue. It is found also in our persistent and pervasive irrationality, in a seeming increase in public demagoguery, and in our failure to produce the political wisdom and statesmanship adequate to the problems of complex modern society. Moral and spiritual deterioration follow from the increasing mechanization and bureaucratization of life that yield alienation and depersonalization.

It is not possible to estimate the share of responsibility for this condition which can be fairly assigned to the school. The failures are failures of the total society. But the schools surely bear a very large part of that responsibility. Obviously, the schools are successful in many things, and there are countless schools that are good to excellent, countless teachers of high competence, countless students who achieve levels of genuine excellence. But the generality of our schools cannot claim full success. Too often their curricula are superficial, their requirements lack intellectual rigor, many of their teachers are incompetent or inadequately educated, or the conditions for proper schooling are wanting. But we seem to have the schools that most of us want because they are the schools we are willing to pay for, so the responsibility rests ultimately upon all of us.

Our great problems may well be a general loss of moral courage and a suspicion and fear of excellence. A dead-leveling mediocrity is a constant threat to any society that has an effective commitment to equality. Whether we can overcome the devitalizing forces that now infect our social order, generate the confidence essential to our future, and develop in our people generally those personal and social attitudes and dispositions that are conducive to high aspiration and achievement depends very much on the schools. This is a monumental moral task that can be effectively attacked only with a supreme effort and a commitment to the worth of education that our society has not fully made in the past.